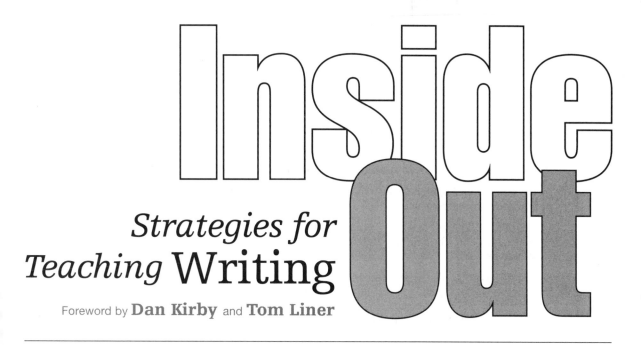

Inside Out

Strategies for Teaching Writing

Foreword by **Dan Kirby** and **Tom Liner**

Dawn Latta Kirby ▪ Darren Crovitz

Fourth Edition

HEINEMANN ▪ PORTSMOUTH, NH

Heinemann
361 Hanover Street
Portsmouth, NH 03801–3912
www.heinemann.com

Offices and agents throughout the world

The authors and publisher wish to thank those who have generously given permission to reprint borrowed material:

Figure 11–1: "Diederich Scale" from *Measuring Growth in English* by Paul Diederich. Copyright © 1974 by National Council of Teachers of English. Reprinted by permission of the publisher.

"Variations of the Five Questions of Media Literacy" adapted from *Five Key Questions That Can Change the World* by Jeff Share, Elizabeth Thoman, and Tessa Jolls. Copyright © 2005 by Center for Media Literacy: www. medialit.org. Reprinted by permission of Center for Media Literacy via Copyright Clearance Center.

"Race to Nowhere" list by Matt Lintner, teacher, Fairfax County, Virginia. Reprinted by permission of the author.

Library of Congress Cataloging-in-Publication Data
Kirby, Dawn Latta.
    Inside out : strategies for teaching writing / Dawn Latta Kirby and Darren Crovitz. — 4th ed.
        p.   cm.
    Prev. ed. main entry under Kirby, Dan.
    Includes index.
    ISBN 978-0-325-04195-7
    ISBN 0-325-04195-4
    1. English language—Composition and exercises—Study and teaching (Secondary).
2. Report writing—Study and teaching (Secondary).   I. Crovitz, Darren.   II. Kirby, Dan, Inside out.   III. Title.
LB1631.K53 2013
371.30281—dc23   2012029503

Editor: Tobey Antao
Production editor: Sonja S. Chapman
Typesetter: Cape Cod Compositors, Inc.
Cover design: Night & Day Design
Cover photo: © Getty Images 78744263
Manufacturing: Steve Bernier

Printed in the United States of America on acid-free paper
17   16   15   14   13   ML   1   2   3   4   5

Dawn and Darren dedicate this fourth edition of *Inside Out* to Dan Kirby and Tom Liner, whose words, attitudes, and savvy ideas live in these pages as they have in all previous editions of this book. Dawn and Darren thank Dan and Tom for trusting them to remain true to what this book has always meant and stood for.

Dawn also dedicates this book to Dan and Cara as loving and supportive family members who tolerated days, nights, and weekends when writing this book consumed her attention and time.

Darren likewise dedicates this book to his wife, Jessi, for her love and understanding, and his parents, for their constant support.

Table of Contents

Foreword

Upon the publication of this fourth edition, *Inside Out* will mark its thirty-second year in print. Over those three decades, this book has served as a text in countless writing methods courses in college and university teacher-preparation programs and in numerous teacher inservice workshops. It has also enjoyed great popularity among National Writing Project directors, and thousands of teacher-consultants have read it in summer institutes. Throughout these years, Tom Liner and I have traveled to every state in the country, speaking and working with teachers and students. As every successful author knows, the books you write take on a life of their own, and over time you become a spectator to your own ideas in print. Tom and I have experienced this process as we wrote three editions of this book and as we worked in person with hundreds of teachers who adopted and adapted our ideas for their teaching. Now in this new edition, Tom and I place this text in the hands of new authors: Dawn Latta Kirby and Darren Crovitz. We are confident that they will continue to preach the gospel of teachers as writers and continue to rail against instructional formulas and inauthentic writing assignments.

Those of you reading this book for the first time may be interested to know about the evolution of *Inside Out* over the past three decades. The backstory is not only interesting but germane to how this new edition is both similar to and different from earlier editions. In the late '70s, I struggled to design a graduate course in the teaching of writing at the University of Georgia. I was determined to offer a course with three purposes: (1) to encourage teachers to read and reflect on the considerable research on writing in the decade of the '70s; (2) to explore the ideas of a group of contemporary practitioners and writers who were using their own experiences with student writers to fashion authentic writing instruction; and (3) to encourage my teacher graduate students to try out new strategies for growing writers, keeping reflective journals about how well students responded to those new ideas. Essentially, I wanted my graduate course to sponsor teachers who were interested in discovering a new pedagogy for teaching writing.

Tom Liner was a published poet and an English teacher at Gainesville High School in Georgia. He was also a graduate student in that class. Tom's journal was rich and engaging, and I found myself writing long responses to his ideas. The Orange Book, as the first edition of *Inside Out* came to be called, began as the result of that extended conversation between a young professor and a high school English teacher. As a class, we explored Vygotsky's notions of the role of inner speech in language development and Moffett's developmental curricular theorizing. We considered the methodologies and remarkable successes of writing teachers Ken Macrorie, Don Murray, Peter Elbow, and others learning the value of free-writing and of teachers as writers. We worked to fashion an underlying theory and model to help teachers map a developmental pathway for their students. In this process, we were strongly influenced by contemporary ideas about language acquisition and sought to adapt that research to the development of writers. We agreed that concerns about fluency should be the beginning point for any writing pedagogy. To that end, *Inside Out* has always supported expressive writing. We also continue to support the journal in its many forms as the most important tool for developing written fluency. Those early journal exchanges between

Tom and me, and many extended conversations on my deck or off camping in the woods of North Georgia, became the essential content of *Inside Out*'s first edition. The spirit of those conversations still informs much of the content of this edition.

Inside Out was originally scheduled to be published by Hayden Books. Bob Boynton, as the English editor at that house, had been instrumental in publishing the works of Ken Macrorie and was anxious to collect authors and capitalize on what clearly appeared to be a new movement in the teaching of writing. Tom and I chatted with Bob at a National Council of Teachers of English conference. He encouraged us to send him a short prospectus. Bob encouraged everyone to "send me a short prospectus." Bob liked our ideas and sent us a contract. We were well into the drafts of that book when Bob informed us that he was leaving Hayden to start his own publishing company. He somewhat sheepishly asked us if we were up for being the first book published by his fledgling company. We assured him that our loyalty was with him. Call it blind luck. In the years to follow, Bob Boynton's genius for finding and nurturing new authors became legendary as Boynton/Cook published the works of the best theoreticians and practitioners in the fields of composition and literature. Being published by B/C became the gold standard for those of us in English education.

The second edition of *Inside Out*, published in 1988, became known as the Blue Book. Tom and I were uncertain as to how to go about revising a very successful first edition: Should we tell new stories? Offer new strategies? We decided to leave much of the book as it was, but to talk back to it and even argue with ourselves as we evaluated our earlier beliefs about teaching writing. We tried to capture those conversations in chapter endnotes. As the work on the revision dragged on, one thing became clear. We needed to bring a high school teacher on board to make sure that we were telling the truth about teaching writing in schools. We didn't settle for just any teacher; we brought in Ruth Vinz. Ruth is one of finest high school teachers I have ever met. She was magic with those kids in Boise High School. Ruth brought new ideas and fresh insight to our manuscript and wrote a comprehensive Resources chapter. Ruth went on to complete a PhD at New York University and has since enjoyed a remarkable career at Teachers College.

After Bob Boynton's retirement, Heinemann acquired the Boynton/Cook line. For the first time, *Inside Out* was to be remade by a publishing house with money and extensive resources. Check out the four-color cover with a real picture on the third edition that Heinemann brought out in 2004. Once again, *Inside Out* enjoyed good fortune: We met Lisa Leudeke, English editor for Heinemann. What a joy it was to work with her. She brought her editorial and coaching expertise to refresh and update the ideas in that edition. She also commissioned extensive market research from users to further direct revision decisions. Lisa pushed us to complete a substantial revision, which led to dropping the '70s language and cultural references, cutting the word *developmental* in the title, adding fresh student examples, and rethinking and completely rewriting the opening and the chapter on writing "the essay." She pointed out that just ridiculing the five-paragraph theme wouldn't change teachers' practices, so we set out to map a new kind of essay-writing process, one drawing heavily from contemporary nonfiction.

For the third edition, Dawn Kirby joined the authorial team. Dawn was an experienced high school English teacher and department head who had taught everything from remedial ninth grade to senior AP courses. Her students called her a "force of nature." She had recently completed her doctoral research on written fluency by working for a year in a classroom with tenth-grade students and their teacher. She brought both real-world knowledge and a deep understanding of current research in the teaching of writing. She also brought her good humor and an annoying habit of challenging us on almost everything we wrote. Karen Hartman, codirector of the Colorado Writing Project, also joined the team to write the Resources chapter. As a former high school English teacher and department chair at Thornton High School in metro Denver, Karen had her finger on the pulse of what questions teachers asked most often: What books should I read for useable instructional ideas? How do I deal with "the grammar issue" in my writing class? How do I survive the grading crunch?

Now in this fourth edition, Tom and Dan hand off their book-child to Dawn and Darren. Darren Crovitz is a remarkable thinker and a fine teacher. He has taught high school and worked extensively in university writing centers. He served a stint in the Peace Corps, teaching English as a second language. Eventually, he found his way to Arizona State University to enter a PhD program in English Education. It was during his graduate studies at ASU that Darren learned to balance both rhetorical theory and process-based writing instruction into a sound, humane pedagogy.

In the Preface, you'll read about what else is new in this fourth edition. I want to reiterate what is *not* new in *Inside Out*, the constants that you will hear echoed in this new edition. Essentially, *Inside Out* has always been about *teaching* as much as it has been about *writing*—not full-frontal, stand-up and tell-'em-how-to-do-it teaching, but a more nuanced kind of instruction. The philosophy of teaching and the instructional activities advanced in this text form a pedagogy of authentic practice. Such a pedagogy is as appropriate for teaching literature or language, dance or swimming as it is for teaching writing. Teaching any complex content or process well cannot be done successfully by relying upon a collection of rules, generalizations, folklore, and formulas. Likewise, deficit models of teaching that focus primarily upon learners' errors and what they *cannot* do are doomed to failure.

We are hopeful that this fourth edition of *Inside Out* continues to challenge the status quo and the corporate writing curricula that many districts foist on their teachers. We are equally hopeful that you will find many new and challenging instructional ideas that will support your efforts to establish a culture of coached practice within your own classroom. What is essential about *Inside Out*—authentic writing pedagogy, immediately useful instructional ideas, and a voice of reality about teaching and writing—is still present. We hope you come to love and rely on this edition as much as teachers have loved and relied on the previous three editions of this book. As always, we encourage you to write, talk, read, reflect, and share thoughts and ideas with one another so that teaching and writing stay in the hands of the experts—the great teachers that you are or want to become.

—Dan Kirby

The Creek in Summer

It is like stepping into the sky.

Water moves, the plunge, white and mirror dark
the fly like a fleck of light touching the pool

Water talks to itself, mutterings
wind high in the canopy, a crow calls

Pepper smell of Hemlocks, sun on rocks
leaf mold warm and sweet water

Copper taste, still and waiting, watching

Sun heat and leaf shadow
the shock of ankle deep spring water

The pull and flex of rod and line
and sudden jerk and run and leap

To pull this day and wood and light
into my hand.

—Tom Liner

Acknowledgments

Dawn and Darren gratefully acknowledge the work and guidance of Tobey Antao and the entire team at Heinemann who helped bring this edition to fruition. We also acknowledge Dan Kirby's guidance and spirited discussions about what a new edition of this book should do and be. Finally, we thank all of the teachers, students, and colleagues whose words appear in these pages and who have "talked writing" with us in classrooms, bars, family rooms, and teachers' lounges; on road trips and plane rides; and at workshops, conferences, and numerous other locations. We learn what we think and what we have to say though our conversations with you.

Preface

This book has a long history. The first edition of *Inside Out* was published in 1981. Now, in 2013, here's the fourth edition, thirty-two years later. That's a long time for a book about teaching writing to be around. Over the decades, some traditions have developed for this book. One is that a Tom Liner poem opens *Inside Out*, and I am delighted that Tom continued that tradition with us. Another is that real teachers contribute their voices and expertise to the book. You will find that still present in this edition, including a new final chapter (Chapter 15: Conversations with Teachers), which features teachers' responses to several of the questions that challenge all of us who teach writing. In addition to teachers' voices, we continue to feature students' voices in this edition. You'll see new students' pieces, and you might recognize a piece or two that was in the previous edition. After all, good writing is good writing, and some students' pieces were just too good to take out yet.

Featuring a wealth of activities to get you going with writing in your own classroom is central to *Inside Out*. You'll find in every chapter multiple activities for working with writing. That's a strong and valued tradition of this book: an abundance of ideas and activities that you can use confidently and effectively in your classroom tomorrow.

Our view of teaching writing hasn't changed fundamentally over the years: It still happens from the *inside out*. That's a phrase that has become quite popular in the last few years among those who write about teaching writing. We're proud that Dan Kirby and Tom Liner, the original coauthors of the book, created that phase and that we've been using it for over thirty years.

As you might expect, we develop this notion of writing *inside out* early and often in these pages. In a new chapter (Chapter 1: Finding a Footing for Teaching Writing Well), we provide insights about what the phrase *inside out* means to us and how adopting this framework will enhance your approaches for teaching writing. In Chapter 2 (Fluency and the Individual Writer), we discuss numerous ways to ease students into writing if they are reluctant, how to lead your students to add an authentic voice and some human life to their writing, and a wide array of activities to promote written fluency for your students. In Chapter 3 (Establishing the Classroom Environment and Building Community), we offer strategies to help you establish a collaborative, productive environment for teaching writing and for having your students work with writing in collaborative ways. In Chapter 4 (Writing Pathways), we lay out the specifics of how to make writing a daily, productive habit for you and your students. Because laying the foundational groundwork for teaching writing is essential to effective instruction and to your students' development as writers, we've taken considerable time to address these aspects of how to grow writers. In Chapters 5–13, we lay out our plans and strategies for teaching writing in the full spectrum of genres, all with the student solidly at the center of instruction, and we end in Chapter 14 as we began, by summing up how an *inside-out* approach to writing enriches your teaching and your students' learning.

Traditionally, the authors of *Inside Out* are writers and teachers themselves who have taught in middle and/or high schools and who are still frequently in middle and high school classrooms. So are we. We strive to keep current with what is happening among students, in schools, and with teachers. To illustrate this point, look at several chapters: Chapter 12 (Writing About Literature and Other Texts), for writing about various texts, including nontraditional ones; Chapter 7 (Crafting Essays), for ways to work with nonfiction in your classroom; and Chapter 13 (Engaging with Nontraditional Texts), for completely new ideas for working with visual, digital, and Web-based texts. Several years ago, we wouldn't have known how to write a chapter like 13 because the area of new literacies has only recently emerged as one having an impact on teaching writing in middle and high schools. As another example of how we've remained current with issues and content in teaching writing, consider how we've discussed working with technology as a valuable tool for teaching writing. The naïveté about technology that appeared in the second edition of this book has disappeared. Ideas for using technology to enhance the teaching of writing and this book have grown up together. Whereas word processing was once a phenomenon in writing instruction, we are now quite comfortable with using the computer for composing and revising. We've long looked to new technologies to enhance our teaching. Throughout this edition, you'll find lots of new ideas and resources, including an entirely new chapter (Chapter 13: Engaging with Nontraditional Texts) for using technology and for incorporating new literacies into your teaching.

Another tradition that we have maintained is that of looking closely at trends, theories, and best practices for teaching writing. Some of these trends bug us, and the authors of this book have always pinpointed ways in which the Emperor of Writing, whoever that happens to be currently, wears no clothing. Like that last sentence, an irreverent tone crops up from time to time in this book, as it has from the beginning. As the trends change, so do the foci of our critiques. Currently, the rash of high-stakes tests and other evaluation inanities have captured our attention. We don't have much respect for standardized, high-stakes testing of writing because those evaluations don't usually measure what they claim to measure. Such tests quantify errors and the teaspoons of writing without paying much attention to individual students' progress and development, authentic content, and evidence of real voices in students' writings. Such testing flies in the face of our model of writing, detailed in Chapter 2, which involves moving students first into fluency with their writing, and then into control and precision. There is definitely a time to correct surface errors in writing, and we discuss when and how to do so in Chapter 9 (Revising Writing), as well as in other sections of the book; but error eradication is not the alpha and the omega of writing instruction.

Traditionally, the authors of this book value teachers and the work they do. So do we, so much so that some current critiques of education set our teeth on edge. Holding teachers' reputations and abilities up for criticism the way that some politicians and so-called education authorities do these days can be nasty stuff. Judging teachers' effectiveness by tracking how closely they follow a somewhat arbitrary and limiting curriculum, by whether they teach for "the test"—a test that generally does little to improve writing instruction and students' abilities to write well—is nothing the authors of this book supported in 1981, and it's nothing the authors of this edition support now. Probably never will. Authentic writing, the topic of Chapter 6, and working with teachers as they become better writers themselves improve writing instruction. Engaging with real teachers as they learn how to teach writing more effectively, with real students as they become better writers, will win out over restrictive curricula and hollow test scores every time. We are also realists, however, who understand the current climate and the demands placed on teachers. We know that you can't ignore high-stakes assessments. In Chapters 6 (Authentic Writing), 11 (Grading, Evaluating, and Testing Writing), and 14 (Mediating Literate Lives: An Argument for Authentic

Education), we provide suggestions about how to prepare your students in authentic ways for testing without having to sell your soul. Being real and connecting with you and your students are our primary goals, just as they were for those who wrote the earlier editions of this book.

Having standards is a good thing, but some of the ways in which teachers are to work with instructional standards border on the absurd. Rigor and learning, having standards for writing and learning, and using authentic assessments are not mutually exclusive and never have been in these pages, in our classes, and in the ideas we share with you. To the contrary, we include an entire chapter (Chapter 11: Grading, Evaluating, and Testing Writing) on ways to assess legitimately your students' writings. In another entirely new chapter (Chapter 14: Mediating Literate Lives: An Argument for Authentic Education), we focus on how and why writing needs to be authentic to the purpose and context for which it is written. As always, we offer a plethora of ideas in various sections of the book for building a comfortable atmosphere in which writing thrives.

As it has from the beginning, this book also contains sound techniques that, when used in your teaching, will promote best practice and help your students grow as writers. Answering the question of "What is good writing?" can be challenging; we know it when we see it, but how do we explain it to our students to help them develop as writers? Several chapters fit together to help us identify, teach, and respond to writing in ways that will guide our students to be effective writers. Specifically, see Chapter 5 (Identifying Good Writing and Emphasizing Voice); Chapter 8 for loads of ideas on how to respond to your students' writings; and Chapter 9 for working with your students to revise their writing in effective, authentic ways. After all of their hard work to craft their writing and move into finished, polished products, students—and you—deserve to celebrate. In Chapter 10 (Publishing Writing), we offer numerous ideas for using forms of publishing to celebrate your students' writing accomplishments, from initial drafts to final products, in short excerpts or full-blown literary magazines. Teaching writing well doesn't happen without savvy teachers leading the way, and we know that's who you are and who you want to be throughout your career as a teacher.

In addition to following some of our valued traditions, we've introduced new ideas in this edition. Some of these new ideas we've already mentioned. Others include techniques for publishing your students' writings in traditional and new venues (Chapter 10), how to improve vastly the research paper and other core writing assignments (Chapter 7), ideas for working with English language learners (Chapters 2 and 5), activities for responding to literature and other texts (Chapter 8), ways of working with new literacies to connect with your students and improve their thinking and writing (Chapters 10 and 13), and examining the big picture of lifelong uses for writing beyond the classroom, including students who are preparing to enter college (Chapter 14).

We invite you to read this book with an eye for capturing the ideas that resonate with you and that will work for your students. We invite you to read thoughtfully, with pencil in hand for making notes and jotting ideas. Teaching writing is hard work; it's also fun, and it should be. That's how writing this book has gone for us: lots of hard work and lots of fun. So, settle in, prop up your feet, and think with us about how to teach writing in ways that improve our own and our students' thinking about all sorts of topics, including writing itself. Turn the page. Our passage is now beginning.

—*Dawn Latta Kirby*

1

Finding a Footing for Teaching Writing Well

Your essential self is precisely what we now need in our schools in order to foster not just a writing community, but in order to foster a community of caring. . . . —**Parker Palmer,** *The Courage to Teach*

We live in a new world of teaching writing. It's a world dominated by curricula that have one clear goal in mind: Students must pass "the writing test." In some ways, this challenge is being met. More instructional time is devoted to the type of writing that is on the test. Many school districts report that 90 percent or more of their students pass the writing test at a "meets expectations" or above level. We are, after all, teachers who want to do the right thing by our students, and the districts tell us passing the test is the right thing—perhaps the only thing—about which we should care. Most of us, however, know that our outcomes for teaching writing need to be something . . . *more*. We know that this new world is not always full of our best practices and our students' most enthused, highest-quality work. The pressure of "the test" has overwhelmed not only our curricula but also our essential teaching selves. As Palmer reminds us, however, our essential selves are critical to successful teaching and learning. Perhaps this evisceration of our essential selves from the curriculum is what we continue to rail against. Ultimately, being held hostage to curricula driven by testing is not doing *enough* for our students, and fostering writing communities in a test-driven environment is highly challenging.

Worse yet, we know that spending more instructional time on writing does not necessarily result in better writing by our students. We can't just teach *more* or *longer*. We must teach *well*. "Testing" and "teaching well" are too often at odds. It takes our most experienced, enlightened, and—in this test-driven environment—bravest teachers' best efforts to improve writing in ways that will carry our students not only through school but also through their lives and careers. The good news is that teachers want to teach well. We return to the university for advanced degrees and participate in seemingly endless professional development in hopes of improving what we do and how we do it. The National Writing Project (www.nwp.org) has had a powerful influence on teachers and on our knowledge about how to teach writing well. As we write, NWP has lost most of its federal funding. Strange days and a new world are upon us. The question becomes, "How will we deal with strange policies, new technologies, diverse students, and high-stakes testing in ways that allow us to teach writing well?"

In some parts of this book, we cheerlead and encourage you try to become a strong teacher of writing. In some parts, we invite you to consider teaching challenges and solutions, enticing you to try some of the new strategies that we offer and technologies that we discuss. Most of this book is an attempt to share our successes in teaching (and some of our failures so you might avoid them), the philosophies and beliefs that guide us as teachers, and the strategies that we have used to work with our students to improve writing.

When Dan Kirby and Tom Liner published the first edition of this book in 1981, they suggested that what young writers needed most was freedom to render experience into words in whatever ways they could muster, and they needed adults who would offer strong support and encouragement for those efforts. Some good ideas are worth sticking with no matter how much schools and curricula change.

Strange Days

Teaching is filled with contradictions and challenges that we strive to overcome in our determination to teach writing well. Let's explore some of them, raising questions about teaching writing well that may stimulate constructive discussion with your peers and colleagues.

■ Strange Notions About Success

High-stakes and standardized testing are hardly new. For several generations, kids have been subjected to on-demand writing exams and standardized tests of one type or another. If testing and prescribed curricula were all we needed to produce good writers, we'd be seeing dividends by now. We'd see not just decent test scores but also reports from colleges and employers about students' excellent preparation, learning, and abilities to write well. Yet, national surveys of educational progress continue to show little improvement in students' abilities to write proficiently. Waves of new standards, test-centered curricula, and more exams haven't really helped. Universities and employers continue to complain that high school graduates cannot communicate effectively through writing. In some sort of surreal and bizarre logic, many educational polemicists think that this situation is actually evidence that we need *more* standards, *more* accountability, and *more* testing. How odd.

■ Strange Notions About Students

One-size-fits-all curricular and standardized exams do not fit the changing, decidedly nonstandardized demographics of contemporary school populations. As a group, our students are more ethnically, linguistically, and socially diverse than ever before. They may bring with them life experiences that have little in common with dominant cultural assumptions. They also bring unique strengths and weaknesses in their language use. Individualized Education Plans (IEPs)—specific instructional sequences for students with special needs—are increasingly common in mainstream classrooms. Although homogenization still exists, especially in urban schools, the once typical suburban classroom consisting of Anglo, middle-class students is a rarity. To put it simply, one size does not fit all when it comes to the teaching of writing. Students need to explore their strengths and improve areas of weakness in ways that inspire rather than demoralize and promote success rather than failure.

Strange Notions About Technology

The recent, spectacular revolution in digital media, online interactivity, and personal communication technology is another indication of changing times. Technology, including the advent of collaborative digital environments and capabilities for immediate networking, has changed how many people read and write daily. This point is especially true of adolescents, who tend to be the most eager adopters of new media tools.

Advances in technology and communications are poised to open new vistas for teachers and schools. When we constructively channel students' interests in gadgets, media, and social networks, we help create sophisticated and agile communicators, comfortable with and skilled in a variety of both new and conventional "literacies." Schools, however, are notoriously conservative institutions; changes can be glacial.

We teachers work with the diverse students who walk into our classrooms. We find ways to connect with our students and get them involved in authentic writing. We prepare them to write successfully for a variety of purposes, including the artificial situations of high-stakes exams. We work hard not to kill the notion that learning to write well can be an enlightening experience. We strive to develop thoughtful, fluent students who are prepared for a full life beyond high school. Ideally, we accomplish all of these goals and provide opportunities for students to discover that writing is a genuinely creative, liberating, and socially transformative act.

Strange Notions About Teaching

The good news is that teaching writing effectively, even in these strange days, is possible. When Dan Kirby and Tom Liner wrote the first edition of this book, they were part of an upstart vanguard of teacher-writers speaking out in opposition to the moss-bound certainties of "composition" and how it ought to be taught to young people. We've come a long way since those days, and a lot of good ideas from those years have found their way into classrooms. Some of those upstart ideas now comprise best practice, including teaching writing as processes, acknowledging the value of students' personal experiences and stories, and promoting students' choices in determining topics for writing. These ideas, commonplace in schools today, were renegade—if not downright iconoclastic—notions just a few decades ago.

The work is far from done, however. Several conservative policy makers—who are rarely experienced teachers—prefer that "good writing" fits a narrow, standardized, and sanitized definition. They want us teachers to boil down writing assessment to a number on a spreadsheet and to abandon concepts like *voice* and *style* in favor of a few test-approved formats. Not everyone is inspired by the idea that effective writing instruction maximizes individual potential and independent voices. In the face of these challenges, we need teachers who are prepared to buck stereotypes, challenge convention, speak truth to the powers that be, and question some very stubborn assumptions.

Stereotype, Misconception, and Identity

Much about teaching writing is a local, private experience: Teachers close classroom doors; set aside the master plans of politicians, experts, and pundits; and get busy helping students improve as writers and thinkers. Good writing teachers have operated this way for decades. Despite the latest newfangled state or district "initiative," writing teachers determine in quiet, sometimes subversive ways, to develop stronger student writers. As much as we might like to view ourselves as philosophical islands or instructional double agents, being able to articulate, support, and defend our teaching decisions—particularly when they conflict with prevailing assumptions, conventional wisdom, and uninformed policy—is more important than ever.

Succeeding as a writing teacher requires a pragmatic awareness of educational politics and the conflicts and questions within our discipline and a solid grasp of public notions about how writing classes should look, what skills are most important for students, and why writing might be useful or important. Public opinion is too often at odds with instructional practices that are informed by research and by teachers' experiences with students.

Writing teachers grapple with presumptions and pronouncements, stereotypes and challenges that usually are not new. In fact, some of the challenges we address next are very similar to those discussed in the first edition (1981) of this book. Our thinking about these issues yields more questions than correct answers. It would be nice to think that we have made substantial progress in changing how the public views what we do. But like vampires and zombies, some bad ideas just won't stay dead.

◼ Challenge 1: What to Do About Grammar

When a new acquaintance learns that you teach English, she may say, "I'll have to be careful with my grammar." It's remarkable how often English and writing teachers encounter this sentiment. It says a lot about what many people remember from their years in English classrooms, namely, that grammatical correctness is what matters most with language use. Teachers of writing, meanwhile, appear as a strange breed of uptight nerd, hypersensitive to spoken and written miscues, and ready to pounce on any deviation.

Although grammar drills are no longer common (at least not by that name), instruction in the nuts and bolts of language use is, reasonably, a part of what writing teachers do. The question then becomes, "How?" How do we best teach grammar? This is by no means a settled question. A raft of twentieth-century studies suggests that grammar taught as an isolated subject has no positive effect on students' ability to write. The idea of teaching grammar in context proposes that we embed small units of mini-instruction as occasions present themselves with student work. Another school of thought suggests that an understanding of how sentences are constructed through an updated linguistic lens helps students. Added to these different approaches are public perceptions of what students should know about grammar (which are usually quite "old school"), along with state-, district-, and school-based policies that may still be based on traditional assumptions.

Whatever the research about grammar instruction might indicate, new teachers often have to learn the hard way. In one of his early teaching experiences, Darren was determined that his students would learn how to use the semicolon correctly in their writing. He lectured them on semicolon rules and usage and created worksheets on which students fixed semicolon errors and created their own correct sentences. His students completed these exercises successfully and generally seemed to be getting the concept. Their subsequent writing, however, revealed no change in their correct use of punctuation, be it semicolons or anything else. We're betting you've had similar instructional experiences. This approach helps our students "learn" an isolated skill—how to do semicolon worksheets—without shifting any new understandings to their own writing.

If writing were a "whole = sum of the parts" process (like building a birdhouse or making a cupcake), our teaching lives would be a lot easier. We could just follow a writing recipe or set of instructions, and learning the rules in isolation (like how to cut wood using a jigsaw, or how to measure and blend ingredients) would build successful results. It's not so easy, however. Good writing is much more than the sum of its parts. Attempting to teach writing as a process of identifying and practicing various components that can then be combined, assembly-line style, into an effective piece of writing just doesn't work.

Grammar instruction isn't going away, nor should it. Given what we know about students and writing, however, teaching grammar traditionally does not equate with teaching writing. Some of the questions with which teachers must grapple concerning grammar include the following:

- How should teachers handle conflicting notions of grammar instruction, whether from administrators, parents, or the public?
- How should progressive teachers deal with grammar instruction, given that certain high-stakes exams may still test for isolated grammar knowledge?
- Are certain grammar concepts ever worth teaching separately from writing? If so, which ones, and how?
- How important is correct grammar use in the bigger writing picture, particularly in an increasingly digital age?

Teaching is full of uncertainty. Will students do well on the test? Will my evaluations go well? Am I teaching enough Shakespeare for the AP exam? These are relatively trivial questions in the grand scheme of our teaching lives and can be answered with a simple yes or no. Other questions, however, are not so easily answered; in fact, we're not sure our questions about teaching have set answers with which we will agree next year or even next week. We ask questions to prompt thinking, not necessarily to provide correct answers. We invite you to think along with us about what seems like today's "right" answer for your teaching context.

◾ Challenge 2: What to Do About Writing Formulas and Formats

When community businesspeople learn you teach English, they say, "What's with kids these days? I can't hire someone without sending them through a remedial writing course. They struggle putting even basic ideas together." Let's gain some perspective by considering this published commentary:

> The rising generation cannot spell, because it learned to read by the word-method; it is hampered in the use of dictionaries, because it never learned the alphabet; its English is slipshod and commonplace, because it does not know the sources and resources of its own language. (Comer 2010, 28)

That's from a 1911 article in *Atlantic Monthly*, and it illustrates an important point to keep in mind: The young have forever been cited for their perceived failure to measure up to the expectations of their elders. This generational bias can be checked in part by reminding ourselves of basic human potential and the tendency of nostalgia to erase our own educational shortcomings.

Writing is an act of creation, which makes writing instruction uniquely different from many other kinds of teaching. We writing teachers impart to our students a body of knowledge, but we also teach habits of mind, choices for self-expression, strategic thinking, and self-awareness. When we do all of this well, our students are able to assess new situations and call upon their skills to literally *create something new* that fully meets expectations. We might reasonably view each act of writing as a uniquely new critical and creative challenge—or as writer and teacher Craig Vetter (2009) notes in wry fashion, each time we sit down to write is an opportunity to find out just how perceptive we *aren't*.

Unfortunately, some students will graduate from high school having learned that writing is mostly the application of a limited range of procedures, templates, and formulas. These limited tools are inevitably insufficient to the needs of real writing situations, leaving students floundering and "struggling to put even basic ideas together," as an employer might say. To adapt a familiar adage: Give a student a methodic formula for writing, and she might pass the test; but teach her to know herself as a writer, and she'll write for life.

Although formulas and prescribed methods might allow our students to write with less difficulty by using tried-and-true formats, we run the risk of excising excitement, creation, and discovery from writing. Doing so contributes to a narrow notion of what it means to write. Our students grow as writers when we encourage them to stray from restrictive, basic formulas and, instead, to follow some imaginative bunny trails. Teaching writing in this way takes more effort and thinking for both our students and us teachers because we may be creating new forms and solutions for writing well.

Students who rely too much on a narrow method—the five-paragraph essay format is a fine example—for their writing restrict their thinking and communicative effectiveness. They may fail to adjust their writing for differing audiences and purposes, for example. Fluent writers, meanwhile, who are able to choose from a variety of possible methods and formats to meet a new writing expectation, may experience the thrill that comes from real learning, from creating an entirely new approach, solution, or response.

Some questions that deal further with writing, thinking, and creating are these:

- How can students best gain skill in assessing and responding to different writing situations successfully?
- How important is creative or original thinking for writing in everyday and professional situations?
- How can teachers prepare students to succeed on high-stakes writing exams without resorting to formulaic tactics?

◾ Challenge 3: What to Do About Rigor

When a college professor who teaches first-year composition learns that you teach secondary school English, he says, "Do me a favor and get serious about prepping these kids for college. Enough with the storytelling. They need some rigor." Anytime we propose that students benefit best from writing instruction grounded in personal relevance, sooner or later we're dealing with critiques such as this one. Mountains of evidence indicate that engagement and motivation are key factors in getting students to become better writers. Whole forests of testimonials from teachers and students speak to personal, narrative writing as a reliable and effective means for achieving this personal engagement. A small but steady stream of practical literature traces ways to build on a personal writing foundation to address a wide range of writing purposes. Yet, for some reason, this is not the landscape that the public and even some of our colleagues (who ought to know better) see when considering the place of the personal in writing instruction.

The experiences of individual writers hold an important place in writing instruction. Personal experiences give our student writers a basis for making sense of the world, for understanding the human condition, for connecting to new ideas, and experimenting with the potential of new forms of text to help them convey meaning. When we focus on students' personal experiences, we are not being softheaded or abandoning rigor. Personal experience tempered by research, reflection, and analysis is an appropriate basis for any type of writing. With these ideas in mind, consider these questions:

- How important is story in modern culture?
- Why use personal writing with students at all? What are its benefits? Its drawbacks?
- Why do some people believe that "personal writing" is less important compared to other kinds of writing?
- How might facility (written fluency) with narrative, memoir, and similar kinds of writing serve students strategically?
- What evidence, examples, and explanation might help change the minds of those skeptical of the practical relevance of personal writing?

We teach within a culture that focuses on analytical, argumentative writing as *the* central academic expectation. During the last twenty-five years or so, expository writing in all of its forms—argument and persuasion being prominent—have dominated high school curricula. It's the type of writing expected on high-stakes tests. It's the writing that seems to represent our cultural currency of knowledge. With this shift to rigorous, academic writing, our students should be wildly successful in college writing classes and with whatever writing they will need for their careers. We don't see a groundswell of public opinion that such is the case.

As you consider what it means to teach with rigor and the place of writing in our students' futures, consider these questions:

- What kinds of writing skills are most important for college?
- What are the qualities of a well-written argument?
- Given that the genres of argument and persuasion already dominate school writing, what do parents, teachers, administrators, and the general public mean when they say schools need more rigor?

▧ Challenge 4: What to Do About High-Stakes Test Prep

In a faculty meeting, your principal admonishes, "Our scores on the state writing exam need to improve. We need everyone on the same page with the curriculum map, teaching the agreed-upon assignments in the established order." For new and experienced teachers, dealing with the existence of state and district writing exams is simply part of the job. So is adapting to curriculum maps, department-level planning, test-prep expectations, committee-determined assignments, and other external interferences that chisel away at a teacher's autonomy. Some schools support sustained collaboration and encourage teachers to have a professional voice about policy decisions. Others operate in a more top-down, autocratic fashion and even shut down regular instruction in English and Language Arts classes in the weeks prior to high-stakes testing to create test-prep boot camps for students. When improvement mandates, school rankings, and even one's job may rely on test scores, the pressure to conform to an approved, exam-prep curriculum may be overwhelming.

Creative teachers face clear challenges when the system seems skewed to encourage uniform, common-denominator approaches to teaching. We absolutely understand this pressure. At the same time, anything worth doing involves some kind of effort and risk. Think of it this way: *If it were easy to be a creative teacher, everyone would be doing it.* When boundaries, limitations, outside requirements, and rigid agendas have constricted your options, the real challenges begin. Succeeding within (and perhaps despite of) the limitations of a system is the real trick.

We offer suggestions throughout this book to help you deal with these circumstances. The questions below help guide our thinking:

- What options do teachers have when departmental or district curriculum expectations conflict with what they know about good teaching, good writing, and student learning? What do such options look like in practice?
- How do we teach writing authentically while still specifically preparing students for writing exams?
- To what extent are high-stakes writing exams accurate indicators of students' writing abilities? How does our thinking about such exams affect our teaching?

◼ Challenge 5: What to Do About Technology

When a friend introduces you to a technology guru who discovers that you teach English, she insists, "Print-based writing is simply not enough. Schools need to adapt to the new literacy demands of the twenty-first-century learner." As we race into a future dominated by technology for business and social purposes, this call for change in our schools has become quite common.

Schools have generally been slow to adapt to recent technology changes, perhaps understandably. Technology is expensive, and most schools have had to make budgetary compromises. We see many classrooms in which students take turns on a couple of in-class computers and teachers share computer lab space. As Herrington, Hodgson, and Moran (2009) have pointed out, there are several contradictory factors involved in how administrators and policy makers view technology. Although a focus on providing "twenty-first-century learning" has led to technology-integration mandates in some school districts, administrators tend to shrink from the innate threats to control, discipline, and established order that Web-accessible technologies create. The result is a policy paradox: Teachers are expected to embrace technology but face restrictions about what they can do technologically with students.

If you are a teacher interested in integrating technology into your writing instruction, you likely exist in a zone of contradictions. Much research indicates that composing with the use of word-processing software helps students write more effectively and revise more often, but how do we teachers reconcile this knowledge of best practice with the shortage of computers and with testing that won't allow students to write on computers? Or consider how the digitally networked complexities of modern communication demand dexterity, judiciousness, and ethical awareness that we could teach our students—if only doing so didn't run afoul of restrictive school policies, including Internet filtering and prohibiting students' cell phone use while at school.

Traditional notions of writing and literacy as being solely print-based and text-centered are inadequate for our tech-savvy students and for the technology-focused world into which they will graduate. Our students benefit from explorations with multimedia and multimodal forms of communication and from exploring the relative contextual merits of each. If conventional writing instruction is all students receive, we are doing them a disservice.

Consider for a moment the growing trend toward immediacy in written expression. IMs, texts, and Tweets may seem as transient as casual speech to young people, but these communication acts are as permanent in their own way as more traditional forms of writing. They also exist within contexts that have their own protocols and genre expectations. The ability for young people to "code-switch" effectively across media and context will be paramount to their future success.

At the same time, we want to be wary of the siren call of futurism when we're dealing with technology, teaching, and writing. First and foremost, the public expects schools to produce students who write fluently and appropriately, an expectation we ignore at our peril.

Some questions that motivate our own thinking about technology and writing include the following:

- How are "digital literacies" defined, and how do they relate to conventional literacy?
- What abilities are most important for students to develop given present and future trends with tech-mediated communication?
- How can writing teachers make best use of technology within the narrow parameters permissible in schools?
- How important is the visual in writing instruction?

Teaching Writing Well: It's Not So Easy

There's no way to sugarcoat it. Teaching writing is challenging; it may be one of the toughest jobs a teacher faces. If you're teaching in a middle school or a high school classroom, you know the depth of the challenges that large classes, students whose first language isn't English, and excessive absences—as well as the challenges we discussed previously—present for teaching and learning anything. Too many teachers work in schools clogged with test-prep demands and follow-the-script teaching expectations. It's not much of a surprise, then, if some teachers try to avoid writing instruction entirely while others adopt the latest "Teach Writing Quickly!" off-the-shelf product to make their lives a little easier.

Effective teaching of writing takes time: time for practice, time to share writing, time to complete pieces of writing, and time to respond to and evaluate all of that writing. Many teachers dread teaching writing precisely because it takes lots of time, in class and out. In addition, the kids may be tough to reach, the curriculum is demanding, and conventional class schedules are not particularly amenable to the teaching of writing. Your frustration is justified. You could certainly choose a formulaic, by-the-numbers path to any writing that you require students to do. No one is likely to blame you, call you on the carpet, or lament what might have been if the circumstances were different.

But wait. Is it possible that you're missing the joy of seeing kids discover their own voices? Is it possible that you have coaching skills and writing talent that you haven't fully explored and developed? Maybe you could find some new strategies for getting your students going as writers and keeping them going. Maybe you could find some revision and editing strategies that students could and would use or transform your class into a community of writers. What if you gave this business of teaching writing a chance, calling upon your essential self to inform your teaching?

Becoming a successful teacher of writing is a journey. That's where this book wants to take you. We want to help you avoid the mistakes that many teachers before you—including us—made as they tried and failed to teach writing well. Maybe it's important for you to know that we are still working on our skills as writing coaches even as we author this text. After years of teaching writing and English, we still have doubts and uncertainties about our teaching abilities. These doubts drive us to experiment, read new research, alter our strategies, devise new materials, and learn as we teach. We continue to learn how to coach writing more effectively. If we cease to learn, we are committing personal and professional suicide. We work hard at being good teachers and writing coaches. More importantly, we invite you to join our journey and grow with us as a teacher of writing.

Inside Out . . . and Vice Versa

Almost every human child learns to speak without formal instruction. Some researchers such as Noam Chomsky suggest that we are hardwired for language. Learning to write and read—learning to be literate—requires training beyond what comes naturally, however. As we learn to write, we certainly tap into our innate, hardwired language-creating abilities. As we become more adept with language, we realize that we have word-choice and sentence-structure options; we have choices about tone and form and style. With this increased knowledge and ability comes the necessity to ponder and select among those options. Much research suggests that we think in a *recursive* manner: Our thinking cycles back on itself in metacognitive, incremental ways. Even as we write this book, for example, we reflect on our past and present teaching and writing experiences, try to bring them alive on the page, and extract beliefs and principles from them—and then we keep writing and reflecting some more. Writing has the potential to be *permanent*, to reside in a written text such as a book. It can resist the obliterating flow of time in ways that spoken words, words that we hear and then are gone, cannot. Writers create. We work a bit like sculptors, giving to shapeless clay or rough stone our steady and patient attention. Though revision and crafting, writing and rewriting, writers smooth the rough edges in our texts. We shape, sharpen, and strengthen our thinking. Form and meaning emerge in our writing just as works of art take shape under the sculptor's tools and hands.

Each student has a story to tell and something to say. All kids have unique and worthwhile thoughts and language in their heads. They all, however reluctant, can be enticed to negotiate the difficult processes of bringing their inner language to the page or computer screen. Likewise, teachers can acquire the skills of an effective coach, nurturing students' meaning-making processes.

To teach writing well, we don't look someplace "out there" for rules, formulas, and mimicry. We begin, instead, by teaching students to attend to their inner language, to their individual sensations, perceptions, emotions, incipient understandings, observations, and perspectives. Writing, like all other acts of creation, develops from the inside out.

▨ Outside In

Although it's important to teach writing from the *inside out*, much of how young people are educated—and so much of how they learn to see themselves in the world—involves taking the "outside in." Even though we're well into the twenty-first century, many school experiences are still based on very traditional, nineteenth-century assumptions about learning. You know how this looks. Teachers dispense information; students listen, take notes, and complete their homework assignments. At the end of the unit lurks a test, so students go through that old ritual of study and memorization. A passing score on the test demonstrates they've remembered enough to move forward, and the cycle begins again.

This scenario is based on a banking model of education in which sanctioned bits of knowledge are placed into students' minds like deposits in a vault. The banking model is very much about getting the "outside in," about putting the right information into kids' brains. State and national standards spell out the knowledge and skills that students are expected to learn. Such knowledge is the currency they are paid for being malleable students. Audits in the form of standardized tests, end-of-course exams, and districts' high-stakes testing ascertain that the implanted information sticks—more evidence of an "outside-in" mentality.

Unless a student lives life completely off the grid, dealing with the "outside in" is a daily, even hourly, challenge. American consumer culture targets teenagers as valuable customers, as consumers who can be swayed by a pervasive stream of visual messages to eat, wear, buy, play, watch, listen, say, do, and think as sociocorporate culture dictates. The digital, plugged-in, smart-gadget nature of contemporary youth culture sells *cool* to kids at the risk of tampering with an adolescent's emerging sense of identity. The "outside" messages barrage the senses, sometimes altering or affecting a teen's "inside" self-confidence.

There is a time and place for bringing "outside" pop culture influences "in," but pop culture, by definition, is transient; it isn't a way of life. The same principle applies to writing instruction. Young writers need to learn about themselves and discover who they are, what they think—maybe even *that* they think—before they have something authentic and interesting to say. When young writers are just starting out, they respond best to an approach that views them as thinking, expressive individuals possessed of a naturally creative spirit, not as test-taking automatons. They benefit from an approach that calls upon your essential self and best teaching practices to work with them from the *inside out*.

Beliefs About Teaching Writing Well

In short, teaching writing can be frustrating and challenging, but it can also be rewarding and a breath of fresh air in a rather stagnant educational context. A prerequisite for teaching writing well is a belief that writing *can be taught*. When you have tried but failed to see progress in your students' writing abilities, it's easy to succumb to the old thinking that writers really are born, not taught. Good writers have the writing gene; being able to write is in their DNA—or else it's just missing. God created some people to be writers and others to be architects. Those creative accidents of the deity just show up in third-period class, all bright and articulate, and they whip out amazing pieces of writing without needing much from us as their teachers and writing coaches. That ideal is not reality for all of our students—just ask any teacher. Fortunately, there's another way of thinking about students as writers.

Our fundamental belief throughout this book is that all students have unique thoughts and language in their heads, that they have personal experiences, stories, and ideas worth sharing. All students benefit from being encouraged to write, to bring the language in their heads onto the page or computer screen. We believe that we can be effective coaches of writing and help our students become better writers, no matter how reluctant they may be and no matter how many doubts they—and sometimes, we—might have.

We hold fast to the idea that writing is an intensely personal and uniquely human act. We see writing as inextricably bound to the individual experiences of feeling, perceiving, and thinking—bound to the processes by which language brings shape and import to what we feel, sense, and imagine. Writing emerges from an ongoing, never-finished, constantly refreshed, and always singular act of creation. Even with all we know about the human brain through decades of inquiry and study in the fields of human cognitive development, neurology, and linguistic theory—even with all that research and knowledge, exactly how language and thought happen and interrelate remain an amazing mystery. Each of us, and every healthy child in the world, is born with minds designed not just for language *use* but also for unique language *creation*. This fact, this ability, is absolutely remarkable, if not miraculous.

▨ What Writers Need

Every teacher shapes an identity through negotiating (and renegotiating) these kinds of issues: What lies behind your teaching decisions? What determines the questions you ask, the assignments you design, the comments you make about student work, your criteria for grading, and your classroom design? What essential skills and abilities are you hoping to impart to your students? What, ideally, will they carry away from your class into their lives as thinking adults?

In the jargon of teacher preparation, working through such questions over and over on the micro and macro levels is called becoming a "reflective practitioner." It's a simple concept to understand that may be difficult to apply effectively. The basic idea is that good teachers never get too settled in their practice. They regularly question their assumptions and rationales, even going so far as to overhaul completely how they teach every few semesters or years. As we reassess our foundation for teaching and ask ourselves questions that may have uncomfortable answers, we are creating *more work* for ourselves. But it's the nature of the work that matters. It's definitely *easier* to pull out the same old worksheet or same old writing assignment year after year. What that doesn't do is offer us intellectual challenges and opportunities to grow as teachers. Revising problematic assignments, designing new ones, experimenting with technologies, and risking failure are part of the process of becoming better teachers. Beware of the teacher—veteran or rookie—who is completely sure of each decision; he is either in a vegetative state or kidding himself. Revising and revamping our teaching lives is one way we stay intellectually alive; it's one way we avoid burnout. If we won't revise and rethink what we do, why should our students? We are reminded that when asked for words of wisdom at age eighty, the Renaissance artist Michelangelo reputedly responded with "I'm still learning." His words might make an appropriate epigraph for our professional lives.

By pointing out some of the challenges that face teachers, we've attempted to pique your curiosity, encourage you to agree or disagree with us, but above all to reflect and come to your own conclusions. We often rethink what we think, and we invite you to join us in this ongoing venture.

Nonetheless, our core beliefs about writing and writing instruction form the basis of this book and essential guidelines that motivate how we position ourselves as writing teachers.

Belief 1: Writing Is Best Taught as a Creative, Social, and Collaborative Act

This assertion might seem like a blunderingly obvious statement because writing doesn't exist unless someone creates it. Teachers may agree with the notion of writing as an essential creative process, but if they run their classes as if students are producing the writing equivalent of widgets, then those notions don't mean squat. Yes, our students benefit from learning a variety of common forms, conventions, and structures in writing. Of course, varying situations call for very specific kinds of writing, be it a company memo, a carefully worded apology, a sales pitch, or a college application essay. Some kinds of writing don't exactly call for inspired invention; no one expects high poetry from a biology lab report. When we consistently forget about or ignore the kernel of creation that lies at the nucleus of each writing act, however, we lose something vital.

At any megagrocery store today you can buy shrink-wrapped items in the produce section labeled as "tomatoes." Uniformly plump and red, these objects may indeed take the form of tomatoes, but they sure don't *taste* like them. They don't taste much like anything actually, and their mealy texture doesn't add much to the eating experience. In the interests of mass production and convenience, these miracles of modern industry were grown far away, picked while still green, sorted by machines, and ripened with ethylene gas while en route to the store. We get something that looks authentic but isn't in any important way.

Does a tomato that doesn't taste like anything still count as a tomato? This is not just a rhetorical question or Buddhist koan. Real homegrown tomatoes may not always look as perfect as those fake doppelgängers at the Giant Food Mart. Each is a little different, with its own character and blemishes. Each takes time to develop and ripen. Almost without exception, however, backyard tomatoes have what matters most: flavor, juiciness, texture, and authenticity.

You see the point of our metaphor. When writing is taught in a way that excises the central creative element, we end up with the literary equivalent of industrial tomatoes, the sad triumph of appearance over substance.

Let's look at another part of this belief: *Writing is best taught as a social act.* The cliché of the writer as solitary, Muse-inspired recluse gradually gave way in the 1970s and 1980s, partly due to constructivist learning theorists who began to insist that all learning was both personal *and* social. Those theorists pointed out that learners and writers needed to construct personal versions of the world around them, but then they also needed to submit those unique versions to peers for response, negotiation, and confirmation. Writing response groups became both a sound instrument for learning and growth and an acceptable element of composition pedagogy. To put it simply, real writing presumes the need—and the expectation—of active readers. Certainly some of what writers do may happen in private, but as an act of communication, writing invokes interaction with others.

The merit of this idea becomes quite clear when we consider the popularity of social networking. Here's a new form of communication that simply didn't exist a few years ago.

Once digital and mobile technology evolved to a certain point, however, social networking arose more or less spontaneously. Give people an outlet for expression and the possibility to interact with others and new communities will form, communities that are guided by shared interests. Traditional writing classrooms that isolate writers or move students through perfunctory "peer editing" as the extent of writing interaction might be rationalized with appeals to time shortages and overloaded curricula. That notion might be understandable, but be aware that such a model represents the opposite of how writing really happens in people's lives, from cyberspace to the workplace.

Writing is best taught as a collaborative act. Writing classrooms may have social elements without being truly collaborative. Think about how peer review typically takes place. Students read one another's work and make comments and suggestions, which is social, but then return to revising their own work alone. Although true collaboration may occur during writing response groups, we improve our students' effectiveness when we teach them explicitly how to interact as readers and responders. It is through this process that the social becomes collaborative.

"Collaboration" as a goal sounds good; but, traditionally, schools are not institutions that promote collaboration. Schools are mechanisms for sorting, classifying, grading, and ranking students based on individual performance. Such a system encourages competition, not collaboration and cooperation. But school is not necessarily like life. If our students are to lead meaningful and rewarding lives, personally and professionally, they need to know how to participate, cooperate, contribute, and connect. A class built on collaborative instead of competitive principles doesn't mean we throw out individual grades or personal responsibility, but it does require that we help our students grapple with a new ethic. Learning to manage and feel comfortable in more interactive structures takes time and some resolve, but the payoff in student growth is worth the pain of change.

Belief 2: Coached Fluency Comes First

Fluency is a term that we use frequently in this book as we talk about writing. Just as readers learn to be *fluent* with word recognition and sentence meaning, and just as speakers become *fluent* in a first and sometimes second language, effective writers also need to become fluent in their written expressions. Capturing thoughts and meanings from the brain and moving them onto the page or computer screen in ways that communicate information, experiences, or opinions—that is, acquiring written fluency—isn't an instant skill for most people. Learning how to be fluent in one's writing requires extensive practice. Written fluency also benefits from coaching by an experienced teacher-writer.

Putting fluency first requires that we allow our students to ease into new, unfamiliar forms. It means offering students many opportunities to read examples of the forms they will eventually write. It might mean deconstructing a form to understand its elements and how they work together within the piece. It means devoting a good deal of time to the *early* stages of writing a piece, namely idea finding, drafting, and experimenting. Oversimplified formulas don't encourage experimentation; instead, they stress getting the *form* right. When developing writers are required to focus on forms, they learn to plug lifeless words and mundane ideas into the formula; they don't learn to create unique expressions and to figure out the form in which the writing might work best.

In writing, all of us probably expect too much too soon. In contrast to the ideas of the late 1800s, we know now that children are not, developmentally, miniature adults; similarly, we also now know that inexperienced writers don't write as do adults, nor should they be expected to do so. Their thinking, sentence patterns, and vocabulary all need time and practice to develop. We shouldn't expect young writers to have all of the elements of form mastered from the beginning.

We suggest that when you begin teaching writing to a new group of students, you declare a moratorium on concerns about rigidly defined forms and structures of writing. Emphasize fluency. Use expressive and reflective forms of writing that offer maximum opportunity for your students to get a feel for producing text without the pressure to meet all of the constraints of a well-defined form. Encourage them to write about themselves and their own experiences first and to value and interact with those pieces of writing. Developing writers need time to experiment with their ideas and words and the connections between the two. Practice in rendering the tangled web of their emotions and imaginations into written language will help writers learn to express their ideas clearly, precisely, and fluently. Let them write and let the forms emerge.

Proficiency in writing requires consistent practice. But just letting students write—mere unguided experimentation—isn't the answer. If students are to grow as writers through practice, that practice must be coached. Someone who knows something about writing must interact with students before, during, and after the practice.

Novice teachers of writing may be dismayed and intimidated by poorly written student texts. Our first reaction to some of the really bad student papers we received was, "There's something wrong with this paper, but I don't know exactly what it is." This can be an exasperating feeling when a student is waiting at your elbow for a response or when you have another hundred or so papers to read. Many teachers end up hiding behind correction marks like *Awk* and *Frag* and *Needs work*, focusing on easily identifiable surface issues.

It's generally true that the best way to get good at diagnosing what's working and what isn't in student writing is to read a lot of student writing. Not much substitutes for this experience and familiarity, but there are some definite strategies that even new teachers might adopt from day one. One of the most effective approaches is learning to read and respond as a *reader*, not just as a teacher. As readers, we don't have to be experts to interact with student work. We are free to base at least some of our reaction on what sounds right, strikes a chord, and makes sense. We might point to places in the piece of writing where we are confused or where we wonder if elaboration might be appropriate. We might ask questions that help to clarify the writer's intention. Instead of filling papers with shorthand that only a fellow teacher readily understands, we suggest that you defer the urge to correct in favor of first interacting as a reader to a writer who happens to be your student.

Writing, sharing, and talking with our students about writing are more important than lectures, conventional rules about writing, and marking papers.

Belief 3: In Writing, the Whole Is More Than the Sum of Its Parts

Schools have always been pretty good at teaching parts and not so good at helping students see the big picture and create wholes. The deductive mind-set of working from part to whole, from word to sentence to paragraph, may sound logical: Begin with the word, next the sentence, then the paragraph; then, when students become *really good*, they get to write a whole five-paragraph essay. Master the parts, get those labels straight; memorize those transitional words to plug relentlessly into every paragraph. This mind-set equates writing to math: It's neat and tidy, and it all adds up.

Except that it doesn't.

Describing a person solely as a collection of a billion cells ordered into a few hundred bones and a couple dozen organs is preposterous. We are evidently more than the sum of our bodies' parts; each of us is uniquely different from every other person in amazing ways. Similarly, in writing, the whole isn't just a collection of parts. The crucial misstep lies in equating foundational knowledge—of letters, grammar, syntax, and punctuation—with operational knowledge, meaning how we put these tools to use. By fragmenting instruction and drilling on one part or one structure at a time, we kill motivation and destroy the very processes we're trying to develop. If that's not bad enough, we also end up with some pretty terrible writing as a result.

When we deal with writing, we are dealing with human acts of creation. Yes, writing is based on fundamental units. But what we each choose to do with these simple elements is what writing is all about. Here's another metaphor: All decent architects understand the basic ingredients of construction. They understand the "rules" for how floors are laid, how brick walls are built, how roofs must be supported, and how homes and buildings are generally constructed. Does this mean they are locked into designing only one kind of structure? Architects are creative professionals, drawing upon their understandings of fundamentals to make something unique, not just to repeat what they've done before. Any architect forced to design the same limited kind of building again and again would likely find little satisfaction from her effort.

We've studied the components of good writing extensively and have worked at coaching writing for many years. We consider ourselves writers who have a sense of good writing when we see it. We also realize that writers fashion subjects in individual ways. We assist our student writers by designing occasions to rehearse their skills and techniques through a variety of writing experiences. We coach them by providing a third eye or ear. We avoid writing exercises taken out of an authentic context, and we make careful judgments about when and how to intervene in students' writing processes.

But writers need to learn the basics first, some will say, *and once they've done that, then they can get creative*. This stance is laden with problems. At what point do we judge a student competent enough to begin using language creatively? How long must they spend in basic boot camp? What counts as "basic" and who gets to decide? And what's the point if, by the time they learn the basics, our students see writing only as an onerous, joyless exercise to be suffered? Consider other creative acts. We hardly prevent toddlers from making up songs until they've mastered standards like "The Itsy Bitsy Spider," nor do we discourage them from dancing unless it's with perfect rhythm.

It's unrealistic to expect students to drill on the parts of language or the parts of a composition for years in anticipation of some far-off future when they are allowed to begin using the parts to explore discourse options. We try to help young writers produce an authentic piece every time they write. There is technical knowledge to be learned; but writing is first enjoyed, read, and communicated. No approach to writing that forgets the joy of singing your own song will work with novice writers.

Belief 4: Writing Assessment Must Support Growth, and Growth Takes Time

Let's be honest. We have assessed writing too early, too often, and in contexts that are too artificial to be informative about how real writing occurs. Some of our grading has been punitive or used shamelessly as crowd control. Many of our assessments tell us little about the writing abilities our students do or don't possess. Grading, assessment, and testing practices are, in many cases, an anathema to the teaching strategies that we know work best with developing writers; not every piece of writing needs to be completely finished and graded. We've heard many teachers lament that students pay only passing attention to the careful marking of their papers. The teachers that we know generally give little credence to students' scores on mandated assessments of writing because they are most often one-shot samples of a student's writing at a particular moment in time, not a sample of the student's best work. Yet, many teachers we know continue to spend an inordinate amount of time alone with student papers, meticulously marking them. Add to these grievances the preparation and class time that teachers may be required to expend on mind-numbing, state-mandated test prep and testing, and we face a serious waste of energy and instructional time that could (and should) be spent on coaching and responding to student writing.

A curriculum that stresses authentic writing in a range of forms and for a variety of purposes and audiences leads to improved student performances in writing. Real language used in real ways for authentic purposes that matter to the writer promotes writing that matters, that others want to read and discuss, and that students value enough to work on and revise. Importantly, such *authentic writing practice raises students' scores on standardized and high-stakes tests*. We don't have to "drill and kill" our students. When writing and the written word live inside our classrooms as part of the intellectual conversation each day, writing and thinking flourish. When we teachers grade fewer papers and take seriously our responsibility to coach writing that is meaningful to students and that demonstrates effective strategies for improving content, appearance, and structures, students grow as effective writers.

Even in this age of instructional enlightenment, the chronicle of many children's experiences with writing in school remains a fitful series of stops and starts. Too often, writing instruction is a patchwork of writing short stories this week, short essays next week, short critiques the week after that, and of delving into literature with no writing at all for the following six weeks. In other words, writing instruction too often consists of a sporadic pattern of quantum leaps and long silences. In too many schools and school districts, we continue to fail to provide enough consistent instruction and practice to reap the rewards of better writers and writings. Just because it's in the curriculum guide doesn't mean it gets taught. And just because it gets taught doesn't mean it's taught well.

For writing instruction to produce good writers, it must not only be well articulated in curriculum guides, textbooks, and inservice workshops, but it must also be practiced by a community of professional teachers who interact with each other to build proficiency over time.

Belief 5: It's About Much More Than Just Writing

We're hoping this final belief doesn't come across as too clever or too cute. This book is obviously about writing and how to teach it well. Even so, whenever we start thinking about the underlying motivation of what we're all doing, we can't help but dwell on the much bigger picture.

Struggle and Accomplishment

When we teach writing authentically and personally, we fight against the prevailing idea that good writers are born with a talent for language and the rest of us are hamstrung by genetic bad luck. We've met plenty of kids who've been taught the heartbreaking lesson that they are not (and can't ever be) good writers. So, why should they bother? This misconception is usually tangled with some other troubling beliefs. Struggling writers often see their halting, disjointed efforts as evidence of a permanent inadequacy and thus a reason to give up. Fluent writers, meanwhile, see these *very same* initial efforts as provisional and expected, the first efforts in a much larger process. Fluent writers aren't born that way. They've just had more experience in seeing writing projects to fruition through persistence, patience, and self-confidence.

This book is a case in point. If there are any phrases or passages that strike a reader as well written, stylish, or compelling within these pages, trust us, it's not because the Muse delivered them, packaged in sparkling perfection. Almost all of our first attempts have to be wrestled onto the page, with clunky sentence structure mirroring our half-formed thoughts. Constant revision is our only secret; if you find areas that seem less elegant or astute, you can bet it's because the polishing process of revision has been inadequately applied.

Part of our work, then, is helping students understand that the struggle, discomfort, and ambiguity so common to work-in-progress are absolutely normal, positive, and necessary. Withholding judgment and getting the whispering critic off our backs in these early stages is a major step forward. At the same time, students have to develop a personal ethic of effort. They need reliable habits of mind and self-discipline. Writing is serious work, with a lot of sweat and effort to go along with those occasional moments of inspiration. Caring enough to stick with it through the confusing and difficult process of creation is essential.

When we help students develop these mental attitudes toward written effort, we're working on much larger life skills like setting realistic but challenging goals, delaying gratification, tolerating discomfort, overcoming failure, and practicing self-discipline. That's a pretty valuable list of skills for success in the world. Every professional or personal endeavor out there worth doing—climbing a mountain, making the basketball team, building a career, or working on a relationship—requires dogged persistence and resilience in the face of adversity. The convenient narratives we often pass on to kids ("follow your dreams," "you can do anything if you put your mind to it," "winning isn't everything; it's the only thing") tend to leave out the hard parts: the grinding work in the trenches, the inevitable obstacles and disappointments. As Tim Harford details in *Adapt: Why Success Always Starts with Failure* (2011), the key to accomplishment is how we learn to handle difficulty, frustration, and defeat. When a student stares down at the garbled paragraph she's just written, what comes next is a microcosm of the test of life. Faced with this challenge, we want student writers to develop the fluency and confidence to roll up their sleeves for the hard work ahead. The alternative—shutting down the effort, and in the process, closing off an entire realm of human expression—is no alternative at all.

Writers and Thinkers

As teachers of writing, we are also teachers of thinking. We'll even say that before you can be a good writing teacher, you have to be a teacher of thinking, first and foremost. This might seem like an odd or uncomfortable idea, but consider all the ways that thinking is woven into writing:

- Good writers use the act of writing to generate and help sort out their thinking.
- Good writers understand the importance of process in writing; in the words of Donald Murray, they see that most writing is actually rewriting.

- Good writers know themselves as writers; they are aware of their strengths and weaknesses.
- Good writers adopt a *thinking pose*: They wonder, ask why, consider reasons, explore alternatives, chase down stray thoughts, hypothesize, and make tentative attempts at developing ideas.
- Good writers consider the social, transactional nature of writing; they are able to see their work through the eyes of others and use this awareness to their advantage.

Can someone be a writer without also being a thinker? It's possible, but the kind of writing produced may not be worth reading. We can live with the idea that our students may be making only modest progress in their writing, as long as they're evolving as thinkers as well.

And Finally . . .

What do we lose if most young people leave school having decided that they have little to say through writing and if they find writing itself tedious and irrelevant?

Whether the result of foregone personal conclusions ("I'm just not a writer") or regressive educational policies that kill motivation and creativity, the corrosive effect on individual potential is the same. We don't need to frame the problem in elaborate economic, political, social, or philosophical terms for the abundantly obvious to be clear: A nation of nonwriters with little confidence in sorting through their thoughts, experiences, and emotions is not a good thing.

Our beliefs about writing fight against this combination of alienation and apathy. We teach writing to help students see themselves as "voiced" individuals, as people who have the ability and confidence to convey their thinking on the page and on the screen, and who can move forward into adult lives rich with the potential that comes from a fluent and literate self-awareness. Now is no time to settle for an impoverished and narrow vision of writing instruction. Our students have something to say—about themselves and about the world in which they find themselves—and we need them to say it.

Works Cited

Comer, Cornelia. 2010. "A Letter to the Rising Generation." In *Youth and the New World. Essays from the* Atlantic Monthly, edited by Ralph Philip Boas, 28–46. Charleston, SC: Nabu Press.

Harford, Tim. 2011. *Adapt: Why Success Always Starts with Failure.* New York: Farrar, Strauss, and Giroux.

Herrington, Anne, Kevin Hodgson, and Charles Moran. Eds. 2009. *Teaching the New Writing: Technology, Change, and Assessment in the 21st Century.* New York: Teachers College Press.

Palmer, Parker. 1998. *The Courage to Teach.* San Francisco: Jossey Bass.

Vetter, Craig. 2009. "Bonehead Writing." In *Essays on Writing*, edited by Lizbeth Bryant and Heather Clark, 35–39. New York: Longman.

Fluency and the Individual Writer

I think the main reason more people don't write is the sheer terror of confronting yourself on the page. Somewhere there are people who—on their first try—can make great writing. These people . . . are not human.

—Ta-Nehisi Coates, *Atlantic Monthly* senior editor

How do words come from the mind and onto the page or computer screen, or become an oral expression? One researcher, Lev Vygotsky, a Russian linguist, postulates that we think in propositions, that is, basically in sentences. He indicates that we are immersed in an endless flow of language, in our *inner speech*. James Miller, one of our favorite writers on writing, builds on Vygotsky's notion of inner speech by saying that "writing is largely a process of choosing among alternatives from the images and thoughts of the endless flow, and this choosing is a matter of making up one's mind, and this making up one's mind becomes in effect the making up of one's self" (1972). Miller's image conjures up notions of discovery, individuality, personal experience, and possibility.

Teaching writing involves helping our students attend to, collect, and select from their inner language flow, and then to spin that language onto the page as text. Much as *Harry Potter*'s Hogwarts headmaster and the wisest of wizards, Albus Dumbledore, pulls memories from his ear before viewing them in the magical Pensieve, when we write, we dip into our inner language flow and pull out ideas and words to put down on the page. We may not know exactly what is coming next even though we have a general sense of what we remember or know or want to express. We begin to impose order as we write one word after the other on the page. During this formative—or inventive or draft—time, writers may feel anxious, sometimes almost panicky, as we try to capture meaning from the flow of language. We may be afraid that something will slip by, that we'll miss that special word or phrase we need to get it said right. Every writer, novice or expert, knows that feeling.

We know that writing is more than magically pulling thoughts and memories from our heads, especially during those times when our students' heads seem empty, devoid of language and ideas. Writing teachers often need to jump-start the student writer's processes for generating ideas by offering heuristic devices, probing questions, or brainstorming tools and tricks. Teaching writing is more than just freewriting and brainstorming.

Nonetheless, we remain adamant about the importance of believing in students' inner language and in nurturing and coaching their efforts to render it as text.

Consider how most of us write. We want the reader to understand and accept our feelings and reasons and postulations. We may write half of the first sentence of a paragraph, stop, scratch it out, and write that half-sentence again, slightly differently this time. The rest of that sentence was there a second ago; now it has evaporated. Something else flashes into our minds, and we finish the sentence. There are long "silences," one of the important parts of this business of writing, while we watch the interior flow of language and wait for just the right word or phrase to surface. We back up to the paragraph before this one, and change a word here and there. We jump ahead, anticipating where we want to go next. Other thoughts intrude, and we reread what we've written to get started again.

This recursive process is something of what writing is like even when it's going well. For those of us who write often, these things, and more—usually happening so fast and so naturally that we're long since used to it—are all part of the *feeling* of writing as it is going on.

Not all writing goes well, even for experienced writers. Elie Wiesel (1996) says, "Writing is painful pleasure and the most difficult part is to begin. . . . Ultimately to write is an act of faith" (336). Any first draft may be halting, awkward, or a bit chaotic. The novice writer needs to know that this feeling of hesitancy and chaos is natural, that even the best writers experience it. Within that initial rush of ideas and uncertainty lies the variety of thoughts and possibilities, the kaleidoscopic flux of life itself from which the writer might capture words, phrases, and concepts that are beautiful and well suited to the writing task. Being able to work though ideas to craft expression is one of the great gifts of being literate humans, and our students need to know they are able to learn to do so.

Writing Processes

When we teach writing, we try to align our instruction with proven methodologies and best practices, with more natural and less artificial processes, with what "real" and "good" writers do when they write. This shift isn't a natural or an easy one for some of our students. They may resist leaving behind the comfort of their personal experiences and usual modes of expression. They may challenge us, preferring to stick with the familiar rather than charging ahead into new territory that is well patrolled by teachers. At times, the best thing we can do for novice writers is to get out of their way and let them write. This is a point that Peter Elbow made long ago. Our job as writing teachers is not to put students through academic exercises or make them conform to what the assessment police are requiring for the latest high-stakes tests. Our job is to make writing a natural and rewarding part of our students' lives, just as it is a part of ours.

The idea that writers follow a "writing process" as they produce text was established by Emig's research in the 1970s. Educators and authors of composition textbooks soon began to promote teaching writing by using comparable methods. Likewise, state and district curricular frameworks also developed a hefty degree of uniformity. As a result, most English and language arts teachers now conceptualize how writing happens in similar ways, and they use somewhat uniform terminology to describe and talk about writing. Brainstorming, jotting, drafting, sharing, revising, editing, and publishing are well-known features of writing instruction in most classes. The idea that writing happens through a process has curtailed the traditional tendency that English teachers once had of giving students a writing assignment without teaching students much of anything about how to *write* whatever the assignment called for. Notions of *process* necessitated that teachers teach the process to their students. That's the good news: The traditional method of teaching writing by merely *assigning* it yielded to teaching writing by teaching "the writing process."

The less than good news is the frequency with which "uniformity" and "consistency" become the ultimate goal of writing instruction. "*The* writing process" implies that there is only one. In fact, many English classrooms have posters on the walls, indicating to student writers what they should do first, second, third, last. Never vary, Young Writer. Stick with the methods for writing that we know will work—the ones represented by those posters on the wall. Write those lifeless but highly organized five-paragraph papers, Student Writer, and you will do well in school and on tests designed to measure your writing skill.

We pause here to note that well-oiled academic sureties are supremely suspect. Dissenters look for cracks in these sureties and generally find them. As with any theory, a new one strives to fill the gaps in the old one. Paradigms—organizing strategies and structures for making sense of complex processes—shift, answering some questions but raising others.

Notions about *writing as a process* arose because traditional writing instruction wasn't producing fresh, original, thoughtful papers. Student writers didn't use outlines as teachers thought they should. Students seemed not to listen very well as teachers spent precious class time, instructing novice writers that every *A* on an outline must have a *B*, that outlines use full sentences or parallel phrases but not both on the same outline. The advanced students learned what to do once they needed to add information beyond small *a* and small *b*. Those of you who did not go to school during a certain era may think you briefly entered an alternate universe as you read those last couple of sentences. Others will certainly recall writing the outline required by the teacher, often *after* the paper itself was written. After all, how do I know exactly what I want to write and in what order I want my thoughts to appear until after I've written something?

Before notions of writing process became institutionalized and singularized (from *a* to *the* process), this methodology provided students opportunities to talk their way into writing to see and hear what they knew about a topic, to jot ideas in any order or form, to write without thinking that whatever came out the first time was what they would turn in for a grade. That's the good stuff associated with writing process methodology. In contrast, the posters on the wall leading in lockstep fashion from brainstorming to drafting, to revising, and to finished product represent the not-so-good simplification of what is a combination of very complex processes: writing.

It comes as no surprise, then, that some theorists and practitioners have adopted a stance toward teaching writing that reacts against rigid methodology and practice—against those steps depicted on the wall posters. In contrast to writing-as-a-process practitioners are those who identify themselves as *postprocess* theorists. They object to a one-size-fits-all methodology for teaching writing. They cast out the simplification and rigidity of "the writing process." They also question what makes an institutionalized notion of writing as a process any better than anything that came before it.

We, Dawn and Darren, aren't sure that we are so simply categorized as *process* or *postprocess* theorists and practitioners. In the third edition of this book,[1] Dawn talked about writing *processes*—plural—that are as varied as the writers who use them. The concept of writing *processes* arose from Dawn's research with tenth-grade writers.[2] As writers ourselves, we know that writers tend to invent their own ways of working. Few English professionals, textbooks, and curricular frameworks acknowledge the idiosyncratic nature of writers at work and the need for individual writers to customize "the process" to meet their own needs and preferences.

So here is our first caution: Avoid the temptation to conceive of writing as one defined process; as a prescription; or as a singular, immutable construct—and worse yet, to present it to your students that way. Think of any *steps* in *a writing process* as an exemplar, a "for example." Swear off haranguing your students about *the steps* as lockstep, ironclad procedures that all student writers must follow. Dawn confirmed in her early research that writers follow unique, even idiosyncratic processes to produce assigned texts (Kirby, unpublished doctoral dissertation, University of Georgia, 1985). She observed tenth-grade writers who began by writing a draft, not by jotting or brainstorming. Sometimes form and structure intrude into writing so that they take precedence in the writer's mind over shaping content, at least for a while. Writing processes are untidy for most writers, even with the automatic neatness of written products composed on a computer. The uniqueness of individual writers' processes reminds us that requiring all students to create a web or cluster before they begin a draft is only slightly different from requiring that all writers turn in a full-blown outline before they proceed to writing the draft. In reality, writers use many different processes depending on their moods, the rhetorical situation, the type of writing, and a host of additional factors.

Books and teachers teach the writing process in steps as though it were a singular phenomenon because it's easier and simpler to do so. We need to keep reminding ourselves, however, that writing processes are recursive, and that writing does not follow neat, separate steps. Most student texts do begin somewhere and end somewhere else, usually but not always with a finished product of some kind. We agree with the assertion that our students' writing is usually better when talking, drafting, revising, reading aloud, and editing are part of the writing experiences that students have; but as students step ahead in these processes, they may also need to step back.

Easing into Writing

A teacher's primary responsibility where writing processes are concerned is to introduce students to a variety of ways of beginning, drafting, revising, and completing their work. More specifically, we need to help student writers wrestle their ideas onto the page and then teach them writerly strategies that will help them shape and refine those ideas into effective texts. Essentially, what process (or postprocess) pedagogy should provide for students is an ever-expanding repertoire of strategies for enhancing their own ways of producing text.

How do you learn to appreciate and accommodate student's differences where writing processes are concerned? We suggest beginning your writing class by talking to your students about what they do when they write. Getting students to talk about their experiences with writing is essential to opening up any authentic discussion of writing and how to make it better. Talk about the hard parts of writing. Ask them about their writing processes. What do they do to get going? How do they revise? How do they know when a piece of writing is finished? When you give them that first opportunity to write in class, write with them and then talk about the writing together, sharing with one another your feelings about the writing and about what you do as you write. Have them do some freewriting—write quickly, without stopping, for ten minutes about whatever comes to mind without worrying about form, correctness, or whether the writing is any good. Ask them to think about writing and, in their freewriting, to talk to you about it on the page as though they were talking aloud to you. Pass out a short questionnaire on writing (see Chapter 3 for a sample) to start and then explore further their thinking.

Another initial activity that we have used with great success is to ask our students to write a narrative about their past experiences, good and bad, with writing. We want these recountings to be genuine, in the student's own voice, and to indicate the good, the bad, and the ugly (or pretty) bits of their literacy development. Sometimes we call these pieces "My Literacy History." At other times, we might call them "How I Learned to Love (or Hate) Writing (and Reading)," or the deliberately irreverent "Me and Writing" to indicate that expression—not correctness or tone or sentence construction—is the point of these pieces. We find that these literacy histories are extremely revealing about our students' perceptions of and connections with their personal growth and progress as literate beings. They tell us the past highs and lows of their previous encounters with reading and writing. We read these pieces and respond in written marginalia as readers of a piece of good writing, not as English teachers determined to correct every mistake or craft a piece worthy of publication. In class, we discuss the pieces with our students as a way of getting them to talk and think about writing.

We also advise that you watch your students writing every chance you get. Make some time each week for at least thirty minutes of in-class writing so that you can coach them while they're at work. We know you will observe differences in how students write, but we think you will notice important similarities as well. Use those observations and the insights gained from reading your students' literacy histories to help you design and select instructional strategies that support and extend the ways in which your student writers work.

Our Model of Writing

From observing and talking with our students and from reading research and methods texts, our approach for teaching writing to *all* students emerges. It is not a lockstep, drills-and-skills, part-to-whole, teach-to-the-test method, but rather a processes approach that builds on the intuitive language resources common to all human beings. We believe that, simply stated, writers' processes move along a continuum from fluency to control and precision. This model of how writing develops has been a hallmark of this book from the beginning when Dan Kirby and Tom Liner were the sole authors (first and second editions of *Inside Out*), so we think it natural to continue to use Tom Liner's terms of seeing writing as a matter of getting it started, getting it down, getting it right, and checking it out. Here's that model:

Fluency ↔ Control ↔ Precision
and
Getting It Started ↔ Getting It Down ↔ Getting It Right ↔ Checking It Out

In our model, fluency is the first consideration. It is the basis for all that follows. Jotting, writing, drafting, brainstorming, and revising will all help writers develop fluency. Fluency isn't a step in *the* writing process. It's a state of written language development during which writers become comfortable with written expression and able to develop and express thoughts with relative ease. Because fluency is so basic to successful writing, your first priority must be to get students writing and keep them writing. Our mantra is, "You can't teach writing if you can't get writing out of your students." You can teach *about* writing, but you can't teach writing. Without that daily practice in a humane and accepting atmosphere, writing is drudgery for most students and grows very little.

Notice also that the arrows between the words on each line point in both directions. We don't yet have holographs and 3-D projectors in our classrooms, or books from which such dimensional models arise, so the words are flat and seemingly linear on the page. The processes represented by the words, however, are far from orderly, flat, and predictable. That notion takes us back to the postprocess theorists. Writing isn't neat and tidy; it's messy. Writing doesn't proceed from one step to another; it's recursive and double backs on itself. Until books can represent multidimensional human behavior through more robust models, however, the best we have are those little arrows and what their double points tell us to remember: Writing consists of processes as unique as the writers using them, and it's our job to foster multiple understandings, experimentation with what and how our students know, and various pathways for working and being successful in our classrooms for all of the students we encounter.

Focusing on Written Fluency

We have found confirmation about the importance of building written fluency early in our teaching of writing by studying other teachers, particularly those in the arts. We have seen art teachers entice students of differing abilities from all over the school into their classes. What art teachers do first is get the kids messing around with art—that is, getting them *fluent* in art—whether the medium is drawing, painting, or working in clay. Dawn loves the feel of the art studio and enjoys watching as students experiment with their own expressions, check out options, and get a *feel* for the medium. Art teachers encourage the good practices and results they see—and there is always something good, eventually. Have you ever noticed that in an art studio, everyone is working on art? The teacher and the students work on their own pieces alongside each other. They practice, becoming more comfortable with the medium, and their artwork gets better. The art develops and becomes deeper, richer, and more complex. By midwinter, the halls of most schools are crowded with paintings and drawings and beautiful creations by the art students—fluency, control, and precision in the art class.

We believe that written fluency brings control in even the hardest and most frustrating cases, but you have to be patient. Dawn worked with teachers in an Atlanta public high school in which 64 percent of the ethnically diverse students were on free and reduced lunch and just over 51 percent of students dropped out before graduation. This urban population was also highly transient; classroom doors seemed to revolve as students moved into and out of the school's service area, continually adding and dropping classes. Inside the classroom, the situation seemed rather desperate. Students slept, hoodies pulled over their heads on their desks, or students stayed plugged in to their music devices while texting on phones secreted in their laps. All of the laws of logic and education said that nothing much was going on in this school, with or without their turnaround expert. If students were developing anything, it seemed to be their plans for what to do once the school day was over. Not enough writing was going on for them to be developing much fluency in anything else.

Two ninth-grade teachers who were graduate students in one of Dawn's classes, however, decided to try something—anything—to break this downward spiral, even if it meant varying from their prescribed curricular materials and district-generated lesson plans, which they did with some trepidation. What would the principal say if he discovered they weren't teaching the same stuff as the other ninth-grade teachers? They decided to change just enough to work on written fluency and to try to get their students writing in journals. The teachers couldn't keep their students from moving, but they could work on fluency in the time they had with the students in class.

These teachers began by asking students about what they liked to do. Sure, there was the usual talk about cars, music, clothes, and sex, but they were talking. Next, the teachers played some of the PG13-rated versions of songs the students liked and asked students to write or just to jot ideas—about the music, their dreams last night, or their favorite movie or TV show. Some healthy and well-controlled teasing began among the students, so the teachers asked them to write a response to a peer's contrary view or to write a convincing piece about why one movie was better than another. The teachers looked for the best in their students' nascent writings and praised clever phrases or well-constructed sentences. Before long, more students were lifting their heads long enough to talk and to write a bit. The teachers handed out manila folders in which students could keep their writings—close enough to writers' journals for now. They began to notice some real thinking and discussion going on in the class, both verbally and in writing. A few students wanted to do more, so they created PowerPoint or Prezi presentations about a musical group they liked, learning how to embed song clips into the slides.

A few other students sat around computers and viewed movie trailers they found online to support their assertions about why one movie was more enjoyable than another. The conversations and topics under discussion expanded, and students started thinking that, maybe, all school time didn't need to be boring. They could bring bits of their lived experiences into class, talk and write about them, and feel as if their writing was sometimes pretty good at connecting with and being noticed by their peers. More words began to come more easily for more students.

Dawn and the two teachers watched with a bit of awe and a lot of excitement as literacy grew almost daily among their students. Because peers were reading their writings, students cared a bit more about spelling and sentence structure, both of which began to improve. Paragraphs emerged where a few jotted words had previously existed. The more the students wrote, the more clues about organization, rhythm, and movement in writing they gained. They watched as their teachers wrote, too, and they listened to what their teachers had to say. The students were learning to write by writing a lot and by writing about ideas and experiences that they wanted to express. At the end of that semester, these ninth graders still had a long way to go, but they could talk civilly to each other, write about what they discussed, and slowly realize that their writing was improving. They had more details and structure and thoughtfulness in their writing. The more they wrote, the more they could write and the better they could express their ideas. Their written fluency was emerging.

Language fluency is necessary for native and nonnative speakers of English. It comes first in our model because little else can happen without some degree of language fluency, orally and in writing. Fortunately, much of what we do to encourage language fluency for our students who are native speakers of English works well with those who are not native speakers of English. We discuss working with nonnative speakers of English—or English language learners (ELLs)—in detail in the last section of this chapter. Knowing that much similarity exists in methods and best practices, we hope, will help you conceptualize how our model might work for all students in your classrooms.

Moving into Control

As fluency develops for native speakers of English (or of any language), control soon follows. Some of the controls in written language come almost immediately. English language users write from left to right across the page. The patterns of our sentences are usually formed in the subject-verb-object order. For some writers entering into control of their writing, their spelling may be rudimentary, syntax may be inchoate, capitalization may be scattered, words may be simple and unsophisticated, punctuation may simply not be there—but you can *understand* what they are saying because you share a common language with them. And that language works in predictable and patterned ways. A large part of this control comes from an intuitive carryover from oral language, but it goes beyond that in writing. When the student writer reaches the point at which she can put words down on paper easily, at which she has found her *voice* and uses it, she will be able to control her writing to a large degree.

We teachers also help out. We coach our students' writing by reading and noticing written language use with them, guiding their revisions of their writing, and coaxing them toward more control without losing their fluency. Much of what occurs throughout our coaching process is the subject of this book, as we stated in Chapter 1: how to help our students become more comfortable and adept with written language.

Many of us encounter nonnative speakers of English in our classes; English may be their second or third language. Vocabulary, syntax, and lack of cultural knowledge can make their initial attempts at getting language onto the page look almost hopeless. We know that some of these students are not really skilled in any language, so the task of making writers out of them seems impossible. We remain cockeyed optimists, however. We believe that helping them talk their way into writing and lowering the bar of our expectations for written texts can give fluency a chance to grow into some control.

By the time students enter your high school English class, a lot of what they need to do is to practice their writing skills and techniques and processes over and over again. If we coach that practice effectively and don't discourage them entirely with our red pen, the controls will come.

We're not saying that all you have to do is get the student fluent in a particular form and he'll suddenly begin to turn out perfect papers. Nor are we saying that you can't help him in many ways to control his writing-in-process with minilessons and instructional activities. We are not saying that writing comes easily for most kids. We are saying that, just as in learning speech, control follows and is closely linked with fluency. *Getting it right* comes from *getting it down*.

Developing Precision

As students become fluent and acquire more control over their written texts, many of them will set higher standards for their writing. They will refuse to be satisfied with just any old word or sentence pattern. They will spend more time revising and crafting texts. In short, they will demand precision in their finished pieces. Precision in writing means choosing the precisely right words, using organization effectively, connecting with an audience, proofreading, and otherwise producing quality writing. We talk extensively in Chapter 5 about the features of good writing. Writers who are beginning to be effective with most of those features are beginning to develop the precision in their writing that is the hallmark of quality. As our students develop confidence and a sense of their own authorial power, our coaching strategies will change with them, giving us opportunities to demonstrate new and more complex text strategies.

Teaching Writing

We're convinced that writing can be taught and learned; we can work with our students to get them to understand much about how and why to write. Writing is wonderfully complex, beautifully intricate, sublimely and frustratingly human—but it's not a magic something that rises from dark depths within us, unknowable and unknown. We know what it is and how it works, and that means we can *teach* it.

What Do Writers Need?

If writing processes are not lockstep and may not look at all like that poster on your wall, how can you design writing instruction that is consistent, flexible, and process-based and that meets the diverse needs of the students in your classroom? Maybe a good way to get a handle on the issues of process is to think about the common ground that all writers share. Of course, writers' needs depend on how proficient they are as writers, but most writers work best when the following conditions and resources are available.

Ideas and Possibilities

If the writing process movement has contributed significantly to the improvement of writing instruction in schools, it is because of its primary emphasis on idea finding. For long years, teaching writing consisted of assigning topics, insisting on an outline, and prescribing a due date for the assignment. Teachers spent very little time helping students find and develop ideas. Now, however, brainstorming, listing, clustering, webbing, zero drafts, freewriting, journals, writers' notebooks, and more are all part of the writing process legacy for ways of engaging writers in the work of exploring and trying on ideas before they commit to a topic and a draft. The term *prewriting* was originally associated with this first step in the writing process model, and the term remains popular even though it sets apart idea finding from drafting when, in reality, writers are bouncing back and forth between idea generation and drafting. To avoid this inaccuracy of the term *prewriting*, Tom and Dan, in earlier editions of this book, coined the phrase *getting it started* to describe the preliminary stage of writing.

Equally as important as teaching students to use a variety of strategies for generating text-worthy ideas is the need to create opportunities for students to share and test those fledgling ideas with peers and potential readers. The interaction between idea finding and focused talk is a strong one. Before we move into writing, we give our students many opportunities to explore ideas and possibilities for their writing by talking with one or more partners. The talk is not random; rather, it is focused on generating ideas or on asking questions about what the piece of writing needs or on whether sections of the piece are as clear as we would like. We have learned to manage some of the chaos and tension that is inevitably present as students spend time generating and exploring ideas for writing together. As long as the noise is focused, productive, and below a dull roar, we encourage our students to continue talking to learn what they think—their ideas—and what they might write—the possibilities.

Excerpts and Examples

Every bit as important as the time for idea finding is the opportunity for students to read and examine excerpts and examples of the kinds of texts they are to compose. When Dawn teaches Contemporary Memoir,[3] she and her students read and examine as many as thirty cuttings from contemporary memoirs. This close reading work gives students a sense of the options of form and layout that the genre may provide. Contemporary Memoirs, for instance, may include prefaces, maps, photographs, chapters, sections, letters, poems, and epilogues. Reading these excerpts aloud will also give students a feel for the language, voices, and syntax that successful writers employ in the genre. Reading and idea finding are compatible processes that feed and enhance each other. We really can't conceive of initiating a writing process instructional model that does not include both reading and writing.

Constraints and Freedoms

We are firm believers that student writers need and want certain boundaries and constraints in a writing process environment. We have seen this question of how much teachers need to be involved in selecting topics for students' writing swing in full pendulum. In the mid-1970s, one school of thought eschewed the notion that teachers should suggest topics for students' writing, probably a lingering idea from many of the individualistic and freedom movements of the 1960s. The logic was that when teachers were too active in students' choice of topics, the writing really became that of the teacher rather than that of the student. Many well-known practitioners of the time professed a "let 'em write" philosophy that ultimately went too far. As a high school teacher during this era, Dawn saw firsthand that students enjoyed both the freedom to find text-worthy ideas *and* some sense of what options and expectations the teacher had for such texts. Such observations still hold true today. Most contemporary writing theorists now suggest that teachers need to be much more active in creating boundaries and constraints for student texts. Even an early guru of student freedom in the classroom such as Don Graves determined quite some time ago that "We've learned that, right from the start, teachers need to teach *more*" (1994).

How do we manage, then, a balance between constraint and freedom? We set limits for our writers: "Yes, you have to write a memoir; no, it can't be a fictitious story." But we also offer freedoms: "Sure, you can stick some of your poetry in there if it fits; and yes, you can make up stuff if it's true to the situation you're exploring in your piece." The teacher in a writing process-style class moves around to offer assistance and support, to clarify expectations, and to listen to students' efforts.

Rituals and Routines

Because writing is work, we have always insisted that our classrooms maintain a worklike atmosphere when students are writing. To maximize the efficiency of writing time in your classroom, we think it is important to establish an agreed-upon set of routines and rituals with your students. These agreements can be quite specific to your needs as a teacher and their needs as writers. "Students working on exploring a topic do this...." "Writers working with a partner do this...." "Response groups use these guidelines...."

Much of the current research on the qualities of effective leaders indicates that, among other traits they share in common, leaders are *intentional*. Teachers are the intellectual *leaders* in the classroom. As such, we advise that you become intentional about how you guide your students into literacy practices. Lead student writers into agreements about working on writing—into rituals and routines that work for you and for your students. In our view, the successful teacher marks the intellectual boundaries for inquiry and initiates a set of expectations or classroom values that establish rituals and celebrate work. We think the writing classroom goes much better with agreed-upon roles and rules.

Coaching

In his seminal work, Donald Schön says that "Students cannot be *taught* what they need to know, but they can be *coached*" (1987). Schön elaborates upon his idea by suggesting that the most effective coaching of student learning happens *while* they are working or "doing." Most writers need some encouragement and feedback while they are struggling to construct a text. Good coaching is not giving advice, however, nor is it telling writers what they should do with their drafts. Effective coaches are good listeners who work both to understand what the writer is trying to say and to discern what specific difficulties the writer is having in saying it. Good coaches ask questions and explore possibilities with the writer, as we discuss in more detail later. (See Chapter 8 for more ideas on how to respond to student writing.)

A Community of Writers

Because learning to write consists of both solitary and social processes, writers need opportunities to work alone and to engage in public sharing of their work. As Parker Palmer says, "The growth of any craft depends on shared practice and honest dialogue among the people who do it" (1998). For that reason, we provide plenty of time for solitary writing in our classes, but we also have students read their drafts to us and to peers and to others they trust. We celebrate finished pieces with displays and readings. We talk together about how to do this thing called *writing*. We become a community of thinkers and learners and writers who work and share and celebrate together.

Teaching Writing Processes: One Way to Begin

One of our favorite ways to introduce students to the practices and habits of mind necessary in our writing classroom is that of The Anatomy. This writing activity is a good starting place—an exemplar—for introducing writing process pedagogy to students because it makes the "skeleton" processes more visible than do some other kinds of writing. It promotes students' exploration and idea finding; it gives students some parameters without shutting out individual options. This model allows us to promote written fluency and a community of writers. It allows space for us to engage in coaching and coaxing the writing along, helping our students shape their meaningful expressions of ideas. You will find versions of this activity—which is grounded in narrative and contemporary memoir[3] writing—in classrooms all over the country. We've used it with students from third grade to retirement age. Like freewriting, we have never known it to fail, a strong claim for any writing activity. To establish the proper climate of collaboration and sharing, do it along *with* your student writers.

▦ Step 1: Remembering and Sharing

Talking is an important part of starting this writing, as it is with most good writings. Ask your students to jot down in a word or phrase three to five memories about which they want to learn more by writing about them. Demonstrate this step before they finish their lists by jotting three of your own ideas on the board. Ask them to pick memories they can locate in a particular place on a particular day, an incident, or a moment. Doing so seems to keep the writing away from vague and meaningless sentiments.

Talk about your memories with them briefly. Choose the one about which you want to write, discussing your choice with them. Let your students help you choose the writing, even if you don't take their advice about which topic to select. This discussion gives you and your students a chance to talk about how writers decide what they will write.

▦ Step 2: Selecting a Memory

Now it's their turn. Ask your student writers to share their list with a partner, just as you have done with them. Warn them not to talk it to death or they won't want to write about it. Give them a ten-minute time limit; then fudge on it if needed. Their job is to pick the one on which they want to work. Talking has lots of benefits for writers, so we frequently use talking as a precursor to writing.

▦ Step 3: Jotting or Other Prewriting on Paper

At this point, demonstrate jot listing, clustering, or webbing as a way of getting started with your writing, and then have students choose their own way of getting some ideas down on the page. The point of all such techniques is to help students get details down on paper so that when they start writing, they won't run out of steam and their writing will be alive.

Jot listing is the easiest technique with which to start. Simply ask students to brainstorm words and phrases in no particular order to use in their writing. The first time we do this kind of writing together, we might ask our students to organize their jot list in categories—such as seeing, hearing, smell, or touch—to focus on sensory details.

Push your students to write down as many details as possible. Often the quantity of details on the jot list predicts the quality of the writing.

Try to get through this part before the end of the first class period.

▦ Step 4: Getting It Down

This is the "zero" draft, the discovery draft. Encourage students to write fast, to freewrite, and to write around the hard parts. Push students to keep writing until they finish a first draft. If a student gets stuck, tell him to go back to his jot list. With this kind of writing, however, not many students get stuck. This time needs to occur in class, not for homework. Students know that what happens in class is the important stuff, so help them know that you value writing by giving class time to it.

Step 5: Sharing

This step involves having students try out, or rehearse, the piece by reading to a partner or a response group. The purpose is not for the student writer to receive criticism. The idea is to let the writer *hear* her piece for the first time. Then, model for your students how to read with your pencil in hand, ready to mark parts of the writing to which you will want to return. The document camera is perfect for allowing students to see you block off confusing areas to which you will return later, put a check mark by the nuggets of good ideas that you might elaborate later, and otherwise model a writer at work. This reading is not meant to be a polished performance. We are reading aloud to hear the piece—really *hear* what has been written. The reading may be halting and tentative. You might pause often to add or strike out words and to make substitutions. Ask questions of your listeners as you read: "Does that part sound right?" and "Did that sentence work?"

Model how to seek help from your audience—who may later be those in writing groups—by asking your student listeners to pay attention to any aspect of the writing that you select. Make it one with which you want help. Tell students what you need before reading your piece to them to set the tone for the listeners as well as for you, the writer.

Step 6: Reworking

There are papers that never go beyond the zero draft for one reason or another. We generally push students to revise, and typically they resist. Using the computer for writing is a big help in encouraging students to revise because fixing writing is quick and easy. Yet, we have students who still prefer to take pen or pencil to paper. Either way is fine. We make distinctions between two types of reworking—revision and editing. Revision and editing deal with substantial aspects of the writing, what works and what doesn't, with moving pieces of text around or cutting chunks of text to improve the piece. Proofreading deals with fixing the surface and usage errors. The actual experience defies neat divisions, but it helps us organize our thinking and our teaching. At some point while students are reworking their papers, we hold a brief conference with them to discuss revising and editing suggestions and ideas.

Step 7: Publishing and Celebrating

Some pieces will be reworked through several drafts, depending on the student's working style and the writing itself. Sometimes a student considers a paper to be finished, but we may ask for more work on such a paper when we see problems in it. Nonetheless, there has to be a deadline for any kind of writing. That's just how it works. Then there is another conference about publishing options, and we help the student to select and follow through with some form of publishing his paper. One form of publishing that we like is the *read-around* so we can show off and enjoy our writings together. For a read-around, each student selects an excerpt from his piece of writing to read to the class. We applaud and celebrate the writer's achievement by making specific comments about the good stuff we heard in the writing.

Moving Ahead with Writing

Once students have followed this "anatomy," we tell them that these are the processes of writing that they'll use for almost all of the writing that they do in our classes. They've just finished a piece of writing on a topic they chose. They've just heard applause and praise. They're working on their written fluency. The writing class is off to a fine beginning.

Language Diversity and the Writing Classroom

Our model of developing fluency, control, and precision resonates with you, we hope, and you're ready to try The Anatomy about which you just read with living, breathing kids. A methodology for teaching writing that emphasizes writing processes also sounds reasonable, and you're ready to give that a whirl as well. You've perhaps heard some similar stuff before in writing methods classes and from your colleagues, and you've taken the pledge to avoid the pitfalls of lockstep procedures. Maybe you even cut your writerly eyeteeth on this or a similar model.

You, however, are not the norm; you actually *like* reading and writing. Good grief, you're even interested in becoming—or, worse yet, you already are—an English teacher! We all know that is *not* the norm. Students like you, you might be thinking, those kids who are bright, future English teachers—you can work with them. But what about the students who struggle, who are not like you in significant ways, and whose first language is not English? Don't they require a different approach to teaching writing? Not as much as you might think.

As we indicated earlier in this chapter, much of what works for teaching writing to native speakers of English is also effective methodology for nonnative speakers of English. Though we cannot delve fully into this topic on which entire books have been written— which we urge you to read—we do offer here suggestions for teaching writing to diverse populations. Given the demographics of today's schools, knowing a bit about how to begin to teach writing to nonnative speakers of English is paramount for every teacher's success in the classroom.

The New Normal

Teachers are increasingly encountering students who are not capable speakers of English, who are not particularly skilled in any language, and who have been humiliated for their lack of academic achievement far too often to find much motivation for staying in school. Teachers often ask us what we "do" to "deal with" the diversity of students, cultures, economic circumstances, and languages in our classes. In several of the school districts near us, more than sixteen different languages and dialects are represented among the student population. How will any teacher effectively handle that much language variation?

Our response, of course, is neither simple nor easy. We see no panacea, no surefire answer, no magic wand. Like most teachers, we want to be highly effective with all of our students, and we work continually toward that goal while realizing the complexities of the contemporary classroom.

To put it plainly, diversity in English and language arts classrooms is the new normal. In a typical classroom, you might expect to find any of the following:

- native English speakers from other parts of the world
- native English speakers from the United States who speak a dialect other than Standard American English
- English language learners (ELLs) at different levels of ability
- students from different countries and cultures
- students from a range of socioeconomic backgrounds, and
- students with specialized educational needs that require an Individualized Education Plan (IEP)

You, as the instructional leader in the classroom, are expected to help *each* student develop as a better writer, regardless of individual background, circumstance, ability, or motivation. If you're feeling overwhelmed, as many teachers in all content areas and grade levels sometimes do, it's understandable. Sometimes, so do we. The sheer variety of students, and just where on a continuum from *novice* to *expert* each student may be in language-learning processes, has important implications for how and what we teach.

But hang on. Let's revisit that earlier sentence and see what happens when we change a few words:

> You . . . are expected to help each student develop as a better writer *through an emphasis on* individual background, circumstance, ability, and motivation.

Upon first glance, you may think we're just playing a semantic trick. The key about semantics, however, is that each change represents a potential shift in perspective. The change in the sentence above is a crucial element in how English and writing teachers view themselves. Teachers so often see students' differences as added challenges (and by extension, added burdens) that we've talked ourselves into a teacher-as-Sisyphus vision, struggling to cope with an increasingly more varied body of students and their individual needs. This outlook is often laden with an unspoken nostalgia for the homogeneous classrooms of the past. Wasn't it so much simpler (and easier) to teach when all the students were basically the same?

Think again. Little is as it seems through the rose-colored lenses of myth and memory. Although the classrooms of a few decades ago might have been less obviously diverse in some ways, the students sitting in them hardly lacked individual differences; and the good teachers working with those students certainly did not ignore individual needs and challenges. We have always had unique students populating our classrooms. Even in classrooms full of students who seem similar socially, linguistically, and ethnically, significant differences among individuals exist and are part of what we consider as we teach for optimal learning.

▇ Focusing Our Expectations

Only in recent years, perhaps, have we realized the importance of individual differences in helping our students maximize their learning. We are not downplaying the challenges of the contemporary classroom. They are legion. But if our philosophies encourage us to *expect* and *value* a range of experiences, talents, and perspectives among the students sitting in the desks before us, then diversity moves to the core of our work. With just a slight adjustment in our thinking, what might be suffered as a perplexing and an onerous challenge shifts, instead, to fruitful opportunity. An emphasis on individual background, circumstance, ability, and motivation is a key part of successful writing classrooms.

English Language Learners as Writers

The prevalent assumption in many contemporary English teacher-preparation programs still seems to be that newly minted teachers will work almost exclusively with native speakers of English. Chances are, however, that you'll have English language learners (ELLs) in your classroom, a fact you fully realize if you are already teaching. How, then, do you go about teaching such diverse students to write, and hopefully to write well? The good news is that much recent research suggests that the elements of effective writing instruction for ELLs are the same as, or very similar to, those recommended as best practice for native speakers.

Fluency First

For both the native English speaker and the English language learner, *personal involvement* in writing topics and an emphasis on *fluency and clarity over correctness* (especially in the initial stages of writing) are commonly viewed as positive practices. This finding doesn't mean that teachers should avoid identifying patterns of errors or directly teaching certain language forms. Actually, nonnative speakers of English may especially benefit from recognizing these points of difference between their native language and English. Nonetheless, the primary goal of writing remains the same for all students: to communicate meaning to readers according to contextual expectations.

Recent research (Ferris 2008) on ELLs and writing yields three broad observations:
1. Second language acquisition takes time.
2. Second language writers' texts are different from those written by native English speakers.
3. Even diligent teacher correction and student editing does not lead to perfect, error-free texts. (95)

These statements align with our own experiences in working with ELL students. In broad ways, they are also analogous to the struggles all basic writers face as they progress to higher levels of language control and proficiency.

Some new teachers with whom we have worked are initially shocked to see the extent to which surface errors dominate the written work of ELL writers. The novice teacher's first reaction might be to reach for the pen and begin a frenzy of correcting each error, followed by a frantic search for a comforting stack of grammar worksheets. These responses might give us a sense of meeting the most basic expectations that parents and administrators have for teachers. Should a parent or administrator pop into any English classroom, few are upset to see students hard at work on so-called *grammar* worksheets or daily oral language or daily grammar practice or whatever other euphemisms such work might be called. The trouble is, of course, that these tactics don't really work for the type of authentic language learning, adaptability, and flexibility that we seek for our students.

Most assuredly, we can and do offer better ways to begin.

An important step is educating ourselves to reset, very deliberately and consciously, our default expectations when working with ELLs. We might begin by fully realizing that second language acquisition is an arduous process. (How much of that French you studied in high school are you using fluently today?) We may expect to see certain written errors in the writing of English language learners. Since the seminal work of Shaughnessy (1979) points out the positive role that error plays in learning processes, we seek signs of progress, looking for strengths in our students' writings. Based on our former experiences with nonnative speakers of English, we prepare ourselves mentally to embrace errors as learning and teaching opportunities. Only *then* do we provide targeted feedback about patterns in English usage and grammar. Most importantly, these beliefs and practices guide what we do for any student in our classes—basic to advanced—regardless of his or her native language.

Effective teachers come to know their student writers' strengths, weaknesses, and idiosyncrasies. We learn to operate on macro and micro levels as we read students' written work. Teachers who achieve progress with their students' literacy acumen provide commentary and seek to determine whether their students are progressing on more comprehensive goals—such as understanding a purpose for writing, audience awareness, and meaning—rather than the micro aims of proper comma usage. We have nothing against using commas well and endeavor to do so ourselves. As somewhat competent writers, however, we are *ready* to focus on micro concerns like punctuation while *primarily* focusing on the macro issues of expression and meaning in our writing. We have benefited from teachers who offered encouragement and noted specific areas in our writing that needed attention—and so will the English language learners in our classes.

The simple truth is that improvement in the surface features of writing is a painstakingly slow process. Decades of research findings indicate that short exposure, such as within one semester, to a teacher's frenzied corrections will not render prose flawless and does little to support a writer's broader sense of control and confidence. Continuous practice within a variety of writing contexts along with some precise, modulated feedback is a much more effective route.

Research and experience also show that the concepts of focusing on fluency and on developing a community of writers, which we believe to be central to effective writing development, also works with ELLs. Specifically, Rollinson (2005) examines the value of peer feedback for English as a second language (ESL) and second language (L2) learners, drawing some familiar conclusions:

> Good writing requires revision; writers need to write for a specific audience; writing should involve multiple drafts with intervention response at the various draft stages; peers can provide useful feedback at various levels; training students in peer response leads to better revisions and overall improvements in writing quality; and teacher and peer feedback is best seen as complementary. (24)

ELL student writers often face particular challenges when required to share their writing in writing groups or in writing workshops. Initially, ELL students may be reluctant to share work for peer review; they may prefer to restrict their oral sharing to same-language peers; and, some may experience a clash among cultural differences about expressing opinions or about the worth of creative kinds of writing. Working within a structured environment with a supportive and caring teacher helps to make dealing with these challenges more about legitimate learning and less an occasion for vulnerability and fear. This atmosphere also supports developing fluency first for ELL student writers.

Bigger-Picture Thinking on Language Learning

Sometimes it's helpful to take the time to consider some of the larger cultural forces that act to shape our conventional wisdom about language. Locating what we do daily within wider social currents is more than just navel gazing. It reminds us that teaching is always, to some degree, political. Here, *political* is not so much about how one votes in presidential elections as it is about considerations of access, power, and pragmatics. Is it reasonable to expect that all people living in a country speak the native language? Is it reasonable that all educational instruction occur only in a country's native language? What happens economically to people not speaking a country's native language? None of these are easy questions with simple answers. Within some countries, just determining one dominant native language is challenging. We can't even begin to discuss these complexities and political facets of language use. (Maybe we'll catch up with you at a conference and sit at the bar to delve into these questions.) Our point here is that education and language learning are tied to large, big-picture issues that have national and international, fiscal and emotional effects on groups and individuals. In this context, something as apparently innocuous as helping children learn English may trigger conflicting agendas, policies, and worldviews.

From elementary school, we're taught the vision of the United States as a nation of immigrants, a melting pot of ethnicities, and a culture that draws its strength from diversity. At the same time, political rhetoric, government policy, and everyday ethnocentrism tell a more ambivalent tale. In general, Americans welcome immigrants as part of our social mythology but expect them to do what it takes to blend in with our national norms.

Consider this rather glaring irony: Even as schools are forced to mainstream nonnative speakers of English on an absurdly truncated schedule, classes of native English speakers just down the hall drone through foreign-language textbook recitations. The idea that two groups of students—for example, native English speakers learning Spanish and Spanish-speaking students learning English—might have something to learn from each other is an idea that seems blindingly obvious even as it is politically untouchable.

This absurd situation, worthy of playwrights Ionesco and Pinter, causes a central question about the breakdown of communication among diverse groups to loom large: What does this isolationist climate mean for you as a teacher of writing?

Using Multidirectional Learning

The concept of *reciprocal learning* serves as a compelling principle for literacy teaching and learning. The conventional direction of learning in school is a one-way street *from* the teacher *to* the student. Reciprocal learning, however, suggests that learning can be multidirectional. (The concept of student peer review is a decent if somewhat limited example of this notion.) In a broader sense, reciprocal learning presumes that everyone in a classroom—including the teacher—can and should learn from one another.

Consider this idea in light of a typical classroom of diverse students. What might they potentially teach one another about language and about using language in written discourse? How are they experts in particular kinds of language use? What insights do they have that, once acknowledged as interesting and worthy of consideration, might benefit all of us as literacy learners? Darren thought about some of the learners he has encountered and their diverse language needs. Look at some of these examples of how language varies across cultures and consider how these observations might help you to work with the ELLs in your classes.

- Dominique reveals that she often finds clues to the metaphorical meaning of unfamiliar English words by scanning their roots for equivalents in French. She knows, for example, that *foot* in English is *pied* in French. She also notices that many English words have the similar root word *ped*. From this observation, she is able to figure out the meaning of words such as *impede* (an extension of "to stop the feet from moving forward"), *expedite* (speeding something up by "freeing the feet from obstacles"), and the adjective *pedestrian* (a person who "goes by foot" rather than by horse or car), which connotes negative, class-based judgments for her.
    - How might you use root words and similarities among language cognates to help your ELL students understand literal and metaphorical meanings of common English expressions?
- In a conversation about English dialect, Maksim points out that some Russian grammar conventions are similar to African American Vernacular English:
    - *Gdze tye nah?* ("Where you at?")
    - *Ktoh ohn?* ("Who he?")
    - *Ohna uchitelem.* ("She teacher.")
    - *Ohn bistri.* ("He fast.")
        - How might an examination of translating common utterances from native languages into English help your students—native English speakers and ELLs alike—appreciate language variations?
- Reyna explains that the word *macho* has very different cultural connotations, depending on how and where it's used. In English, the word seems to carry negative overtones of aggressive pride. In her home country, the word has a positive sense, describing a man who is responsible, hardworking, and family-oriented.
    - How might a discussion of various culturally-based connotations of words help your students distinguish denotation from connotation and become more aware of cultural context and word choice?
- Marta observes that the word *happy* in English has a different use than the equivalent word in her native Polish. Americans, she says, use the word quite freely to describe many situations, but Poles reserve it for rare moments of joy. She sometimes struggles with how commonly Americans use the word, thereby robbing it of the power she usually associates with it. She adds a final note: "To me, Americans are always smiling, even when they're not really happy."[4]
    - How might a discussion of commonplace words and their meanings give your students an added appreciation for the ways in which language highlights issues related to class, culture, and gender?

When our students understand the quirks, cultural representations, meanings, metaphors, similarities and differences across languages and other linguistic features of words and phrases, they begin to think about language variations and how to deal with them. Nonnative English speakers might learn much about tone and style by thinking about commonplace expressions in English and how they do or do not transfer to their native language—and vice versa. Any time our students learn more about language—any language—they are considering elements that are important for writing such as tone, style, metaphors, and an author's distinctive voice in her writing. Not only do we promote cross-cultural curiosity and multidirectional learning among all of our students, but we also offer our students opportunities to approach language with a fresh perspective, one that may transfer into their creative use of words and phrases in their writing.

Building Communities for All Learners

Shared notions of language use build community, an essential feature of all writing classrooms. Within caring and respectful communities, the tendency to judge and classify others on superficial merits becomes harmful. Caring and respect need to exist before students are comfortable enough to explore language and work at building fluency—written and oral—in an unfamiliar context.

To build communities within which our student writers are free to explore ideas and express themselves, we relentlessly work against bias and ignorance by consciously encouraging open-mindedness, respect, and communication among our students. Our students become aware of our genuine excitement about diverse languages and cultures. We offer opportunities to our students from other cultures to teach us about both the unique and the usual for them. As insights and understandings of others emerge for our students, we may lead them into productive and more extensive understandings of what it means to be a member of a literate community.

We all use language to construct reality and define what is important to us, individually and as a culture. Seeing the world from different points of view requires students to grow toward reflective, metacognitive thinking, especially about their own language use and what they think they know. This journey may be a tough one for our students, but the concept of lifelong learning about ourselves and others is one of the most important ideas that teachers impart to our students. In the writing classroom, such open respect and exploration are essential if fluency, written and oral, is to flourish.

Fluency for All

Fluency is critical to the writing classroom and to all developing writers. When we create safe, supportive, and nurturing environments and opportunities for students to practice spoken and written language use and encourage them to do so often, we begin the work of building confidence, widening perspectives, and refining what we think and how best we might say it.

Practical, philosophical, and perhaps political and legal challenges await teachers who pursue inclusive approaches and attitudes in the literacy classroom. Personal disclosure is risky in a traditional classroom, especially for ELLs or students otherwise perceived as *different*, as existing outside mainstream culture. For good writing to occur, our students need to explore what it means to be human and literate. Creating a classroom climate that promotes linguistic, cognitive, and cultural fluency helps our students engage in meaningful expression, reflection, and literacy learning. Such a climate best promotes fluent personal expression for all students.

NOTES

1. The third edition of *Inside Out* (2004, Heinemann) was coauthored by Dan Kirby, Dawn Latta Kirby, and Tom Liner.
2. These findings emerged from Dawn's research for her unpublished 1985 doctoral dissertation, "Toward a Definition of Written Fluency" (University of Georgia).
3. For more information on teaching Contemporary Memoirs to enhance reading and writing abilities, see Kirby and Kirby (2007).
4. Marta's example is borrowed from Mary Besemeres' article "Different Languages, Different Emotions?" (2004).

Works Cited

Besemeres, Mary. 2004. "Different Languages, Different Emotions?" *Journal of Multilingual and Multicultural Development* 25 (2&3): 140–58.

Coates, Ta-Nehisi. 2011. "Bad Writing." Available at: www.theatlantic.com/entertainment/archive/2011/02/bad-writing/70916. Accessed January 29, 2012.

Ferris, Dana. 2008. "Myth 5: Students Must Learn to Correct All Their Writing Errors." In *Writing Myths: Applying Second Language Research to Classroom Teaching,* edited by Keith Folse, 90–114. Ann Arbor, MI: University of Michigan.

Graves, Donald. 1994. *A Fresh Look at Writing.* Portsmouth, NH: Heinemann.

Kirby, Dan, Dawn L. Kirby, and Tom Liner. 2004. *Inside Out, Third Edition.* Portsmouth, NH: Heinemann.

Kirby, Dawn Latta. (formerly, Bruton). 1985. *Toward a Definition of Written Fluency.* Unpublished doctoral dissertation, University of Georgia.

Kirby, Dawn L., and Dan Kirby. 2007. *New Directions in Teaching Memoir: A Studio Classroom Approach.* Portsmouth, NH: Heinemann.

Miller, James E., Jr. 1972. *Word, Self, Reality: The Rhetoric of the Imagination.* New York: Dodd, Mead.

Palmer, Parker. 1998. *The Courage to Teach.* San Francisco: Jossey Bass.

Rollinson, Paul. 2005. "Using Peer Feedback in the ESL Writing Class." *English Language Teachers Journal* 59 (1): 23–30.

Schön, Donald. 1987. *Educating the Reflective Practitioner.* San Francisco: Jossey Bass.

Sergiovanni, Thomas. 1996. *Leadership for the Schoolhouse.* San Francisco: Jossey Bass.

Shaughnessy, Mina. 1979. *Errors and Expectations: A Guide for the Teacher of Basic Writing.* New York: University of Oxford Press.

Wiesel, Elie. 1996. *All Rivers Run to the Sea: Memoirs.* New York: Schocken.

3

Establishing the Classroom Environment and Building Community

A learning space must be hospitable—inviting as well as open, safe and trustworthy, as well as free. . . . [It] must have features that help students deal with the dangers of an educational expedition: places to rest, places to find nourishment, even places to seek shelter when one feels overexposed. **—Parker Palmer, *The Courage to Teach***

The thought of taking or teaching a composition class does not always inspire students or teachers. Perhaps because of writing assessments and lingering sour tastes in our mouths about the way writing is too often (mis)taught and (mis)critiqued, students may enter our English/Language Arts classes with some negative feelings and nagging fears. They sniff the air for tension, weakness, and fear—or for ease, comfort, and excitement—gauging us and their peers. Before we have a chance to say the first word to our students, they begin making inferences and judgments. Does this classroom look inviting? Does it look like a place in which I can be comfortable? Does it contain interesting books, posters, and *objets d'art* and of pop culture that catch my eye? Will I be able to see and hear everyone in the room? We know from the work of Malcolm Gladwell in *Blink* that humans make snap decisions and judgments within two to three seconds—or less. Gladwell calls this quick cognitive activity *slicing* information, and we do it within the blink of an eye. We teachers may forget that fact, thinking that we have all semester to get to know and work with students.

What happens during the first few days and weeks of our classes is critical for any successful teaching experience, meaning that we can't overlook or take for granted those crucial first impressions. Are we intriguing our students or setting up some barriers that we'll later need to overcome? Some attention to the basics is essential for those first snap judgments to go our way. What is the physical setting—the way the room looks? What is the psychological setting—the way the room feels, the vibe and energy of the room? What are students asked to do first—express their thoughts, or sit down and be quiet?

If we are to change the sterile physical spaces in which most of us teach into welcoming, intellectually exciting and safe spaces, appearances and our first activities are fundamental to how the writing classroom functions. The impressions work for or against our efforts to create a sense of community, expectation, sharing, and interest. We want our students to come into the room, meet each other and us, and very quickly feel like working on explorations through reading and writing, talking and listening, thinking and creating. Each day, we want our students to enter with a "What are we going to do today?" energy.

The Way the Room Looks

We don't want to spend too much time talking about how to decorate your room. Interior decorating is, after all, a personal matter. Tables versus desks, carpets, and workshop designs have all been described elsewhere. The important point to make about decor is that there should be some obvious indications that you believe that the physical environment is important, and these touches need to be present even in a rather basic cinder block classroom setting that leaves little to your personal tastes or preferences. Maybe you're stuck with a windowless room with brown carpet and the same desks that two generations of students have occupied. Maybe the so-called technology in the room is an overhead projector. Nonetheless, doing *something* with your room is a signal to students that you care about the writing and learning environment. The opposite is also unfortunately true, so take the pledge: You will do *something* with that room to make it a warmer, less barren place.

Remember one thing: The focal point of any good writing class is the display of student products. Elementary teachers do a good job of showing student work. Smiles and gold stars are everywhere. Teachers of young children don't go to this trouble because they're softheaded. They know that displaying student work builds pride and enthusiasm and dramatically enhances motivation.

A Word About "The Writing Class"

Throughout this book, we use terms such as "writing instruction," "the writing class," and "the writing classroom." Unless you live and teach somewhere in a writer's heaven, you probably will not have the opportunity to teach a middle school or high school "writing class." When Dawn first began teaching sometime after the Dark Ages ended, writing and literature were separated into individual courses. Dawn taught classes such as British Literature, but also Advanced Writing and Creative Writing, not to mention Advanced Grammar. These days, English instruction is most often integrated, with English and language arts teachers being responsible for teaching literature, grammar, writing, speaking, viewing, and listening all in one course. These catchall classes may be called something like Ninth-Grade English, English 10, English Block I, or numerous other "in this class I teach everything related to English" names.

For the sake of simplicity, we refer to "the writing class" to mean the part of any class in which you teach writing. We trust you to make the mental notation of what we mean.

Creating a Comfortable Writing Environment

Writing might not be every student's first-choice activity. Shocking, we know. If we are to grow effective writers, especially among those students for whom writing is a bit threatening or intimidating or just plain awkward, attention to the space in which students are to work is necessary. The room itself needs to feel welcoming, alive, productive, and fun. Here are our tips for creating an effective and a comfortable writing environment.

▨ Create a Place in Your Class for Student Products

Let students know that writing is the primary business of your writing class by making written products the *center* of attention. Have a poets' corner, a graffiti board, a gallery of finished pieces. Display (framed, laminated, or glued on colored mats) some of your favorite pictures, and encourage students to post creative responses around them. Use 3-D displays and mobiles. Use the ceiling, walls, and floors. Various products exist to help make your room a 3-D writing environment, including easy-to-use paints designed to work like white-boards. Paint an area, let students write on the paint with dry-erase markers, erase every so often, and begin again with new writing. We also have had success with the following ideas.

- Encourage students to display drafts and unfinished pieces of writing by designating a "works-in-progress" area.
- Have a quotable quotes display with typed excerpts from student journals (with author's permission, of course).
- Take pictures of your students while they're writing and enlarge them, using your computer or the user-friendly equipment found in most photo-developing shops. Post them around the room.
- Post some of your own writing, as well as the writing of other teachers and adults in the school community. (Maybe the custodian is a secret poet . . . ask him.)
- Post pictures and short biographical sketches of the authors of the displayed products.

Get creative about making students' writings the focus of your classroom.

▨ Create a Comfortable Room Arrangement

The number one priority in room arrangement is that it be a place where you feel comfortable. If you feel good about your room, chances are the students will, too.

We know teachers who divide their classroom into specific work areas to give student writers a functional place to be during the various businesses of writing. When there's enough space in the classroom, they designate a writing area, a responding area, a resource area, a revising area, and a brainstorming area. They place chairs or small couches in a circle or semicircle for group reading and discussion of written products. They and their students move among the areas, providing help, consultation, and responses when needed. Students know which behaviors are appropriate in each area. The classroom hums with activity but is quiet enough for writing and revising to occur. Teachers provide redirection and reminders if students are chatting or wasting time.

Many teachers and some students need quieter, more structured-looking environments. Some physical spaces in which we teach just don't adapt easily to rearrangement. Do what you can with the space that you have. Don't apologize. Arrange the classroom your way.

Some really good writing teachers have desks in rows and surprisingly conventional-looking rooms—except for the mass of books, posters, and student products. Maybe your tendencies toward details and order make you just feel better with rows; but even rows can be rearranged and grouped for readings and brainstorming. Dawn prefers a large rectangle of tables in the middle of the room or clusters of desks throughout the room, and she frequently rearranges the furniture to accommodate the task at hand. Her students become skilled furniture movers.

We also like music in the writing class. Set up a small set of speakers, and load an iPod, a smart phone, or another device with a large library of different kinds of music—especially instrumental tracks. (Caution: A fully loaded device can easily store $500 to $1000 worth of music, so lock up the equipment in a storage cabinet at night or transport it to and from the classroom daily.) The music comes on at the drop of a hat: when students enter the room, as background music for workdays, or to stimulate a variety of creative responses. Students may also contribute music to the class play list—within reason. No X-rated lyrics and distracting rhythms. Music energizes and soothes, and we don't teach writing without it.

The Way the Room Feels

Far more important to the successful teaching of writing than the way your room looks is the psychological climate—the way it feels.

A good writing class must feel like a safe place. Writing is scary business; sweaty palms are the order of the day. Good writing teachers work hard at reducing fear in the writing class. If you expect students to experiment, to try things out, then you'll have to convince them that they are safe and won't be shot down in flames.

Offer support and plenty of figurative pats on the back. Ask questions that show you are genuinely interested in what students have to say. Encourage students to externalize their feelings; extend empathy when the going gets rough. Tell them about times you've had difficulty getting ideas to work on paper. Show them examples of the way you struggle through drafts by showing them the actual marked-up and crossed-out drafts of some piece of writing on which you are working—maybe even your own version of the assignment you've asked students to do. Hold frequent idea-sharing sessions in which you encourage students to talk about their work. Dawn holds *press conferences* in which students present their writing ideas or problems and listen as fellow students respond with helpful ideas. However you structure these conversations of *writerly talk*, we advise making them a regular, weekly occurrence in your class. To foster the reflective atmosphere essential to quality writing instruction, offer extended periods of class time for students to find, draft, share, and refine ideas. You'll foster a classroom community of writers if students know you care about each writer's progress.

Metaphors for the Writing Classroom

Like many creative spaces, a classroom in which authentic writing occurs may seem utterly chaotic or cathedral quiet. Students may work individually, in groups, and one-on-one with the teacher—sometimes all during the same instructional period. Reading, talking, writing, and reflecting occur throughout the room, each student using the techniques that help her to generate her written texts. What are the students doing? What is the teacher doing? It just depends on where the writers are in their processes.

The variety of instructional techniques common to the writing teacher's repertoire may not look like what happens in classes of other content areas. A casual observer might wonder what learning and what instruction are occurring. We have even known of principals who visit a class during a writer's workshop, look around briefly, and tell the teacher, "I'll come back when you're teaching."

The work of teaching writing is not always teacher-centered nor focused on the front of the room. Techniques for teaching writing are varied and complex enough that managing the parts and pieces of writing instruction may be difficult, especially for the novice writing teacher. As we work with our college students who want to become English teachers, and as we seek explanations for the secondary students with whom we work about what it is they will be doing with writing, we find that the compact potency of metaphors often help students, parents, and administrators understand what we are doing.

A Writing Preserve

When our teaching is going well, students treat our classroom as a refuge, a haven for experimenting and trying out words. We don't tolerate cheap shots and verbal jabs. Having a visual reminder or slogan to that effect keeps that caveat in students' frontal lobes. During the first week of school, we post a large "No Hunting" sign on the door because writing and learning occur best in a supportive, protective environment. As we discuss throughout this book, having a supportive environment doesn't mean that we adopt a Pollyanna attitude toward writing or that everything that everyone writes is praised or that we don't criticize one another's work. *No Hunting* simply means "No cheap shots." We cut short anything that hints at a volley fired across the bow of the student writer's ego. The writing class must not become a hacksaw operation where people criticize each other's failures. If a piece of writing is bad, then we tell students that it "didn't work." It either needs to be reworked or filed. If it needs reworking, then specific, constructive suggestions are helpful to the author. Offer suggestions such as, "How about throwing out that first paragraph and beginning here?" or "I want to know why this character felt he was a failure." Suggestions offered in the spirit of coaching a writer to rework a piece so that it becomes a better piece of writing serve to improve writing and keep the writer's ego intact.

If the piece has no potential at all, then simply suggest that the writer file it in her writer's notebook. The writer's notebook is a kind of working repository of all the ideas, drafts, false starts, experiments, revisions, and reflections that a student has worked on. Throughout the semester, students return to their notebook to read the pieces within it, looking for ideas that can be repurposed, quotations that might fit their current writing, and other nuggets of inspiration. It serves as a wellspring for new ideas that occur to students as they review the work it already contains. A writer's notebook may be virtual or physical, as long as the teacher has access to it to help the student recognize effective writings that hold promise for future efforts. *Notebook* may be literal or metaphoric. Many of our students have kept their writing in a literal notebook. Others prefer a file, a box, or some other container, or an online space. What's important to us is the work that's going on in the notebook, not the specifics of the medium.

Beginning again is often the best remedy for an ineffective piece of writing. Note that "file it" does not mean fold, spindle, or mutilate it. The piece that didn't work goes into the student's writer's notebook as evidence of the student's overall work and effort to write. In the writer's notebook, the piece is an artifact that is available for review by both you and the writer; the piece may even be resurrected later.

It's so easy to wound writers. "That piece didn't do a thing for me," or "I won't read this piece until you learn how to spell" are comments that cut deep. None of us would feel heartened by such a response to our own writing. Not only are student writers likely to be discouraged by such comments, but they may also hear indictments of personal—not just academic—failure in such cutting remarks. Students often find it difficult to separate comments about their writings from comments about them as people. Remind yourself often that students are most vulnerable when they submit a piece of genuine writing. Proceed with caution; put away the hacksaw.

The Writing Studio

After the first few weeks, we generally stow the signage and simply continue to model the tone and type of responses to writing that we expect from our students. By then, we have established the values of the writing studio[1]: practice, practice, practice; being at work; re-visioning the writing; studying the craft of other writers; creating an atmosphere of sharing and discussion; reading and talking about writing; and practice, practice, practice. We have established the rituals and routines of the writing community (see Chapter 2), and we are able to identify the contributing members of the community as separate from the poachers.

What comes to mind when you think of the traditional image of the writer at work? Most often, the writer is depicted as being alone, in isolation in a dark garret, hunched over his papers, hair askew from the frustration of seeking the right phrase, the exact image, the precise word.

What comes to mind when you think of an artist at work? The images that occur to us are quite different from those of the writer. We think of artists, surrounded by myriad paints and implements, standing in large, well-lighted rooms with separate easels for each person. A model or a series of objects sits at the front of the room while the artists render their individual representation of what is before them. The art teacher walks around to each artist, gazes at the canvas under construction, offers a suggestion, guides a brushstroke.

We borrow the concept of the studio classroom from our observations of how artists work. Like an artist in a studio, surrounded by his canvases in various stages of completion, our students are awash in writings. Some writings appear in published books, some are written by the students themselves; some are finished and others are awaiting another time, another piece in which they may appear. Like bare canvases, computers and papers populate the writing studio, awaiting the touch of the writer. The work—the writing—is the focus. The teacher writes herself, pausing to respond to a student's question, offer a response, suggest an alternate word or image. Writers are at work, all crafting their own expressions and renderings of experience.

A Liminal Space

Another way to think of the classroom is that it can act as a *liminal space*. *Liminality* refers to the qualities of a threshold, a boundary area, or a borderland. In literature a *liminal figure* is someone capable of crossing normally impervious boundaries and of negotiating the values of different worlds. This role usually grants the character more than the usual power, perspective, or insight, though these abilities come at some cost. These characters tend to be heroes, prophets, rebels, and tricksters. Some of our favorite liminal characters from fiction include Huck Finn and Hester Prynne, Frodo Baggins and Luke Skywalker, Harry Potter and Arnold Spirit.[2]

Liminality is also characterized by a shift in conventional roles, expectations, and actions and by the concept of *communitas*, in which the typical power relationships between people are temporarily set aside in an effort to encourage fellowship, honesty, and understanding. Liminal spaces are spaces of change, growth, and shifting meanings, with potential rewards for those venturing into them.

To say that the writing classroom might function as a liminal space suggests that the traditional teacher-student power dynamic is purposely subverted at times, such as when the teacher reveals herself as a writer or responds to students' work as a reader rather than an evaluator. It also suggests that a sense of community arises spontaneously through trust, mutual respect, and shared experience; no one can dictate it into being. We can't force our students to feel a sense of shared values or to believe in themselves as a group. Although we teachers guide our students' interactions and offer opportunities for shared trust, these feeling must have genesis among the class members themselves. As we think about this type of *esprit de corps*, we're reminded of that classic piece of office satire, the management memo dictating that "the beatings will continue until morale improves." In a writing class, the morale needs to improve fairly quickly and grow stronger each day.

Venturing into any new territory may be challenging. Just watch students on the first day of school in the lunchroom. They wander in search of a friendly face and observe clusters of students to be sure they aren't crossing boundaries into another group's table. Students who venture into new peer groups or into new imaginative territory in their writing are acting as liminal figures, finding themselves changed—often significantly—by their experiences.

Students who are willing to enter new experiences with anticipation and to follow the teacher's lead, even when it seems fraught with dangerous self-reflection and revelation, will have the opportunity to plumb their own thinking, emotions, and lives for meaning. They may effect a kind of personal evolution, seeing themselves as hybrid thinkers or as mental border crossers. We've seen these transformations often enough to know that those who venture into liminality are precisely the students who contact us years later and praise our teaching. That in itself is a rather powerful motivator.

Beginnings

Feelings of competition, grade-grubbing (the "Is this going to be graded?" syndrome), apathy, and even outright hostility are all factors that may work against you in the writing class. Teachers need to meet these attitudes head-on with some serious anxiety-reducing, community-building activities.

After the first impressions have registered in students' minds, the first days and opening activities in any writing class are critical. Because you want students to write often, because you want them to write honestly and openly, because you want them to share their work and respond to one another's work, and because you want them to accept criticism and to work on revising their writing, you have many new attitudes and behaviors to develop in your students. If you want them to function as an audience for one another's writing and to become careful critics of their own and others' writings, then attending to the psychological climate of the class is essential. The following starter activities will help you get to know your students and help them get to know one another. They also get students talking, thinking, and writing.

A few words of advice about these starter activities: Don't try to do all of them. You'll overwhelm the students and take the focus away from the purpose of such activities, which is to improve the climate and psychological context for writing. We suggest strongly that you ask students to react to the selected activity *in writing*. Writing their responses reminds them that the central business of this class is getting words down on paper.

These activities and others that you may have used are not instructional fluff. Putting students at ease, having a bit of fun, thinking metaphorically, getting to know one another, learning to listen actively, and developing collaboration result from activities like these and are the cornerstones of successful writing classes. In addition, writing from sources of personal knowledge increases students' potential for learning and for writing in an individual, authentic voice. When used with follow-up writing activities, these beginning activities cause the class to come together as a unit without lessening the seriousness of the writing class or turning the teacher into an entertainer. Rather, they pave the way for more authentic interactions among students and for more genuine writing throughout the school year.

The First Writing

On the very first day, we ask students to freewrite for ten minutes on their feelings about and experiences with writing. Freewriting is an excellent way to begin a writing class. As we discussed in Chapter 4, freewriting involves writing quickly for about ten minutes, putting thoughts onto the page without stopping, editing, or even worrying about the quality of the writing. Initially, we ask students to write about themselves as writers. What is the history of their experiences with writing? How do they feel when they write? Have they ever written anything they're proud of? Have they had any disasters with writing? Here are some typical student responses:

> Writing. Actually writing is not that important to me—I prefer verbal expressions. All of my writing career I have received good grades on content and rather poor grades on grammar. This improved only somewhat last year after Trad. Gram. and Theme Writing. I get my ideas from my experiences and what I've read. I love to read. My major problem with writing is subject matter—how unoriginal. Anyway—in my journal, I just write down what I'm thinking about—very seldom do I get out and create something. I don't have time and like I said, I'd rather talk or read than write. Even now I've got writer's cramp.
>
> *—Laura*[3]

> I have had bad experiences with writing since the first days of school. The main problem has been that I was assigned to write and *had* to write on the teacher's topic in the teacher's style. I love to write. I dream of someday writing a book that will be the most profound literary work ever; Nobel Prize in Literature and all that.
>
> *—Todd*[3]

These excerpts are honest and full of information for the teacher of writing. Use them to talk openly with your students about some of the problems and frustrations of writing. Engage them in lively conversation about the many ways and processes of writing. Talking about writing should reduce some of the tension in the writing class. Dawn follows up the freewriting and discussion with a more finished product on the students' individual perspectives about themselves as writers. Display these finished products or excerpts from them in the room, accompanied by each writer's picture. These displays are great tools for Parent Night or Open House at your school when parents want to see what their students are doing in your class.

Names

Names are important. Spend some time each day for the first week or so helping students learn one another's names. Don't leave this name-learning process to chance; teaching writing, sharing writing, and working to improve writing go better with names.

We go around the room a time or two with the old name chain: Say your name and then recall and say the names of everyone before you. Use the "who are your neighbors" activity in which you point to a student and ask her to name the person on either side of her. Ask students to create names for themselves that consist of an adjective beginning with the same letter as their first name, like Daring Dawn or Dashing Darren, and then to write a few lines about why that adjective describes them accurately. Encourage students to remember the name by remembering each peer's attribute.

There's nothing new here, but students tell us, "This is the first class in which I've known the names of everyone in the room." When students know each other's names, they feel more like a community and take more interest in responding personally and authentically to each other's work. If you're not the name-game type, ask students to make name cards to stand on their desks. Ask students to call one another by name. When a student hesitates and can't remember a peer's name even after a few days together, Dawn "introduces" them to each other—"Sarah, meet Chien-pin; Chien-pin, meet Sarah"—and does so as often as necessary until everyone learns the names of everyone else in the room. Of course, that means that Dawn must also learn students' names quickly, a challenge for teachers who may encounter well over one hundred students a day in their classes. Use name cards, make mental name associations, have students say their names when they begin speaking to the class or to a small group, use a name chart to indicate who sits where, take pictures and label them with the student's name—but do whatever it takes for everyone to learn all names. Writers' names are important. Work at it.

Lives

No less important than names are the students themselves. Who are they? Where do they come from? What do they do well? Motivating students to participate in your class will be easier if you get them to invest something of themselves in the class at the beginning. Self-disclosure—sharing something about themselves—is a subtle and important way to do so.

Remember also to share some tidbits of your own reading, music, and movie preferences; stories of yourself as a young student; or humorous life stories with your students. Not only are you modeling what you want students to do, but when everyone in the writing classroom, including you, is open and responsive, community and confidence building increase.

The least threatening of these activities is probably a simple writer's questionnaire that asks students how they spend their time, where they live, their favorite music, the latest book they read, their favorite movies and television shows, and so on. See Figure 3–1 for an example. Be sure to tell your students the purpose of such questionnaires: to know them and their interests better.

Figure 3–1. Writer's Questionnaire

WRITER'S QUESTIONNAIRE

Name: _____

What do you like to be called?

How do you like to spend your weekends?

Do you have a job? Where?

What kind of music do you like?

Who is your favorite singer or group?

What shows do you watch on TV?

Do you write poems or stories on your own? If so, describe them.

When was the last time you wrote something you really liked, and what was it?

From *Inside Out, Fourth Edition*. © 2004 by Dan Kirby, Dawn Latta Kirby, and Tom Liner from *Inside Out, Third Edition*. Heinemann: Portsmouth, NH.

◼ Sentence-Completion Survey

Another low-threat activity is the sentence-completion survey (see Figure 3–2). This activity lets the students set the level of openness. If they feel safe in your class, they may be very honest. If they are still uncertain about the class, they may provide superficial answers.

Figure 3–2. Sentence-Completion Survey

SENTENCE COMPLETION

Instructions: Complete the following sentences. Write as much as you wish on each one. Your answers will be kept confidential unless you wish to share them.

1. I'm not happy when _____.

2. Sometimes I wish I were _____.

3. I'm pretty good at _____.

4. My friends think I'm _____.

5. Writing assignments are _____.

6. When I get home from school, I _____.

7. I'm afraid of _____.

8. School is _____.

9. The most important thing to me is _____.

10. I have hopes that _____

_____.

From *Inside Out, Fourth Edition.* © 2004 by Dan Kirby, Dawn Latta Kirby, and Tom Liner from *Inside Out, Third Edition.* Heinemann: Portsmouth, NH.

The follow-up on the sentence-completion activity is teacher response to what the students have written. Read the sentences carefully and write personal comments and observations on several of them. Select some of the most honest, humorous, or serious completions to share with the class without identifying the authors. The point at this stage is what is said more than who said it. Look for interesting turns of a phrase, surprises, humor, metaphors, and other techniques that give the responses a lively, authentic voice. Letting your students hear those voices gives student writers ideas about how to expand and improve their future writing.

These three activities acquaint you with your students' attitudes toward writing, their interests, fears, and hopes. You also help students overcome writing problems, aid them in finding writing topics that interest them, and monitor their attitudes toward writing when you take the time to know something about the way they feel.

Caution: Self-Disclosure Ahead

A word about self-disclosure: Activities such as the ones that follow work well in a composition class because they involve students in talking about themselves and their own experiences. Personal experiences are the beginning writer's best resources. Talking before writing is priming the pump. The disclosures your students make during these activities also reveal information about them that a skillful teacher will use to motivate them further. You may learn which student is an artist, loves motorcycles, reads widely, lives on a farm, is a musician in a band, or works in a mortuary. The effective composition teacher stores these nuggets and uses them at appropriate times to suggest topics, draw out students, cast them in the role of expert, or simply engage them in spirited conversation.

Move slowly with this self-disclosure business. Remember that you are teaching writing, not conducting psychoanalysis. Your purpose in helping your students to open up a bit is to accustom them to letting go of fear, sharing their writings, and becoming more open to constructive criticism. Self-disclosure activities are not designed to pry into students' lives, to embarrass them, or to single them out. In general, the more you know about your students and the more they know about one another, the more a climate of openness and safety prevails. These are precisely the conditions that foster maximum growth in a writing class where students work closely with the teacher and with one another.

Finally, be aware that almost every school district has an explicit policy mandating that you report possibly illegal or dangerous activity. We recommend that you make sure students understand your responsibility when it comes to delving into sensitive subjects. Many schools require that teachers read everything that students write for class, so in essence, nothing they write will be totally private. This may sound a little scary, we know, but it's really a matter of setting common sense and agreed-upon boundaries. Done right, you can frame this conversation with students as a matter of self-regulation and control, of writers making informed choices based on a solid knowledge of consequence and audience.

Invitations for Peer Dialogue

The writing class strives to be a community whose members are exploring and experimenting with language, expression, thinking, and the art and craft of writing. We need to get to know our students in the writing class. They need to get to know each other and us. Most teachers will engage in these activities at the beginning of a new class when it's most obvious that students don't yet know each other. We have found, however, that returning to these activities throughout our time with a group of students is helpful for giving us new insights about each other and for maintaining an atmosphere of discovery and exploration. The more comfortable we are with a group, the more we all open up and tell deeper truths. The next series of activities will open dialogues among student writers through role taking, interviewing, connecting with pop culture, and other explorations among student writers while you model the openness you seek.

Letter to Yourself[4]

Ask students to write a letter to their future selves in which they describe how they feel as students, writers, and thinkers at this moment in their lives. What are they confident about, if anything? What do they feel they need to learn? How do they see their future selves? This may seem a bit weird to students (though weirdness can be a useful quality in a teacher), but encourage them to be honest—after all, it's not like they don't know who the reader is. Provide envelopes and ask them to seal their letters within, and then squirrel them away somewhere. In the rush and novelty of a new school year, most students will quickly forget this assignment. At year-end, with a flourish, produce these now ancient pieces. Ask students to read these as they'd read a letter from someone they used to know. What surprises them? How do their former and current selves differ? What advice do they have for their former selves, and how has their self-awareness shifted through the year?

Recalling and Reimagining the Past

Students walk into our classrooms with experiences, preferences, and opinions about almost everything. Use their lived experiences and personal attributes to advantage as you encourage your students to open up and become part of the writing community. The following activities build upon who our students are or would like to claim that they are.

The Lie Game

This is a personal favorite and one we have used for years with great success in our classes. Versions of it are widely used and are now classic icebreakers. The idea is for students to reveal something a bit surprising, noteworthy, or unique about themselves.

Ask students in your class (if you have a large class, select fifteen volunteers) to think of something that has or might have happened to them in the past—for example, "My father was an Olympic swimmer," or "I broke my nose in fourth grade," or "We have ten aquariums in our house and one hundred guppies." Caution students not to reveal anything they don't want others to know. Give them a minute or so to think about something. There is one basic rule in this game: Whatever they tell about themselves must be wholly true or wholly false. No half-truths are allowed. (For example, "We really have only fifty guppies.")

Ask the students to take out a sheet of paper and number from one to however many students are participating in the Lie Game.

Begin the game by telling something about your past. Tell a good lie: "I was on a high school basketball team that went to the state tournament," or "Right after college, I spent a couple of years hanging out in Hollywood, trying to make it as an actor." Alternatively, tell a revealing truth: "I played center on our high school basketball team the year we lost the state championship," or "I played the lead in our high school musical when I was a junior." Whatever you tell them, make it a good one. Your lie or truth will be a model.

After you have made your statement, ask students to mark *True* or *False* beside number one; even if only some students participate in the telling, all may join in this part of the game. Continue around the room. Keep it moving. Ham it up a bit. When all players have made their statements, go back around in the same order and ask the person who made the statement to give the correct answer. How good was each student at lying or at detecting a lie? What surprising facts did you learn about each other?

The purpose for the Lie Game is rather obvious. First, it's a talking activity. Second, it's a composing activity. Third, it's a self-disclosure activity and a good way to get the writing class moving. And yes, we call it a *game* to emphasize the lighthearted nature of this activity and to let students know that we have fun sometimes even as we learn.

Toy Stories

Ask students to write about their favorite toy from their childhood, detailing why they found it so compelling and memorable. Then pair students to share their stories. Next, ask them to write about a toy they remember yearning for but never actually owning. Why did they want this toy so badly? What were the circumstances that prevented them from possessing it? How did it feel to go without? How do they feel about it now? Students again share their work with partners; ask for volunteers to share with the class.

This kind of shifting focus on a topic serves multiple purposes. It gives students some practice with sifting through their memories and writing specifically, while the transition from fondness to unrequited longing reminds them of different emotional and intellectual perspectives that they will be able to use in other writings. Discuss these shifting emotions with students to pinpoint words, sentence structures, and other techniques that help readers identify feelings.

Creating Visual Portraits

Plan at least one activity that involves students in creating a visual portrait of themselves. This focus on visual images is an attempt to satisfy our natural impulse toward image making as well as promote the use of visualization in the writing class.

Coat of Arms

You may have seen this activity before; it's been around awhile. It works in a writing class for the same reasons the Lie Game works: It lets students share some of themselves in a nonthreatening way. Although students may complete this activity on a computer—using clip art or personal or Internet picture catalogues, or by pulling information from their social networking page—we deliberately go low-tech with a variety of our in-class activities. This is one of them. All you need for this activity is a facsimile of a shield (see Figure 3–3 for one example) divided into sections and some specific instructions (see below).

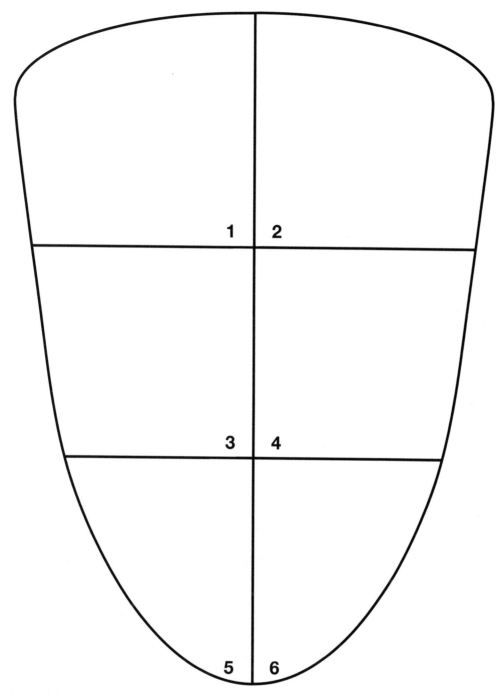

Figure 3–3. Coat of Arms
© 2013 by Dawn Latta Kirby and Darren Crovitz from *Inside Out, Fourth Edition*. Heinemann: Portsmouth, NH.

Tell your students not to worry about artistic results, and model your own artistic ability by illustrating that a vertical line with a circle on top of it may be a tree, a balloon, or the beginning of a stick figure person. It's fun to do this activity with your students. As a follow-up, students may share, in small groups, the drawings on their coats of arms, explaining the significance of the symbols. To enhance the visual nature of this activity, you might elect to post these coats of arms on a class website or to display them on the classroom walls and hold a gallery walk.

Students draw their responses on corresponding sections of the shield, to prompts like the following:

1. Draw two things you do well.
2. Draw the place where you feel most at home.
3. Draw your favorite person.
4. Draw your favorite possession.
5. Draw something related to the profession you hope to have as an adult.
6. Draw something related to your best academic subject.

As a variation, other value questions may be used, like the ones that follow:

1. What is a personal value that you will always hold?
2. What is something you're striving to be or become?
3. What one thing do you want to accomplish by the time you're 55?
4. Draw three activities you do well.
5. What is a personal motto by which you live? (We allow words for this response.)
6. What trait do you value most in your best friend?

With younger students—or with older ones if you just prefer it—you might use generic silhouettes of male and female children's heads in profile instead of shields.

▓ Logo, Slogan, and Epigraph

Very similar to the Coat of Arms, this activity gives students an opportunity to create a personal logo that incorporates their name, surname, nickname, or initials. A list of real-life logo examples may help students grapple with design elements such as color, font, shape, and image. Logos and slogans are iconic; they convey meaning in highly compressed form. Along with their logo, students craft a personal slogan. Help them recall logos and slogans with which they are familiar: PlayStation 3's "It Only Does Everything," Nike's check-mark-like swoosh and slogan ("Just Do It"), and Lance Armstrong's yellow bracelet and "Live Strong" motto.

Finally, students locate a quotation to serve as an *epigraph*, a written statement that personally resonates or provides further insight into each individual's identity. The quotations do not need to be familiar or famous. In fact, the personal connections to quotations that come from family histories, conversation, and everyday observations may be more effective for conveying meaning. All three elements—logo, slogan, and epigraph—are then brought together on a one-page hard copy or electronic display.

We sometimes make this activity more challenging by asking students to choose an epigraph that seems to complicate or contradict the other characteristics they have revealed in their logo and slogan while still being essentially true to the individual. This work involving deeper thinking and cognitive dissonance reminds students of the complexity of preferences and variations of personality in all of us.

Personal Collage

This one is a classic. Students search for online pictures, use clip art, cut pictures from magazines, or draw representations of their interests, talents, family life, home, pets, personal traits, and the like. Students may write a few paragraphs explaining the most significant of these pictures to those who may view the collages. Post these around the room along with a photo of each student to help everyone learn names.

Secret Box

Raid the shoe store for shoeboxes or ask students to bring them from home. Armed with scissors, glue, and a stack of magazines, ask students to decorate their boxes with pictures, words, or advertisements that reveal something about themselves. "Aha," you say, "a variation on the personal collage." Exactly. The outside of the box should illustrate readily known information, the *outside* of the student's interests, hobbies, talents, and so forth. The secrets go *inside* the box. Ask each student to put three artifacts in the box that reveal something about his inner self. Pair the students and ask them to explain the outside of the box to each other. They should reveal the secrets inside only if they feel comfortable with their partner.

Road of Life, Part 1

For this activity all you need are paper and pens or markers. Ask the students to make a map of their lives from birth to present. Tell them to illustrate the hills and valleys, the thrills and conflicts. Give them time to share the maps with at least three classmates. Collect the maps and decorate your walls. (See the next section, page 61 for Road of Life, Part 2.)

Behind the Mask

Use butcher paper to cut out a huge mask, or give students construction paper to make their own masks. Supply them with a stack of newspapers and magazines and ask them to cut out and paste words and pictures on the mask to form a message from behind the mask.

Cross-Family Comparative Collage

This activity is another spin on the traditional collage. Students pair up, ideally with someone they don't know. On the halves of a shared poster sheet, they assemble a family collage using photos, images, memorabilia, and other artifacts that they bring from home for this mixed media display. As they're creating the representations of their families, ask them to consider explicit similarities and differences between the two families, making written notes on the collage. Post their work around the classroom.

Integrating Technology

Activities with strong connections to technology resonate with our online-oriented and digitally savvy students. Before we detail these activities, however, it's important to remember that—most of the time—the technology itself is not the focus of the exploration. What *is* important is the thinking that students demonstrate regardless of the instructional approach or tool.

You'll need to assess your technological landscape before attempting these activities. Are online writing options even feasible for you and your students? Are sufficient computer resources and lab space available? Does your district encourage or frown upon online applications? If you find yourself in a school with sparse technological resources or at the mercy of restrictive online policies, don't toss out the entire concept of technology-assisted thinking and writing activities. Instead, consider ways that students might reproduce digital work through analog media.

Translating technologies across media requires students to get innovative; it'll take some thinking and effort to render what is taken for granted in cyberspace into our everyday "meatspace." By thinking and using their creativity across platforms and contexts, our students demonstrate what they can do and expand their literacy in multiple mediums.

Our students generally love working with the media options that technology affords, and with guidance they produce some impressive work. But we can't stress enough the importance of checking out online sites and applications. No teacher likes unpleasant surprises in the middle of a class. Do your homework; go through the sites carefully and engage in the processes of creation yourself *before* you jump in with these activities.

Finally, speak up. Talk with your administrator about the exciting educational uses of technology that you come across. Many "nontechie" administrators have an impression of teens and technology colored by stereotypes of nonstop texting and mindless gaming. Make a detailed case for the specific, applied use of digital technology in your classroom, and you just might change some minds.

▩ Creating Avatars

Avatars—digital representations of oneself—are a common part of online interaction. A variety of student-friendly avatar creation sites can be located with a simple online search. When you settle on an appropriate site, ask students to create an avatar that represents their public persona—how others see them—and one that reveals a more personal side. Students print both avatars and use them as either an oral or a written introduction to their peers. Again, displaying such work is easy to do and gives your classroom a real student-centered focus.

One caution: Some avatars have exaggerated physical features, making them not only unrealistic but also R-rated. Preview the sites and the possible avatars that students may create with an eye for what is acceptable in the context of your teaching.

▩ Glogs and Similar Online Resources

A variety of online multimedia applications may open new ways for students to describe themselves through more than words. Glogster is a popular poster-making site that features embedded media options; Museum Box allows a similar mixing of text, image, and other elements. Many others exist. Turn your students loose to see what they create as they visualize and write about themselves. If popular online applications are blocked at your school, challenge students to create interactive 3-D posters using traditional paper crafts, found objects, and other materials. The newest online app, site, or program can be "repurposed" through more conventional materials, and in the process students practice some higher-level thinking to justify the decisions they've made.

Visuals with Words

Many students have artistic and design talents, on the computer and off. This activity allows those with such talents to enhance an electronically produced item or to create their own; those without design talents will feel the surge of excitement that comes with seeing an artistic rendering of their writing.

After students have completed one of the initial interest or sentence completions activities in this chapter, or once they have written any piece about themselves (such as a portion of The Anatomy in Chapter 2), have them load the piece of writing into one of several online resources that will create a "word picture." Wordle and Tagxedo are a couple of our current favorites. These sites allow students to select color, font, and directionality of the words on the page, along with other options. Students may filter out the most common words (articles and prepositions, for example) so that they don't appear in the final product. What results is a colorful rendering of the piece consisting of the key words in the original piece of writing. (For an example, check the link to the online Additional Resources at www.heinemann.com/products/E04195.aspx, on the Companion Resources tab to see a word cloud of this chapter.)

Road of Life, Part 2: Virtual Tours

Online photo-sharing sites such as Flickr and Picasa, along with tools such as Google Maps, easily allow students to create virtual tours of places and spaces relevant to them. This activity may use geotagging, a method of adding GPS (Global Positioning System) data to photographs, to help students create their virtual tours. For example, a student interested in astrophysics may geotag Cape Canaveral. Students interested in hiking may geotag favorite locations they have walked. Along with the geotag, students add commentary about why and how the space is important to them. Learning how to upload, organize, and geotag photos and videos is a relatively simple process. Recruit a couple of the more tech-minded students in your class to serve as guides and assistants for others. Also provide links to quality student virtual tours on your class blog. And remember, kids don't need to reveal personal information—such as a picture of where they live or of their family members—that they prefer to keep private.

Creating Metaphors of Self

Comparing one thing with another is a natural human inclination. In these activities, students create metaphors of self in words or through a shape that represents them, and they then exchange ideas and information about themselves with their peers. These activities often require critical thinking as well as imagination; they also may require more time to develop fully than do some other opener activities we've discussed. Use these activities not as icebreakers necessarily, but as ways of offering students opportunities to expand their vocabulary, sense of figurative language, and transfer of knowledge from one context to another.

◼ Impressions Word Game

This brings students together and works well several weeks into the course after the students have become comfortable with one another. Students talk among themselves, share humorous perceptions of one another, and learn something about themselves. In the process, they practice creative uses of language and vivid detail. To begin, prepare a grid or table like the one in Figure 3–4.

Divide the class into groups of five students, give each student a copy of the grid, and ask them to write in the names of each person in the group. Now your students are ready to go. Ask them to fill in the blanks. A few suggestions:

1. If your students have not worked in groups much, structure the activity carefully.
2. Make up the groups any way you wish, but we like random groups for this activity.
3. Tell students to be as *specific* as possible: If it's a car, what kind? What color? Any unusual details to note about it, like a dented fender or bumper sticker?
4. During the sharing phase, be sure that all students receive some positive feedback quickly.
5. Maintain a positive atmosphere.

For follow-up, ask the students to respond to the activity by writing in their journals what they learned about themselves.

◼ Wire Sculpture

All you need for this deliberately low-tech activity are pieces of floral wire about eighteen inches long. Before you give each student a wire, spend some time talking about symbols and logos. We are all familiar with logos such as those of the Red Cross, the interlinking circles of the Olympic games, McDonald's golden arches, the Nike swoosh, and others. Ask students to begin thinking about a logo for themselves. What symbol would best represent them? Pass out the wires and ask the students to shape the wire so that it becomes a personal logo. Sometimes we use one of the following ideas:

1. Students shape the wire so that it makes a statement or represents an idea about something important to them.
2. Students shape the wire so that it becomes a *lifeline* that graphically depicts important events in their lives.
3. Students shape the wire so that it characterizes someone they have known for a long time.

As follow-up, have students pass the finished creations around the class and discuss the following:

1. Invite students to discuss what the shape says about its creator.
2. Have the creator discuss his wire to explain its significance.
3. Have each creator explain his creation to at least three other class members. (Free movement around the class is required for this activity.)
4. Have each creator write a short paragraph about the significance of his creation. Mount the wires on construction paper and tape the written paragraph to the back of the paper. Set up a display of the sculptures and invite students to browse.

Group Members' Names	Three Words	A Specific Car	A TV Personality or Celebrity	A Food Item	An Animal

Figure 3–4. Impressions Word Game

From *Inside Out, Fourth Edition*. © 2004 by Dan Kirby, Dawn Latta Kirby, and Tom Liner from *Inside Out, Third Edition*. Heinemann: Portsmouth, NH.

Variations of this activity can be done with straws, clay, paper, or paper clips (especially those of differing colors and sizes). Manipulating a wire and then talking about the creation allows the student enough psychological distance to be more open and honest about himself. It also moves our tech-savvy students into another kind of analogous (and yes, analog) thinking, which they may not get much of a chance to do anymore.

Making the Familiar Strange

Students are often so accustomed to their surroundings that they long ago stopped attending to the details of where they spend most of their time. Good writers need to incorporate details and sensory triggers into their pieces if they are to capture the reader and draw her into the piece of writing. We like working with several activities that encourage students to notice the details of their familiar routines and places as though they were seeing them for the first time. One of our favorites follows. With this activity, we can easily connect to literature and to other content areas such as anthropology.

Mini-Me

This activity allows students to consider what is important to them and to think metaphorically about how to represent those values, people, places, and activities in pictures. Students may draw their pictures for this activity, go to an online source of free pictures, use clip art, or use any combination of these to create their pictures. As a disclaimer, the title of this activity has nothing to do with the character of the same name that appears in the *Austin Powers* films; it is simply an abbreviated, and much catchier, way of saying "a miniature or symbolic representation of me."

Give students a silhouette of a human figure. We like to use generic forms like the one shown in Figure 3–5. Students then consider the literal and metaphorical functions of primary body parts like the feet, legs, spine, head, heart, arms, and fingers. For example, legs support the body. What and who, metaphorically, holds them up and supports them in their lives? The brain contains our thoughts. What worries your students? What goals and ideals motivate them? Once they have brainstormed some of the applicable functions and metaphors, ask students to fill in the body outline with pictures that represent what is true for them. A word of caution: Advise your students to keep the naming of the body parts G-rated.

Once the body form is filled with pictures, have students write about some of the parts that are most important to them. You might post these completed writings and body forms on your classroom walls and add a photograph of the student. This display is again one that focuses interest on the student and helps students to get to know each other. It also is an impressive display for Parent Night or Open House.

Martian Anthropological Observer

Ask students to take the perspective of a Martian Anthropological Observer (MAO) and report on the day-to-day rituals and routines of a particular Earthling (i.e., themselves). Their goal here is to strip away the taken-for-granted assumptions about normal behavior and to render the everyday as strange. Taking an alien's point of view on commonplace activities is entertaining and enlightening. It may also give your science or math student experts a chance to put the terminology of their favorite content areas to good use while encouraging writing across the curriculum. Our students often surprise us with how clever and incisive they are when using such a lens.

Figure 3–5. Mini-Me

© 2013 by Dawn Latta Kirby and Darren Crovitz from *Inside Out, Fourth Edition*. Heinemann: Portsmouth, NH.

The MAO is similar to the classic Nacirema activity in which the familiar is made strange in order to gain new perspectives on what we take for granted. (Note that *Nacirema* is *American* spelled backward. For more details, search the Web for numerous explanations and activities using this humorous anthropological exercise.)

Benefits of Initial Writings

By using these strategies, we provide student writers with multiple opportunities to engage in a wide, imaginative array of activities. They are learning about their peers and recalling their experiences, both of which help students generate the subject of self. They've written, talked, created visual representations, and leaped into metaphors. They've practiced many of the strategies they'll use to generate writing. Through these activities, your students have functioned as author and audience. This is a classroom in which you have already encouraged a community of sharing, listening, and advising. Fluency and community building are well underway, opening the door for deeper levels of exploration, writing, and learning.

NOTES

1. For more information on the studio classroom, see Kirby and Kirby (2007).
2. In order, these characters appear in Mark Twain's *Adventures of Huckleberry Finn*, Nathaniel Hawthorne's *The Scarlet Letter*, J. R. R. Tolkien's *The Lord of the Rings* trilogy, George Lucas' *Star Wars* saga, J. K. Rowling's *Harry Potter* series, and Sherman Alexie's *The Absolutely True Diary of a Part-Time Indian*.
3. Laura Jacobs and Todd Williams were students at Cedar Shoals High School in Athens, Georgia.
4. For more ideas for initial writing, see the link to the online Additional Resources at www.heinemann.com/products/E04195.aspx, on the Companion Resources tab.

Works Cited

Berman, Jeffery. 2001. *Risky Writing: Self-Disclosure and Self-Transformation in the Classroom.* Amherst, MA: University of Massachusetts Press.

The Breakfast Club. Dir. John Hughes. Universal, 1985. Film.

Gladwell, Malcolm. 2005. *Blink: The Power of Thinking Without Thinking.* New York: Little, Brown & Company.

Kirby, Dawn and Dan Kirby. 2007. *New Directions in Teaching Memoir: A Studio Classroom Approach.* Portsmouth, NH: Heinemann.

Palmer, Parker. 1998. *The Courage to Teach: Exploring the Inner Landscape of a Teacher's Life.* San Francisco: Jossey-Bass.

4

Writing Pathways

I write every day for two hours, but it's what I do during the other twenty-two hours that gives me something to write about.
—Don Murray

Most of us have heard some version of the adage, "Writers need to write every day." Certainly, we are able to locate books by and interviews with authors who profess that their success comes from the discipline gained by sitting down to think and express thoughts daily. Few people actually follow this advice, however, and maybe that's as it should be. What are we going to write about if we are prisoner to our own thoughts? We agree that writers need discipline—the discipline to work hard, study the craft of writing, and practice, practice, practice writing. At the same time, we know that most of the students in our classes are underexperienced—at least in the ways that lead to good writing. Life is at the heart of writing. We might argue, in fact, that great literature could not be written if the authors did not experience the joys and defeats of their lives.

So what experiences do student writers need? We think they need to live life joyfully and fully (at least during part of each day, and we think it tragic that some of our students aren't able to do so); they need to read, view, listen, talk, and think about pop culture and current newsworthy events; and yes, they need to write every day in our classes. They may not sustain this habit throughout their adult years, but they need the immersion in writing that we bring them while we have them captive. The ritual of writing every day improves writing. You know it, we know it, and our students will come to know it throughout their time in class with us. Meaningful writing that leads to meaningful thinking and then to more writing and more reflection and more writing (you get the idea) is one of the ways students understand how writing—and all forms of literacy—will improve not only their abilities to write but also their abilities to think critically.

The Power of Routine and Ritual

It's hard to underestimate the human need for routine and habit. Each of us, even the most nonconforming of souls, has favored patterns of behavior: a morning cup of coffee while scanning sports scores, a weekly workout routine, previewing tomorrow's activities before sleep. It's relatively easy to develop routines for what we like to do, but the more difficult tasks require the discipline of routine if they are to occur regularly and reliably.

Setting up daily writing as a class routine takes planning and commitment, especially when more and more content is crammed into the curriculum. Students may think it odd to write for five or ten minutes each day. We generally hear some whining for the first few days when we're working to establish this routine. Because we are adamant and write while they write, our students soon accept this expectation as just part of what we do in class. "You're in Kirby's class? Get ready to write *every* day!" or "Dude, Crovitz? He's crazy about this writing thing!" are comments that we frequently hear in the hallways. Writing routines work by establishing dedicated time for students to put in the work that builds fluency. If you're following the guidelines we describe in Chapter 3 for creating and sustaining community, you may find, as we often do, that routine morphs into ritual. Is this a good thing? We think so.

Routines become rituals when they are tied to social circumstances that carry meanings beyond simple convenience or habit. A Friday vocabulary quiz, for example, is a traditional routine in many English classrooms; it's one of dozens that might typify our expectations for our students' evidence of learning. Few students will rejoice in this routine. By contrast, *rituals* connote meaningful connection, buy-in, and shared values beyond the somewhat arbitrary requirements of schooling.

The bonding potential of ritual comes through a simultaneous commitment to the individual and to the group. Think about how people come together to form a team identity. Coaches are fond of saying, "There's no *I* in *TEAM*"; yet, teams rely on the contributions of uniquely talented individuals, pulling together for a common cause and toward achieving common goals. The secret for building such camaraderie is *trust*. The average teenager is acutely aware of what can happen when trust is misplaced, even among their friends. What, then, exists in the typical classroom environment to reassure students that building trust among their peers, who may not be *friends*, is worth the potential risk? We find that outlawing mockery and insults, insisting relentlessly that our classroom is a "No Hunting" zone, allows students to feel less wary about revealing pieces of themselves. We've seen amazing progress academically and personally in classrooms where caring and trust are at the forefront. In such a space, taking a risk is less scary because *we all have agreed to take risks* for the sake of everyone having an opportunity to grow as writers.

Nothing here is mystical. We teachers absolutely need to model treating everyone with respect and caring. Consistently, we will brook neither snark nor cynicism, cattiness nor contempt. We have to talk the talk, and then walk like we mean it. We lead by example, taking risks in front of our students, sharing our writing about emotionally tough topics, and finding personal insights in our writing as we work through it. When we model openness, caring, and risk, our students generally get on board. Are *all* of them buying in to this new way of being and interacting? Maybe not—at least not right away. For those too-cool-for-school types, a private request or two—*We need you. We need to hear your voice. You have something to say that we need to hear.*—often generates some initial trust. For the few die-hard apathy-heads, Darren has positive results from taking a different tack: *You don't care? That's okay. Fake it. Because even though you're faking like you care, we won't know the difference. Deal?* Maybe that sounds like a violation of a core trust, but we are pragmatic and flexible about the minutia in service of the greater outcomes. We've found that, given a chance, some students who seem to be the biggest roadblocks to building community will emerge as vital players later on. They just need a little more time to trust (or to fake it).

Finally, let's consider what rituals or rites of passage ultimately provide for individuals. Giving up a little bit of control, autonomy, and authority for the sake of group identity and dynamics has the potential to pay big dividends. Rituals traditionally serve as transition points in life, symbolic movements into new identities and roles. We like that analogy. Done right, we in writing classrooms welcome students who may be unsure of themselves as writers and as beings of worth. Unique social processes involving rituals of risk, reward, sharing, and group assistance foster the emergence of writers who are stronger than before in their confidence and abilities. They are the writers emerging from our very deliberate and thoughtful efforts to care, include, nurture, and honor individual worth and capabilities.

Focusing on the Writing Environment

No doubt, you are realizing that we think it essential to create a unique environment for the teaching of writing, one that our students probably can't get elsewhere in the crush of schooling. We are firm believers in the notion that the writing portion of class inherently *feels different* from other activities and aspects of instruction. We urge you to exude welcoming warmth and to offer reassurance of safety. Students walk into a kind of time warp when they enter our classes. They experience time to experiment and receive encouragement. They anticipate that we will prod them perhaps more than just a bit, asking them to rework and revise and, above all, to write and then write some more and then keep on writing.

Such an environment does not occur by chance or by the "I don't know what to do during fifth period; I think I'll have them write something" method. A writing class is, of necessity, carefully planned to maximize flexibility. This view is one of the true koans of our teaching.

Writing Daily: Fluency First (Getting It Down)

We do daily that which we love and that which is required to keep us alive. Writing does not fall into either category for many of our students. Most teens would hardly consider their daily quasi-writing, like the ubiquitous texting of teen's interactions, as *writing*. Moving teens into meaningful daily writing requires established routines and rituals to be successful.

Many of our student writers seem inordinately worried about getting it right before they get it down. As a result, they write in a halting, overly cautious, and tentative manner—one that is far from fluent. Time spent in developing fluency may help students write with more ease and comfort, putting off concerns about correctness until they have writing worth fixing. Personal writing is the natural place for students to begin to develop fluency by rendering experiences into words. We suggest that you begin your support for growth in fluency by providing students with lots of opportunities to write about what they know and feel.

Encourage them to express themselves in their own words. Note the insight that acclaimed writer Toni Morrison (1998) offers:

> When you first start writing—and I think it's true for a lot of beginning writers—you're scared to death that if you don't get that sentence right that minute it's never going to show up again. And it isn't. But it doesn't matter—another one will, and it'll probably be better. And I don't mind writing badly for a couple of days because I know I can fix it—and fix it again and again and again, and it will be better. (200)

When we teach student writers, we begin with only two real, attainable goals: to build a feeling of confidence in students that they *can* write, and to help the student find a voice in writing. Building confidence is our first job. As tender as the ego of the beginning writer is, there is little wonder that many of our students dislike and fear the experience of writing. Thankfully, a little success goes a long way.

The Journal

One indispensable tool for successfully helping students expand their language and writing repertoires is the journal. The journal provides immature writers with some of the regular, daily practice they need to become comfortable with writing. No matter how good the assignment and no matter how inspired the teaching, students cannot develop as writers if they write only once in a long while.

Now before you panic at the idea of a mountain of journals to grade every weekend from 150 or more kids who have written their hearts out every day in your class, calm down. It doesn't work that way. Journals are not designed to be—and should not be—red-penciled. The idea of journal writing is to develop fluency and to eradicate fear of writing. Correcting every error that students make in their journal writing will not promote those goals.

Instead of being corrected, journals need to be read and celebrated and responded to by a real audience—you and fellow students. Peer reading and responding is one way to take the pressure off you, and the reactions and comments of peers will often mean more to the new writer than will yours. You'll need to develop procedures for peer responding in your classroom (as we outline in Chapter 8). Dawn tells her students that specific comments are more valuable than are generic "good job" responses. She models specific comments such as, "I like the part about . . ." and "I could really relate to the part where you talked about . . ." and "When you mentioned getting your sister's room after she went off to college, I remembered. . . ." *Sharing* writing is important for its own sake and is a powerful motivator for further writing. And if you work it right, peer reading will help you alleviate some of the paper load.

One technique is to use computers for journal writing. Many students prefer writing on computers because of the ease with which changes in the writing may be made, even in midword as it emerges fresh from their minds. When we work in well-equipped classrooms, we project our computer screens for the class to see our writing as it emerges. After ten minutes of sustained writing, the students and we play musical chairs, moving progressively around the class to sit down at another person's computer and read the journal entry. Not everyone will have time to read every entry, but give students enough time to read several. Next, we ask, "What did you see that was interesting or that you liked?" With an especially shy or reluctant group of students, we might begin these conversations among small groups of five students who have read each others' screens; then, we build up to whole-class discussion. Either way, we get the conversation about writing to flow.

Managing Journals

What typical requirements come with journals? That's up to you. Some teachers expect a page a day and collect journals weekly. Some teachers use the first ten minutes of class for journal writing; others prefer that students to do all of the writing at home. The choice is yours. In the beginning, you might want to get the habit going by giving some in-class time to journaling. Dawn usually requires four pages a week and collects them four times during a semester. Of course, the idea is that students will write more than the minimum. Darren has experimented with not collecting journals at all, but expecting students to demonstrate evidence that their work has emerged from their journal explorations. Regardless of how often you collect journals, the idea is to feature lots of opportunities for sharing journal writing in class before journals are collected. We ask for volunteers during the first few minutes of class to read something pithy or funny or thought provoking from their journals. We provide opportunities for response groups during class, and we have students read to us from their journals during conferences. Because working with journals is so integral to our classes, we know at any given time what each student is writing and the progress she is making with her latest effort.

Journals are not static tools. That is, we begin by expecting and praising quantity; we move into praising the quality of a few lines in an entry; and we ultimately focus on the thought-provoking nature of the content in the journal entries. We progress toward helping students develop writing with legs, writing that has the potential to go somewhere, to become a more polished piece. As we maintain an emphasis on the journal as a working, evolving collection of writing that students will mine for future nuggets of new writing, we find that the journal becomes much more student-directed. The journal begins to belong to the individual student, not to us, the teachers. When students own their writing, they invest more of themselves and their time in it. That is the ultimate goal of all writing, and journals help our students make that journey.

With that goal in mind, our work with journals takes on new perspectives. We do not read papers at home at night, and we do not grade journals on the weekend. We have learned to read during breaks in our day, before and after school, and on the train during the morning and afternoon commutes. We have learned to read fast, to skim journals for the gems of writing that we always find there, and to respond briefly with a question, an exclamation point, or a concise but meaningful comment. Of course, some parts of the journal will connect with you, and that's when you'll respond with more detail and depth, but responding to journals is a way to encourage writers, not note their every nuance. The task is not impossible.

We usually do assign grades to journals, holding students accountable for the number of pages assigned for the journal each week or for bringing forth new pieces of writing from gems begun in their journals. We count. We count the number of new pieces arising from the journal or the number of written pages and give them credit for the percentage of the minimum that they completed. When we're counting the number of pages, for example, we give our students full credit if they completed the full number of assigned pages. We don't give full credit for half-pages, and we don't give full credit for pages that have exorbitant margins or quadruple spacing just to fill the page. We redirect students who aren't getting the point or following directions. Their journal work is important, and we make sure that students know how and why their journals are important writers' tools. We take time with getting journals started and with making sure everyone is on the right track, we praise the writing, and we make sure that we're hearing from everyone regularly in class during those sharing times before the journals are due. This combination of praise, sharing, responding, and credit for journal writing has been successful for us, and the journals have been invaluable writing tools for our students.

Freewriting

Freewriting is the bread and butter of the writing classroom, one of the key practices to promote fluency in writing. We use it frequently with our students. It is the writer's first and most basic tool. We start with freewriting in students' journals and go back to it whenever students seem threatened by a new assignment, stuck in their thinking, or otherwise in need of limbering up their minds.

Have your students write for ten minutes without stopping or thinking about what they'll say next. The important thing is to keep the words flowing across the paper. They are not to worry about spelling, punctuation, or usage. If they can think of nothing to say, tell them to write "I've got nothing to say" over and over until something occurs to them. This exercise should be repeated for several days initially so that freewriting becomes almost automatic for students and so that they can do it without balking. Getting over writer's block and the threat of an empty sheet of paper or a blank computer screen is one of those tricks that fluent writers have internalized. Freewriting helps defang the anxieties of creation by making writing a low-stress, normal activity.

Middle and high school students generally enjoy freewriting, probably because it's a nonthreatening way to write, and it removes the restraints. After a while with daily practice, patterns in their writing begin to emerge and individual voices begin to grow distinct. That's why we usually don't assign a topic for freewritings; they are *free*.

Freewriting Variations

Once the students are accustomed to the idea of freewriting, we like to have them play around with some possibilities as they write.

Brain Dumps

"The human mind," writes Garrison Keillor (2002, 291), "is like a cloud of gnats." How very true. Help your students calm the gnat storm with five minutes of mental peace. From the tumult and clamor of the school hallway, the journal provides a quiet zone: to rant, to ramble, to blow off steam, to get it out, to settle the mind and clear the air.

Focused Listening

Ask students to *listen* carefully as they freewrite, recording the sounds they hear around them. Or ask them just to concentrate on listening while they keep their writing going without paying particular attention to what they're putting down until the ten minutes are up. This activity helps build sensory awareness of the details that help to enliven writing.

Mood Music

Have students freewrite to music, and use different kinds of music to set different moods as they write. Students particularly enjoy this stimulus, perhaps because they like to ridicule our music choices. Darren is fond of Zen-type ambient music, atmospheric and meditative; Dawn goes for smooth jazz. Freewriting to rock music changes the vibe in class radically, which changes again if we use Beethoven or Tchaikovsky. At first we use only instrumental music so the lyrics will not distract the students, but later we have them freewrite to songs also, reacting to the lyrics as they write. We discuss how the lyrics and musical arrangements of Lady Gaga or Billie Holliday or The Smiths make us feel; we discuss tone and voice and style, all tools of artists, including singers and writers.

Here and Now

You may want to pick a time for this exercise when your students are particularly agitated about something, or one of those days when the room seems to buzz with excitement or sinks into a gloomy silence for no particular reason. Ask the students to record the date and the time and write four words that capture how they're feeling here and now. Tell them to think about the four words they have recorded and to expand on one or more of them. For example:

> August 29, 2011, 12:30 AM. Tired. Anxious. Sleepy. Excited. I'm both anxious and excited by thinking about the book. Can I do this right? Will people want to read it? Will they think this version measures up to the others? The deadline is starting to loom large in my thoughts. Maybe Dan can reassure me, or Darren can respond to what I've just added to the chapter. I've got that online workshop to fit into my schedule somehow, too. And, what am I going to do with my classes tomorrow?

It's a good journal exercise, or you may want to do it as a Quickie (discussed later). However it's used, it helps students get in touch with themselves and gives them something real to say in their writing. Try several Here and Nows, and choose the best one from each student to be expanded, edited, and published.

Poetry and Prose

With our students who are practiced at freewriting, we read them a poem or a brief prose passage and have them freewrite about it without planning or preparation of any kind. They may respond to what we read to them, make a personal connection to it, recall another piece of similar writing, or perhaps create a companion piece in another genre. That is, if we read a prose passage, our students may elect to get the beginning of a poem going in response. This activity is a way to get those gut-level reactions to a piece of writing down on paper. The purpose is to get feelings and ideas out that then might be ordered, with more thinking and talking, into a more complete paper. If you are particularly interested in having your students work with poetry—either writing it or responding to it—we note that the Poetry 180 website features daily poems for the high school classroom. We have used it often to find an appropriate poem to read to our students and about which they then freewrite.

Time-Outs

Freewriting is not just for the beginning of class. Any time a class discussion gets heated can be a good time to call a time-out, offer a well-chosen question, and ask students to "give me five minutes." Out come the journals, the room is suddenly quiet, and both teacher and students write furiously for five minutes. Afterward, call on one student after another to read. No comments; they must read what they have written. At some point you can read your own, with no more nor less fanfare than anyone else received. And then the questions and the argument continue.

Meta-Writing

We often start a new class by asking students to freewrite about *writing*. The results are sometimes surprising. Students reveal their feelings about writing, positive and negative experiences with writing, and mention teachers who helped or hindered their progress with learning about writing. Some students wax philosophical about writing as a great cultural art or the joy of well-turned song lyrics. Some write a poem about writing, which is perhaps one of the most interesting meta-writings we've received. Leaving the topic broad gives students the freedom to follow their thoughts.

Spontaneous Writing: Quickies

During the first days in class, get students into the daily habit of writing by having them write a Quickie—a half-page of writing in ten minutes or less—at the beginning of each class. Personal subjects work well for these. Here are a few suggestions.

1. Given the choice of one, and only one, of these things, which one would you choose: money, fame, friends, or love? Why?
2. Tell about something that makes you happy.
3. Tell about something that makes you sad.
4. Talk about something you really dislike.
5. What *color* do you feel like today? Talk about why you picked that color.
6. Tell about your favorite song right now.
7. Plan the menu for the school cafeteria for a week. You may include anything you wish. Why did you make these selections?
8. If you were a character from a television show, who would you be? Tell about what you would do in one episode of the program.
9. Imagine that you stayed out of school today. Where would you go? What would you do?
10. You are an artist painting your masterpiece, the painting that will make you famous for generations to come. What is the painting? Describe it.

Focused Writings

After students are accustomed to freewriting, we begin to focus a bit more the ideas they explore. By focusing their writings to some degree, our student writers begin to explore a range of ideas and to see what surfaces that might be promising for future and further work. The following ideas get students going with focused writings. Periodically, have students cull their journals for pieces worthy of further work and development.

Snapshot Writing

Sometimes, students need a concrete prompt to get them going with personal writing. One technique that works well is to use a snapshot. The instructions to students are simple: "Bring in a photograph in hard copy (not just on your phone) that is important to you. It will be posted in the room for a few weeks, so don't bring in one that will embarrass you or that is so precious your mother will kill you if something happens to it. No boyfriends or girlfriends, please."

Dawn has brought in an old snapshot of herself in elementary school, standing at the base of the Washington Monument. Darren uses an old photo of himself surf fishing on a lonely Florida beach. We tell the stories behind the photos, laugh it up, and then write about the photographs. After the pieces are drafted, edited, and proofread, we put the pictures and writings together on the classroom walls. For days afterward, we find it generally difficult to get students in their seats and away from reading the walls.

Here's Christina[1] with an example:

> Beside me on the ground is the other dog, a large, intelligent shepherd mix called Shadow. Pointed and velvet ears lay flat against a think, ebony ruff to shield from the wind, and he looks away from me, almost longing. Shadow takes solace in half-sitting on the fringe of the tide, letting each wave surge up gently under his forelegs and stomach. He's getting old, ringing up nine this December, and I'm glad to see the quiet big guy do something he enjoys before he's unable to.
>
> "Shadow," I call softly, just to see his beautiful dark muzzle turn toward me, even if it's only by a little bit. He's always been that way, so aloof, like he's smarter than all of us.

We like Christina's creative mix of physical description and subtle insight here. She shows us how recording sensory details can be a doorway to deeper understandings.

Movie Soundtrack

Soundtracks do more than simply accompany images or film. When done well, a soundtrack contributes to a story, offering an interpretation of the script and enhancing the visuals of the movie, perhaps even *suggesting* the visuals. The advent of video-hosting sites such as YouTube means that a vast array of short videos featuring particularly well-done or unusual soundtracks with no narration or dialogue are easily available to teachers. To capitalize on this type of composing, play soundtracks before showing the video (or hide the video by blocking your projector or turning off the monitor) and have students write an imaginary script to match the soundtrack. Or, they might freewrite using the soundtrack as the stimulus. Then show the video and have students turn their papers over and record their reactions on the back.

A quick YouTube search for "soundtrack" yielded more than three million hits; you probably have your own favorites. Just as teachers maintain a collection of interesting readings, activities, and assignments, it's now just as easy to create a library of useful video clips.

Memory Writing

The purpose of this exercise is to encourage student writers to use their best resource—themselves—as the material for narrative writing and to impose some controls on that material.

Tell students that they are to concentrate on capturing the essence, the particular detail and feeling, of each incident as they engage in this activity, working without much concern for grammatically perfect or complete narratives.

The students delve into their memories, recent and distant, to see what vivid images come to mind. We generally use instructions similar to the following:

> You are to go back in time to capture four incidents in your life. Each incident may be important or trivial, but it should be one that stands out in your mind. Record it as briefly as you can, but make it as real as you can.
>
> 1. Go back in time twenty-four hours. Remember one incident from yesterday. Record it.
> 2. Go back in time a week and remember something you were doing on this day seven days ago. Record it.
> 3. Go back a year for this one and record an incident you remember from about the same time of year. Concentrate on the particular details.
> 4. Now concentrate really hard and go back as far as you can. Record your first *clear* memory.

We have students look for concrete details and vivid verbs in this writing. How did they make the memory live on the page? What connections do they see among the experiences?

Then and Now

This is another memory exercise with a different twist. Have students look back into their memories and compare a person or place they remember *then* with their perceptions of the same person or place *now*. Here are a few suggestions of Then and Now subjects with which we have had success:

1. Your backyard when you were six years old and now
2. Your bedroom then and now
3. Church then and now
4. School then and now
5. The family car then and now
6. A close relative then and now

Remember to keep the writings short unless the student gets involved in a memory and wants to continue it. Your purpose at this point is to provide the stimulus to get students started as writers, not to exact long expositions.

Extending the Writing

As students become familiar with these kinds of regular writing activities, you might begin looking for opportunities to extend their writing beyond a ten-minute experience. You'll find that some of the prompts we've described will resonate with students so that the students may be interested in continuing to work with the piece, crafting it to become a more developed piece of writing. You certainly shouldn't feel compelled to turn every freewrite into something larger, but be on the lookout for opportunity. If students seem fired up by a particular activity, or want to keep writing and discussing, it may warrant some extended attention. The Name Piece activity that follows is one such example, and you will find a variety of others online in the Additional Resources for this chapter. The link to the resources is at www.heinemann.com/products/E04195.aspx, on the Companion Resources tab.

▇ The Name Piece

This activity is a favorite of ours and is one that we've noticed as gaining increasingly widespread use over the last few years.

First, we read several excerpts from published writers in which they have written about names. Tobias Wolff (2000) has a good piece in his memoir *This Boy's Life* about his name, Toby, and about how he once wanted to change his name to Jack. Sandra Cisneros (1991) has a piece about the names of her characters, Esperanza and Magdalena. Scott Momaday (1987) has a piece about tribal names. The Name Piece is out there in published literature; go looking for it. Once you've done this assignment a few times with students, you will be able to gather student examples that are equally as impressive.

After we have read and discussed these name excerpts, we ask students to write their full names across the top of a page so that each name is a separate column. Then, as in the excerpts, we ask students to jot what they know about each of their names. Who named them? Are they named after someone? Do they like their names? Do they have nicknames? Do their names show up in songs? And so forth. We keep the jotting going for a while, and we complete our name chart on the board as students write their own charts. Then, we briefly discuss the jottings on our name charts with the class. Next, we put students in pairs to tell the stories of their names.

After this sharing of about five to seven minutes per partner, we debrief as a whole class. What was particularly interesting in the partner discussions? Did we mention anything similar to what one of the published authors mentioned?

Next, have students write a draft piece that tells the whole story of their names. The next day in class, we share and respond to our drafts. The discussions are lively. Not surprisingly, some students don't know a lot about their names. They may need to do some family interviews or conduct some research. The following is a Name Piece by a student who did just that to find the information she needed to write a rich piece about her name.

> **Sadiqa Adero Ihsan Edmonds.** Isn't that a mouthful? I love my name but it took me a while to be able to say it all at full speed. I first blessed the world with my presence on a Friday, March 2. I was born at 610 Albert Court around noon.
>
> Even though I was born on a Friday, I wasn't named until Saturday, March 10. Of course, my dad had already picked out my names before I was born, but my parents made the decision to name me in a very special African naming ceremony. African names are believed to be very meaningful in a person's life by the people of certain African tribes, so my parents decided to use a variation of the naming ceremony used by one of these tribes.
>
> That Saturday, March 10, a lot of relatives and friends of the family came to participate in my naming ceremony. The first thing that they did was sit in a

circle on the floor. My parents were at the head of the circle and everyone else sat around from the eldest to the youngest, the eldest being by my father, and the youngest by my mother. My parents talked about my birth and how my being born would help us as a family. My father whispered my name in my ear, and then announced it to the people in the room. So other than my father, I was the first person to hear my name.

After this my father passed me to the eldest person, who was my Aunt Ossie. As each person passed me around, they each would whisper some words of wisdom in my ear. In the African villages, this was done to show the baby's acceptance into the community. By doing this, my family showed that they accepted me into the family. After this was finished, everyone had a big dinner of certain foods.

The names my dad gave me were *Sadiqa*, *Adero*, and *Ihsan*. *Sadiqa* is my first name. It's Arabic for "friend." My dad chose *Sadiqa* as my first name because he believes that the essence of a relationship both outside and inside the family is a friendship, and if friendships can be formed inside a family it makes the bond stronger than just having the same blood.

My first middle name is *Adero*. It's from East Africa and it means "life-giver." Dad chose this name because he wanted me to breathe life into everything I do and every one I meet. My second middle name is *Ihsan*. It's also Arabic and means "performer of good deeds." My dad chose this name because he wanted me to do pretty much what the name says, perform good deeds.

My last name is *Edmonds*. I acquired this from my dad. My great grandfather's name was Tony Edmonds but everyone called him Papa Tony. Although his father was a slave owner named Bardlin Edmonds and his mother was an African princess removed from her African village by force and sold into slavery, Papa Tony was not a slave. His mother was given the name Susie Robison by her slave owner.

Although she was subjected to the pursuit of her slave owner, she still had children from the mate of her choice.

Papa Tony was a man who built his own businesses. He built a school and a church for black children to attend. The church is still attended. I was able to see it. The school has been torn down after integration but my dad was able to visit it.

My parents chose to give me African names and to celebrate my joining the family by an African naming ceremony so that I'd have a full appreciation for my African as well as my American heritage. They want me to appreciate what my forefathers have done to overcome their oppression.

—*Sadiqa*[2]

We especially like this starter activity and use it at the beginning of each new writing class for several reasons. One, it helps all of us to learn each other's names. Two, students know more about their names than we do, so they are writing from authority and expertise. Three, this activity is modeled after real, published writing but remains personal and contextualized. Four, sometimes students want to learn more about their names, which can lead to research on genealogy websites, looking through the family Bible, or conducting some Action Research on their names by interviewing family members. (See more about Action Research in Chapter 7.) This piece is a hit with students, who love to write about themselves; they usually spend time revising it, indicating that they value the piece; and the Name Piece almost always becomes a piece that students work to revise, showing us that it resonates with students.

By the way, the naming ceremony mentioned here in the piece by Sadiqa is very similar to the one portrayed beautifully in a children's book by Deborah Chocolate (1995) titled *On the Day I Was Born*. We recommend that book along with the other sources we named here as good exemplars for use with your students.

"Stacking" and Backward Design

From freewriting to quickwrites to targeted prompt responses, starter activities can help create the climate of regular writing that students need to develop fluency. But with just a little forethought on your part, these exercises don't have to function as only isolated islands of practice. Your larger unit goals can and should trickle down into the daily work of the classroom in a variety of ways. This doesn't mean that every lesson has to be explicitly tied to or governed by specific larger themes, but just that having broader destinations in mind positions you to take advantage of day-to-day writing for its reinforcing and cumulative potential. Wiggins and McTighe (2005) call this concept "backward design." We like to think of it as *stacking* (as in stacking the deck); that is, we purposely order learning experiences of increasing complexity so that students build on what they've already accomplished as they move into new learning. It's not a revolutionary concept by any means; but in the frenzy and stress of a school year, it's easy to lose sight of how smaller writing tasks might become the threads of larger tapestries. For a thorough example of how to use stacking with memoir writing, see Kirby and Kirby (2007).

Tilling the Soil

We use many metaphors when teaching writing, looking for the connotations that will resonate with our diverse students. For this one, we suggest that you might imagine some daily writing exercises as *tilling the soil* for more elaborate work in the future. Thus writing prompts that help students explore family dynamics, roles, relationships, and tensions might be a good way for students to begin grappling personally with themes that will show up in another week or so in texts such as *Romeo and Juliet*, *Death of a Salesman*, *Ordinary People*, *The House on Mango Street*, or many others that may have a spot in your curriculum. Writing that deals with experiences with degrees of phoniness, types of reputations individuals may acquire, and issues of social class might be a prelude to themes found in *The Catcher in the Rye*, *The Great Gatsby*, or *Speak*. You get the idea. While students may not see the destination right away, you're thinking about both the small and big picture and planning writing experiences accordingly.

Let's look at an extended example using the Name Piece as a starting point.

Naming and Identity as an Extended Unit: One Example

The Name Piece is a great way to get students into extended writing because it deals with a topic about which everybody has some insight, expertise, stories, and experience. *Naming* may become part of an extensive thematic unit dealing with the concept of *identity*. Such a unit might be guided by the following kinds of questions, which in some curricula are termed *essential questions*:

- To what extent is identity determined more by one's family, one's culture, one's individual beliefs, or one's actions?

- How might different situations change who you are or how you are seen by others?
- How might you define or characterize a person's *real* identity? How would we be able to tell *real* from *fake*?
- How might a *persona* be different than an *identity*?
- Under what circumstances, if any, might it be acceptable to put forth a *false* identity?
- What does one's appearance (clothing, hairstyle, etc.) or possessions have to do with one's identity, if anything?

With such questions as an overall framework, many different kinds of writing (and many different texts, not just the classics) become relevant. Such a unit might go in multiple directions. As we brainstormed a short list of possibilities that extend on the theme of *naming and identity*, we generated the following, which clearly is not a sequenced list of formal assignments:

- Family Name Investigation: Where does one's name/surname originate, what did it mean, and how has it evolved?
- Place and Naming: How were names of schools, subdivisions, neighborhoods, towns, counties, and states determined? What do they mean? What did they used to be called? By whom? Why did they change? What do these changes signify?
- Nicknaming: How are nicknames assigned? What rules, if any, apply to nicknaming? Can a person choose his or her own nickname? Who gets to decide?
- Fame and Names: Celebrities, musicians, and artists have a unique freedom to rename themselves. How does such naming translate in terms of power, influence, and authenticity?
- Character and Impression: How do authors use naming to affect our understanding of characters? Examples abound, from the Harry Potter novels to video games to popular animated films to just about everything Nathaniel Hawthorne ever wrote. Students might envision their own alter ego persona, create a backstory that explains the traits of their character, write a story, and use simple moviemaking technology to visualize and narrate these events.
- Creation and Naming of a Fake/Hoax Creature: Naming doesn't always need to be for real things. Have you ever heard of the *Octopus paxarbolis*? The name seems to be created from Latin and means "peaceful tree octopus," which is a totally fictional name for a totally fictitious animal. We like the Pacific Northwest Tree Octopus website for the way it cleverly mimics the language of scientific study and environmental advocacy (see http://zapatopi.net/tree octopus/). After studying how language, image, and graphics combine to create the illusion of scientific validity on this webpage, students might design similar tongue-in-cheek eco-sketches for creatures of their own creation. Such writing would necessarily require geographical, biological, ecological, and etymological information delivered in an appropriate voice and format, accompanied by appropriate informative multimedia. Knowledge of Latin, pop culture, and other social media are rich with opportunities for playing with names.
- Product Names: Students might investigate the associations and implications of product names, from snack food (Funions, Doritos, Skittles) to prescription drugs (Allegra, Celebrex, Flomax) to SUVs (Wrangler, Explorer, Highlander).

- Controversies in Naming: Ask students to explore local or national issues related to naming. Because what we call something or someone is often laden with stereotypical assumptions or culturally insensitive language, public naming may change over time. Some specific topics that we have used to invite inquiry include the following:
  - the renaming of natural areas based on changing ethnic, racial, and gender sensitivities (e.g., Squaw Peak in Phoenix renamed Piestewa Peak)
  - the retiring of certain sports team names and mascots (e.g., the Redmen of St. John's University becoming the Red Storm)
  - proposals to ban public signage in Spanish (in Georgia, one such proposal was ironically supported by a representative whose district included the city of Villa Rica)
  - President Obama's opponents referring to him by his full name (Barack Hussein Obama)
  - The use of loaded or politically correct language in political conversations and definitions (e.g., *torture* vs. *enhanced interrogation techniques, progressive* vs. *socialist, secretary* vs. *administrative associate*, etc.).

Students might seek to understand the opposing rationales in a specific conflict or debate in preparation for entering the conversation themselves.

Here's an incomplete summary of the subjects and thinking that the list above implies: narrative control, expository writing, connections to multiple disciplines, consideration of root words and morphemes, connotation and denotation, narrative, plot, speaking and listening, understanding media representations, viewing and visually representing, scientific voice and naming principles, understanding the effect of nonverbal rhetorical elements, audience awareness, research of various kinds, and the basics of argument, such as establishment of a problem, selecting evidence, and building a case. How many Common Core standards (or other content and learning expectations) are potentially met here with just a bit of thinking, reframing, and judicious planning? We can think of several without much effort. Not bad for a unit that begins with an innocuous Name Piece.

This is what thoughtful, reflective teachers do. They look for ways to build on thematic threads from lots of different angles, with lots of different texts and writing activities. No doubt you've already thought of some other writing possibilities related to *naming and identity* as well. And that's the idea. As students come to know the subtleties, lines of inquiry, and real-world conflicts around a theme, they become more well-rounded thinkers in their own right. Don't be surprised if they come to class excited by (and even eager to write about) some local naming issue they've suddenly recognized. Finally, don't feel restrained by this particular theme. This approach works with any significant topic that arises in the natural course of the curriculum and your instruction.

Place and Context: A Second Example

Let's look at another example of stacking. This one begins with a Life Map activity that asks students to sketch from memory a neighborhood or familiar place from their childhood. As they draw, they label specific places on the map that were important to them in some way, maybe because they contain a story or a peculiar bit of lore, or because they harbor something else interesting or unique. One of Darren's Life Maps (he has several since he lived in lots of places as a kid) is in Figure 4–1. It shows the neighborhood he lived in near Oscoda, Michigan, when he was eleven years old. You can see that some of the areas have labels and short explanations that suggest their relevance, but he's also used numbers to indicate more in-depth stories, events, memories, and facts about this place. That's the way Darren's mind works—with details and lots of depth and backstory. Your students may not want to number and label. That's fine as long as they can still talk through what is represented on the map.

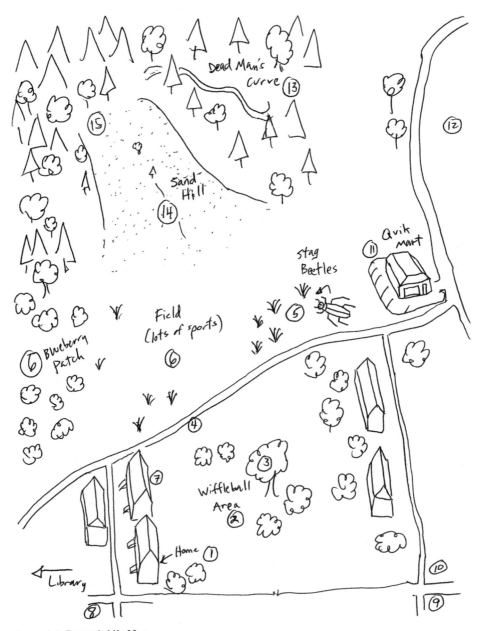

Figure 4–1. Darren's Life Map

Life Maps are great activities to get students writing about subjects they know and care about. There's something about the act of diagramming a place from memory that jogs loose episodes and events that might otherwise remain hidden. Life Maps help students practice fluency and, in the need to get right the details of a particular incident or experience, precision. But Life Maps can also hint at deeper ideas—ideas about the importance of place and memory, of connection and community, of stewardship and the sacred—that with a little forethought can be used to our advantage. Consider the following questions:

- What is *essential* about a particular place (i.e., what element, if removed, would change the fundamental quality of a place)?
- How much does a particular place influence who we are as individuals or a community?
- What is the connection (if any) between memory and truth?
- What does it mean to have *roots* in a place? How does such a metaphor affect how we make sense of physical space?
- Is it better to try to preserve a place that has special meaning, or to let it change?
- How do certain places invite or inhibit connection with other people?
- How does the way we experience a place relate to its meaning?
- How do issues of legal ownership relate to meanings of place?
- To what degree should we honor or preserve the special or spiritual spaces of others?
- How does *context* change how we interpret place and meaning?
- How important is the concept of physical place in a digital age?

These are just a start; you've probably thought of several more already. With such questions as a platform, our initial Life Map might morph into a gateway activity for a larger unit dealing with *place* and *context*. Our prospective plan could incorporate some of the following pieces of writing, with students lastly writing a final reflection about how all of their pieces reveal important information about them. Try writings like these with your students:

- *Where I'm From*: The Where I'm From poem is a great way to move from a personal map to a personal statement of identity, place, and heritage. It also eases students into poetry writing, which can be challenging. (See our ideas that follow about how to engage your students with poetry writing.) Students use a framework of "I'm from . . ." statements to create a portrait of themselves using specific visual detail, figurative language, and metaphor. We are consistently amazed by the evocative work students produce with prompts like this one. Like the Name Piece, the Where I'm From poem has become an increasingly common writing activity in classrooms, for good reason.

  Here's a Where I'm From poem from Cara. She makes references in the piece that she would need to explain to us if we were to understand them fully, but her use of symbols and metaphors help. Also note that she writes a reflection about her poem, telling us what she was trying to accomplish in the piece and how she feels about her work. This type of information is invaluable for teachers of writing. We often ask students to write similar, if more in-depth, reflections about pieces of their writing.

Where I'm From

I'm from the air,
From running and flying,
And climbing until I fell.
I'm from cold mountain air,
Sun-dried summer days,
And the breeze of stillness
Or of movement.

I'm from fire.
I'm from the duplicitous destruction of hard work
And a lifestyle past.

I'm from the water,
From swimming until my little-kid-blonde hair
Was green,
And catching frozen raindrops
On my tongue.

I'm from the earth,
From towering trees, pines and beeches and aspens;
From the twenty-foot boulders I climbed at four,
And the tall golden grass I hid in.
I'm from wooden beams and rolls of insulation
Carried on the broad shoulders of hard work.
I'm from watermelon seeds,
And fishing with my parents
In a namesake pond
With a surface like a mirror.

And I'm from my dad;
From cowboy boots,
Too-big-for-me suede ten-gallons
(The kind that actually looked good on someone),
Pickup trucks in red and silver
And the twangy, well-worn melodies
Of Tim McGraw;
And my life then:
The quintessence
Of living in the West.

I'm from my mom.
From the blinking and winking

Of "city lights"
And whispered good nights;
From Kissing Hands
And Three Trees
And "one last minute."

I'm from the others, too—
From my wonderful sister,
My Vince Vaughn-like brother-in-law,
And their two kids.
I'm from the memories I can't recall
And the people I know
Only through a frame.
I'm even from my half-brother the ghost
And his wife and kids
Who have grown up year by year
Without my knowing.

Yes, this is where I'm from.
I know all of these things,
These nostalgia-inducing
Things
And so much more.
But what I don't know,
What I can't wait to see
Is just what the future
Holds in store for me.

—Cara[3]

Reflection—Where I'm From

The assignment was to write a "Where I'm From" poem and incorporate the requisite literary elements into it. I'm really proud of this poem. I put a lot of thought into it, and I do believe that it really reflects where I'm from. The writing is an expression of myself, and it's a very personal piece. This has almost everything important about my past (the things I'm willing to share with the general public, anyway).

—Cara[3]

- *Can You Really Go Home?* A personal sense of place is almost always wrapped in layers of memory. These memories can be bittersweet when we realize that the place we remember is no longer the same. Nostalgia and regret sit side by side with fond sentiment. Ask students to think of a neighborhood or city in which they once lived, or ask them to recall a school they once attended. What were they like during that time of their lives? Could they return to that place as they are today and be content, happy, or satisfied? How might the places have changed? Would those changes likely bother them? Is it true that "you can't go home again"? If our identities are linked to particular places, what does it mean when those places change? The topic invites extended personal research from students.

- *Setting Versus Place*: *Setting* is one of those literary terms that's been too often reduced to a multiple-choice quiz answer: *Elsinore*; *Oceania*; *Maycomb, Alabama in the 1930s*. Investigating *place* beyond its simple geographic sense means getting into the historical, social, and political forces that may have affected characters and events. When students ask how the idea of *place* in a story influences (or even determines) the characters and their conflicts, that's complex thinking.

- *Access and Impact*: Natural spaces and scenic areas raise some interesting questions about public access and use. Beautiful areas draw visitors, but too many visitors tend to make such areas less beautiful. For example, building a road so that everyone can enjoy a stunning mountaintop view might seem like a good idea, but it can lead to overcrowding, pollution, and a spoiled environment. What's the solution to such situations? On a related topic, should a very rich person be permitted to *buy* that mountaintop and make it private property? Students might explore local issues of this kind to understand competing beliefs.

- *Maps and Metaphors*: Maps are fascinating tools, reducing the three-dimensional world around us into two-dimensional (and even virtual) forms. What goes on a map is, essentially, a process of defining what's important. Political, physical, demographic, migration, and ecological maps can each stress different facets of a place. What kind of new insight might students be able to bring to local maps, maybe with patterns of teenager activity, wildlife, public art, or some other offbeat focus? What do maps tell us about what we consider important . . . and not so important? And what do the certain place-focused terms—such as *manifest destiny*, *the heartland*, *Homeland Security*, *The New South*, *land development*, *gentrification*, *the exurbs*—tell us about our assumptions?

- *Transformations*: The Mannahatta Project (http://welikia.org/explore/mannahatta-map/) is an interactive multimedia map of what the island of Manhattan might have looked like in 1609. Is it possible for students to research and recreate something similar—in some form—for their own communities? If turning the clock back four centuries is a bit much, how about fifty years? This kind of work might even draw on archival research and oral histories, and produce something that has real relevance beyond the classroom.

- *Cemeteries and Memorial Space*: Cemeteries are obviously places of shifted context, as what might otherwise be a park, field, hillside, or neighborhood serves a different purpose. Visits to cemeteries (or other public spaces dedicated to remembrance) can inspire all kinds of writing, from horror movie fiction to more subtle reflections that deal with mortality and meaning.

- *Digital Versus Analog*: Going back to the original Life Map writing, what possibilities (and what drawbacks) might there be in creating an online Life Map instead of drawing one on paper? Google Maps (for instance) allows users to create their own maps and routes with embedded images, audio, video, text commentary, and many of the other features common in online environments. If a student were to propose such an alternative, how would you respond? Would you be skeptical, reluctant to deviate from your expectations for the class? Or do you instead see some potential in a new medium and how it might represent personal histories and stories in different ways? What is gained by drawing your neighborhood from memory versus finding an actual online map and annotating it with hypermedia? What is lost in opting for one approach over the other? What habits of mind and ways of seeing are reinforced by each option? How might one inform or add dimension to the other? And how do these options play out in your overall goals, for what you want students to be able to do, eventually?

Again, we're proposing many possible pieces of writing and a general framework for how they might fit together for study and exploration. We stack experiences and readings and types of writing for our students so that they live inside genres and inside their writing to understand both better. Our aim is to set up explorations for writing that reveal opportunities to our students, unearth some of their assumptions, and keep us all from getting too satisfied with what we think we know. You know your students, your school, your goals. With experience, we all get better at recognizing the creative possibilities of these situations, deciding what's appropriate and what isn't, and leveraging various options for students to demonstrate what they've learned and can do.

Bottom line, we want you to begin (or to continue) to tap your own creativity as an imaginative professional. Our hope is that any ideas we mention in these pages might ultimately serve as inspiration for your own experiments. Imagine, design, and test-run new writing ideas to see how students respond, and use whatever helps you in books like this one to begin writing the texts of your own professional life.

Pathways for Writing Poetry

Another way to extend writing is to switch into various genres. One of the genres we enjoy exploring with our students is that of poetry.

If you've already explored various themes and types of writing with your students— perhaps including the Where I'm From poem and themes of place, identity, and belonging as we discussed previously (see pages 83–85)—you're already tiptoeing up to and all around poetry. And you haven't passed out yet, nor have your students.

Whether you're in the second week or the second month or the second semester, we hope that you have already worked with your students and poetry. Too many teachers cram all poetry reading, writing, and discussion into one two-week unit, usually right before a holiday because the students will be hyper anyhow, so why not let those creative juices flow into poetry? That timing may work okay for some of the poetry that you do with your students; but stuffing poetry into one isolated, short unit doesn't work at all.

The more that you integrate poetry into all areas of literacy study and writing that you undertake with your students, the more you accustom your students to working with the genre—to reading, writing, responding to, and transacting with poetry. After you've read quite a bit of poetry with your students, we'll bet they will begin to suspect that they might just find a poem or two they could like. They're lowering their guard just a bit and letting notions of poetry play around in their minds. We won't go for full commitment to the genre yet. Your students are still feeling their way along and getting used to the idea that they can handle poetry. Heck, you may be trying out and growing accustomed to the same ideas. That's okay, and that's why we started by tiptoeing into poetry.

Perhaps you've noticed by this point in your journey with us as you read this book that we are proponents of writing for all sorts of reasons, not the least of which is to figure stuff out. We write drafts to see what we have to say. We write responses to texts to understand them better. We write nonfiction and narrative and opinion pieces and memoir and essays and all sorts of genres to get inside them, figure them out, see what we can do with them. We write to learn—to see what we might learn from and about multiple texts and genres. All of these types and reasons for writing create some of the many pathways for writing that we address in this chapter and throughout this book.

Working with poetry—though the mere word chills many a student and teacher's heart—is no different. In short, one way to minimize the trepidation that students and teachers often feel about poetry is to roll up your sleeves, flex your fingers, and write. Yes, engage your students in writing some poetry.

Here's another key point: Write some poetry yourself and share your poetry (or attempts thereof) with your students.

Now, before you slam this book shut and throw it against the nearest wall, stop and think a minute. We understand literature and other texts more richly by getting inside the author's style and voice and purpose, by relating to her topic, by feeling what the author guides us to feel as we read and transact with her work. When we *write about* what we read, we build meanings that are personal and relevant. And when we *write ourselves* in multiple genres, we understand the genre, the experience of working with the genre, and the possibilities for opening up the genre that we wouldn't know just by skimming over a few pieces from thirty thousand feet. We learn by getting into the form and the writing and by doing them firsthand.

That's our model for teaching writing. We don't just *talk about* writing; we write. We don't just *talk about* various texts and genres; we write them. It's also part of our model for understanding what others have written. We understand by *doing*, not by having a flyover. Get in and get dirty and get to work with the writing, reading, reflecting, drafting, crafting, and learning to be a more literate person.

We aren't suggesting that you leap into complex sonnets or rondels (Look that stuff up; it's good for you.) as your first foray into poetry writing. But we are suggesting that as you read poetry with your students and study its parts and inner workings, you will enhance your comfort with the genre and your students' depth of understanding of the genre by writing it. Stiffen your upper lip. Keep reading this chapter. Let's see how to write some poetry ourselves and with our students.

Pointers for Writing Poetry

Studying any kind of text naturally leads to writing it ourselves as we work within a readers-are-writers, writers-are-readers model. Because it offers a way into personal expression and inventive ways of meaning making, forays into poetry writing may be especially inviting for student writers.

In poetry, as in all writing, good writing is *honest* writing. The writer risks feelings with us, and we respond to the words because they touch our feelings through shared human experiences. The subtleties of form, the intricacies of vocabulary and literary device, the technical aspects of the poem, and the erudition of allusion will doubtless contribute to the experience and to our pleasure in the work. Our students don't need to have control of all the form and technique that enriches poetry to begin writing some of it. As we've stressed throughout this book, students need to gain fluency with any type of writing before they are able to move into control and precision (see Chapter 2). We strive for fluency first, for some risk taking and sharing of feelings, and we'll add the rhyme scheme and meter a bit later as we work with poetry.

Before you move into writing poetry with your students, we invite you to consider the following points and to reflect upon how they apply to and affect your teaching:

1. *The growth process in writing poetry is the same growth process operating in all forms of writing.*

   Most teachers are intimidated about writing poetry although they may teach it effectively. Usually, students are not given an opportunity to write poetry or, worse, they are expected to start generating Petrarchan sonnets or haiku (the more difficult of the two forms to write!) the first time students attempt any poetry. The results are predictably dismal, and teachers are further convinced that students cannot, and should not, attempt to write poetry or understand it with any legitimate depth.

   Poetry grows the same way prose does. It's not a mysterious process. Especially in poetry, content and form intertwine to enrich the text. The natural spoken rhythms of language help form lines and even stanzas as the student writes more. You may want to suggest alternate forms for a particular verse, but such crafting of writing happens in later drafts and revisions of a piece of writing. The best thing you can do at the beginning is to let form be controlled by content and emerge from content.

2. *If you don't have a plan for writing in the classroom, with many options and with personal writing encouraged and supported, then poems won't be written.*

   Writing benefits from being planned, but students need the freedom to explore their own forms of expression at least some of the time and perhaps especially with poetry. When students are ready to try new forms of writing, especially those first few times, support their efforts fully. In other words, students must have the freedom to start someplace. Whenever possible, remove the restrictions, give them their heads, and be receptive to their efforts. Class environment is crucial, and you set the tone.

3. *Encourage students to write what they want to write—at least most of the time.*

   We do live and work in the real world of schools. We know that standards and common cores and testing require you to work on specific types of writing with your students. As we've indicated before, however, real writing is authentic writing, and authentic writing serves students well on high-stakes tests. As long as the student is writing about what's important to him, then his writing is real, it's motivated, and it's likely to improve. When students begin to write poetry, it is almost always personal, as is all real writing. As immature writers grow, their writing will naturally become less egocentric. They will strive to reach their peers, and perhaps eventually a wider audience. That growth will move them gradually away from what is sometimes painfully personal writing. The intimate nature of these early efforts, however, puts a heavy burden on the teacher. Tact and sensitivity are required when a student writes about personal topics—in any genre.

4. *At this point in the writing, quality is not the most important consideration.*

Expectations of Wordsworthian prosody will only stop the student from writing. Lower your standards a little; *invite* students to give this poetry writing thing a whirl. At first, emphasize honest writing and honest responding. Understanding and recognition are what students are seeking. Save the criticism for when they are more accomplished and confident, for when they are moving into some control and precision with the genre. Encourage them to practice. Take a risk yourself. Respond with a poem of your own. Give them lots of opportunities to write and share their poetry.

5. *Gently push students to widen their audience.*

Display poetry in your room. Publishing student poetry in the classroom is easily done and is the best possible way to encourage more poetry writing. When others are regularly reading and responding to their writing, students work hard at shaping and fine-tuning their poems. Student readers are always the best audience for student poets.

6. *Many kids really do like writing poetry. Encourage them.*

There's a kind of freedom in writing poetry that appeals to many students. They feel less threatened by poetry than by prose writing. Because poetry is usually an intense and brief writing experience, students are often able to write and rewrite a complete draft in a class period and get immediate satisfaction from the finished product. They also receive an immediate response to what they have written, which is especially important for those students for whom writing—in any genre—is an ordeal that threatens failure. Positive responses encourage writers and make them believe that they *can* write something that others want to read.

7. *When you teach poetry writing, also offer prose as an option—at least sometimes.*

Just as students have the choice of writing poetry when the assignment is to write prose, students should have the choice of *not* writing poetry in any given situation. Understandably enough, some students are afraid of poetry. There is evidence that most writers must write prose before they can write poetry. It's not unusual even for an accomplished poet to begin a poem with a prose sketch. Be alert for students' prose pieces robust in images and wordplay that might easily be turned into poetry (the reverse is also true, of course—poetry might become prose sometimes). Students learn a great deal about their language by switching forms with a piece of writing, that is, by turning a piece of poetry into prose or a piece of prose into poetry. There's also the option of prose poetry, a form of writing popular with modern writers and one that has many possibilities for the classroom. The best way to encourage reluctant poets, however, is sharing with them and the class the writing of their peers. They see that it's not so hard after all and will often try it themselves the next time.

8. *Understand that poetry follows most naturally from fooling around with poetry.*

To teach poetry by parsing lines, unstringing iambs, and calculating rhyme schemes is a barren exercise unless students have done a lot of writing, sharing, and talking about poetry previously. Reading is important, of course, to the poet. Put off the classic poets until later. Instead, get out poets like Mary Oliver, Tom Wayman, Nikki Giovanni, Billy Collins, and even the songwriters to whom your students listen all the time. It's time we declared a moratorium on the Great Symbol Hunt in poetry teaching and, instead, allow students to create their own symbols. Even if students never write very good poetry in your class, they will learn about poetry by playing with it. We have students write poetry to understand the genre from the inside, from the writer's perspective. Then, they will enjoy reading poetry more.

9. *Writing poetry is one of the best ways to study language.*

As students write and share and write again, they begin with their knowledge of words from spoken language. They expand on that knowledge very quickly, which is one of the benefits of working with poetry by reading and writing it. Every time students grapple with a different image, a subtle emotion, or an elusive rhyme or line ending and have to hunt for a word that fits, their language grows. Every time they ask you, "What's the word for this?" or say, "This word doesn't sound right here," they're growing as users and writers of language. (They may also come to appreciate a thesaurus!)

10. *Grade poetry very carefully and gently, just like all writing in your class.*

Many teachers don't give students the opportunity to write poetry because they don't feel they know enough about how to grade it. However, the approaches to writing we are suggesting will revise your grading strategies and make the question unimportant. Consider these alternative methods to red-pencil grading that we have found particularly useful when students in our classes write poetry.

Early poetry from the student is *not graded at all*. It is read and responded to; it is shared and published in some form. It may be displayed in the room, or photocopied and passed around, posted to a class blog, or read aloud. The student is given credit for doing the assignment. Consider a point-based grading system for students' early poetry efforts. A portfolio or folder may be used to hold the writing so it may be examined in a private conference; then decide on the grade.

Or, selected pieces may be revised for careful (and perhaps gentle) grading after the student has more practice with writing poetry. Once a student is a practiced poet and begins to demonstrate control of poetic form, insist on revisions to encourage the student poet to attempt new techniques with poetry. The student picks the specific works to be revised.

As with all writing, respond to your students' efforts as a *reader* and to your students as *writers,* not as the great unwashed masses who don't know their iambs from their dactyls, even if they don't. Teach them that stuff later, after they have gained some experience and fluency and excitement with poetry. The grade is negotiable, depending on the extent and kind of revision done, but the grade is not given until the revising is done.

11. *If the poem is just plain* bad, *look hard for something good in it—especially if it is an early poem from the student.*

> Search for an interesting image, a well-done metaphor or simile, a phrase, even just a word. If there is nothing in that poem you can honestly applaud (but there almost always is), then you are reduced to merely offering encouragement, which also helps immature writers. If the poem is from a student you know is practiced enough to exercise some control, and if you are asked for a response, be gentle but be honest. Your judgment as an informed reader is important. Don't be afraid to exercise it when the time is right.

With poetry, as with most writing, students benefit from immediate responses to their writings. Because poetry is a short and an intense experience, it lends itself to the kinds of pieces that might be drafted, and perhaps redrafted, in a single class period, yielding fast results. Look for ways to celebrate and *publish* students' poetry to keep spirits and efforts high. Remember that developing techniques and trying out new forms and ideas are important for developing student poets.

Literature textbooks are full of poetry. Websites are devoted to poetry. Poetry of all types is readily available. Read lots of poetry as you prepare to read and write poetry with your students. Bring poetry into the classroom and ask students to respond to it. (See our ideas for responding to poetry in Chapter 12.) When your students find a poem that resonates with them, ask them to try the same format, types of verses and metaphors, similar rhyme schemes and meters. That concept lies at the heart of the Where I'm From poems—writing the *same type and format* as used in an existing poem, and changing it up to include personally meaningful content. Using poetry with clearly identifiable formats and patterns—such as cinquains, diamantes, and even sonnets—helps your students explore poetry with a safety net under them.

For a variety of student poetry samples, see the online Additional Resources for this chapter. The link to these resources is at www.heinemann.com/products/E04195.aspx, on the Companion Resources tab. Following is one more way to have fun with poetry.

▧ Strange Poetry

Working with poetry seems to be such a *serious* undertaking most of the time. Not all poetry is serious; some is quite humorous, and some is just plain odd. Go down that road sometimes to introduce variety into your materials. Find three of the *strangest* poems and/or songs that you can. Play the songs and then read them aloud with students. Then give these instructions: "I want you to write something *really strange*, Johnny Depp or Tim Burton strange. It can be a poem, a song, a sketch, or something else—but *it must be weird*." The results are always entertaining.

Some classic favorite strange songs are Kottke's "Morning Is the Long Way Home"; Dylan's "Changing of the Guard"; Crosby, Stills, and Nash's "Winchester Cathedral"; Carly Simon's "De Bat"; and just about anything by Frank Zappa or Beck. Classic favorite strange poems include Francis' "Summons," Monro's "Overhead on a Saltmarsh," and selections by Corso, Ginsberg, and Ferlinghetti. As a variation, Dawn includes an excerpt from one of Francesca Lia Block's young adult novels about adolescents on the fringe of society and formats it as found poetry or as prose poetry. If you use an author like Block, do so with caution; her work has been frequently censored.

The point here is not to drop off the deep end of reason; it is to play around with the varied nature of texts, including poetry. Not everything is English class needs to be life-and-death serious. Mix it up and reflect on questions like these with your students:

- Why would poets choose to write something off the beaten path—something that is just *strange*?
- What thoughts come to mind as you read these unusual poems?
- Amid the oddities, what in the poem is rather sensible or perhaps a tangent that you actually follow?
- What social, cultural, or political commentaries might these poets be exploring?

Once students have begun to read some poetry, explore different types and purposes for poetry, understand something about the varied style of poets, and otherwise muck around with poetry, they are ready to continue wading more deeply into the range and possibilities of the genre. Go with them, and enjoy the journey.

Pulling It All Together

Our goal in the last three chapters has been to paint a picture of a certain kind of writing classroom, from physical layout to community building to initial forays into written self-expression. We hope that the activities we've suggested are helpful in the process of creating such a space for you and your students.

The caveat here is that our advice takes the path of general recommendations highlighted with specific examples. If some of the actual writing prompts and explorations work for teachers "as is," that's fantastic. We want this book to be useful to the teacher who needs a good idea fast (like late on a Sunday evening). But be wary—especially if you're new to the field—of using isolated assignments too often. Yes, borrowed prompts may get students writing. Keeping them writing and moving them forward as writers, however, relies on knowing *why* you're choosing specific learning experiences in a systematic way.

With all the recent angst about teacher accountability and measures of effectiveness, the core trait of *creativity* is too often overlooked. Good teachers are imaginative professionals, and the creative challenge of diagnosing student needs, envisioning what they might be capable of, and designing pathways to these goals is a big part of what drew us to the classroom. Depending on your teaching situation, the big picture objectives may already have been determined for you. In other situations, you'll have the latitude to define those broader destinations. Whatever the case, you will have a measure of creative freedom in imagining just how students experience writing, build on what they're learning, and grow as thinkers and communicators. Absolutely, borrow what you need—that's part of your own teacherly experimentation. Adapt and adjust along the way to fit the needs of your students, and change what needs changing.

Authoring and Gaining Authority

The experience of authoring a work is powerful; it builds self-esteem and self-efficacy. When students have authored a work in their own voices, when they have seen readers nod their heads in agreement and in recognition of shared experiences, and when they have received praise for their efforts, they feel as if they "know stuff" that others want to hear and that others will like. They feel like an authority, at least of their own experiences and expressions. That's a powerful and self-enhancing feeling. That is part of the power of writing authentically about subjects that only you, the writer, know best. Initially in the writing class, our job is to help students write in their own voices about their own areas of authority—their own experiences, feelings, and perceptions. We begin small with tasks easily finished, like a freewriting about a person they know. We encourage our students to experiment with written expression, to try out many written forms, to fool around with writing. Instead of demanding an impossible perfection, we encourage trial and error and an attitude of try-it-and-see-what-happens. We encourage students to work beyond their zones of comfort in writing, to start with what they know and like, but then to move into less familiar territory in their writing. In this way, students expand their language and writing repertoires. They are expanding their thinking and learning. While all of that is happening, the writing community in the class is growing stronger.

◾ Who Owns the Writing?

Once students see that they can write—and that can be a big job itself—what we hear almost at once from some of them is, "What do you want us to write about?" Years of conditioning have taught them to rely on the teacher for this information. When we tell them that they are the writers, they don't like it. "I don't have anything to write about!" they cry, and the tug-of-war starts. Students try to give the authority for their writing to the teacher. Refuse to take it.

In her observations of classes, Dawn found that students are adept at getting teachers to do some of their work for them. She observed one student say to a teacher, "I don't know what to write." The teacher read what the student had written so far and then made detailed suggestions for what the student should write next. The student, being smart in more ways than one, proceeded to write what the teacher had suggested. The teacher loved the paper. Although this is a humorous, if bittersweet story, it points out the overreliance that students have on teachers as idea givers and as those who control the writing. We suggest filling your classroom with reading, writing, and talking while considering points of view and alternate ideas. Try lots of "What if . . . ?" or "Let's think about. . . ." Break the habit of handing out your ideas as good ideas for students; refrain from it in yourself and in your students if you want them to author their own, authentic writing instead of just churning out your assignments.

⌐ *Pathways and Destinations*

This chapter gives you some of the starters we have used to make the job of finding something about which to write less threatening. We have found that these activities are generally catchy and interesting to adolescent writers, but we remind students that these activities are intended to give them practice and to help them find things on their own about which to write. Without that intention and attitude, these activities can become as artificial and arbitrary as those dreadful summer vacation essays. Remember that *the writing belongs to the writer*. Imposing a topic, even a good one, doesn't help the growth of young writers. Your curriculum may demand certain kinds of writing, and you may have to compromise, but there are usually ways to give students some control over the writing while still teaching them how to be successful on the mandated tests required by most districts.

Another notion that may help you is not to be too concerned with originality. Writers steal from other writers. Consciously and unconsciously we copy ideas, techniques, novel twists, and even vocabulary we like when we read the works of others. It is natural and healthy for your students to borrow from each other and from their reading. Good ideas are catching, and they should be.

We try to grant our students the authority of the writer over their own writing. We maintain our authority in managing the classroom so it is a safe, friendly place in which to write and share and talk about writing. We also insist that they do write, and we set deadlines. But our only real authority derives from being a writer with more experience than they have who is willing to show them how. Their writing belongs to them.

NOTES

1. Christina was a student in Marsha Kindrachuk's class at McCleskey Middle School, Marietta, Georgia.
2. Sadiqa Edmonds was a student at Albany High School, Albany, Georgia.
3. Cara Kirby was a student at Harrison High School, Kennesaw, Georgia.

Works Cited

Chocolate, Deborah. 1995. *On the Day I Was Born*. New York: Cartwheel Press.

Cisneros, Sandra. 1991. *The House on Mango Street*. New York: Vintage Press.

Keillor, Garrison. 2002. *Lake Wobegon Summer 1956*. New York: Penguin.

Kirby, Dawn Latta, and Dan Kirby. 2007. *New Directions in Teaching Memoir: A Studio Workshop Approach*. Portsmouth, NH: Heinemann.

Momaday, Scott. 1987. *The Names*. Tucson, AZ: University of Arizona Press.

Miller, James F. Jr. 1972. *Word, Self, Reality: The Rhetoric of the Imagination*. New York: Dodd, Mead.

Miller, James E. Jr., and Stephen N. Tchudi (formerly, Judy). 1978. *Writing in Reality*. New York: Harper & Row.

Morrison, Toni. 1998. "The Site of Memory." In *Inventing the Truth: The Art and Craft of Memoir*, edited by William K. Zinsser. Boston: Houghton Mifflin.

Wiggins, Grant, and Jay McTighe. 2005. *Understanding by Design*. Expanded 2nd ed. New York: Prentice Hall.

Wolff, Tobias. 2000. *This Boy's Life: A Memoir*. New York: Grove Press.

5

Identifying Good Writing and Emphasizing Voice

If proper usage gets in the way, it may have to go. I can't allow what we learned in English composition to disrupt the sound and rhythm of the narrative. **—Elmore Leonard, "Writers on Writing; Easy on the Adverbs, Exclamation Points and Especially Hooptedoodle"**

Features of good writing are not immutable, universal, and eternal, contrary to much that we hear in contemporary educational circles curtseying to politico-palaver and popular opinion. Definitions and determinations of good writing actually depend on the context in which the writing occurs. Context considerations about good writing include *when* (1800s or 2012?), *where* (Australia or the southern part of the United States?), *why* (entertainment or persuasion?), *who* (Maureen Dowd or Ayaan Hirsi Ali?), and for which *audience* (readers of the *New York Times* or *Fangoria* or *The Source*?) the writing is situated. We would prefer to think that the aim of most school writing instruction is to help students achieve good writing full of detail, strong verbs, flare, and an identifiable voice in multiple contexts. We seriously question, however, that such is the case. Instead, we generally see a focus on writing that is formulaic, correct, and relatively bland; we see writing that expresses mainstream opinions and throws in a few surprising vocabulary words from the SAT prep class.

Is that good writing? If what we want are great scores on high-stakes tests, then yes, it is. But how many of us read those test-driven papers for fun? How many of us read a magazine or newspaper article and think, "That would get a 3 on our school district's test of written proficiency?" We think the answers to those questions are rather obvious.

In his typically heretical manner, Elmore Leonard, in the earlier quote, rejects "rules" in favor of effective, real writing and voice. If you've read any of Leonard's work, you know he practices what he preaches. Hallmarks of Leonard's writing are consistent mood and tone and a strong voice within the novels, short stories, and essays that he writes. Yet, his writing is not so riddled with idiosyncrasies and errors that we can't follow it. As a highly successful contemporary writer, Leonard has developed his own "rules" for good writing and sticks to them. Sandra Cisneros, another highly successful writer, also developed her unique style, voice, and forms for writing—many of which violate most "rules" taught in composition classes. If you've read her highly episodic novel, *The House on Mango Street*, you've seen how effective a story she can weave. Pulitzer Prize–winner Annie Dillard eschews a few established rules of writing herself, using one-word paragraphs, fragments, subjects, and verbs up front in sentences—and a legendary ability to capture detail and authorial voice in her writing. We could go on, listing many more good writers and what they do that isn't taught in most secondary English classes. What makes successful writers successful, in part, is their ability to find and use "good" writing as they have wrought it into being over years of work, blazing new ground for writers and, in the process, sometimes ditching established "rules" in favor of effectiveness.

Neither our students nor we are yet in that vaunted position in life, however. We need to follow a hefty chunk of the "rules" for teaching, writing, and life in school. Few writers, even the published ones, have the leeway of Leonard, Cisneros, and Dillard. Some of our colleagues assert that student writers need to know the rules before they know how to break them for good effect. For writing done in school and for school purposes, possibly so.

As teachers of writing, what do we collectively know about *good writing*? We know our students need to write relatively well to pass our classes. We know that students need to write well enough to pass standardized and high-stakes tests. We know that most jobs require competent writing and that some high-level jobs require lots of writing. Our students are probably going to need writing for a range of purposes, from writing emails to writing short articles for newsletters and staff bulletins. Some of our students will need writing for creative, artistic expression—poems, short stories, memoirs, family histories, or the next great American novel (even if only their family reads and admires it). Most colleges demand a well-written personal piece for admission. We know that good writing gets published and the other stuff doesn't—usually. We know we are capable of producing it ourselves, and we coach our students to do the same. Right? Well, yes and no.

Defining Good Writing

As English preservice and inservice teachers, we are supposed to know what good writing is. And we do. Just ask us. We grade papers based, in part, on how *good* we think the writing is. We revise and edit our own writing until we think it is good enough to share with peers or to send off for publication. We read newspaper and magazine articles and think they are good pieces, or we shake our heads and wonder, "How did *that* ever get published?" So, take a moment—right now—to get a piece of paper or turn to your computer screen and write a definition of *good writing*. We'll grade a few papers while you write your definition.

So, how did that go? Did the definition of *good writing* flow from your brain onto the page or onto the computer screen? Or did you start, hesitate, cross out or delete, and try again—and perhaps still not get something that fully captures what you think good writing is? We suspect the latter.

For most of us, the definition of *good writing* resides in our tacit knowledge. *Tacit* knowledge is what we know but may not have verbalized or acknowledged even to ourselves. Tacit knowledge differs from *overt* knowledge, which is the stuff we know we know. Because our notions of good writing are often tacit, we may need to think and explore the concept a bit to teach elements of good writing to our students. So, what is good writing?

What Is Good Writing?

What we propose are working criteria for good writing in the English classroom, touch-stones that will give you a systematic review of the most important qualities of good writing that you can identify, encourage, and build on in student writing. The criteria that follow are listed more or less in order from the most basic to the most sophisticated. That fact does not necessarily mean, however, that your students will demonstrate that they can write in a recognizable human voice before they begin consciously to use words rich in sound effects and imagery. Nor are the categories mutually exclusive. In the act of writing, many things happen at once; and the mental processes are incredibly complex, especially when the writing is going well, which makes any linear tracking of writing processes and development faulty. The criteria are listed in a linear fashion for convenience and clarity and for an indication of the most common developmental patterns that you might find in your students' writing.

We believe that you can expect to find these qualities to some degree in the writing of *all* your students in *every* set of papers you read. It's not only the exceptional paper written by the rare and brilliant student that has good writing in it.

There are two main attributes of good writing, to which all other qualities are related. Good writing is *interesting to read*, and good writing is *written with technical skill*. The first and most basic requirement we make of anything we read is that it interest and/or entertain us. Without that, it becomes drudgery. Good writers create and keep the inter-est of their readers. This aspect of writing is where we need to begin in teaching quality in writing to our students.

A reader's interest cannot be sustained for long, however, unless the writer demonstrates some skill with the techniques of writing. The craftsmanship with which words, sentences, and paragraphs are manipulated in an essay—or aspects of writing such as dialogue in a short story or imagery in a poem—affect our judgment of a work and either frustrate us or add to our pleasure as we read. Therefore, the two important questions for us to ask when faced with a stack of student papers are as follows:

    1. What are the qualities that make writing interesting?
    2. What are the attributes of technically skillful writing?

What Makes Good Writing Interesting?

Good writing is interesting in a variety of ways. We focus on some of the elements that make writing interesting for the reader.

    1. *Good writing has a voice.* Good writing talks to you with a real voice; it has the recog-nizable imprint of the author on it. A lot of rhetoric and composition texts talk about *style*. A writer's voice on the page *is* his style. That human sound is what makes a piece of writing real for us. That's the reason bad translations are so frustrating to read, and that's why best sellers are not written like doctoral dissertations. Notice the human contact and individual voice in this piece:

> I looked down at the terribly small piece of chicken on my plate—somehow there
> just didn't seem to be any justice—I always received the smallest piece possible.

The girl sitting next to me looked at me for a slight moment as though I was a creature from another world and then turned back into her own small world—herself. She laughed a high inhuman laugh that seemed to pierce the whole room with sound.

First I thought she was laughing at me and my measly portion of chicken—but only of news of how her ex-boyfriend had received a blow in the eye which now wore the colors black, blue, green, and a tinge of red.

I thought how she would look that same way but then another devilish thought entered my mind.

"I hope she gets fat!"

—*Tracy*[1]

Tracy is beginning to find her voice as a writer, and in places in this piece, we hear a very human voice talking about an irritating neighbor in a crowded school cafeteria. There is a hey-I've-done-that-too kind of feeling about the piece that gives it recognizable humor. We share experiences and feelings with the writer because she speaks in her own voice.

To have a real voice, a piece does not necessarily need to be written in first person singular. Consider the following:

Waiting eagerly behind the dark stage wings for her music cue to enter into brightly colored spot lights. Lights with cool and warm colors. Nervous, tense muscles, and pounding heart. Thinking over her part before darting on stage to do her dream ballet.

—*Lynn*[1]

Good writing is *honest* writing. Lynn takes a chance with her reader, sharing something very important to her. There's no mistaking that the "nervous, tense muscles, and pounding heart" are hers. If a teacher's only remark about Lynn's paper is to put "FRAG/–30%" in the margin beside that phrase, then the teacher will have proven to be an insensitive pedagogue and a poor rhetorician. Published writers frequently use fragments for effect in their writing. Student writers can do so, too, but the effect needs to contribute to the tone and mood of the piece, not just result from sloppy punctuation. Such latitude helps students develop their written voices and produce effective writing. Lynn risks herself a little with her reader. Our responsibility as teachers and as readers is to be receptive, to *listen* to the writer's voice, and to encourage the writer to use her voice when she writes.

My name is Alyssa. Alyssa, the fancy name that flows like a river. It sounds like a ribbon being sliced in two as if flutters down a staircase to the level below. The name that belongs to a princess in some faraway land. It doesn't fit me, not at all. It's too fancy, too flowy. It almost makes me feel uncomfortable when people say it. It makes me feel older, more . . . proper. Not like me.

I like to lounge around in sweats with a Starbucks hot chocolate in my hand. I watch cheer competitions on TV during the commercials for *Dr. Phil*, *Intervention*, or *The OCD Project*. I'm into psychology, eating disorders, dark stories, and Peter Pan. I love music and my best friends more than anything.

That's not an Alyssa, and I figured that out in seventh grade. I realized that my name didn't fit me. Alyssa isn't the girl who got a bloody nose in Bring Me the Horizon's mosh pit at Warped Tour, not the girl that wants to be an adolescent psychologist or write a book of all her journals and what went on in her life in middle and high school.

—Alyssa[2]

Good writing is *real*. Alyssa turns inward, probing the spaces between surface impressions and reality. We connect with her candid observations, her sense of chafing at labels, and her ability to have us follow her thinking through the piece.

If you want your students' writing to have a real voice, then you will have to accept their individual voices and be accepting of what they have to say. We realize that our students' voices will differ from those of each other and from our own adult voices. Some students have fluent knowledge of another language; we encourage them to use that knowledge in their writing. If a phrase can't be effectively translated, use the Spanish or Japanese phrase, giving enough context clues to help the reader figure out much of the meaning. We fully support the notion of multiple voices in our classes. Everyone's voice is different, and it is the combined variety and impact of those voices that will enrich our classrooms' learning environments.

If students submit papers that are stilted and dead, ask them to "tell me about it" when they next write. Structure ways for them to *talk* about it *before* they write it. Help them find their voices by freewriting often (see activities in Chapter 4). In fact, the only way that students will find and refine their voices in their writing is to practice using that voice on the page regularly, preferably *daily*.

2. *Good writing moves.* Good writing starts here and goes to there, and it pulls the reader along with it. Whether it's a narrative or an elegant argument or a poem, there is movement and order to it. Good writing also gives us enough variety, enough changes and twists and turns and sometimes surprises, to keep us interested and reading.

A sense of order appears in student writing first as the straight chronological this-happened-first-and-then-this-and-finally-this order of the narrative. Lynn's piece has less than fifty words, yet it shows this kind of order—a ballerina waiting, her nervousness growing, and the beginning of the dance anticipated.

You will also find that students will begin to place special emphasis on the first and last sentences of their writing. They feel the movement and order of the piece and are looking for ways to strengthen it. Look at these opening lines from two students' pieces:

You know it. We all do. This is the book of the Dead.

—Jade[3]

The clouds played tag in the night sky. The stars whispered to each other. Bonfires burned to the last log.

—Meagan[3]

Jade and Meagan open with unorthodox lines. Jade piques our curiosity and asks that we trust her to reveal what "we all" know. Meagan experiments with strong verbs, figurative language, and personification, trusting her audience to read beyond literal meanings to understand the mood she is setting.

Kathy writes a pithy piece with a strong opening line:

> She was in a bad mood anyway. He kept on bugging her, so finally right before
> the curtains opened she agreed to go and buy him popcorn. Secretly she had a
> crush on him, but he was sitting next to another girl. It was a very scary movie,
> when she came back the theater was silent. She walked down the aisle with a big
> bucket of buttered popcorn. He was sitting directly behind her, when she started
> to hand it to him, both of their hands slipped. In the silence of the movie, all there
> is to hear is—"DUMBASS!"
>
> —*Kathy*[1]

With a casual and natural-sounding ill will, Kathy's opening line moves readers toward
the climactic ending of a too-loud and embarrassing vulgarity uttered in the silence of a
dark movie theatre. Tracy's writing about the frustrations of the cafeteria has a similar
movement, but there the action is all in the flow of thoughts and feelings of the writer.

Some students' writings seem to begin anywhere and end nowhere, with no sense of
order at all, but a close reading shows that most have some kind of movement somewhere
in the paper. If the writing doesn't seem to "move," ask students to add specific action verbs
(*saunter* rather than *walk*, for example) for starters. Perhaps remind them to focus on their
point for the piece of writing: What are readers to know or understand as a result of reading the piece? As young writers grow, some of their writings will become very complex. The
place to start to develop a sense of movement in writing is with simple narrative order and
with the invitation to "tell me about it."

3. *Good writing has a sense of humor.* Good writing often laughs. Laughter keeps us
sane and helps developing writers take themselves less seriously, which helps them to
develop a more even tone in their writing. Good writers don't take themselves too seriously
even when they're writing about a serious subject.

> *Ugh, another one of those dreaded projects Ms. Boyd assigned*, I thought to
> myself. Mostly because the last time I did this, it didn't exactly work out so well.
> Hopefully, everything will work out as planned. I mean, I'm making a cereal box.
> How hard could it be, right?
>
> —*Wayne*[3]

> If you are reading this, then you must be interested in the culture of the Inter-
> net, a veteran to it, looking to see how accurate it really is, or a teacher having to
> grade it. Regardless of the cause, I welcome you to this foreboding world full of
> trolls and magic. In case you don't already have one, here's a coupon for one free
> Internet to get you started. Just cut it out and redeem it at your local Internet
> retailer.
>
> —*Sam*[4]

> As I gain the crest of the mountain I see in the fading light the solitary figure
> of my father as he loads his muscular arms full of firewood. I walk up silently
> expecting not to be heard but his keen ears catch the noise of what I thought
> were silent footsteps. He turns and with a quick dodging motion I barely escape a
> flying piece of wood. He laughs and I open the door for him.

No words are spoken until he notices that my hands are empty of game.

"Where's the meat?" he says as he throws another piece of wood on the fire.

"Still in its skin, I guess." I laugh at my remark and he looks at me sternly and I get the message that he'd rather I keep my remarks to myself. A silent period takes place as we sit down to eat supper.

—Billy[1]

Each student takes a risk by using humor to good effect. Wayne reveals his less-than-enthusiastic attitude toward schoolwork, discarding the façade of the diligent student. His payoff, however, is an immediate connection with his readers, including the teacher he is gently teasing. Sam experiments with irony and humor, trusting his readers to catch on. Billy's excerpt reveals a relationship between a boy and his father that is handled with a light touch.

Laugh with your students when they are funny. Keep your silence when their humor falls flat or misses the mark. Remind them that most jokes—the classic humorous expression—are short and pithy and that editing their writing closely may emphasize the humor. Encourage them to write in their own voices and not to take themselves or any subject too seriously.

4. *Good writing is informative.* Good writing *says* something. It adds to our experience. Good writing adds up and makes the reader feel that her time has been well spent. Good writers grow from the author's unique experiences and knowledge, from the writer's individual areas of authority.

If you browse the Internet long enough, this has probably happened to you. A friend sends you a link to a video. You click on it expecting to see the video your friend described. Suddenly, you hear the drum fill that begins Rick Astley's extremely ridiculed song "Never Gonna Give You Up." This indicates that you have been tricked using a technique known as Rick Rolling. Although the song was released in 1987, it hadn't gotten much attention until April 1, 2008, when YouTube linked all their main page videos to this song. Ever since then, this video has been the primary technique for pranks. In meme years, Rick Rolling is rather old and should be retired.

—Sam[4]

He's a large one I thought as I saw the track in the soft moss that ran beside the creek. I unslung the battered 30-30 Marlin from my back and even as I did it I could see the moss rising back from the track. I clicked the safety off, this track was fresh, very fresh. I had no intention of running into a big brownie at this time of the evening. The sun was setting and the woodland around me was taking on the murky shapes of coming night. I turned silently and started away slowly and carefully with my rifle still cradled in my arms.

—Billy[1]

Sam knows his way around Internet culture, and his expertise leads to confident writing. Billy's area of authority is hunting. He writes about it well because he *knows* it well.

All writers, even the most inexperienced student writers, have their own areas of authority. Tell your students that they have unique experiences about which to talk. Teach them to reach into their memories for those experiences that will say something to their readers.

Backstage at a ballet performance is one of the most hectic places imaginable. Costumes are hanging everywhere. The smell of hair spray, sweat, and ballet bags fills the room. The make-up lights are hot and very bright which practically causes your make-up to run before getting it on. People are nervous, fidgety, scared. I noticed that some were very quiet, going over steps in their minds, and others were nervously chit-chatting, trying to take their minds off being scared. The excitement in the air is thick. Curtain is in 5 minutes.

—*Susan*[1]

Susan, like Lynn, is an aspiring ballerina. She gives us a glimpse into that world and shares her feelings about it as only someone with her experience and perspective can. She gives the readers information.

Ask students what they know well, and then encourage them to write about that. Challenge your students to move readers into their worlds, however briefly, and take part in their experiences. That's what Billy, Sam, and Susan also do in their pieces, which helps us derive meaning from what they have written.

5. *Good writing is inventive.* Good writing says something new, or it says something old in a new way. Writing is infinite in its possibilities. The perception, emphasis, voice, concerns, and, perhaps most important, the *imagination* of each writer is different from those of every other writer. Consider these examples:

During the day the living picnic in the cemetery, but at night the dead come out to play.

—*Skyler*[3]

. . . the giant bleached skeleton of a barkless tree, its face smoothed by the elements. Once proud and tall, its mammoth bones now topple over, half-buried in the earth.

—*Christina*[3]

Skyler uses parallel structure creatively for rhythm and emphasis, while Christina draws an extended analogy to describe a scene.

Even quiet writings, those that have almost no overt action involved, may suddenly flash with the writer's inventive phrasings.

Photoscript Final

An older man, about fifty years old, sits at a roundtop table. A cup of de-caffeinated coffee, sipped noisily at one minute intervals, is in front of him to the right. A pack of cigarettes rests, at an angle, on the plate-sized, half-full, ceramic ashtray to his left. His rugged, aged semi-line-creased face is covered from the cheekbone down with a salt and pepper beard. His upper lip is invisible in the multi-earth-colored mustache. He sits with his right elbow resting on the table with his forehead planted in his palm. The smoke stained fingers are visible in his dark brown fine hair. On the table in front of him he reads the words off of the paper that he has written. He destroys the still image, in what seems only a split second, to light a cigarette, sip the coffee, clear his throat, then he resumes the position. His smoking cigarette strategically and instinctively finds its place in the right hand, between the yellow fingers.

—*Richard*[1]

Richard's description is static, until there is a brief flurry of activity that returns to stillness, which emphasizes the statuelike quiet of his subject. It's finely done with a subtle touch that makes the piece memorable. This is pretty sophisticated writing for a student writer.

Encourage your students to explore new ground in their early drafts, trying techniques, words, and voices that they don't normally use. Try lots of brainstorming to help them find ideas about which to be inventive, and perhaps even create a "word wall," a list of spiffy words that your students might use to build connotation and metaphor as a way of highlighting inventiveness in their pieces. A word wall may change often, depending on what the students are studying, reading, and writing. Most of all, work with your students to read together writing that is inventive and to discuss how the author accomplishes that goal.

What Makes Good Writing Technically Skillful?

Although good writing shows the writer's ability with usage, diction, and sentence structure, it also does much more. We next discuss some of the features that contribute to writing that is technically skillful.

6. *Good writing has a sense of audience.* Good writing anticipates its audience. The writers are aware of their readers and their needs as the writing progresses. Writers sometimes directly answer questions readers might ask; at other times, writers talk to the *you* reading the piece. Writers pay their readers a compliment when the writing contains allusions or an intricate and well-formed argument because they trust that their readers will comprehend their points and appreciate their techniques. Good writing always conveys the feeling of *contact* between a real person writing and another real person reading.

I thought about the old, dirty graves that had been neglected. I thought that we should do something to make it nicer. This is why.

—*Olivia*[3]

With those declarative three words, "This is why," Olivia speaks bluntly to her readers, urging them to take action and leading into telling why they need to do so.

Sometimes the writer plays with the reader. Even in a private piece, the feeling for a reader out there sharing the experience of the writer adds to the enjoyment of the work. This next piece by Richard was intended as a personal writing, perhaps one that others would not even read.

Cocoon
I float in peace in my cocoon—fluffy cotton walls, not visible to sight but soft to the touch. Air sweet. Sweeter than honey to the taste. Being suspended as I am in total weightlessness my mind is free, free as the wind is free to blow and take residence any place it pleases. Having this freedom I travel to the limit of boundless thoughts—Here I can be sad but not cry, happy but not smile, wonder

but not be confused, find answers to questions not asked, war with the real, be at peace with fantasy. I have been shaken and torn away from my cocoon—I want to return—I never want to leave. If you see me but cannot find me—that is where I shall be . . . I was really there—

—*Richard*[1]

Although it's private, Richard cannot resist a playful nudge to his reader as he ends his fantasy. One of the most important steps in the growth of the immature writer is when he becomes aware that there is an audience out there. Richard seems to have reached that awareness.

If your students need help with audience awareness, see the activities we suggest later in this chapter and get them to experiment.

7. *Good writing uses detail, but not too much detail.* Good writing is selective. The writing evidences the selection of just the right details from the chaos of sensation that threatens to overwhelm the writer; the writing particularizes the experience for the reader. The details are vivid, they suit the piece of writing and the audience, and they create clear images in the reader's mind. Along with the writer's voice, perhaps it's the selection of detail that makes what is said more *real* to us.

As I was sitting in the library, I noticed an old man at the table beside me. He looked like a retired soldier. His face was old, dark, and wrinkled as if from the worries of war. He was rather fat and very tall. He was dressed in a khaki shirt and pants, and the pants were tucked into a pair of old boots. The boots were faded green and looked like they'd been through hell. He was reading Douglas Reenan. It looked like a rather boring book. His briefcase before him was stacked full of books and old papers which were yellow at the edges. His glasses were lying on top of the briefcase. There were more books lying on the table—American Espionage and war books. His eyes began to droop. He put down the book, rubbed his eyes and leaned on his knees with his elbows. Then he picked up another book and began reading in the middle of it.

—*Susan*[1]

The old jewelry boxes the women in my family used to doll themselves up have the mixture of fragility and strength that is my name. The tiny mahogany drawers, brass knobs, black velvet lining, and gold leaf insignias echo my name. My name looks like my grandmother's hand and the way her skin seems like paper. . . . My first name is like an embroidered napkin used by high society for afternoon tea parties framed by strong white pillars. My middle name is like a melancholy oak tree watching the generations pass by silently.

—*Caroline*[2]

Susan particularizes the old man with his khaki shirt and pants tucked into boot tops; she includes the titles of a couple of books he is reading, and she includes the detail of the glasses lying on the briefcase. Her description has a photographic reality because she chooses to include small details that help the reader visualize the man. Caroline, on the other hand, offers a pastiche of carefully selected images resonant with place, family meaning, and cultural insight.

The student writer who is beginning to find a voice and who has a sense of audience will be able to use details effectively with little trouble. Sometimes, we just have to alert the writer to the impact that using such details adds to her writing. We show students many models, pointing out effective uses of details and vivid verbs and evidence of a fine eye at work. We encourage as much close observation for writing as possible. If they are ready, such instruction helps most student writers to notice more details and to improve their use of details in their writing to make it feel more real.

Much more difficult is the task of teaching students to cut and edit their writings. Economy with words seems to be an ability that comes very late in the growth process of writers. Many writers, especially student writers, are reluctant to throw away any of the words they've worked so hard to put on the page. Sometimes, students recognize that their subject matter calls for economy rather than lush description. Several of the students' writings in this chapter would benefit from some careful cutting. The economy in Lynn's piece about the ballerina about to go on stage probably comes as much from her subject as from anything else.

Student writers need to be comfortable with using detail before they are able to learn what they need to edit out. A Hemingway's ruthlessness doesn't come along very often. Any real success we've had teaching students to tighten their writing has been done individually and almost word by word. That kind of revision is complex and subtle and demands careful coaching during your conferences with your students.

8. *Good writing uses words that sing.* Good writing is rich in imagery and associations, strong in rhythm and repetition, and filled with wordplay. The skillful prose writer uses the language resources of the poet, choosing words that are effective in sound and metaphor. This is sophisticated stuff for most student writers, but you'll find that some of your students show signs of skill with wordplay. Below, we use some new student examples and highlight the techniques from examples previously used.

Rhythm, Repetition, and Variation

Laugh. It was a joke. I think it was a joke. . . . Mr. Rogers blaring on the screen, the phone ringing, the door bell buzzing, and the already burnt spaghettios burning again. . . .

—Alice[1]

With her use of repetition and light touch, Alice lets readers see and feel the scene, laughing at the notion of reburning already burnt food.

During the day the living picnic in the cemetery, but at night the dead come out to play.

—Skyler

Paradox, Words That Play with Each Other

Here I can be sad but not cry, happy but not smile, wonder but not be confused, and find answers to questions not asked, war with the real, be at peace with fantasy.

—Richard

Imagery, the Dramatic Scene

As I gain the crest of the mountain I see in the fading light the solitary figure of my father . . .

—*Billy*

The smell of hair spray, sweat, and ballet bags fills the room.

—*Susan*

Alyssa, the fancy name that flows like a river. It sounds like a ribbon being sliced in two as it flutters down the staircase to the level below.

—*Alyssa*

Association, Metaphor, and Simile

His upper lip invisible in the multi-earth-colored mustache. . . . He destroys the still image. . . . His smoking cigarette strategically and instinctively finds its place in the right hand . . .

—*Richard*

. . . the giant bleached skeleton of a barkless tree, its face smoothed by the elements. Once proud and tall, its mammoth bones now topple over, half-buried in the earth.

—*Christina*

Emphasis, the Right Verbs and Nouns and Adjectives

Mouth agape, Henry stared . . .

—*Beth*

The clouds played tag in the night sky. The stars whispered to each other. Bonfires burned to the last log.

—*Meagan*

Sounds of Speech, Real Dialogue

"Where's the meat?"
"Still in its skin, I guess."

—*Billy*

Good writing seems to flow. There's nothing halting or awkward about it. It *sounds* easy. Like a good gymnast or archer or guitar player, the good writer makes a very difficult task seem effortless to the audience, and like them, achieves this apparent ease through practice, through caring about what is done, and through careful attention to detail. As James Dickey (1968) puts it, "I work it over to get that *worked-on* quality out of it."

Working it over—and over, and over again—and listening with a practiced, sensitive ear each time is the only way we know for student writers to make their words really sing. See our suggestions in Chapter 9 for helping your students become better revisers.

9. *Good writing has form.* Good writing is graphically well designed. It has a presentational sense. In this criterion, we are ultimately concerned with the writer's ability to visualize the work *in print* or as part of some multimedia presentation that may include print.

A feel for form in writing is most obvious in a student writer's poetry.

> *So came the night;*
> *It dropped down upon me*
> *I was blanketed by purple blackness*
>   *and everything was dry*
>   *and everything was wet*
>   *and everything was cold*
> *And my head fell forward in sorrow*
>   *But it was useless.*
> *I saw it in the shadows, in the*
>   *corners, behind every tree, every*
> *opaque object; but I still saw it.*
> *It creeped behind me and my*
>   *spine melted in the heat*
>   *of Death's passion.*
> *It grabbed me and held me*
>   *squeezing my last breaths*
> *into the fog.*
>   *and everything was dry*
>   *and everything was wet*
>   *and everything was cold.*
>
>   *—Lynne*[1]

Lynne has learned to use the line in her poetry—line endings and beginnings for emphasis, and line indentations to build her refrain. She *sees* the poem as it would appear printed and manipulates its form accordingly (and rather surprisingly in a few lines). She wants the poem read straight through, for example; there is no stanza break to create a pause.

Composing on the computer opens even more possibilities for the manipulation of form and of how the writing appears in print. Elements previously available only to experts and professionals are now routine options for us because of the sophistication of common word-processing software. Writers may easily insert images in their written products; use font style and size and color for effect; enhance finished products with shadings, borders, tables, bullets, or print overlays; and, for online documents, include hyperlinks and a variety of embedded media options. As much as our students will be attracted to these features, part of our task is to help them be judicious and intentional in their choices. We suggest that students experiment, but also that they are prepared to explain and justify their decisions about what they included in their pieces.

Concern with form is properly one of the last aspects of writing that you'll take up with student writers. To insist on too rigid a concern for form alone will only teach students to create a hollow shell or to consider form and appearance before substance. Some students seem never to have a feel for it, although most have at least some sense of form. They know to write in paragraphs, for example—unless, like some of our most able writers, they create new forms to suit their treatment of a subject.

Form-finding is legitimate writing behavior even for young writers. Encourage your students to experiment with form and presentational options. Show them pieces of writing that use different presentational forms, from shape poems to graphic novels to stream of consciousness pieces. Most students like to work with how their writing will look on the page or computer screen, but they need a piece of writing from which to work, and they need to know why—for what purpose or to create what impression on the reader—they select one form over another. Discuss form with your students often to heighten their awareness of its affect.

10. *Good writing makes sense.* It is clear. We get the message. The writer knows what she wants to say and is able to communicate her ideas and her points clearly to the reader.

In all of the student examples in this chapter, and even in the entire book, the sense of what the student writers are trying to say is clear. We may want to word the ideas differently or put them in a different order, but those are mainly stylistic considerations. The meaning that the writers are trying to convey to readers is present in their writings.

When writing makes sense and is clear, all of the previous elements of good writing that we have already mentioned in this chapter work together in concert to convey and to develop the writer's point. The writing is interesting and skillful in ways that contribute to the overall message of the written piece.

Writing that makes sense leaves us with an "Aha," not a "Huh?" In fact, when students wander in their writing, lose their way within the direction of a sentence, or move inchoately from one idea to the next, we often just write "Huh?" in the margin. The writer gets the point ("I'm lost here") and knows that this is a section of the piece in which her writing has become muddled. In conference, we work together to determine how to recapture the flow of ideas—by word choice, sentence structure, the inclusion of more details, or a more effective ordering of ideas.

Having students read their writing aloud to a partner helps them determine places in the writing where clarity and sense fade. When readers hear their words and attempt to read the words actually written—not just the words intended—they pinpoint what needs to change in the writing to improve the sense of the piece. Short of that, a responder can say, "Do you mean . . . ?" again letting the writer know what is and is not making sense to others.

The idea of making sense is basic to good writing, but achieving sense is not always as easy as it sounds. We think in convoluted, interwoven ways, making our precise thoughts and ideas sometimes difficult to capture in clear form and diction and order. *We* know what we mean when we write; why don't you? Nonetheless, genuine responses focused on helping the writer to express ideas clearly will eventually improve the writer's awareness of her ability to make sense in writing.

11. *Good writing observes the conventions of mechanics and usage.* Good writing observes those social conventions of written discourse that are expected by literate readers. Punctuation, spelling, and consistent usage are the most obvious. Notice that we list these conventions of *correctness* almost last in the criteria because we believe that eliminating surface errors is one of the last aspects of writing that student writers should consider. Recall again our emphasis in Chapter 2: Getting it down precedes getting it right. Once our student writers are somewhat accomplished, they need to know that their readers will judge what they have to say, at least in part, by their ability to spell, put commas in the right places, and select the right endings for verbs. There's nothing wrong with insisting that competent writers also become competent proofreaders.

Finally, there's one more category. It may be the most important one.

12. *Good writing is what you like (and what the writer likes)*. We believe that our working criteria are of practical value in your classroom, but we realize that you're the expert in that room. You're the final authority for your student writers, and you have the responsibility for teaching them to write as well as possible in the time you have with them. Don't be afraid to trust your own judgment about what is good and bad in their writing. Make your own list of criteria to use with them—referring to district and state standards and institutionalized rubrics, if you must. Think about your list, and discuss it with your students. Revise it frequently, but use it systematically.

Ultimately, what we're trying to teach student writers is to recognize and pursue the good in their own writing, to make sound judgments about what is effective human expression and what is better changed or discarded. What we're trying to do is to make them the judge of quality in their own writing—to help them become people who see and feel quality, and who care about it in their writing.

Coaching Good Writing

Note that all of the features of good writing that we discuss relate to a sense that the writer took care with what she wrote. When writers care about their pieces and work on them to make them *good*, our job as audience and readers, as James Dickey classically reminds us, is "to be able to feel and see and respond to what the poet [writer] is saying. . . with as much strength and depth as possible" (1968). Considered this way, good writing is writing that touches readers on a personal level. It's writing to which readers respond.

Good writing is our goal, and a level of correctness is certainly expected for final products and for writing that has been thoroughly peer-reviewed and teacher-coached. Writing that is free of surface errors is what we'd ideally expect to see in polished work. It's a tenuous thread, however, when the "goodness" of writing hangs on whether students avoid a narrow range of errors in spelling, punctuation, diction, and formal usage. Teaching writing with correctness as the first or only criterion is deadly to getting the best writing from our students.

You may be thinking, *What's wrong with students learning to write correctly? Don't they need to demonstrate that they can spell, punctuate, and create sentences according to common expectations?* Absolutely. The key question is about timing: *When* do we focus on correctness? Too much emphasis on surface correctness too early destroys motivation, especially for beginning writers. Even for our good student writers, the error avoidance approach to teaching writing generally results in pieces that are a bit dull and predictable.

Before focusing on formal correctness in their writing, students need to be working on deeper concerns about making what they write *worth reading*. A perfectly correct piece of writing that says nothing is an exercise in pointlessness. In fact, it may be a step backward, perpetuating the fallacy that what's most important is how writing *looks* instead of what it says. Think of it this way: Would you rather have an ugly, rusted-out old beater of a car that runs, or a shiny new sports car that looks great but has no engine? That old clunker might be a little hard on the eyes, but it can take us places—and with enough attention, repair, and polish, it can eventually end up looking pretty good as well.

We emphasize finding and nourishing quality in the writing of our students rather than obsessing from the get-go about surface errors. Let's continue with the automotive analogy. Imagine a broken-down old car sitting in your driveway. As any sixteen-year-old with a limited budget knows, the most important thing is to *get the car running*. The whole point of owning a car is its potential for transportation. If it can't do that, it might as well be in the junkyard. Knocking out the dents, replacing the mismatched door panels, adding fancy wheels, polishing and detailing—all of that stuff can wait until we have the thing revving to life with the turn of a key. We don't focus *only* on the engine—decent tires and matching doors and a functional steering system help—and making the car look attractive also has its benefits. The point here is that we address the essentials first, before worrying too much about appearance.

Donald Murray (1979) talks about the "listening eye" of the writing teacher. We like this classic phrase. This listening eye is the sensitivity the teacher must develop to see (or hear) the good aspects of writing by even the most immature student writer. One of our first jobs—and maybe the most important one—is to look for potential in the often-stumbling attempts our students make. You're listening for the sound of that engine in a student's writing. Is it sputtering and backfiring? Barely turning over? Or is it humming along? Murray points out that some sign of skill in any area in a paper is hopeful. Perhaps it's only a few words in the whole paper, but we can begin to build from that strength. We're listening for the sounds and signs of that internal dynamo that fuels all good writing. We're searching for the small sparks in student writing that can be fanned and fed.

Listen carefully when you read those first attempts of your students, and train yourself through practice to be sensitive to the good features that are there. Peter Elbow (1998) reminds us that "a person's best writing is often all mixed up together with his worst. It all feels lousy to him as he's writing, but if he will let himself write it and come back later he will find some parts of it are excellent. It is as though one's best words come wrapped in one's worst." What our students need first is for us to help them see their best words that are usually hidden by their worst. Skip the detailed criticism and offer, instead, encouragement in those areas where it will do the most good.

Sometimes improvement comes almost spontaneously from practice and sustained praise. Your persistence in insisting on some writing being done every day and your open, receptive attitude will probably bring out more potentially good writing and cause more real growth in your student writers than anything else you do, but you still need a clear idea of what you're looking for when you pick up a student's paper. Otherwise, even your best intentions, carefully planned writing activities and opportunities, and most positive reactions are random, perhaps confusing, and finally ineffectual.

After your students have started writing and after they're accustomed to writing daily, then you'll need to approach their writing systematically, looking for the best aspects of what they are doing and helping them see the good and how to grow with it. First, you get them writing; you can't do anything until they're no longer afraid to put words on paper. Then, the work of growing good writers begins by growing the good in their writing. Remember our mantra from Chapter 2: Get it down before worrying about getting it right.

A Writer's Fingerprints: Voice (and Style)

Voice is at the heart of the act of writing. As the writer moves from talking into writing, she tries to hear clearly the flow of language in her head and capture it on the page, hoping you will hear her talking to you and be moved by what she has to say.

When you read good writing, you *hear* the sound of another human being talking to you. A writer's *style* is the *sound* of a voice on the page. The natural place to start with a beginning writer is with his or her own voice. Early in working with writing processes, beginning writers need to learn how they sound when they write. Our job as teachers is to help student writers find a voice in each piece they write.

Alice has found a voice with a clear tone in this moving and personal piece.

> I once felt like writing a poem about the moonlit door. Or the wooden lady whose face holds more secrets than her mind can speak. Or since silent spring never leaves, spring will always come.
>
> I once felt like writing about broken colored glass lying on a clear floor with the sun sparkling. I thought of mysteries with passwords to unknown hideouts. And human detectives with houses of dreams where there lives an old-fashioned girl that is someone's little princess. And when she glimpses that girl in her mirror, her wonderland through the looking glass will hold love for little men and little women.
>
> I once felt like writing about closing doors and opening windows, learning to pretend, to live in fantasy, of courage and war and love that I have not felt but that will be tomorrow's poem. For then it will be today and I will learn of love to come. For tomorrow is the future of today.
>
> —*Alice*[1]

Alice is able to use voice very effectively. There's more involved here than just using the first-person "I" in the writing. This prose poem has a serious subject, the mysteries of growing up; it's a little melancholy, but hopeful, even though her irony flickers in places in this piece. Writers learn to use different voices. Each voice needs to be individual, identifiable, and suited to the purpose and audience of each piece of writing.

Hal demonstrates his sensitivity to voice in this short piece.

Staying Alone

> I know when I left that I left the light on. And that paper wasn't on the floor. Someone is in here, I know it.
>
> Oh, don't fool yourself, no one got in.
>
> I guess you're right. I'm just nervous. I'll just lock the door, the windows, and check under the beds and in the closets. No one got in.
>
> I know I heard a voice when I finished washing my face and hands. And I know someone is here.
>
> Ah, you're doing it again, no one got in.
>
> No one got in. That's easy for you to say. You're just me, I'm you. And I'm scared. I guess I'll just watch *Saturday Night* and fall asleep.
>
> No one got in.
>
> —*Hal*[1]

Hal talks to himself with one voice that is afraid, the other reassuring—and both voices are his. "You're just me, I'm you." We hear throughout the piece the sound of a fallible, very human person.

Our approach to writing instruction helps students discover and strengthen their individual voices in their writings. A great deal of practice with writing about subjects close to them and important to them is necessary. Giving them choices in the writing class, the freedom to explore their own expressions in their own ways, is also important. Your genuine, positive response to the good in their writing is essential, more important than anything else you do. In your responses to their writing, listen for students' effective voices and point out indications of their effective use of unique, authentic, and personal voices in what they have to say in writing. Watch for opportunities to make comments to your students such as, "This is *you*," and "This *sounds like you* talking" as you read their work. Mark their papers to indicate where they sound real, genuine, like themselves. Use every opportunity in class to point to passages in their writings that clearly reveal their voices. Encourage students to ask themselves "Does this sound like me? Do I hear myself in this paper?" after they have completed a piece of writing. Do whatever you can to create an environment in which students are aware of, and encouraged to use, authentic voices in their writing.

Because being aware of their voices in writing is so important to young writers, we don't try to move student writers away from personal expression too early in their development as writers. Don't be too anxious to get them through the personal stuff and on to "more serious" writing. For the good writer, all writing that is *serious* is personal. Accomplished writers do not remove themselves from what's important to them. Even a writer as formal as Henry James (1889) had this advice for young writers:

> Oh, do something from your point of view; an ounce of example is worth a ton of generalities . . . do something with life. Any point of view is interesting that is a direct impression of life. You each have an impression colored by your individual conditions; make that into a picture, a picture framed by your own personal wisdom, your glimpse of the American world. The field is vast for freedom, for study, for observation, for satire, for truth. (in Miller, 1972b, 94)

Encourage students to write from their own points of view, to use the unique expressions of their individual voices so that they can create their pictures of experiences with their written words.

Tuning Your Voice

Although mature writers have a voice on the page that's relatively constant throughout their writing, they adapt their voice in a particular piece of writing to their purpose and to the anticipated demands of their audience. In a way, the workings of purpose, audience, and voice are so inextricably mixed in the act of writing that they can't be separated. However, it's important for us to focus on voice as the aspect of writing closest to the writer. Once they begin to find their voices in writing, student writers further need to find out the range of their voices and what their voices can do.

It's more difficult to talk about a writer's use of voice and exploring ways of using voice than to show it in operation. Listen to this:

> The legend of Junior Johnson! In this legend, here is a country boy, Junior Johnson, who learns to drive by running whiskey for his father, Johnson, Senior . . .

and grows up to be a famous stock car racing driver. . . . Finally, one night they had Junior trapped on the road up toward the bridge around Millersville, there's no way out of there, they had the barricades up and they could hear this souped-up car roaring around the bend, and there it comes—but suddenly they can hear a siren and see a red light flashing in the grille, so they think it's another agent, and boy, they run out like ants and pull those barrels and boards and sawhorses out of the way, and then—ggghhzzzzzzzhhhhhhgggggzzzzzzeeeeeeeong!— gawdam! there he goes again, it was him, Junior Johnson! with a gawdam agent's sireen and a red light in his grille! (Wolfe 1965)

There is no mistaking the voice of Tom Wolfe. Like the voices of other traditional classic and modern classic writers, his voice rings true decades after it was written. The excitement, the feigned innocence, even the sound effects make us hear the experience as though we were sitting around in a North Carolina country store, listening to a backwoods orator tell us about "The Last American Hero" and how he fooled the revenuers that time. But when Tom Wolfe talks about Las Vegas, his voice changes.

This is Raymond talking to the wavy-haired fellow with the stick, the dealer, at the craps table about 3:45 Sunday morning. The stickman had no idea what this big wiseacre was talking about, but he resented the tone. He gave Raymond that patient arch of the eyebrows known as a Red Hook brush-off, which is supposed to convey some such thought as, I am a very tough but cool guy, as you can tell by the way I carry my eyeballs low in the pouches, and if this wasn't such a high-class joint we would take wiseacres like you out back and beat you into jellied madrilene. (1965)

This time the pace is slower, and we hear the deliberate sarcasm of a jaded craps dealer, a "very tough but cool guy."

The voice is always Tom Wolfe's; it is his trademark and not to be duplicated. Yet, he alters his writing voice to put us closer to one experience or the other. He adapts his voice automatically to suit his purpose. That's what skilled writers do; that's what makes their writing resonate with readers across time; and becoming flexible and adaptable with their voices is what we can teach our student writers to do, too.

Studying Published Authors

We, Dawn and Darren, cannot teach writing without also reading lots of writing ourselves and with our students. Our students do the same, reading each other's texts and current newspapers and magazines. They read fiction and nonfiction from the mid-1900s to now in order to see how writing evolves over time. One of our favorite activities involves students' bringing in their favorite books and reading a passage aloud to the class. Then, we discuss how the author wrote, her writer's craft, and which of the writerly techniques in the passage students might use in their own writing. We have great fun with these discussions and hear from myriad sources what our students like to read.

Even though most of us cannot truly write as do our favorite authors, even when we try, we learn much about voice, style, and the craft of writing when we study closely what published writers do, how they connect with their audiences, and how they establish their signature voices and styles. A time-honored method used by writers to perfect their own style is to model their writing after that of authors they admire.

Two caveats are in order. Caveat 1: We're definitely not suggesting that we go back to the copybooks of an earlier age, nor are we suggesting that students learn to write by following the examples of Milton, Swift, Pope, or Franklin; but there's nothing wrong with—and much to be learned by—having students discuss, critique, and try out the techniques of published authors.

Caveat 2: Some refer to any published text that we use with students as an example of good writing as a "mentor text." We are not especially fond of that term. Teachers and other *people*, not texts, mentor student writers. When we use published authors' works in our writing class, we use them as *exemplar* texts, or texts to notice, or texts that illustrate certain writer's techniques. Leave the mentoring to real people interacting with other real people.

With those stipulations in mind, consider the following passages.

Exemplar Text 1: Rich Details

> My first indication that food was something other than a substance one stuffed in one's face when hungry—like filling up at a gas station—came after fourth grade in elementary school. I was on a family vacation to Europe, on the *Queen Mary*, in the cabin-class dining room. . . .
>
> It was the soup.
>
> It was *cold*.
>
> This was something of a discovery for a curious fourth-grader whose entire experience with soup to this point had consisted of Campbell's cream of tomato and chicken noodle. I'd eaten in restaurants before, sure, but this was the first food I really noticed. It was the first food I enjoyed and, more important, remembered enjoying. I asked our patient British waiter what this delightfully cool, tasty liquid was.
>
> "Vichyssoise," came the reply, a word that to this day—even though it's now a tired old warhorse of a menu selection and one I've prepared thousands of times—still has a magical ring to it. I remember everything about the experience: the way our waiter ladled it from a silver tureen into my bowl; the crunch of tiny chopped chives he spooned on as garnish; the rich, creamy taste of leek and potato; the pleasurable shock, the surprise that is was cold.

You probably have a hunch that a chef wrote this piece. But who? Did you think the author might be Julia Child, Charlie Trotter, or Martha Stewart? If you've read anything else by them or seen one of their appearances on television, you probably thought something was a little "off" in the passage—it didn't ring true to their style. Good instincts.

That's Anthony Bourdain (2000), the celebrity chef, on his awakening to food. His writing is almost as lush as his food. Notice the rich detail. Bourdain uses a personal voice, paints himself as a young and naïve child awakening to elegant food, and savors both a memory and a specific dish. Yet, he ends with a bit of the critical flair for which he is also known. Shifting from past to present and from reverie to critique brings the reader on a roller-coaster ride of emotions, responding to the situation, details, and voice.

Exemplar Text 2: Irony

Kurt Vonnegut, an author who was a forerunner of many contemporary writing techniques, also knows how to ensnare an audience. Vonnegut's signature voice and style stem from his fine use of scathing irony.

> [This book] is so short and jumbled and jangled . . . because there is nothing intelligent to say about a massacre. Everybody is supposed to be dead, to never say anything or want anything ever again. Everything is supposed to be very quiet after a massacre, and it always is, except for the birds. . . .
>
> I have told my sons that they are not under any circumstances to take part in massacres, and that the news of massacres of enemies is not to fill them with satisfaction or glee. (Vonnegut 1969, 19)

Notice that the last sentence is the kicker in this piece. Students are able to learn how irony works and then try it out, placing it strategically in their pieces of writing.

Exemplar Text 3: Addressing the Reader Directly

Another effective technique is to talk directly to the reader. When authors break the invisible wall between their writing and the reader, they draw the reader into the writing. In memoir, writers do so by qualifying their memories, saying, "I remember it this way," or "I think it happened like this." At other times, they may put asides or their interior thoughts in parentheses or italics. Here's Frank Conroy, writing about being in a contest as a boy in the 1940s to win a coveted black beauty diamond yo-yo:

> [He] smiled and held up the prize, turning it in the air so we could see the four stones set on each side. ("The crowd gasped. . ." I want to write. Of course they didn't. They didn't make a sound, but the impact of the diamond yo-yo was obvious.) (1967, 113)

Or, look at Joan Didion, writing about her year of extreme, almost insane grief after her husband fell forward into his dinner plate one night, dead. She reads an article about a psychiatrist's recommended treatment for "established pathological mourners" and brings the reader directly into her thoughts as she argues with the psychiatrist-author:

> *Were you there?*
> *No. . . .*
> *I don't need to "review the circumstances of the death." I was there.*
> *I didn't "get the news." I didn't "view" the body. I was there.*
> I catch myself. I stop.
> I realize that I am directing irrational anger toward the entirely unknown [doctor]. (2005, 56–7)

In drama, this invisible wall is called the *fourth wall*, the one that metaphorically stands between the audience and the actors. Several contemporary playwrights break the fourth wall as a way of informing the audience about the meaning of a scene or as a way of drawing the audience into the action of the play. Consider, for example, how the Narrator, Tom, addresses the audience in *The Glass Menagerie*. This technique works much the same way in other written genres, from poetry to fiction to memoir.

Activities with Exemplar Texts

Let your students try their hands at working with exemplar texts. Select a favorite passage from a classic work, a contemporary classic, young adult literature, or popular fiction. The passage might include pithy dialogue, vivid descriptions, intense emotion, vibrant action, or some other hallmark that students will readily identify. Discuss the style of the author with your students. What makes the writing work? What makes it *classic*? How do audiences today view the author's style as compared to audiences during the time when the work was first written? How long will the popularity of recent works and authors last? What modern themes and issues have wide audience appeal?

After this analysis and discussion, have students select a subject about which the author might have written and try to write in the author's style and voice but not in the author's exact words. How might Mark Twain, for example, write about contemporary issues of class, ethnicity, and gender? How might Hemingway write about contemporary views of animal rights issues or using animals in laboratory testing? How might J. K. Rowling write about the Salem witch trials? If Stephenie Meyer wrote about issues related to aging, how might that go? Without guidance, students' results may become silly or ludicrous. This is a good time, perhaps, to remind your students how literary absurdity works in the hand of a masterful writer. Prompt your students to give this activity a solid try.

Hearing All Voices

Each student in our classes is unique. They have differing opinions, looks, perceptions, religions, cultures, experiences, mannerisms, and methods of expressing themselves. Some of them are monolingual, some bi- or trilingual. Some speak English as a native language; some don't. Whatever the student knows from personal experience and the language that flows in his head impacts what he writes. Whatever he reads—including exemplar texts—impacts what he writes, as do his dreams and aspirations, values and beliefs. It's the same for all of us. We are unique, and our writing rings with authority when we delve into what we know and what we care about for our writing.

The diversity in our classes is a source of richness. Tap students' varying experiences, languages and cultures, viewpoints, and knowledge to enrich the conversation and then the writing in your classes. When students bring the full force of their complete backgrounds into their writing and into the conversations that surround their writing, their voices ring with greater authority, the writing resonates with readers, and the power of the written word again asserts itself as a powerful tool for learning and for human expression.

As you read the remaining sections on voice in this chapter, ask yourself how you might help each writer in your class tune his unique voice; express himself from the power base of his culture, language, and experiences; and use his voice to connect with his readers. When students feel that authority and power, they understand the value of becoming writers—not just for today and not just in your class, but for life.

Activities for Exploring Voice

Too much of what we teach in school is not a voice people want to read; it's only one expository voice, and a limited, restricted one at that. Compare, for example, the five-paragraph formula theme with the exposition of Tom Wolfe. The activities that we suggest here will encourage your students to grow stronger in their own voices, to be more aware of what their voices can do, and to move away from that impersonal school voice that Miller (1972), classically calls "the prose in the gray flannel suit," playing on the title of the novel by Sloan Wilson about the 1950s striving, but not quite succeeding, "man in the grey flannel suit."

These activities do not yield pieces that you collect, read, and return with a grade. The emphasis in the class is on "hearing" the sound of the voice in the writing. That means the writings need to be shared *aloud*, and they need to be *discussed in some detail* in class. A great deal of reading aloud and much open discussion about what is distinctive and interesting, moving or funny, personal and unique are necessary if these activities are to be helpful in showing student writers what their own voices can do. We're working on exploration and experimentation, on fine-tuning writers' voices, *not* producing finished products. Think of the singer who warms up her voice prior to the concert; that's what we're doing here: warming up student writers' voices.

Try this entire series of activities over several days. Don't have that much time? Select an activity or two for students to complete and make connections to other writing your students are already doing. We urge flexibility at all times so that our ideas blend readily with what, who, and how you need to teach.

Who's Talking?

This activity gives students the opportunity to stretch their voices by putting on the voice of someone else. Ease them into creating a *persona*. Give students these instructions:

Write about a *situation* twice, as two different people in that situation would see it. Each time you are to be one of the persons in the situation and speak with that person's voice. You may put your people into any situation you like, but here are some choices of characters for you to use:

1. a local and an out-of-towner
2. a man and a woman
3. a young kid and an elderly person
4. a teenager and a parent
5. a worker and the boss

Your students, of course, should be free to suggest their own contrasting characters. Tell them first to visualize each person in the situation and to imagine that person talking before they begin to write. They'll also find it helpful if they use the first sentence of each contrasting voice to set the scene and get into the character. As they write, check to make sure they're using the first person. Often *I* will switch to *he* or *she* before they finish a piece. Emphasize again that they're speaking with the character's voice.

Ask students to read aloud their pieces in groups of three or four peers. Instruct the members of each group to underline the words and phrases that indicate that the student author was speaking with the character's voice.

Keep realistic expectations. Even professional writers find it difficult to keep a *persona* in character and sounding authentic. Your students will enjoy this kind of writing, but they'll require a great deal of practice before their characters begin to have a personality of their own. Students are learning how to writing in varying voices, not becoming novelists.

Who Owns the Voice?

This activity leads students into the rather sophisticated techniques of *tagging* a character. It requires the skills of detail selection, repetition, dialogue, and pacing. For that reason, we suggest you use it after your students have had a good deal of practice with voice in writing and are beginning to have an intuitive feel for voice when they write.

Have students write a brief piece, trying to capture the voice of someone known to the entire class, such as the school principal, the football coach, the Latin teacher, a TV personality, a famous politician, or a local radio personality. Ask them to pick someone with distinct speech mannerisms. They're to write the piece as a short monologue using *I* and assuming the voice of their subject. Then, read the papers aloud without identifying the speaker. The class tries to guess who owns the voice.

Follow up the activity by selecting two or three of the best or most interesting monologues and asking *what the clues are* to the speaker's identity in each case. Make a list on the board of key phrases and word choices that identify the speakers, and point out important uses of repetition in the writings.

Who Was That?

Use a recording or a videotape of an impressionist and talk about how an impressionist works. Point out how they *select* and *emphasize* certain voice qualities and mannerisms. Also talk about what impressionists do to create a character that a writer can use—selection, repetition, and exaggeration. Excellent clips might be found from episodes of *Saturday Night Live*. Because the TV show's trademark is irreverence, use caution when selecting which clips to use with students.

How Did He Do That?

Select a clip from a TV show with a memorable and identifiable character. Try clips from the classic television show *Taxi* in which the character Jim is featured, or from *Seinfeld* in which the character Kramer is prominent. For more recent examples, use clips featuring Sawyer in *Lost*, Sue Sylvester in *Glee*, Dwight Schrute in *The Office,* Charlie or Alan Harper in *Two and a Half Men*, Barney Stinson in *How I Met Your Mother*, Abby Sciuto in *NCIS*, or Gregory House in *House*. Ask students to notice their mannerisms, which are quite distinctive.

Help students understand how characters' mannerisms, dress, movements, facial expressions, hair, clothes, speech patterns, intonations, and word choices all distinguish or *tag* the character. Lead the discussion by asking questions such as: What's distinctive about the way he talks? What are a few details about each character that are exaggerated and unique to that character? What is his speech pattern? Does he elongate some words and misuse others? What are his unique mannerisms? Does he wave his hands or thrust them through his hair? Analyses such as these indicate how a few repeated and exaggerated characteristics are used to tag a character.

Additionally, students may examine passages from literature, seeking similar ways in which authors make characters come to life on the page by tagging them. For example, look at descriptions of classic characters such as Boo Radley in *To Kill a Mockingbird*, Willy Loman in *Death of a Salesman*, Shug in *The Color Purple*, or Lennie in *Of Mice and Men*. Or, for more contemporary examples, consider Bean in *Ender's Game*, Edward Cullen in *Twilight*, and Katniss Everdeen in *The Hunger Games*. What makes each character memorable?

Will You Remember Me?

Ask your students to create a memorable character, including dialogue, in a few pages. They may model their characters on those from movies, TV shows, books, or the comics. Tell them to be particularly aware of the character's voice and mannerisms, to concentrate on *seeing* and *hearing* the character as they write. After they have the character captured in a first draft, encourage students to go back to *emphasize* the characteristics of voice and action to make their creation stand out. Share the finished characters aloud with the class.

Writing Well—And Liking It

We are always amazed, and a little amused, at the relief in students' eyes when we say, "Yes, this is English class. And yes, you may use *I* and *you* and contractions when you write. Maybe even fragments effectively." Of course they may. Don't the authors you read do the same? Yes. The question is, who has been telling our students that they shouldn't do those things—and why? Forget those tired models of writing. Formal essays are written mainly in English class and usually then as an excuse to "get them ready for college" or to "pass the test"—which can usually be passed anyhow with a piece of writing that exhibits a fresh, lively voice; some inventiveness; and a respectable degree of control with language, form, and the traditional conventions of written expression.

Who are the writers you most enjoy reading? Bring them into class—when you can and still keep your job. Who are the writers your students like best? Bring those into class, too—again, when you can and still dodge censorship issues. What are those favorite authors' voices like? How do we know their writing is *good writing*? Or is it? Do we enjoy reading some authors whose writing is not all that skilled? Sure. Some of that writing is just plain fun and relaxing. Discuss what good writing and favorite authors offer us as readers. When you share favorite writers, you enhance writing *and* reading; you bring literacy to life. When your classroom is awash in reading and writing, voice and quality in writing improve. Try it. It works better than threats of not passing the test, not getting the job, or not getting into college any day of the week.

NOTES

1. Tracy, Lynn, Billy, Beth, Susan, Alice, Richard, Susan, Lynne, Kathy, and Hal were students at Gainesville High School, Gainesville, Georgia.
2. Alyssa and Caroline were students in Jama Branham's class at The Walker School in Marietta, Georgia.

3. Christina, Jade, Meagan, Wayne, Skyler, and Olivia were students of Marsha Kindrachuk in Marietta, Georgia.
4. Sam was a student in Kyle Jones' class at North Gwinnett High School in Suwanee, Georgia.

Works Cited

Bourdain, Anthony. 2000. *Kitchen Confidential.* New York: Bloomsbury.

Cisneros, Sandra. 1991. *The House on Mango Street.* New York: Vintage.

Conroy, Frank. 1967. *Stop-time.* London: Penguin.

Dickey, James. 1968. *Babel to Byzantium.* New York: Grosset and Dunlap.

Didion, Joan. 2005. *The Year of Magical Thinking.* New York: Alfred A. Knopf.

Dillard, Annie. 1990. *The Writing Life.* New York: Harper Perennial.

Elbow, Peter. 1998. *Writing Without Teachers.* 2nd. Ed. New York: Oxford University Press.

James, Henry. 1889. Letter to Students at the Deerfield Summer School, London. In James E. Miller, Jr. 1972a. *Theory of Fiction: Henry James.* Lincoln: University of Nebraska.

Leonard, Elmore. 2001. "Writers on Writing; Easy on the Adverbs, Exclamation Points and Especially Hooptedoodle." Arts. *New York Times.* July 16, 2001, 1.

Miller, James. 1972b. *Self, Word, Reality: A Rhetoric of the Imagination.* New York: Dodd, Mead.

Murray, Donald. 1979. Workshop on Writing at Georgia State University, Atlanta, GA.

Robbins, Tom. 1976. *Even Cowgirls Get the Blues.* New York: Bantam.

Vonnegut, Kurt. 1969. *Slaughterhouse Five.* New York: Dell.

Wilson, Sloan. 1955, 1983. *The Man in the Grey Flannel Suit.* Introduction by Jonathan Franzen, 2002. New York: Four Walls Eight Windows.

Wolfe, Tom. 1965. "The Last American Hero Is Junior Johnson. Yes!" March. *Esquire.* www.esquire.com/features/life-of-junior-johnson-tom-wolfe-0365.

6

Authentic Writing

Writing with authenticity means: writing with your own true voice, writing that is personal and human, unique to you, reflecting your experience. Writing with clarity and simplicity to allow your readers to learn who you are. . . . Being open, honest and real. Writing from the heart. —**Joanna Patterson, *Writing with Authenticity***

Writing that happens in the context of school is rarely authentic, nor does anyone except the teacher usually read the stuff. Why? Like the Velveteen Rabbit, it isn't real yet. For writing to be real, it has a form, purpose, topic, depth of thought, creative spark, voice, and fluent ease that appeal to multiple audiences who live beyond the hallways of the schoolhouse.

Would you be surprised to know that Patterson's quote, above, is written for bloggers? It's part of her advice for those who would write on the Internet about topics they know in hopes of finding a wide audience of real people who will read and follow each new posting. Anyone may start a blog; an agent and publisher are not required. Because of its accessibility and ease of updating, the Internet is one of the most *real* venues for contemporary writing that we know. Not everyone will be into blogging, just as some may not write a memorable and beloved Shakespearean ode. It's nice to know, however, that both odes and the Internet offer our student writers different opportunities to try their hands at authentic writing and to grow their writing through practice and audience response.

Prolific and award-winning writer Elmore Leonard also offers sage advice to writers in his essay, "Writers on Writing" (2001). The subtitle of his essay, "Easy on the Adverbs, Exclamation Points and Especially Hooptedoodle," already gives student writers a major clue about "rules" for achieving authentic writing. In his somewhat irreverent manner, Leonard goes on to say, "Try to leave out the part that readers tend to skip," and "If it sounds like writing, I rewrite it." Leonard clearly has a grasp of what authentic writing needs.

We also encourage our student writers to eliminate most adverbs, to edit their writing thoroughly, and to write in their own voices. (See Chapter 5 for our comments on voice, and Chapter 9 for revision suggestions.) Giving snippets of advice to student writers, however, isn't enough to help them develop a comprehensive concept of what it means to write effectively and authentically. To teach writing effectively, we, Dawn and Darren, needed to develop a comprehensive framework to organize our thinking about what and how to teach and about how to work most effectively with our student writers. Through trial and error, observing and listening to our students, we have created a framework for teaching writing that works for us. It's complex enough to accommodate theory and best practice, but practical enough for students to bring self-awareness and informed choices to their writing.

At the core of our framework is authenticity. *Authenticity* in writing involves writing for real audiences (not just the teacher) about a topic important to you (not whatever topic was assigned) for a reason important to you (not just to the makers of high-stakes tests) to communicate a real message ("Go see this movie." "Let me tell you about my gaming community.") in a form (essay, poem, letter, book review) that enhances your message ("I will persuade you." "I will tell you about my experience." "This is important for survival.").

In this chapter, we invite you to think constructively, creatively, and confidently about some of the ways in which you and your students might approach authentic writing.

Writing in the Context of Schools

Most students' writings live in the isolated, structured, and inhibiting silo that we call *school*. Too often, our methods for teaching writing send students the implicit message that *school writing* is a genre that exists outside school. It doesn't. We can't wander into the local bookstore and find the section labeled Great Writing from Our Local High School even if we have some darn good student writers in our classrooms.

Since the seminal research of Britton et al (1975), we have known that students write primarily for an audience of teachers as evaluators: School assignments are written according to a teacher's expectations, read by the teacher, and graded by that same teacher. Good students want to make the teacher happy, so they try to give the teacher what he wants, which will result, hopefully, in a high grade. Those are the rules of school.

The only problem with this simple equation is that we don't stay in school forever. A teacher will not stand at our shoulders throughout our lives, dispensing topics and ideas for revision.

We leave school to become functioning adults, professionals, parents, family members, and citizens who write for broader audiences than the teacher. We inevitably explore various purposes for writing and topics other than those allowed by schoolwork. We branch out to forms that help us relay *our* message rather than one chosen by a teacher. In short, writing is not just for school and not just for an audience of teachers as grade givers. For that reason, we need to think about writing and teaching writing from a larger perspective than one that is limited to school.

Recently, Dawn had a somewhat frustrating conversation with a colleague, Gail, who is a language arts coordinator for a large school district. They lamented the point that narrative writing gets little instructional attention. "The only kind of writing within the district that really counts is strictly expository," explained Gail. "Our writing standards and assessments are focused on persuasion and argumentation." Dawn commented that various modes of writing—including narrative—might help to strengthen an argument, clarify a point, or drive home a persuasive message. "Yes, but that's not really how we teach writing. We want students to know narrative writing when they see it and not confuse it with persuasive writing." For Gail, following the mandates of her school district means teaching students that the modes of writing are isolated and distinct: The point of narrative writing is to tell a story; of expository writing, to inform; of persuasive writing, to convince.

The message that Gail's district is sending—perhaps deliberately, perhaps unwittingly—to students, teachers, administrators, parents, and the public is that students don't need to think about whether the modes of writing overlap and complement each other. Overall, the district is achieving good scores on district and state writing tests as compared to other districts' scores in the state. Isn't that really all teachers and parents need to worry about?

You may be nodding your head, agreeing that all is well in Gail's district. A closer analysis of the scores, however, reveals that few students are improving their ability to write. That is, many students meet expectations, but very few go on to *exceed* expectations. The approach that Gail's school district takes is so literal that it rips the guts, the creativity, the critical and analogic thinking, and all the other messiness from the act of writing and teaching writing. Compared to the multiple purposes, forms, and modes involved in any type of real writing—including those that corporate America wants to see their new hires able to perform—these school-based, test-aware, static methods and labels are artificial, stilted, and overly simplistic versions of how we write and communicate.

What to Write: Finding Authentic Topics

You may be thinking, "This *authentic writing* stuff is all well and good, but what does it mean for what I do in my class on Monday morning? What are my students going to write about?" A traditional, somewhat cynical response might be "Whatever the teacher assigns." Sadly, that answer is often too close to the truth.

In contrast, consider these situations that prompted curiosity, inquiry, and results:

- A scientist observes that when he presses the side of his eyeball slightly, his vision seems to warp; from pursuing such simple initial observations, he redefines an entire branch of physics.
- A bedridden writer, reflecting on how the taste of a favorite cookie brings back a wave of childhood memories, creates a classic work of fiction.
- An engineer accidentally knocks a spring from his desk, watches it slink down to the floor, and invents one of the world's most famous toys.

Do you recognize Sir Isaac Newton's inspiration for the science of optics, Marcel Proust's *Remembrance of Things Past*, and engineer Richard James' observation leading to his invention of the Slinky? (We didn't make this stuff up. Google it.)

The seeds for writing lie in the flow of students' lives, even in mundane and monotonous moments such as watching a spring fall from a desk. By overtly noticing details ourselves, we help our students become people who *pay attention*—to *attend* to the places, events, personalities, and moments around them. Get your students into this habit by pointing out the curious, the inconsistent, and the unexpected in current or historical events, in the literature they read or the music they listen to, or in the actions of people around them. Help your students make the normal strange (and the strange, normal) whenever possible. Gently dispute settled thought and custom. Use "Why?" as a crowbar, opening up space to speculate, challenge, and wonder.

Common cultural conventions—food, clothing, speech, and public behavior—are excellent subjects for helping students develop this combination of observation and speculation. Is a guinea pig a pet or a food item? What is acceptable behavior while riding in an elevator, and why? Should boys be allowed to wear kilts to school? Probing everyday matters hones critical faculties in a social space and gets students accustomed to the conversational give-and-take—or, formally, *dialectic*—that experienced writers convey.

Helping Students Actively Explore Potential Topics

Many English teachers have taken the pledge to acknowledge the value of student-generated writing topics. In the conventionally organized curriculum, however, the pledge is only partial and the freedom of student-selected topics is often limited to personal narratives and other "creative" kinds of writing. Once students move into argument and research, fun time is over and the pool of acceptable topics dries up, making classrooms rather static and staid places.

To combat that tendency, we pose controversies and ideas that we know will get our students fired up. We often begin by introducing our own uncertainties and a variety of ways of looking at an issue. Students take over and learn from one another's knowledge and experience as they discover ideas or concerns about which they genuinely want to find out more.

We use ideas like the following to engage students in topic exploration.

▨ Virtual Experiences

For inexperienced writers, topics cannot be too far removed from their knowledge and experience. Because most of our students are terminally underexperienced, we create virtual encounters with ideas that offset their limited knowledge. As with all writing, previous experience as a reader, person, and thinker counts. Experience precedes writing effectiveness.

Intellectual stimuli, including problems and puzzles to which students connect and extend their personal experiences, are essential. Photography, works of art, video clips, digital culture curiosities, news sources, fiction, poetry, personal experience, artifacts, and experts in the field invite students to shift their perspectives and see their subjects through a variety of lenses. For an example of one type of virtual experience to explore a topic, see our discussion of geotagging in Chapter 3.

▨ Exploring a Topic Before Writing About It

Have you ever had a hot idea for a piece of writing that just didn't pan out? Sometimes, ideas fizzle because we don't spend enough time thinking deeply about them. To help your students think through possible topics for their writing, provide class time for them to try some of the following:

- Imagine what might happen if they met a member of their intended audience. How might that conversation go? Ask them to create and enact one or two scenarios.
- Select a topic of interest, anything from nature conservation to having better food choices in the school cafeteria. What problems and dilemmas arise if the situation is not addressed or if their opinions are not heeded? What positive outcomes could result if their writing is successful?

- Envision a televised debate about their topic. Who would watch the debate? Who would be the ideal spokesperson for their viewpoint, and why? What is engaging and stimulating about their topic? If the topic seems limited or boring, what might they do to enliven it?
- Where they would go to learn more about their topic? What fact-finding junkets or field trips could they take? What would they need to learn? How would they find the information?

Any topic may become more specific in the writer's mind after engaging in some deep thinking and reflection about it. Devise your own questions for your students to explore as they generate their topics, and encourage them to work with a partner to do the same as a routine part of their idea generation and refinement. Considering these types of questions works well before students begin writing or anytime students are "stuck" in thinking further about their topic.

Heuristics

Guided thinking procedures may help students develop richer ideas, particularly if the teacher models this kind of thinking for the students. Sequenced and guided questions, which cause students to think about a topic in an orderly progression, are helpful. The old journalistic heuristic of Who? What? When? Where? Why? and How? is a classic example of directing a writer by posing leading questions. Heuristics stimulate and guide writers; avoid using them to create a stepwise formula for students to follow. Our questions lead students deeper into their topics. Try questions such as, "What are the key terms related to your topic?" and "What are the two or three central ideas related to your topic?"

Clusters and Webs

Brainstorming of all kinds is helpful in generating a plethora of ideas. The genius of clusters and webs is that they make thinking *visual*. These techniques are not just for narrative writing. These strategies help writers get their thinking and ideas on the drawing board so that they can work with them more concretely. Taking the time to construct order from ideas that are represented visually is a real help to many writers, particularly those who have limited capacity both to generate ideas and to construct text models of them simultaneously.

These visual representations let students follow their natural thinking, finding fruitful and sometimes surprising topics and ideas for their writing.

Storyboards

In the same way that clusters and webs work as visual representations of thinking, storyboards help students think about arranging elements of the message they want to deliver into a logical presentation. Have your students create PowerPoint-style slides of their ideas to keep them focused as they create the supporting documentation for those ideas. If they aren't adept with the computer or if there are not enough computers available in your classroom, have your students draw the "slides" related to their topic and experiment with the most effective order in which those slides should appear. These slides and their sequenced order—the storyboard—comprise the topic at a glance. The storyboard functions as a space in which to generate ideas, but with far more flexibility than a traditional outline offers.

Metaphors, Analogs, and Stories

Many of our students construct meanings and build individual understandings based on their culture, ethnicity, and life experiences. The directness of conventional essay expectations is aberrant to students whose cultural pattern is to approach ideas indirectly through metaphor and story. Essay strategies such as Aristotelian logic, a "cut to the chase" presentation of ideas, or the typical five-paragraph strategy of "tell 'em what you're gonna tell 'em, tell 'em, and tell 'em what you told 'em," may totally baffle some students. Encourage students to use a method of organizing ideas that seems natural to them. After students have a jot list or a rough draft of their topic, ask them to ease into the topic by thinking about how to begin their writing.

Ask students to try several partial drafts about their topic, with each draft beginning in a new way. Which beginning is most effective in attracting the reader to the topic? Which one helps to clarify what the topic is, exactly? Which one sets the mood or appropriate tone for the topic? Some different ways of beginning pieces of writing that we have used with success include the following:

- a quotation
- an anecdote
- a personal experience
- a picture
- a song's lyrics
- a poem
- a memory

Invite students to share each of their beginnings with a group of peers to see how they respond to each technique.

Talk, Talk, Talk

Most of our students would rather talk about a writing assignment than actually construct text. Why is that? Talk is cheap, disposable, difficult to assess, and easy to revise or redo. Writing is more difficult to disavow, more permanent, easier to critique, and riskier, revealing flaws of both logic and linguistic ability. Encourage students to talk extensively about their ideas before drafting them into text. Create opportunities for your students to rehearse their main points, titles, opening sentences, and supporting details with peer partners. Encourage the partners to become an active audience, recording important ideas as the writer talks. Provide time for partners to discuss problems and potential text structures or organizational schemes for the piece.

Who Reads Writing? Considerations of Audience

Conversations about topics for writing will inevitably lead to considerations of audience. The concept of audience is more than a corner on the rhetorical triangle. *Audience* consists of the real people that you imagine reading what you have written. The better the writer knows and envisions her audience, the more finely tuned the writing is likely to be.

To get comfortable with writing is to experiment with what works on others. Writers work on creating a distinct voice, connecting with their readers, and selecting precisely the *right* words to convey messages to readers. One of the most desirable sensitivities to cultivate in developing writers is a heightened ability to conceive an audience as they write.

Many traditional writing assignments either define audience in very limited terms or omit considerations of audience altogether. Formulaic persuasive essays, research papers, typical homework responses, and similar assignments have only one expected audience: the teacher. As much as we hope that most students really want to impress their teachers with their work, the reality is less rosy. Because most school writing happens under mandate or duress, students learn the warped lesson that their work is not really responsible to the expectations of a real audience. It's no wonder that many of our students possess little sense that their writing should meet real readers' needs for clarity, organization, examples, details, information, or entertainment. Many students even find it unbelievable that others are interested in what they've written.

There's something ironic (or just sad) about this situation. Most teenagers are very audience-centered with their language, seeking to amuse, astonish, and impress their friends with stories, jokes, and witty comebacks. Teens are hyperaware of who said what to whom and why. They are attuned to the image they convey to others through their rhetorical choices—even though they would not phrase their choices in those terms. These same savvy students lose touch with the concept of audience when they face traditional writing assignments.

Students usually write for audiences that include, among others, themselves, friends and other peers, a trusted adult, and you as the teacher and/or the evaluator. Less experienced writers need practice to personalize an audience. Try having them envision the people to whom they are writing by asking them to work through questions such as the following:

- How old is the typical person in your intended audience?
- What do the members of your intended audience value?
- What do the members of your intended audience already know or think about your topic?
- What interests does the typical person in your audience have? How might you connect with those interests to draw your reader into your writing?
- What is unique about your intended audience?
- How much like you is your intended audience? How different?

With increasing skill, students begin to internalize such questions about their intended audiences, and they are ready to venture into writing for larger known audiences such as younger children or older relatives. Much public writing occurs for general unknown audiences such as congressional representatives, corporations, specialized groups, and the general public—groups that our students don't know well but about whom they are able to engage in some logical conclusions.

Writers generally learn about audiences by starting with oneself and gradually broadening out to the general public. As the audiences become more abstract, a greater degree of writing skill is necessary to bridge the increasing distance between the writer and the reader. Meeting the needs of a general audience becomes more challenging than writing for oneself. While students develop an increasingly skilled repertoire of audiences for whom they write, your role as a sophisticated and caring responder continues. The key is to be *one* audience, not the *only* audience.

Students need practice communicating with real people if they are to muster measured thoughtfulness and a sense of audience interaction in their writing. As Gerald Graff (2000) puts it, traditional advice on how and what to write "is more paralyzing than helpful because it factors out the social conversation that reading, writing, and arguing must be part of in order to become personally meaningful" (48). To write is, very often, to enter into a conversation—to engage with others about ideas, agreed-upon assumptions, and points of difference. These are experiences that our students need if they are to write well. A well-developed sense of audience develops one way—through experience. Unfortunately, a discussion about imagined audience or a few exercises on word choice will not be all that developing writers need to hone their sense of audience. They need many opportunities to adjust their writing for real audiences, letting the interplay of writing and audience teach indirectly what no direct teaching can. Encourage students to practice and experiment with writing for various audiences, to read their writings to variety of audiences, and to learn by doing.

Thoughts on Form

Form in school involves one *format* most of the time: the five-paragraph "theme" or "essay." It's liberating for teachers of writing and their students to focus *less* on mode and format purity and *more* on how all modes, literary and rhetorical devices, and the recounting of facts and personal experiences contribute to an effective piece of writing when strategically selected. Doing so may take some courage.

Mention the word *form* in the company of writing teachers and you're likely to hear some very strong opinions in response. An emphasis on form—on structure—has dogged the teaching of writing for decades. In our test-happy era, slick form-focused methods are packaged and sold to teachers as panaceas for low writing scores.

Writing that follows a formula usually looks like what many think school writing should be. It has discernable paragraphs of fairly similar length. It has a controlling idea stated in an identifiable way. It has an opening, a middle, and a closing. Writing that has *form* or *structure* also is clearly organized, has sentences and paragraphs, and addresses a main point. The difference is that *structure* works in the service of meaning, while *formula* works in the service of rather simplistic and often mandated writing.

Consider this analogy. Imagine that you own one, and only one, container. You must carry, store, or drink from that one container; it's all you have. The container is a bucket. You want to pour yourself some orange juice? Get the bucket. You need to mix ingredients for a cake? Get the bucket. You need to move into a new home? Yes, get the bucket. You'll be making numerous trips between your old and new home with only a bucket to transport all of your possessions. People watching you will think you've lost your mind.

There are hundreds of specific, contextual situations that demand a variety of containers: a bowl, a paper bag, a freight train. The same idea applies for writing forms. Effective writing uses an appropriate form or structure—an appropriate container—to deliver its message. The writing situation governs the appropriate writing structure that writers opt to use. A single structure doesn't serve all purposes for writing, nor do skillful writers try to make one form fit all writing. Except, perhaps, in school.

Formulaic Writing, aka The Five-Paragraph Paper 5

The most prevalent structure for school writing is the five-paragraph paper. The formulaic five-paragraph essay (FPE) is the metaphoric phoenix of writing instruction. In article after article, researchers and practitioners alike have "burned" the form, explaining the FPE's drawbacks and limitations. Yet, it arises anew from the ashes. For each new generation of teachers, it springs back to life and is taught to a new generation of student writers as The Way to Write an Essay. As a writing form, it has an astonishing, nearly mythic, resilience.

Why does the FPE—and formulaic writing in general—have such strong appeal? First, it's a rather reliable way to get students to produce writing, any writing, on a blank piece of paper. In fact, when the FPE form is combined with more specific rules about thesis statements, topic sentences, and sentence types per paragraph, even lackluster students might write an entire essay by sticking to an easy-to-follow script. For teachers who struggle to get some students to write *anything*, this can be a highly attractive option, especially when students will need to produce writing on demand for a district- or state-level proficiency exam.

Second, the FPE is simple to evaluate. All highly formalized writing is fairly straightforward to grade. One question is key: Does the writing follow the formula? If yes, then the grade is likely a good one. If no, flashes of creative genius may earn a few points, but no good grade will be given to writing that doesn't follow the formula.

Because they are so highly structured, FPEs are often boring to read. Why? Most FPEs are heavy on structure and light on inspired and interesting content. In this era of do-or-die testing, a formula-driven piece of writing is generally enough to pass a class or move to the next grade level or give evidence that the student should be allowed to graduate.

Stop and think about that last sentence; reread it.

If the only reason we are doing something is to avoid negative consequences, we are unlikely to do more than minimally necessary to complete the task. Student writers need more authentic motivations to generate positive attitudes toward writing and the effort it takes to produce effective writing.

Third, FPEs live in schools. They simply don't exist outside of school. An overreliance on the FPE sends students the very clear message that writing is more about appearances—about structure—than content. Whether the author knows and writes anything worth saying seems to be less valued than having the thesis statement and the paragraphing right. This is perhaps the most troubling point about FPEs and the subtle message they send. In reality, how often is a writer able to "prove" a point in five easy paragraphs, and how often is that the most effective choice about the structure of the writing, given its purpose and audience?

We invite you to engage in that conversation with your colleagues to learn what you and they really think about FPEs specifically, and formulaic writing in general. Once you know what you think, consider how it affects what and how you teach writing. In the meantime, here's what we think.

Is Formulaic Writing Really So Bad?

Many teachers argue that the FPE focuses the student writer, necessitating clear and organized pieces of writing. Perhaps. It is certainly one of the building blocks of thinking about organization, purpose, and placement of main points. Unfortunately, the FPE is mechanistic. Reliance on the FPE truncates an examination of other forms, other ways of making an argument or presenting a case. Is it really so bad? Only when formulaic writing becomes the privileged writing in the classroom, the first and last resort, the default, the preference, the ultimate achievement.

Successful writers experiment. They figure out what form and artistic devices best suit a particular writing situation. Having options and not being afraid to use them distinguishes a skilled writer from one who has only a single, inadequate option.

High-Stakes Writing

We define *high-stakes writing* as any writing that students produce under pressure, in which they have little or no interest, and for which they may suffer adverse consequences if the writing falls short of expectations. Writing tests, by definition, are situations replete with high-stakes writing. Students aren't writing for fun or from interest, but because they are being compelled to do so. It doesn't end with testing, however. Schools are full of situations in which high-stakes writing occurs: exams, unit tests, timed writings, research papers, documented argumentation papers, and a range of written projects that count for a high percentage of a student's course grade.

Such writing is far from authentic. It's writing that is stressful and that students will seek to avoid but can't evade because high-stakes writing is usually evaluated or graded. In situations involving high stakes, students seek ways to cope with their stress. One common and unfortunate coping mechanism for high-stakes writing that students may try is plagiarism.

Before you face your first case of plagiarism, it's helpful to think about the causes and consequences of plagiarism. Also think about how to avoid it. How might you, as the teacher, lessen the lure of plagiarism for your students? We offer some of our ideas next. As you read, we invite you to brainstorm strategies that will work for you and to reflect upon how you will adapt our ideas to your teaching

Addressing Plagiarism

If your teaching of writing focuses on authentic writing and on the types of activities we've described, you're building a sense of confidence and control in students while also reducing some of the typical problems writing teachers face when they sit down with a stack of papers. One of the more serious of those problems is plagiarism. When writing is authentic, there's little, if anything, to plagiarize. The student writer is engaged in the topic and with the writing, expressing unique ideas to which she feels a connection. When students plagiarize, try to see it as a wake-up call that they aren't yet personally involved with the writing. The writing is not yet authentic for students who plagiarize. Regardless of the reason for its occurrence, plagiarized writing regularly inspires deep frustration among teachers and students.

Plagiarism occurs when the student writer (or any writer) passes off someone else's work as his own. Plagiarism is generally treated as a blend of fraud and stealing. Consequences range from receiving a zero on a plagiarized paper to suspension. These punishments and plain common sense communicate to most students that plagiarism is to be avoided.

Why, then, do some students still plagiarize? Let's examine some possibilities.

Reason 1: Students Don't Know the Rules

This explanation (much like traditional attitudes toward grammar errors) seems to be a default assumption, in part because the solution is then quite simple: Just tell students the definition of plagiarism, explain the rules for citing material, and provide the details for correct MLA documentation of sources. Throw in a discussion of the consequences for breaking the rules, and ignorance is no longer an excuse. Seems easy enough.

Not so fast. Consider that even in middle school, most students will have heard these rules (and the riot act) before. Why will one more rant make the rules abundantly clear this time? Consider, also, that teens are lax with similar rules, such as those related to music downloading and sharing, and notions of public access to materials become more complex. Entire industries have developed from the modern remix culture in which texts, including music, are borrowed, spliced, and repurposed without much regard for citation doctrine. Some teens may sincerely have difficulty seeing the point of strict citation rules.

Because most students find it hard to believe that their *own* writing has value and might deserve acknowledgment, they are highly unlikely to intuit the need to document scrupulously the use of another person's words. ("Words are cheap," or so we're told.) Ideally, however, we want students to understand and believe that the words and ideas of others carry value. Just telling kids "It's important" isn't working, or else we wouldn't still be talking about widespread plagiarism issues.

Try this. Discuss with your students the fact that authentic writing needs room within it for multiple voices, perspectives, and opinions. Writing is a kind of conversation in which everyone needs to know who said what. That's where documentation comes in. It provides space for others and is polite behavior. If you talk with your mouth full, wipe your hands on your shirt, and burp loudly at a dinner table, relationship consequences, such as fewer dates and dinner invitations, usually follow. Similarly, if students ignore conventions of documentation, they put themselves at risk with readers and damage the writer-to-audience relationship.

Reason 2: Some Students Are Just Lazy, Sneaky, or Plain Amoral

All students may not put forth an honest effort every time they write. Most will, under the right circumstances, but there are no guarantees. Even with the most enlightened and energetic teaching, a few students may decide not to do the work, and others may occasionally try to pull a fast one. When we come across an instance of obvious cheating and plagiarism, we treat it as a student's contextualized choice or reaction, not as a symptom of his overall moral failing.

Refuse to see your students as reprobates. Once started, this syndrome is fatal for the classroom community and toxic for your own professional well-being.

▦ Reason 3: Students Panic

It's the night before the research paper is due, and Kelly is scrambling. She's blown off working seriously on the paper until now, and she's horrified to realize that a last-minute writing marathon will not rescue her from this mess. Pressure mounts. She needs to get enough of the assignment done to scrape by with a C—or maybe a D—because her parents don't appreciate failing grades. Everything looks and feels like a hopeless mess. The paper needs to be a minimum of eight pages; she has two, and it's almost 1 am. She copies and pastes some "research" she finds on a website into her skeletal essay, adds some quotation marks around a few paragraphs, tosses in a couple of topic sentences and a short "In conclusion" section, prints it out, and throws in the towel. At least the misery is over, and maybe it'll be good enough to pass.

We suspect that something like Kelly's microdrama is a too-common experience for some students. A paper produced in this manner will likely fit some definition of plagiarism, with its unattributed material and borrowed filler dumped in as a last-ditch effort. Taken in perspective, these problems seem more a result of poor planning and desperation than a plot to deceive. Questions arise in most teachers' minds about why our students procrastinate to the point of such misery.

In cases like this one, work with your students on planning and timelines for completing projects in a reasonable manner. You may even need to impose a few due dates along the way for large projects so that both you and your students have a chance to stop the train wreck that is on the way. With practice, many students will internalize these strategies and begin to use them independently, helping them avoid situations that lead to a tendency to plagiarize and take other risky shortcuts.

▦ Reason 4: The Writing Assignment Is Predictable, and Abundant Materials and Options to Plagiarize Exist

Plagiarism only happens when we assign writing that is, well, plagiarizable. Producing sample papers for commonly assigned topics is a thriving Internet business, we're sad to say. Even students who don't pay for papers outright easily locate massive chunks of boilerplate content that, when inserted in a paper, may carry the sheen of authenticity. Generic assignments lacking specific relevance, choice, or opportunities to incorporate individual interests are easy targets for poor writing and for plagiarism.

Opportunities for plagiarism are mitigated by a healthy dose of forethought about the design, content, and scheduling of writing tasks. Even traditional assignments may be tweaked in small ways to make them locally unique. Your district demands a conventional research essay? Fine, but add crucial facets that require individual reflection and personal connections to the student writer. Try requiring a narrative thread that reveals the relevance of the topic to the writer's life or context, insights of classmates woven into the evidence, a sustained connection to a local event or news story, or a section linking this writing to previous inquiries undertaken by the class.

▦ Reason 5: The Stakes Are Too High

Having a single deadline for a heavily weighted piece of writing is just asking for trouble. We think of the joke about college classes: The first-year student enters a large auditorium filled with three hundred students taking Biology 101. The instructor enters, takes roll, and says, "Your paper on gene splicing that counts for 75 percent of your grade is due in six weeks. See you then." This is, of course, hyperbole, but students often feel that type of pressure for any long-term, do-or-die piece of writing.

For types of writing that require extensive time and effort by students, try creating specific checkpoints and charting out stages for project completion. Combined with alternative grading and feedback processes, checkpoints and planned stages for having various parts (a first draft, an annotated list of resources, a revision based on peer response) of the project due help more students stay on schedule. It also helps undo some of the paralysis students might feel when confronted by a significant and complex task.

We also advise devising projects that build upon one another—the "stacking" idea from Chapter 4—so that one piece of writing lays the groundwork for another. For example, a memoir piece might inform a problem analysis, which then morphs into a formal proposal. There's no need for students to leave their previous writing behind like a string of isolated and deserted islands, visited briefly and then forgotten.

With some reasoned effort, you really can lessen the opportunities for students to plagiarize their writing in your classes.

Specific Recommendations for Quoting, Paraphrasing, and Documenting

The conventions of quotation, paraphrase, and documentation are important, especially in formal academic contexts that depend upon establishing credibility with an audience. Our recommendations for dealing with these topics follow our same Fluency–Control–Precision model. Students need experience working through the process of manipulating outside information, including multiple opportunities to build confidence and a sense of control in low-stress situations, to refine their tactical abilities.

To address issues of ownership that underlie appropriate referencing, Darren uses comparisons to hip-hop and rap sampling, trademarked images, and clothing designs as a means to open discussion about the real ramifications of using someone else's ideas or work ethically, legally, and fairly. What if you designed some cool and unique skateboarding T-shirts only to find that someone else had seen your designs and begun printing and selling them himself? What if you discovered that your original comedy skit had been ripped off, posted on YouTube, gone viral, and generated lots of advertising revenue for someone else? Why are the controlling rights to published songs and music such a big deal? Why do Major League Baseball teams sometimes prevent Little League and high school programs from using imitations of their logos?

The parallels to incorporating outside information into one's own writing may not always be direct—at least initially—but that's okay. What's central here is a framework for understanding these concepts that focuses more on *reasons* than *rule following*. If it makes sense that a person's unique ideas, artwork, lyrics, and designs in fashion, music, and other creative spheres may have monetary value, it's not a huge leap to understand that one's own words might have a similar kind of merit.

Once this foundation for appropriate referencing has been discussed in ways that make sense, we're ready for more nuts-and-bolts matters. But even that discussion takes place in the spirit of conversation, rationality, and response. Consider the passage below.

> *World of Warcraft* is a very popular video game. There are millions of people who
> play this game almost every day. "MMORPGs were the fastest growing segment

of the video game industry from 2005 to 2010." Another popular online game is *Gears of War*.

This kind of "floating" quotation is common in students' writings. (We sometimes call it a *ghost quotation* since it comes and goes so mysteriously.) While we experienced readers immediately detect several problems with this passage, students often don't. Construct opportunities to help your students see things from a *readerly* point of view. Consider this sample interior monologue of a reader (in brackets below) working through this passage:

> *World of Warcraft* is a very popular video game. [*Okay, I understand the focus here on a certain video game. That's clear.*] There are millions of people who play this game almost every day. [*Here's a bit more on the popularity of the game. I'm with you. So far so good. But wait; what's this next thing? Quotation marks?*] "MMORPGs were the fastest growing segment of the video game industry from 2005 to 2010." [*Suddenly there's someone else talking here. Who is it? The writer? Is it someone else? And what the heck are MMORPGs? Now I'm totally lost.*]

The goal is to help students see that outside material doesn't stand alone well; it doesn't make much sense on its own. Quotations are strangers amid our own words and thoughts, and they need help to get along, just like a newcomer to a party needs an introduction to avoid awkwardness. Also like social situations, a name and a context help everyone feel at ease. Consider the merits of this piece with its proper citation:

> *World of Warcraft* is a very popular video game. There are millions of people who play this game almost every day. According to *Jacked In*, a top magazine for gamers, "MMORPGs were the fastest growing segment of the video game industry from 2005 to 2010." Another popular online game is *Gears of War*.

This piece isn't perfect, but it's a step in the right direction. As readers, we are introduced to an authority on the subject before encountering the actual quotation. We still might need some help on the whole MMORPGs business, but we are set to work on improvements step by step.

Discussions about integrating quotations are just that: discussions, not lectures or rule recitations. Use examples with your students that illustrate how a potential reader might react, line by line and word by word. Students don't necessarily need to know that the technical term here is *attribution* and that it can actually occur at the beginning, the end, or in the middle of a quotation. We'll get to those options later, just as we'll get to block quotations and other related topics. In the beginning, emphasize taking care of the reader when working with outside material. This approach is consistent with our model of fluency to control to precision: Students need to build confidence and fluency with how to cite works appropriately through practice, and we need to allow the time and space for their fluency to grow into control and precision.

Knowing how to manage quotations, paraphrases, and citations are both more important and less important than students may think. On timed writing exams, the ability to attribute outside sources smoothly and confidently is an indicator of writing proficiency—one of those subtle flags that results in higher scores because it tells a scorer that *this student knows how to write.* It's less important, however, because many proficient writers use quotations sparingly. Students learn that quoting is characteristic of much formal writing, but they may then draw the mistaken conclusion that using a bazillion quotations is a yellow brick road to good writing.

Students benefit from knowing how to contextualize and use quotations sparingly. As a rule of thumb, we recommend that any quotation be followed by two or more sentences from the writer that explain, situate, or otherwise comment upon this outside information. As with all such advice, students are free to experiment with their options as they gain control and a sense of audience expectations.

Many times, writing flows more smoothly when students paraphrase rather than quote outside sources. Paraphrasing is the real indicator of fluency when dealing with outside material, and it's no surprise that students tend to avoid it. To put other writing "in your own words," and do it well, student writers really have to do the following:

- Read the outside material.
- Comprehend it, which usually requires rereading it.
- Summarize it, which takes some time and effort to do accurately.
- Evaluate its interest, importance, and relevance.
- Decide which ideas in it are worthy of discussing in their own writing.

These complex cognitive operations all happen before anything is actually paraphrased, which requires some focused effort and thinking. And it takes time. In comparison, simply finding a sentence to quote looks a lot easier. The process of thinking about other writing—letting someone else's idea settle (or marinate or gestate or whatever metaphor you like best) in your thoughts and relating it to your own thinking is essential to advanced academic writing. Reading well goes hand in hand with writing well. The ability to summarize often gets pawned off as a low-level skill, but it's actually a key strategy for many kinds of writing. Students have opportunities to practice this thinking-centered work in many classroom contexts that focus on concision ("Summarize, in one sentence, the essential tensions our discussion explored today") or elaboration ("Write a paragraph that explains the primary points of the essay you reviewed").

Finally, you won't be surprised that we take a similar real-world discussion-focused angle on documentation formalities. We don't waste time on the minutiae of citation formatting; we use handbooks and websites for that detailed stuff. We focus again on *reasons* (why include source information at all?) and *metaphorical explanations* (such as in-text citations acting as hyperlinks to sources on an end-of-text list) that demystify and help students gain a measure of understanding and control of the process.

We encourage you to pursue lines of discussion with students that move this topic away from arbitrary drudgery toward practical, low-stress understanding. You'll still get to those deeper questions of responsibility and fairness without the antagonism and drama. Renee Hobbs' book *Copyright Clarity* (2010) is essential reading for teachers interested in educating themselves about issues of permission, fair use, and acknowledgment when using the work of others. We're all familiar with copyright as legal protection for creators, but Hobbs explains that *users of copyrighted material have rights too.* Her book does indeed help to clarify a murky, rumor-ridden subject and is thus helpful for students and teachers alike.

Primarily, we urge you to focus with your students on writing that is authentic. It's the best—and least likely to be plagiarized—type of writing in which students may engage.

Writing as an Essential, Lifelong Activity

Teaching writing is hard work. It is work our students often do not appreciate. What we English teachers know that our students may not, however, is that writing is a lifelong activity that exists well beyond school, just as reading does. We want students to be lifelong readers, writers, and learners. One of the key ways to *learn* is to *read* and *write* about what you *think*.

For most of us, writing becomes a volitional activity. We discover that we need or want (or both) to write; we have a message we want to convey to someone "out there," whether that is someone in our family or the general public. Most of us ultimately will *choose* to write to convey meaning at least a few times in our lives. We will choose to engage in authentic writing.

In short, we teach writing because it exists in the real world and is imminently useful outside of school. Our students have something to say, voices and media through which to say it, people who want to receive their meaning, and valid reasons for wanting to convey it. Writing is a real-life, relevant activity that encompasses all manner of professional, communicative, and creative challenges. By writing, we work through problems and solutions, we think about topics important to us, and we make meaning that we may elect to communicate with others. What happens in your classroom ideally provides students with perceptive skills in identifying issues; flexibility, confidence, and experience in addressing unique situations; and the rhetorical savvy to choose apt strategies appropriate to the circumstances. In short, it provides them with all they need to engage in authentic writing as a lifelong pursuit.

Works Cited

Britton, James, Tony Burgess, Nancy Martin, Alex McLeod, and Harold Rosen. 1975. *The Development of Writing Abilities (11–18)*. London: Macmillan Education.

Graff, Gerald. 2000. "Disliking Books at an Early Age." In: *Falling into Theory: Conflicting Views on Reading Literature,* edited by David H. Richter, 41–48. New York: Bedford.

Hobbs, Renee. 2010. *Copyright Clarity: How Fair Use Supports Digital Learning.* Thousand Oaks, CA: Corwin.

Leonard, Elmore. 2001. "Writers on Writing; Easy on the Adverbs, Exclamation Points and Especially Hooptedoodle." Arts. *New York Times.* July 16, 2001. p. 1.

Patterson, Joanna. 2007. "Writing with Authenticity." Confident Writing: The Art of Writing for Non Writers. Blog. Available online at www.confidentwriting.com/2007/08/writing-with-au-2. Viewed May 1, 2012.

7

Crafting Essays

Close the door. Write with no one looking over your shoulder. Don't try to figure out what other people want to hear from you; figure out what you have to say. It's the one and only thing you have to offer. —**Barbara Kingsolver**

Let's face it. Many of our students' essays come under the heading of "passing along information of which we are in no great need." More unsuccessful teaching of writing has been done in the name of essay writing than any other form. Sadly, teaching the traditional essay poorly does not just produce bad prose. Too often in our effort to teach the essay, we inadvertently teach kids to give up the very skills and instincts that have made them good writers of narrative and poetry. Worse, we miss a great opportunity to lead our students to discover their own beliefs and to become thoughtful and articulate spokespersons for those beliefs.

In contrast to the deadly boring exercises typically called "essays" in schools, the contemporary essay is alive and taking on new forms and finding new readers. Take a look at a fine piece of nonfiction by Lewis Thomas, a well-crafted essay by John McPhee, a memoir by a contemporary Southern writer like Janice Ray, or contemporary essays such as those by Cynthia Ozick or Barbara Kingsolver or Michael Chabon. Notice how these writers blur the sharp lines of form, putting all of the elements of good writing to work. Perhaps even more importantly, observe how the essay functions not as monologue, but rather as a conversation between the writer and the reader. We encourage teachers and students alike to read and explore many examples of the modern essay to get a sense of how the form and its content have been reborn as a more artful literary *genre*.

Contemporary essays borrow heavily from narrative and descriptive writings. The contemporary essay as literary nonfiction is an easily accessible and popular form. It is, for us, the expositional form of choice in our teaching. Literary nonfiction blurs the lines among many genres of writing; it is highly literate, using the figurative language of fiction such as metaphor, foreshadowing, and character development; yet, it is nonfiction, essay writing. We see the popularity of contemporary essays in best-selling magazines and journals, and in collections of the best essays of each year.

Literary nonfiction generates new possibilities for understanding the self and others via inquiry and reflective processes that both pose and attempt to answer questions. Our classrooms have become livelier places because inquiry lives in them. Our students' minds are engaged in making meanings, drawing conclusions from data, and in finding answers. Research no longer equals regurgitation.

It's time to reconsider our assumptions about the essay and to see it as a lively form in which a writer tries to create an authentic communication with a reader. It's time to see the essay, as Alan Lightman suggests, "not as an assignment to be dispatched efficiently and intelligently, but as an exploration, a questioning, an introspection" (2000). It's time to see the essay as an opportunity for our young writers to enter larger conversations with thoughtful, knowledgeable, and measured voices.

What's to Be Done?

For us, using the same strategies that we use when we teach students to write poems, short stories, or chapters for a book are appropriate for teaching students how to write essays. First, we get them excited about a subject and get them talking about it with peers. We encourage them to read numerous examples of the *genre*, and we look with writers' eyes at many models as we work on a particular essay. We encourage students to jot, to write notes to generate ideas for the essay, and to write exploratory drafts to think through their ideas. We create opportunities for them to read drafts aloud to other readers. We admonish them to read whatever they can get their hands on that helps them clarify their ideas. We ask them to check to see if what they've written represents their thoughts and ideas. Subject, language, and form work together when they get rolling. We show them how to move pieces of text around and try them out. As they work at the difficult task of making sense of the subject for themselves, the pieces start to fit together naturally. We encourage them to tinker with language and reflect on expression until it feels right. We remind them that writing processes take a long time and that their writing will get messy and frustrating, but that's the road all writers take toward shaping a meaningful essay. At the end of this process, if all goes well, they have found ideas worth communicating and a suitable form in which to express those ideas. What follows are ideas on how to engage students in these challenging processes.

Introducing a Variety of Essay Forms

We have found it useful and refreshing to introduce students to new and alternative formats in which to couch their ideas: critiques, reviews, white papers, belief papers (Here I Stand), editorials, investigative reports (I-Search), anthropological pieces, case studies, college application essays, historical pieces, change pieces, performance essays, scientific treatises, problem–solution pieces, speculative pieces—all of these writings have been useful to us in our teaching and to our students as they work on writing insightful essays.

■ White Papers

Technically *official reports*, white papers present an analysis of the state of things and possibly a position or recommendation. This form requires writers to have a solid grasp of their facts and information and to document their writing with solid evidence. White papers usually either recommend a particular course of action or lay out plausible alternatives. The voice is measured and reasoned. Large corporations, city governments, environmental groups, and various federal agencies write such pieces; plenty of models are available online. We have used white papers as outcomes for group inquiry and research during which students identify a pressing, problematic issue and then propose a solution or options for resolutions. In that case, various members of the group author sections of the paper. When composed and featured on a wiki or other online platform, white papers can serve as a public mission statement for larger ongoing projects.

Critiques and Reviews

Critiques are the backbone of writing for the college English major, but we aren't born knowing how to do this type of analytic writing. To ease students into critiques, Dawn has her students write movie reviews. She begins by having students brainstorm a list of favorite movies, new and old. Once they have a good list of titles, they talk to a partner about what makes that particular movie a favorite. Is it the action in the movie? Is it the lead actor? Is it the cinematography? Is it the soundtrack? After that, Dawn shows students the opening segment of two radically different movies. Students then discuss the features of the two opening segments that are noteworthy. Next, students brainstorm potential features of a movie that they might critique: acting, direction, cinematography, special effects, writing, editing, music, casting, originality of story line, and so on. After that, Dawn and her students go online to read reviews of favorite movies written by professional critics or local reviewers. They study the purpose and order of each paragraph in the review: plot summary, features of the movie, strengths and weaknesses of the movie, and the reviewer's professional analysis and personal opinion of the movie. Then, they write their own critiques.

Critiques and reviews help students practice audience awareness and anticipation. Part of the challenge is to write in such a way that a reader gets a sense of the text under critique—the film, article, advertisement, or story—without having actually read or seen the original. Conveying that level of familiarity and detail means describing and summarizing effectively: being complete but also being concise.

Here I Stand Papers

This type of essay encourages students to clarify their own opinions and beliefs and then to go out on a limb and state publicly where they stand on a particular issue. The *I* voice is important in these papers, but the *I* must engage the *you*, so the writer has a real responsibility to anticipate the audience's needs for understanding this position. The writer needs to acknowledge that there may be other legitimate viewpoints. We want the writer to come to a strong statement of her position, but we try to encourage the student to avoid inflammatory rhetoric so as not to create a "My way or the highway" tone for these pieces.

I-Search Papers

Ken Macrorie (1988) developed this form as an alternative to the traditional term or research paper. It's a classic that is still in frequent use because of the ways in which it bridges personal and research writings. Here, the student writer investigates a topic to which he is personally connected in some way by past experience, avid interest, family circumstances, cultural connections, linguistic links, or in other ways. Then, the student finds unique data sources to plumb for information. Instead of using traditional research, the student conducts interviews with key informants such as family members or notable people in the community who are knowledgeable about the topic. Perhaps the student writer devises a survey and then conducts it with the affected members of the culture or linguistic group. After the data are gathered, the student writer determines findings from the data and draws conclusions about the topic under consideration. The final I-Search paper includes information about *why* the student was personally compelled to the topic, about *the process* the student decided to use to gather data, about *what* the data are and what they revealed, and about the conclusions the student drew as a result. This type of *I-Search*—not mere *re-search*—helps the student to find personally meaningful answers to inquiry rather than regurgitating information found in some Internet or traditional research source.

Editorials

We like editorials for several reasons: There are many examples of these around, topics have a broad range, and the form and voice are quite flexible. Like white papers, students need to have accurate facts and information in hand; and like the Here I Stand paper, they need to be aware of the audience out there as they write. Asking students to direct their efforts toward an on-the-fence, skeptical reader offers them the opportunity to think strategically about how to phrase their positions moderately and reasonably.

Investigative Reports

Caution: Opportunities for getting into hot water ahead. There are, no doubt, many injustices and potential targets for investigation in your school. Before you send your students on a muckraking quest, however, be sure that your administrators want the harsh light of student investigation turned upon the school culture. We have found many students energized by the opportunity to research an issue that bothers them about their school. Favorite topics include whether athletes receive preferential treatment in some classes, why our school has certain restrictions that the neighboring high school does not, and why we pay parking fees and they don't. An investigation requires strong interview skills and a well-designed plan for collecting information. We always require that students show us their plan for data collection before we give our blessing to their hunt for truth.

Anthropological and Case Studies

For this type of writing, we lead students to find an environmental, a social, or a cultural issue (or some combination of these) that they want to investigate: What effect has the new freeway had on the marshes located beside it? A formerly rundown area of town has been renovated, and both the city government and local retailers have spent several hundred thousand dollars on the project; are the people in that area better off than they were prior to the renovation? A nearby school is expanding its course offerings to include classes held at downtown locations and online; is the quality of education improving for the students taking the more convenient courses?

Their job in this kind of writing is to analyze an issue or problem with a specific purpose in mind. No one gathers data or examines a subject randomly—we must have a reason for setting off on this kind of work. Purposes can range from self-education ("I just want to find out more about this problem") to informing others ("How can I explain the complete situation to an average person so that it makes sense?") to motivating some kind of action ("After they read this, I want people to care enough to attend a town hall meeting to voice their opinion about new biking trails").

Your job is to help students to focus on the issue in a step-by-step process:

- Guide students to find an issue they want to stick with for a while.
- Help them form questions to guide their inquiry.
- Work with them to decide whom they need to interview, whether surveys would yield useful data, what public records they need to read, and what locations they need to visit.
- Question them about what eye-witness reporting or descriptions would be helpful in detailing the problem.
- Ask them to explain how their purpose for undertaking this investigation will affect how they write their final paper.

In addition to asking students to write about their guiding questions, data sources, data collection methods, and conclusions, also invite students to reflect and write about the challenging aspects related to the inquiry. If they were to continue this study, what additional information might they need? Have they reached definitive answers to their questions? This kind of writing and thinking not only leads students to sharpen their powers of observation and inquiry but it also helps them to develop multiple perspectives on the world around them.

College Application Essays

Most college entrance applications still require a biographical essay or some other writing that asks for personal disclosure. We frequently offer students an opportunity to develop a personal essay that is both measured in voice and well documented in content. Such an essay also tests the writer's ability to speculate about the essay's audience and the hidden criteria that audience may bring to the reading of such expectations of a particular audience. Recently, Kyle L. Wray, Associate VP for Enrollment Management and Marketing at Oklahoma State University, has stirred the pot of the traditional college entrance essay. His initiative was to move to more thoughtful and comprehensive prompts requiring the student to synthesize, analyze, and throw in a cup of creativity as well with prompts such as the following:

- "If you were able to open a local charity of your choice, what type of charity would it be, how would you draw people to your cause, and whom would it benefit?"
- "Today's movies often feature superheroes and the supernatural. If you could have one superpower, what would it be, and how would you use it? Who would be your archenemy, and what would be his or her superpower?" (Jaschik 2011)

Writing contexts change; even something as traditional as the college application essay is in flux. That's why students need flexibility and knowledge about how to craft writing for the specific audience and occasion at hand. Admissions committees don't have to be mysterious and inscrutable entities. They tend to look for well-thought-out and well-crafted prose with a sense of individuality and confidence. Practice helps. Offer your students a series of traditional and more avant-garde topics to try and perhaps discuss the merits of each; but prepare them for both. Doing so extends their flexibility with written essays.

Historical Pieces

Pieces in which students trace family histories or the history of a place or in which they chronicle a particular cultural tradition in which their family participates are always favorites in our classes. Histories of particular family members give students the opportunity to learn about their own family and to celebrate a relative. These pieces invite the use of narratives and of interview data as well as offering student writers the chance to do a little historical investigation.

Change Piece I—Evolution and Revolution

Change pieces engage students in looking at a phenomenon or a set of ideas over time. Our best students have written change pieces on such diverse topics as "The NFL Quarterback: From Johnny Unitas to Michael Vick," "Jazz Trumpeters: Dizzy Gillespie, Miles Davis, and Wynton Marsalis," and "The Evolution of the Racing Bicycle." This form particularly lends itself to the performance essay (discussed below), with writers free to add photos, art, and music to supplement their essays.

Change Piece II—Influence and Impact

Pop culture offers endless fascination to students, and we leverage this interest by asking students to investigate and explain the more subtle relationships that exist among artists, musicians, films, and similar phenomena. Online resources are especially useful for these inquiries. As an example, Darren has had great success with directing students to *Rolling Stone* magazine's website, which offers an artist directory with information about hundreds of musical acts including listings for "related artists." Lady Gaga's entry lists Madonna, David Bowie, and Christina Aguilera as related artists, information that naturally raises questions. How is Gaga's music related to or impacted by David Bowie's work? What does Gaga borrow from Madonna? How, in turn, has she influenced later artists in specific ways?

Change Piece III—Analog Versus Digital

For this piece, we ask students to delve into the growing gaps between traditional analog and more contemporary digital information. We think the growing divide and difference between analog and digital texts, tools, and communication open interesting ground for students to investigate and analyze. What are the pros and cons of one-stop online sources of massive information as compared to that of traditional encyclopedias? What is beneficial about using an e-reader to read a novel electronically instead of reading a hardcopy, paper, and bound edition? If I want to get in shape, should I do it the old-fashioned way of walking and lifting weights, or will I have better results if I use a video program designed to feel like a game and to challenge my balance and endurance? Darren also extends the analog and digital dichotomy a bit to include older and newer forms of media: Is it more fun to play an online game such as *World of Warcraft* or a dice-and-paper game like *Dungeons and Dragons*? Why do teens text more than talk on a phone? The contemporary default opinion seems to be that digital is best, but young people are well positioned to interrogate and tease out issues connected to the status quo and the avant-garde.

Performance Essays

One of the best ways for students to learn about how an audience will "read" their essays is to create a two-part essay assignment. First, students compose essays that they believe other students will find interesting and engaging. Then, plan a time when students perform their essays for the class. We use some of the many essays that are read on National Public Radio as examples of how to perform the essay; Garrison Keillor's *A Prairie Home Companion* radio show is another good example. Students are free to use props and visual aids to illustrate their points and entertain listeners. Some of our favorites are essays about music, art, and pop culture. An alternative to a physical performance is creating a digital film, an attractive option for the budding cinematographers and directors among your students.

Scientific Treatises

Essays that advance scientific ideas or explain scientific phenomena in layman's terms can be interesting and entertaining. Look at the work of Isaac Asimov, Stephen J. Gould, Jane Goodall, Loren Eiseley, Stephen Hawking, and Annie Dillard, for example. Often science students are some of our most original and passionate thinkers. Encourage them to read and employ the techniques of the contemporary science writers found in journals and magazines such as *Discover, Audubon, Wired,* and *National Geographic*, or websites such as Slashdot.org and BoingBoing.net. You might challenge students to render a concept or controversy into accessible "person on the street" language, or task them with explaining a complex idea to a younger student who is having trouble understanding it. These situations keep students from simply parroting technical jargon while requiring them to process, comprehend, and reimagine concepts from different perspectives.

Problem–Solution Pieces

Dawn has her students brainstorm problems that they see around them, either at school or in their neighborhoods. Students discuss their lists with a partner to hear themselves talk about the problem. The writer selects a problem, offers *one* best solution, and writes a paper in which he argues effectively for that solution. In the past, some of Dawn's students have chosen as problems the cost of extra fees included in college tuition, city bus routes that are inconveniently scheduled, the issue of putting a trash landfill near a particular neighborhood, or the high cost of car insurance for students. The solution must be realistic, cost-effective, rational, and believable.

Statistics and data may help students support their arguments, so some research and documentation of sources may be necessary. Another strong factor is personal experience: How is the writer directly connected with the problem? Such personal experience lends the writer a voice of authority, which is an important feature for a proposal. Problem–solution pieces, or *proposals*, as they are sometimes called, are a type of writing that students may have to do in the "real" world of business, so we stress the connection to future writing on the job.

Multiple Solution Pieces

A variation on the problem–solution piece is a piece that asks students to examine a complex problem and to propose more than one possible and plausible solution for ameliorating that problem. A notable model for these pieces is former President Jimmy Carter, who has authored multiple solutions for intransigent problems in third-world countries. In the writers' papers, there is no one best solution, but rather the writers offer a cost-benefit analysis for several alternative solution scenarios that may be equally effective for solving the problem under consideration. Obviously, some groups will prefer one solution over another, but the idea is to become the think tank expert for the affected groups facing the problem. These papers challenge the writer to develop a thorough understanding of an impasse and to engage in a careful analysis of the various groups that are at odds. Multiple Solution Pieces must speak with reason and persuasion to multiple audiences. These pieces offer good practice for entering the diplomatic service or for being a teacher.

Proposals, Modest or Otherwise

Another slightly different twist on the problem–solution paper addresses the tendency of students to offer advice on complex problems with little thoughtful deliberation. Proposal writing requires students to construct a careful analysis of a problem or a need. The analysis must make use of data and be submitted to a panel of peers for scrutiny. Other writers usually vigorously critique frivolous or half-baked analyses. Then, as the problem analysis is reworked and writers begin to develop solution scenarios, they conduct feasibility studies and ultimately develop a budget and justify the economic and social viability of their proposal. That sounds pretty sophisticated—and it is—but we have had relatively average student writers author proposals on such diverse topics as altering the school's daily schedule, forming a more representative student government, financing school clubs for rock climbing and fly-fishing, taking field trips to exotic places, and initiating service learning projects in the community. Of course, we welcome satiric proposals if they are terribly clever and well done.

What's Next?

After students have worked with topics, drafts, and forms, it's time for them to work with voice and language choices in their essays.

Helping Students Write Their Way into Drafts

We have found that the pathway from brainstorming ideas to writing a successful draft can be a tortuous journey for some of our writers. The energy and fun of thinking about and playing with a topic is difficult to sustain as the writer stares at a blank page or screen and contemplates how to begin. Students need to live with their topics awhile—a few days, a week—collecting and recording ideas, information, and opinions from many different sources. Finding an interesting topic and watching it grow and take shape in the mind is important groundwork for effective essay writing. Organization and structure grow naturally from such explorations because the exploration itself begins to suggest its own organizational scheme.

We encourage students to write exploratory pieces to extend their thinking about their topics and to begin to organize what they know about a topic. Writers gain control over their knowledge base when they write out what they are thinking, connecting, and questioning. The following are some of the exploratory pieces that we use with our students.

Here and Now

Take the Here and Now concept explained in Chapter 4 and use it as a specific tool for advancing thinking by giving students a chance to practice and play with a subject. Students explore in short notes what they know and need to know. Tell students that Here and Nows are written right now, reflecting what they are thinking today about their topics and what knowledge they currently have. These are in-the-present writings that may help students see what they already know, hear what they have to say, and discover interesting questions.

Here and Nows can be recorded in a Thinker's Log. Use these entries to nudge students along. Help them keep their topics lively by consistently bringing in new bits and pieces of information, contrasting viewpoints, or downright puzzling and confusing ideas related to their topics. By the time the students sit down in earnest to compose their essays, they will likely have ten or more pages in their Thinker's Log of resource material and of personal reflections recorded in their own voices. The Here and Nows have been the bait on which they nibble. They have thought through their subject in a variety of ways and become more expert and interested.

Dispatches and Bulletins

We love the Annie Dillard quote from her book *The Writing Life*: "When you write . . . you go where the path leads. At the end of the path, you find a box canyon. You hammer out reports, dispatch bulletins" (1990). Ask students to write dispatches to you or to their writing response groups on where they are in their topic exploration. What are their big questions? What sources have they found that are especially helpful? About what contradictions and unresolved issues are they stewing? How do they think their essay might develop? What kinds of information and specific details do they yet need to find? How are their work habits? When will they be ready to attempt a draft? What kind of specific help do they need right now? These dispatches confirm for student writers that they own the writing on which they are working, and it makes them accountable to other potential readers as well. Dispatches also inform the teacher about where each student is in the essay-writing process and who needs what kind of coaching and encouragement.

Speculative Pieces

Encourage your students to ask themselves questions about their inquiry and writing, and then try to answer them. What would this piece be about? What would be difficult about trying to write on this question? Where would a good place be to begin the piece? Are my ideas clear in my own mind? Would a title help me now? What else do I need to know about my topic? Can I create a map for this piece yet? What are the chunks of text I already have that I can use? What other chunks do I still need to write? These meta-pieces turn students inward to examine their own thought processes and direct them away from the need for constant coaching and advice from others. This writing problem is theirs to solve.

Blast Pieces

These are espresso pieces written with energy and drive. Tell your students not to wait until they have all their ducks in a row. Tell them to assemble as many pieces of the topic as they can and then to *blast* into a draft to assess where they are in its development. You might organize your class so that on a given day they all do a blast piece. Or tell them to practice at home by setting time limits and goals: "Tell yourself you're going to write for thirty minutes or two pages or until dinner time." Remind your student writers to write as hard and as fast as they can to see if they can push through their inertia and fear into a rough first draft. Tell them not to quit too soon, but to go as far as they can. Encourage them to find the flow, to let the writing energize them. Then put the piece away and return to it later for a scan and to mark good stuff and begin again.

Spider Pieces

In Whitman's poem, "The Noiseless, Patient Spider," the spider begins to construct a web by spinning out single filaments, one after the other. Initially, the filaments just float in the air and fail to connect. But finally, one of those threads catches hold, creating a solid anchor around which the web can be spun. Students can compose short pieces in the same way, looking for their hook filament piece. Provide a series of in-class practice sessions for spider pieces in which your students try writing an opening or a conclusion, or they try writing in different voices and for different readers. Encourage them to shift tense from past to present. Suggest that they shift person from third to first or vice versa. Help them to see their topics from different angles and different vantage points. They don't need to try to link these spider pieces. As writers, they are looking for a hook or an anchor piece, some idea around which they will be able to spin their essay.

Opposition Pieces

Some topics are not cut-and-dried. They may be ambiguous and lend themselves to contrasting viewpoints. Many solid ideas have an upside and a downside. Structure an opportunity for writers to explore the contrasts and oppositions in their topic: then and now, good for some and bad for others, sometimes but not always, "It was the worst of times and it was the best of times." After they have written on several sides of their topic, ask them to see if they can construct a consensus piece or at least find a balanced and measured approach to the topic.

Talking Pieces

Some student writers do their best writing when they relax and just engage in an internal monologue. Give them permission to write notes to themselves. Suggest that they talk to a partner about the problem they're having with the topic or with the drafting. Tell them to talk about the events of the moment. They might make excuses for their frustrations with the essay. They could blame others. Encourage them to talk to themselves as a way of breaking the tension and stress they are feeling about the writing task and to talk themselves into new understandings.

List Pieces

Perhaps the ultimate stalling strategy is to make lists. We all kill time waiting for inspiration by jotting a list. Suggest to those students who appear to be really stuck that, at the very least, they can make lists of things they need to be doing and thinking about where to begin their essays. Initially, they may not make lists about the essay assignment; they may drift into "What do I have to get done before prom?" or "What is due in all of my other classes by the end of the semester?" Those are favorite stalling lists. Give them time to list anything; then, tell them to put away anything that isn't related to their topic. Admonish them to gather together as many viable writing ideas on their topics as they can and to stare at them. Provide opportunities for them to share those lists with someone else. Encourage them to set some goals and some deadlines. Challenge them to promise someone they'll have a draft to share by a specific date.

Exploring Drafts

All of these written explorations help students discover what they don't know about their topics and the holes in their thinking. Such gaps are not only the stuff of literary deconstruction; they are also the catalyst for more reading, research, writing, thinking, and planning. Once students' thinking begins to gel, they are ready to write exploratory drafts of their essay.

Recall our model of writing progression from Chapter 2: Writers develop *fluency*, then *control*, and finally, *precision* with their writing. We might say this concept a bit differently by indicating that writers need to "get it down" before they "get it right." Drafting precedes fixing, revising, crafting. Once student writers have engaged in a variety of explorations, they are ready—or about as ready as they will ever be—to draft. See drafts as one more way that students work on written fluency. Help them to move into drafts with optimism, accomplishment, and the realization that drafts are evolving—not finished—works.

After students have several drafts under their belts, they're ready to work on getting it right—that is, on crafting.

Guiding Principles in Crafting Essays

Essays are variable in tone, purpose, style, and content. Essays may be as varied as the writers who compose them. Really good essayists have a distinctive voice, manner of expression, and defined range of topics on which to expound: the national debt, the ills or benefits of technology, how robust American businesses are and what they need to do to improve, or even the latest fashionista must-have items of clothing. With such variety, what principles hold together as a group of best practices, guidelines, or instructional techniques to yield our students' best writing? As you have been reading this chapter, you have probably been thinking about how you will use some of these ideas with your students or how you might adapt them to suit your expertise and personality. We encourage you to continue that type of thinking as you read our ideas for how to lead students to move from idea to finished product, from rough draft to a crafted essay.

Use the Draft as Discovery

Encourage students to carry all of their preliminary thinking from logs and jottings into the draft-writing phase. Because students may find essay writing more complex than other types of writing, you may find they need considerable time for drafting their pieces. Try to keep them from committing to a final draft too early. Encourage discovery drafts, recommending that they delay outlining or other formal organization structures until they have fully explored their topic. Outlines often enslave inexperienced writers, taking away the opportunity to discover spontaneously an organizational structure and an appropriate scheme for developing ideas. A discovery draft shows a student writer where the paper is light on content, where transitions are lacking, and where more thinking is needed. The draft forces students to resee the topic they are exploring. These exploratory or discovery drafts, which may be written in a timeframe of twenty to sixty minutes, depending on how much time you have, serve as a commitment by students to get the ideas with which they have been working onto paper.

Even more important, the discovery draft is a place where new ideas are born and new information discovered. In a classic analogy, James Britton et al. likens the writing of a draft to a person "pushing the boat out from shore hoping it will land someplace" (1975). Confident writers push the boat out fearlessly because they have been out before and know it will not drift indefinitely. Unpracticed writers need more support and encouragement during the discovery draft because they may be less sure about where a piece is going. Many writers discover what they know by playing around with a topic, turning it over in their minds, jotting down ideas, and working them over in informal writings.

Encourage Students to Use Their Own Language

We're not suggesting that student essays be couched in teenage slang, but neither should they be laden with adult jargon. The best language for essay writing is language the writer knows. To borrow the words of others or to falsify one's own language is to doom the individual voice in essay prose. The debate around the use of the *I* pronoun in essay writing still exists, but contemporary writers are very likely to use the personal pronoun in their published works. We try to blunt the argument about the use of *I* by teaching students that there is an *I* that means *me* and an *I* that really means *us* or *we*. Is that confusing? In the hands of a good essay writer, *I* is not an egocentric or arrogant pronoun; rather, it is an inclusive one that speaks not only for the writer, but also for the reader. Arguments about whether the *I* pronoun is appropriate are futile at this point. The piece itself and the writer's own language resources dictate appropriate pronoun and diction choices. Inexperienced writers lacking in intuitions about appropriateness may merely need suggestions and feedback from their audience.

We support and encourage a student's attempts to find a unique voice. Rather than lock students' voices out of the writing, we encourage students to tell us what they are trying to say. They usually can. After they have told us their ideas orally, we nod and say, "Yes. Now, go write that." Students have words. Maybe we'll help them reconsider the exact word choice later (that's part of revision, after all), but students need to get beyond the fear of formal language and into the making of meaning. If language interferes with meaning, we need to help, but we do not need to inflict our voice on their writing.

Encourage Students to Use Personal Allusions or Cite Personal Evidence

The contemporary essay is rarely impersonal, detached, and devoid of expressive detail. In the past, in our attempts to help our students distinguish between informal and formal writing, we have overstated these differences or even described the division as a dichotomy. Effective essays, the kind people actually read and enjoy, are impossible to dichotomize. That's what we're finding in contemporary literary nonfiction. The writer uses what works for the expression of meaning; the writer is not limited by format. In a classic explanation of the ways in which literary techniques apply to any type of writing, Nancy Martin and colleagues suggest that

> Much effective writing seems to be on a continuum somewhere between the expressive and the transactional. This applies to adult as well as children's writing. What is worrying is that in much school writing, the student is expected to exclude expressive features. . . . The demand for impersonal, unexpressive writing can actively inhibit learning because it isolates what is to be learned from the vital learning process—that of making links between what is already known and the new information. The [effective] essay writing task asks the student to reconcile what he/she already knows with new knowledge or experience. As a student develops as a writer, he/she should be more able to bring appropriate inner resources to bear on knowledge of the outside world. (1976)

Are you surprised by how many years ago that was written and by how contemporary the issue sounds?

Sadly, too many of us have continued to teach exposition as a nineteenth-century phenomenon, ignoring the new, more exciting directions essay writing has taken. We've been using the wrong models—models that do not represent the range of contemporary exposition. Writers such as Loren Eiseley, Tom Wolfe, Rick Bass, Annie Dillard, Maxine Hong Kingston, Joan Didion, and Alice Walker, to name a few, have certainly found new ways to enliven essay discourse.

Discovering New Ways to Introduce Traditional Assignments

Stop for a moment and consider some of the traditional assignments English teachers make. It isn't that they are bad. It's the way we have approached them. Good student writing in the essay mode can happen only infrequently if we use the old "throw out a topic and ask them to write on it" approach. We want to free constraints and anxiety; we want, instead, to pique curiosity and interest. Here are some suggestions for doing old stuff in new ways.

Reviving Comparison and Contrast: Making It Meaningful

The comparison and contrast assignment has always been an English teacher's favorite. Unfortunately, it's an easy assignment to formulate, and easy for students to produce shallow, saccharine analysis as they try to fulfill the assignment. Rather than writing a formula on the board and telling students to go to it, we use a more inductive approach, which also generates some good writing in the process. As part of the process of writing a contemporary nonfiction form such as memoir, which can be the basis for a comparison and contrast piece, we ask student to do the following:

1. Think of a favorite place or artifact as it looked when you were a child. Be specific, not general. Remember a favorite room, part of the park near your house, a toy such as a bike or doll, a desk, a wall with pictures on it—whatever. Try to choose a place that you visited across a period of time or an artifact that you owned for a number of years. Now, jot some notes about this place or artifact. Be as concrete and specific as you can. Remember the details. See the place or artifact in your mind. For this part of the brainstorming, Dawn chose to recall her first desk, one that she and her father bought together when she entered middle school, which she kept with her in college, and that followed her into her first house as an adult.

2. Share the notes. Try ideas on one another. In large classes, the sharing goes on in small groups. Take enough time for this step. New ideas and details occur to students as they discuss the experience with each other.

3. Now, think of the same place or artifact in the present, or at least several years later. Again, jot notes. See the place or artifact. Be concrete. What feelings do you have about the place or artifact?

4. Share the notes again. Allow time for discussion.

5. Ask, "What have you learned about yourself that you didn't know before you began reflecting on this place or artifact?" Jot some notes in response to that question. Sometimes these insights come to students immediately; sometimes they get stuck. If they get stuck, tell them to relax and work on this later. They may need to write more before the insights grow.

6. Write out a discovery draft. Begin at the beginning or begin at the end or begin in the middle—but begin. Don't interrupt the writing-out process. Give students plenty of time. Let them shape the piece, using their own intuitions.

7. Share the discovery drafts, reading them aloud. Talk about beginnings and endings. Talk about transitions. Talk about concrete detail. Talk about language and diction. Talk about anything that concerns you or your students.

8. Talk to your students about the *genre* of comparison and contrast. Because they've just engaged in a mental process of comparing and contrasting something meaningful to them, they'll understand the point and see the possibilities of the *genre* for explication.

Students may elect to rewrite, revise, or file their individual pieces, depending on their involvement in the writing and their assessment of its worth. We find that our students often continue working on this piece and choose to include it in their memoir collection for their final product.

Rethinking Research Papers

Ah, the research paper.

If the five-paragraph essay is the zombie that won't stay dead, the research paper is the living fossil, the reptilian behemoth from the jungles of the past still clumping through classrooms and devouring huge chunks of the calendar. Everyone knows the beast should be extinct—or at least confined to an exotic park or museum—yet, there it is, year after year, still dominating the scene.

No doubt, the cognitive gymnastics and myriad skills associated with researching and writing about a particular topic are essential in just about any academic or professional sphere. The ability to ask critical questions and pursue avenues of inquiry, to sift through various sources of information to assess their worth, and to weave outside voices and material into one's own emerging thinking are useful in the personal and future professional lives of our students. To that end, research-oriented writing of some kind is an appropriate part of just about any course.

During a time long ago and in a place far away from contemporary methods of conducting inquiry, the spirit of research got lost. Like other kinds of writing assignments that have become institutionalized, *research* has too often become an exercise in tedium for teachers and for our students. What students actually produce is usually the opposite of what real research is all about. Students generally hate writing research papers and teachers usually dread grading them, perhaps more than any other type of writing. Some research paper assignments last eight weeks or more, becoming a march of drudgery toward a destination that, in the end, hardly seems worth it. Do we advise abandoning the research paper? In the traditional sense, yes. Do we advise excising inquiry and real research from the curriculum? Emphatically, no.

Inventive teachers find new ways of dealing with the traditional trappings of the English classroom. Consider the case study that follows, which demonstrates how two teachers collaborated to revamp the research paper for their students.

Case Study: A New Idea for Dealing with the Research Paper

Part of the fun of writing a book is meeting people, exchanging ideas, and talking about what really matters as we endeavor to teach English and, especially, writing. Two such teachers whom we "met" via their writing and in email exchanges are Erica DiMarzio and Ryan Dippre.[1] They have been teaching about five years each, are fans of earlier editions of *Inside Out*, and are mixing up their methods for teaching traditional assignments. One such assignment they have tackled is the age-old research paper.

After we exchanged several emails, Dawn asked Erica and Ryan, who coauthored a recent article in *English Journal* (DiMarzio and Dippre 2011) that caught our attention, to write about their new approaches to inquiry, research, and the role of each in their teaching and in their students' learning. What they wrote for us follows.

As you read their ideas, think about methods you might use to freshen up, revamp, or even gut how you teach inquiry, research, and how to manage information. What will you take from this book and from this case study to enhance your teaching and your students' learning?

RESEARCH PAPERS AND SOCIAL REHEARSAL
By Erica DiMarzio and Ryan Dippre

A Common Problem

The start of the research paper is perpetual springtime for teachers: a new beginning, a chance to "get it right" this year, another opportunity to make the research and formatting easy and fun once and for all. This time, we say, it'll work. This year the logic will be clear, the sources will be found easily, the notes organized effectively, and the papers will be superior without exception.

But it rarely turns out like that. There is always some mixture of success and failure. Some students become interested in their topics and run with them, while others struggle—or fail even to struggle—and turn in work that indicates clearly that the students did not take advantage of the weeks of class time committed to the project.

As the time for the research paper drew near for us, we felt a mutual mild apprehension about using the research paper described in our sophomore curriculum guide. The unit was clear and well organized, but we felt that it didn't fit well with the group of students we were teaching. We knew something different was in order, but we did not know what that "something" was.

We began by looking at the research paper itself. What was it about the research paper that caused our students to struggle? The formatting was not much of a problem—until they had to do it on their own. The use of sources to support their points seemed easy enough—when done piecemeal in smaller essays. Organizing an essay was not a challenge—as long as the paper was relatively short. Formatting, using sources effectively, and organizing an argument: They could all be done independently, but not together. The pieces seemed to be there, but the puzzle was still in the box.

In the end, we decided that what was keeping our students from using their skills was the social nature of the research paper. In other writings, students are discussing something they know in depth through readings, class discussion, personal experience, and conversations with others. The writings in those cases give students the space to explore their ideas in their own ways, apart from everyone and everything else. In a typical research paper, however, students don't have the exploratory and reflective space they are used to; instead, that space is given to the arguments, ideas, and theories of the sources they found, which are so expertly expert that the author's knowledge was written down, copied, and given a place in a library. Students need to use these experts in an efficient manner to convey a complex argument for an extended number of pages, often more than they have written to date in their lives.

The encroachment of the social sphere of expert writers on our students' writing spaces seemed, to us, to be the crux of the entire problem. Students are working to find their own voices in writing, and creating that voice while juggling elements of traditional research only complicates an already difficult situation. But how could we fix it? How could we teach our two classes full of teenagers to argue with conviction for an extended period of time?

An Obvious Solution: Music as a Springboard

The answer, to paraphrase Springsteen, was akin to finding the key to the universe in the engine of an old, parked car. How do we get a teenager to argue? Did we really just ask that question? Teenagers, as parents the world over no doubt know, can argue eloquently and at length when they feel they have something worth fighting for. Our solution? Give them something to fight for. One of the tenets we held to in past projects and in our teaching in general was the concept that in order to excel on challenging assignments, students need to be provided with engaging choices. Clearly, if students are interested in what they are writing, they will be more capable of coming up with adequate details and will be more invested in the multiple-step revision process required to turn out complex, engaging writing. The solution was to use what our group seemed to know best: music. What better way could there be to reach our students who inundate us daily (okay, more like twice hourly) with their desperate pleas of, "Can we *please* listen to our music while we work on this?" We decided that using music as a springboard for research and the analysis of that research through writing would allow our students to see the project through to completion with both a high level of interest in the topic and a comfort level with using expert sources to communicate their theses.

The Project
Choosing the Bands
The task that fell to us next became more challenging than we initially anticipated, namely that of choosing a manageable list of albums that we knew had significant cultural value and represented various genres and time periods. This job seemed easy enough until we realized that we must also be personally comfortable enough with each album/artist to be able to aid students in their interpretations of the songs and research connected to them. Ryan's affinity for classic rock proved extremely informative, but Erica's eclectic interests that spanned the gamut of more obscure genres from musical theatre and female vocalist folk to reggae sent her fleeing to colleagues with more mainstream musical educations for help. After much discussion and reorganization, we composed a final list for students that contained major albums from various eras in American history and diverse genres of music.

Addressing Social and Historical Issues
Convincing our students that the music they listen to was linked to the social circumstances and historical events around them was not difficult. Convincing them to express those connections in their writing, however, was a bit more of a challenge. To help our students work with these connections, we encouraged them early in the project to use additional sources of information. We tried to show them that the music they were listening to on their iPods was tied to the development of music over time; we wanted them to understand how increased knowledge about the relevant social and historical events related to the songs would, in many instances, help them better interpret and understand the lyrics. Structuring the assignment a little further—such as requiring a recap of the importance of the album early in the paper—helped our students see these connections. We also allowed our stronger writers to depart from our structures, which enhanced their decision making and creative freedom.

Thankfully, the Internet is rife with music enthusiasts, and finding histories of both individual groups and worldwide music movements was not difficult. Using the packets we gave them, students were able to document important items and, over time, see connections throughout different bits of information that they collected. Putting multiple sources in one spot before our students began writing was an important step, and we fervently hope that they apply that strategy to research writing in other courses. Once our students had collected their sources, however, they still had to move from research notes to organized writing, which was a difficult step for many of them.

Using Sources
Although we had students working with and recording information from multiple sources early in the project, they were still uncertain and hesitant about using sources in their writing. The earlier problem of students' being unable to find a place for their own voices was somewhat alleviated, but it was definitely still a problem. We needed to

convince our students—one at a time, in some cases—that they could use the sources they found to support their arguments. In this case, direct questioning about their arguments worked best. We asked student several guiding questions such as "What was going on at that time to prove your point?" and "What can you say to convince me of your claim?" We also structured the required sources to lessen the chances of having an encyclopedia-style paper presented to us. We asked students to use the following sources:

1. album (this means another song or the inside jacket)
2. lyrics (online)
3. one professional analysis of the album (allmusic.com)
4. one review of the selected song
5. one outside reference (sales, marketing, fan base, etc.).

Our initial concern with this list was that we were not giving our students enough leeway to explore the library. Since our library was inadequate to meet the needs of any but the types of biography-oriented research papers that gave our students so much trouble, however, we decided that having an Internet-heavy research paper was a chance worth taking.

In retrospect, the direction that we gave our students did not diminish the returns on the project. Indeed, we felt that it prevented students from feeling overwhelmed and allowed them to expend their research and writing energies in effective ways. Our students were able to use their sources as we structured them to bootstrap their own arguments to a higher level, and our students had much less trouble with working their own arguments, attitudes, and styles into their writing. Our structuring gave students some of the writing space that they were used to, which freed their creative and argumentative energies.

Analyzing the Works

Students were required to accomplish two different goals with the analysis segment of their work. First, they had to explain to us the importance of the album in the history of music. Second, they had to select one song (or several, as some did) and analyze it for strengths and weaknesses in message, melody, or a combination of both. If our students struggled with the analysis—and many of them did—it was less an inability to analyze and more a difficulty with putting their analyses into words. Nonetheless, this section of the paper gave us what we were looking for: an opportunity for students to express themselves, using rational argument about a subject with which they felt they had some command.

We fostered this sense of control through modeling—Ryan's students may have listened to more Bruce Springsteen than they ever wanted or expected to in their entire lives—and one-on-one discussions with students while they were working in class. We also combined our classes several times, which crowded the library, but also gave our students who were working on the same album a chance to compare notes and discuss ideas. Creating an environment of research that was open to collaboration without falling into plagiaristic issues was difficult but worthwhile, as we saw in our final results.

The Results

The outcome of this project was positive for most students in both of our classes. It began with high student interest and motivation to complete the initial research, a result, we believe, that came from the appealing nature of the topic. When our students needed to compose logical arguments and use their research to convey their assertions, our students were undeniably more capable of exploring their own ideas through their writing than we had seen in past research assignments. We attribute this improvement to the fact that they were more comfortable completing the writing because they were invested in the topic and because they were working from what they truly knew best.

But what about that one technique of research writing with which our students had so often struggled in the past: the ability to seamlessly use the ideas of others to logically support their arguments? Regardless of varying levels of instructional support that individual students required, we found that, for the most part, our students were able to embed their research within their papers to effectively support their theses. We found that with an interesting and manageable topic, thorough modeling and conferencing about their theses and the ways our students could support them, and through the support of their peers for brainstorming and revision, our students were able to argue with confidence and certainty for the length of time the research assignment dictated. In the process, our students found their own strong voices among the many others (those of their cited experts) that they used in the creation of the work.

We find lots to like in what Erica and Ryan did. They collaborated and encouraged their students to do the same. They gave students some parameters but did not restrict them to the point of creative strangulation. They drew on students' existing knowledge and encouraged more inquiry to augment that knowledge. They allowed students to find an authentic reason to ask questions and to seek answers. They realized that traditional sources of information might not be contemporary enough and therefore encouraged students to use the Internet to seek valid, applicable information.

What interests your students? (Okay, yes *that*, but clean it up so your administrators and constituent parents won't freak out when your students begin their next research project.) How might you build on students' interests and encourage students to form authentic questions that they *want* to answer? What new writing techniques and what contemporary resources might your students devise and discover as they work on a topic of interest to them?

As Erica and Ryan found out, what students produce under such stimuli—including using their prior knowledge, shared meaning making, and collaborative social interactions— may be considerably better writing and more authentic research than we teachers usually extract from students when we abide by the strictures of the traditional research paper.

Real Research

Why does research happen in the real world?

This is an important question to ask because our response helps clarify why we ask students to do it. First, research does not happen in a vacuum. No one simply decides to "do research" for no apparent reason. Even professionals who are assigned research tasks that they themselves didn't generate—people such as legal aides, graduate assistants, and corporate analysts—are responding to a real need for research. Research—inquiry—is motivated by a need or desire to learn more about some topic, as Erica and Ryan led their students to understand. Through research, we answer questions, find information to help us address a problem, or locate materials to help us work through a puzzling situation. Consider these scenarios:

- A homeowner notices more blue jays and fewer cardinals around the bird feeder.
- A criminologist sees a spike in burglaries on certain days of the month.
- A backyard gardener wonders why his tomato plants failed to thrive this year.
- A sociologist wonders about why bowling leagues aren't as popular as they once were.
- A media specialist wonders about the rise of fads such as "planking" and flash mobs.
- A teenager is puzzled by the popularity of oversized clothing.
- A parent is confused about which video game system to buy for the family.
- A film buff wonders about the possible influence of Alfred Hitchcock on Quentin Tarantino.
- A high school football coach wonders why his players seem less energetic during Tuesday afternoon practices.
- A teenager is frustrated that a popular fast-food chain has yet to build a restaurant in his part of town.

Each of these situations has a common element: a person is genuinely curious about a problem or question *that doesn't seem to have a simple answer.* This second element is important, as it separates research from simple fact-finding. We may be puzzled by a question like "What's the capital of Albania?" but it's a different kind of puzzlement than that caused by a question such as "Why is Abercrombie and Fitch such a prevalent brand of clothing at my school?" The answer to the former question may be found in a few seconds with an online search; the second takes some sustained inquiry to reach an adequate answer.

Social critic Neil Postman has written that schools often fail to teach students a crucial skill: the art of asking good questions. Instead, schooling emphasizes the opposite—the search for answers (ideally, the *right* answer). Asking good questions presumes an observant eye, a sense of curiosity, and the value of fresh ideas. It may be the case that traditional schooling (ironically, tragically) has deadened these qualities in many students, as the old saying implies: Students enter school as question marks, and leave as periods.

Authentic research awakens our students to the puzzles, curiosities, and problems that exist around them. The typical teenager is not exactly a stranger to complaint, curiosity, and criticism, all of which might become the basis of inquiry. Our job is to move students from simple kvetching to organized inquiry around a topic.

Breathing life into the old research paper assignment is challenging, but we are inspired to do so when we consider this question: Who enjoys the traditional research paper and what do they learn from it? The responses do not encourage us to maintain the status quo.

Our students fear traditional research papers as complicated ventures that take large doses of planning and discipline. Teachers hate reading and grading these massive—and massively dull—papers. Media specialists dread having us teachers and our thirty students per class in the library for two weeks or more, surfing the Web aimlessly and misfiling resource books. Parents are anxious about the fact that one project, on which their children spend hours and hours, may still fall short of expectations and adversely affect their children's final grades in our classes. On the other hand, many high school English teachers think they fail their college-bound students by not assigning the beastly research paper. What a dilemma!

A clear path out of the predicament does exist: Enliven inquiry in our classes. In large measure, the value of the research project lies in the related inquiry processes. Knowing how to ask authentic questions and find legitimate data to support claims are at least as important as the final product. Effective inquiry projects are problem-solving experiences that challenge students and that leave them, at the conclusion of their work, with a positive feeling and increased knowledge.

To dispel the notion that only hunchbacked, nearsighted scholars in the bowels of a dusty library conduct research, students benefit from a model that guides them to work through the conceptual framework of conducting research as a meaning-making process to answer real questions. They need reality-based techniques for being successful researchers. The ideas that follow are designed to present students with situations and frameworks that position *research* as a logical and meaningful outgrowth of real questions.

▨ The Action Research Project

The very term *action research* seems to be an oxymoron to most students. But it doesn't have to be. As we work with students on conducting research, we focus on the quality of their questions that drive the research. Without good questions, students aren't motivated to find good answers. What issues or problems exist about which students want to know more and perhaps change the status quo? We also focus not just on what they find out, but on *how* they find it out. Books and the Internet are powerful tools, but so are surveys and interviews—sources that are rarely used by students in authentic situations. To focus less on product and more on inquiry as a meaningful activity, we follow a process similar to the following.

1. *Generate a class topic of interest to most students.* You might bring in an editorial, lyrics from a contemporary song, a short story, or a poem to get students started. Pick something that will generate mixed and rather complicated reactions: mandatory education, pros and cons; the individual's responsibility to society; students' responsibilities to the school community, or teachers' responsibilities to students. Or perhaps even try tough topics, in the right situation, such as school violence—if your students, administrators, and parents can handle it.

2. *Check out the topic in subjective and objective ways.* Use fact and fiction in Here and Nows. Have students write short reactions and keep a Research Log while they explore the topic.

3. *After several days of seeing the topic from a variety of viewpoints, each student or a group of students working together formulates questions about the topic.* The questions should reflect the complexities of the subject and avoid yes-or-no responses. Spend time with students helping them word their questions precisely.

4. *Ask students to answer these questions using their Research Logs for preliminary responses.* Fill in information with further investigation—readings and interviews with classmates and people in the community.

5. *Explore a range of online resources—including Wikipedia—to find out what we know and what we don't know.* One of the big problems about traditional research papers is how students too often "research" and present already settled information as somehow "new." Repeating the basic facts on any

subject is not research. How are students to know what information is already well established and accepted, however? A one-stop spot full of readily accessible information is a good place to test the information waters. What about a topic is being debated? What remains a mystery?

6. *Explore interview options.* Who in the community might have some insights about the question being researched? Who in the community might be able to offer some historical perspective? Who is most affected by this issue? Help students to formulate questions that knowledgeable community members might be able to answer, teach them how to conduct an interview that is more informative conversation than rapid-fire Q and A, and then help them sort through the data they gather from their interview sources. What are the new insights? What are the surprises? What are the conflicting viewpoints among those interviewed? These are all inquiries that will spark discussion, reflection, and more research, as well as some conclusions, eventually.

7. *Expand the students' repertoire for tracking their information and notes.* We encourage students to track their notes and resources. We know die-hard English teachers who insist that students use antiquated methods such as tracking their work and references on literal paper note cards. For some students, note cards may serve as useful manipulatives. Most students whom we know, however, are able to use a computer to catalog, categorize, and track information, sources, and almost anything else related to research. They quickly become adept at using specialized tools created for students engaging in research, using software that allows students to manipulate data in a variety of ways, or using a format the students themselves specifically create. Although some teachers may cling to their (t)rusty methods and devices, we prefer to show students how to use computers for more than surfing and gaming. In addition, we value having our students think through ideas in their own language; they use their Research Log reflections, Here and Nows, interviews, and information shared with classmates. Ideas in books or online sources won't make sense unless students have first built meaningful connections to many of the issues related to their research topics. We find that our students know how to cut, paste, and copy digitally or analogically. We push them to think, not merely regurgitate.

8. *Begin discovery drafts in which students explore findings and sort through ideas.* Students work their way toward a more formal paper through a series of short papers.

One thing we've found in following this procedure is that students learn the process and are able to apply it for individual research at any future time. They have learned a way of collecting information and transforming it into an opinion paper.

The same process can be used with individual topics if your students have previous experience. It's tough for students and teachers when thirty students, covering thirty different topics, spread their books and notes over a huge library or hog all of the available computers. Students, all needing help at the same time, may easily get frustrated. We like to have several students work on various facets of the same subject. Each provides expertise and helps the others. The collaborative effort helps them explore the topic more thoroughly and brings other viewpoints to individual ideas. They follow each other through the exploratory discovery drafts and serve as a response group through the final paper.

The Multigenre Paper

The multigenre paper is exactly what it says it is—a form of exposition that employs many modes and *genres* of writing in one product. Tom Romano (1995) has popularized the form, and we have taught versions of the multigenre paper to students from middle school to college. The concept is modeled after Michael Ondaatje's novel *The Collected Works of Billy the Kid* (1970), which is itself a blending of fact, fiction, and supposition based on facts about the life and times of Billy the Kid.

When Dawn teaches the multigenre paper, she has students focus on one person or event about which they are passionate and about which they want to research and write for a month or even for an entire semester. Careful selection of the subject matter is essential to the success of the final multigenre paper. Once the topic is chosen, students begin conducting research to find out the facts about their person or event. Once students have a factual core of knowledge from which to experiment and build, the writing begins. We encourage students to stretch beyond their comfort zones as writers. They try unrhymed poetry, narrative, drama, obituaries, journalistic pieces, interviews, description, interior monologue, and other genres as a way of exploring their topic and explicating it to readers of their multigenre papers. They squirm with the Grammar B requirements—the deliberate breaking of some traditional grammatical rules to achieve impact in their papers—as Romano explains. But the most fun comes in the production and celebration of the final product.

We encourage students to consider presentational format as an additional mode of expositional meaning. One student who chose to write her multigenre paper on a famous Scottish battle encased her final multigenre collection in a handmade tartan cover complete with pin. Another student who chose to write about Georgia O'Keefe presented her final multigenre collection as an artist's portfolio that opened vertically and featured reprints of some of the art pieces alongside the student's original writings. Students also experiment with bindings, paper, and font color and style. Some creative students have hand-printed letters that were to have been written by the person who was the subject of their multigenre collection, and others have gone so far as to singe the edges of the pages that were to have been partially consumed by a fire. One industrious and talented student discovered that the person about whom she had written was an admirer of watercolor artwork, so she created an original watercolor on every page of her multigenre collection.

On the day that the final multigenre collections are due, ask all of the students to clear their desks of their belongings and place their multigenre collections on top. Then, lead students in conducting a walk-around during which everyone circulates among the desks, looking through the final products. After about twenty minutes, students return to their seats and discussion ensues. We usually begin by asking, "What did you see that you liked?" The compliments flow and the writers glow from the effects of praise.

Such writings and presentational considerations give students another lens through which to view exposition and research—not as deadly dull assignments, but as creative, meaningful expressions of self and of information. Students shape a message and deliver it to readers through a range of forms. When the writer's message is received by the readers, the inquiry process moves from the dusty, dusky library to the full light of celebratory achievement.

Additional Research Ideas

By now, you are not surprised to learn that we like to push beyond the traditional to explore new and emerging methods and ideas. The following are some of the additional ways in which we bring research and genuine inquiry into our classrooms.

▨ Arriving at Questions

Consider a research assignment in which students *end* with a question (or questions) rather than a specific solution. For example, Jamie is interested in researching why her neighborhood does not have any sidewalks. She has to walk to the bus stop on the shoulder of the road, which is dangerous, and it's worse in rainy or snowy weather. Her possible research—examining city and county requirements for developers, interviewing residents, and investigating other communities—might lead her to a position statement: "The city should pay to have sidewalks installed in our neighborhood." More interestingly, her inquiry might also lead her to deeper questions for consideration, such as the following:

- What services should a town, city, or county reasonably provide?
- At what point do the drawbacks of business regulations outweigh the benefits?
- How do we define "quality of life," and what role should government play in its promotion?
- What do local people expect from the taxes they pay? How much more in taxes would the average resident be willing to pay per year for new sidewalks?

When students are able to formulate these types of rich questions as a result of research, we think they have arrived at a good learning destination.

▨ Common Ground: Bridging Divides

Because most global problems, debates, and issues are fairly complex, a range of nuanced, differing opinions—rather than simplistic "one side against another" positions—usually exist. Further, most people have understandable reasons (based on experience, education, and background) that ground what they think, and disagreement doesn't mean that one's opponents are automatically wrong. The Common Ground research project asks students to focus on the various stances toward an issue in order to come to a more complete understanding of why people believe what they believe. After seeking commonalities and neutralities, student writers have the option of positioning their emerging beliefs within the existing spectrum of opinions. We also challenge our students to seek and articulate which foundational beliefs—which common ground—they share with various factions before moving into discussions about what separates particular stances. By focusing first on unities and commonalities, students often find it difficult to advance arguments seated in pettiness, prejudice, and predictability.

▨ Obscured Voices

"History," as Winston Churchill famously postulated, "is written by the victors." We might expand Churchill's observation somewhat to note that mainstream narratives—from news reports to folklore, from traditional notions of success to perceptions of what it means to be an American—are governed by conventional assumptions that emphasize certain viewpoints and ways of thinking while sidelining, ignoring, or silencing others. Potential topics are as diverse as our students; for example, consider the power, race, and economic implications of questions such as these: What aspects of everyday life are obscured or ignored in volatile national debates about immigration? What is it like to be poor in a culture that views wealth as a sign of an individual's significance? What challenges meet a student who bucks conventional notions of masculinity or femininity? This kind of deep inquiry is not always welcomed; only you can judge if you and your students might delve into these or similar questions without loss of income and integrity.

Blue Sky Research

It's a sad truism that the rhetoric of education often bears little resemblance to reality. We say we want creative and critical thinkers, but our high-stakes tests measure low-level learning. We say we need to educate "outside-the-box" innovators if we are to succeed in an emerging global economy, but legislators and others discourage inspiration and innovation in how schooling is conducted.

Let Blue Sky Research lurk on your teacher radar, so that when a student approaches you with a "crazy idea" for a research project, you hesitate to snuff it out and get the whippersnapper back on the straight and narrow. As the educational writer Alfie Kohn has noted, it's impossible to force students to feel intrinsic motivation. When that distinctive firework does spark, we want to be ready.

If You Can't Beat 'Em . . .

When our students hear a simple question or know they need to find information, where do they look first? Right. They go online. Online encyclopedias of information (you can name one or two such sites without much thought) that are "crowd produced"—that is, consisting of documented (hopefully) information on a specific topic written by myriad contributors who want to add to a public resource—are almost inexhaustible resources for, well . . . almost everything. Our students may think these sites are the gold standard for writing almost anything that requires them to gather information, to conduct inquiry. Because we English teachers worry about the reliability and validity of sources of information and because some of the information on some sites might be questionable, working with processes and methods of valid inquiry provides us a rich opportunity to discuss with our students what, exactly, makes an online source verifiable, authentic, and trustworthy. Some questions we might ask our students to help them assess the reliability or online sources include the following:

1. When was the site last updated?
2. Who authors the site?
3. What are the credentials of the site's authors?
4. What agency or corporation or group sponsors the site?
5. Does the site's sponsor have a vested interest in leading the public toward specific information or certain conclusions? If so, does the site contain biased or one-sided information to guide public thinking in that direction?

6. How does knowledge about the site's authors and/or sponsor affect how I interpret the site's content?
7. What types of information am I likely to find from sites that end in .com, .gov, or .edu, or other designations?
8. How do information and data compare across several sites? If one site is an outlier in the general stream of information, why?

Online resources are one venue for gathering information. Students may be surprised to learn that some valuable information is simply not available online; they may need to turn to hard copies of books, professional journals, newspapers, and other information sources. Questions about sources of information and a need for multiple sources are necessary for almost any type of inquiry. Quality resources of information—whether online or in hard copy, from personal interviews and data gathering—not only enlighten our students, but they also serve as the basis for new questions. When students conduct meaningful inquiry, they help to fill the gaps between what we do and do not know.

The Creation of Meaning

In their best incarnation, online encyclopedic sources—such as the ubiquitous Wikipedia—constitute a rather amazing phenomenon and offer valid research-related potential. Recently, we sense a shift in our colleagues' attitudes about such sources, from "don't use it at all" to "use it wisely if you do." Far from the stereotype of chaotic free-for-all of misinformation, many of these online encyclopedias are self-regulated with specific editing guidelines. That fact challenged us to think carefully about the entries in these sources and how we might use them as teaching tools, not merely first-line pop-ups to questions posed.

For example, this project is more challenging than it first may seem: Darren's students wrote or amended their own online encyclopedia entries, using a range of entries in Wikipedia as a model. His students considered elements such as the style, tone, details, and precision required for this type of writing. They learned that encyclopedic writing must be evenhanded and fact-checked, detailed yet concise, tonally neutral and stylistically restrained. Try it yourself. It's an enlightening activity.

Darren also discusses with his students the topics that do and do not rise to the level of warranting an entry in an online encyclopedia. Some sites make these discussions and decisions public, and students might consider the points of view expressed in those discussions.

Alternately, students might begin research with an analysis of a specific online encyclopedia entry to generate questions and seek to close gaps in what they know. Some of our enterprising colleagues have also constructed their own classroom Wikipedia-inspired sites with students responsible for researching, editing, and maintaining subject-specific information. Online encyclopedias—whether Wikipedia or its next iteration—are not dying out anytime soon. Rather than stick our heads, ostrichlike, into the sands of denial, we prefer to embrace the phenomenon and explore how genuine inquiry and shared knowledge support learning. We encourage you to do the same and to discuss with your students what you all learn about online resources for inquiry.

To a Wider Audience: Exploring Digital Culture

For students who are immersed in or who identify with Web 2.0 applications and digital platforms with a social dimension, exploring topics from a subculture viewpoint and representing them to wider audiences may hold great appeal. In the spirit of the Dispatches and Bulletins writing we describe on page 147, student writers might seek to explain quirky trends and esoteric communities to a mainstream audience. Sam's discussion of "Rick Rolling" is a great example. (See Sam's piece in Chapter 5 and his complete project in the online Additional Resources. You'll find the link to the online resources at www.heinemann.com/products/E04195.aspx, on the Companion Resources tab.) Encourage students to consider the digital networks, communities, and affinity spaces in which they participate. For example, anime, machinima, fan fiction—all of which your students can likely explain to you—are legitimate subculture topics for writing. How are your students secret experts in certain areas of knowledge or skill? What might they share about their worlds that will enlighten the larger classroom community?

New Attitudes About Research: From Agony to Enthusiasm

As student writers explore new approaches to research, they might also experiment with ways to transform the look of traditional research. Wiki and blog platforms allow for easy hyperlinking, embedded media, and a variety of interactive tools that broach new possibilities for writing. Darren's students experiment regularly with online research options. For both teachers and students, such work requires flexibility and a willingness to experiment with the possible rather than the predictable.

We began this chapter by talking about how often the teaching of the essay is drudgery for teachers and students alike. We end this chapter by sharing the fun we have and how much our students learn when they expand their range of expositional writing, blurring genre, conducting Action Research, considering both the medium and the message, and challenging assumptions. We've tried to convey our enthusiasm to you and give you some ideas for generating new essay forms for your students. Have we communicated our message? Have we answered some questions and raised others? If so, our exposition has been successful.

NOTE
1. Erica DiMarzio and Ryan Dippre teach at Delaware Valley High School in Milford, Pennsylvania.

Works Cited

Britton, James, et al. 1975. *The Development of Writing Abilities (11–18)*. London: Macmillan Education.

Dillard, Annie. 1990. *The Writing Life*. New York: Harper Perennial.

DiMarzio, Erica, and Ryan Dippre. 2011. "Creative and Critical Engagement: Constructing a Teen Vision of the World." *English Journal* 101 (2): 25–29.

Jaschik, Scott. 2011. "Beyond the Standard Essay." *Inside Higher Ed*. August 29. Available at: www.insidehighered.com/news/2011/08/29/oklahoma_state_university_gets_ready_to_ask_broader_questions_in_admissions.

Lightman, Allen. 2000. *The Best American Essays of 2000*. Boston: Houghton Mifflin.

Macrorie, Ken. 1988. *The I-Search Paper, Revised Edition of Searching Writing*. Portsmouth, NH: Boynton/Cook.

Martin, Nancy, Pat D'Arcy, Bryan Newton, and Robert Parker. 1976. *Writing and Learning Across the Curriculum, 11–16*. London: Ward Lock.

Ondaatje, Michael. 1970. *The Collected Works of Billy the Kid: Left-Handed Poems.* Toronto: Anansi Press.

Romano, Tom. 1995. *Writing with Passion.* Portsmouth, NH: Heinemann.

8

Responding to Students' Writing

Remember your humanity, and forget the rest. —**Bertrand Russell**

Writing in isolation without lively response is like singing in the shower or dancing in a coal mine: They are solitary activities devoid of feedback, appreciation, or reaction. They may be pleasurable diversions, but without some response from an audience, they do not get much better. Most writers, and particularly your students, need the reactions of other human beings both during and after they write. More to the point, they will demand to know what *you* think about their writing. Thus, the critical moment in any writing class is when beginning writers put their words in your hands. "Well, what do you think?" "You don't like it." "It isn't very good, is it?" They watch your eyes. You can't fool them with facile praise.

Over the years, students have developed a kind of self-preservation instinct in writing classes. They try to figure out what teachers want and then give it to them. They have also learned to insulate themselves against the criticism of the writing teacher. If you're successful in drawing them out, in getting them to take a chance with language, then you must also accept the burden of bringing them along with sincere and measured response.

The secret of building good writer–responder relationships lies in the *touch* of the responder. Overly harsh, picky, and niggling criticism will spook any writer. The *only* way to help writers improve is to draw them out slowly with honest encouragement and support. We hear a little murmuring out there from those who label this kind of responding as softheaded because it doesn't discriminate enough between good and bad writing. The successful writing teachers we have observed are an idiosyncratic bunch, it's true; but they have one strong similarity. They draw out writers by searching for the good in their writings and by looking for potential with the same vigor some composition teachers waste on the great fragment hunt. Successful writing teachers never sit around in smoke-filled rooms, ranting about how badly their students write or reading the latest collection of fault-ridden papers to horrified listeners. Far from ridiculing students' writing, the careful teacher-as-responder gives students' writings a careful, thoughtful, and considered read.

Students peg in a heartbeat any dishonesty or insincerity in their teachers and in the responses they receive. Disingenuous responding has no place in the writing classroom. When you respond to students' writing, you enter into a transaction with students from which each of you gains something positive. You promise to focus on improving the writing in real and genuine ways, and students promise to listen and to try to improve. Responding as an authentic and caring reader, as a coach, and as a fellow writer is essential for developing an effective responding relationship with your students. Respond to writing early and often.

Effective writing teachers have a positive mind-set. Good writing teachers, because they have a backlog of miracles, know that students' writings are full of clues to hidden potential. Successful responding technique is at least 50 percent mental. Get your mind right and resolve: "I will look for the good. I will go with anticipation to my students' writings."

Responding as a Person

You may need to spend some time practicing this responding business. Teachers are frequently unaware of the extent to which they act as correction machines rather than as receptive people. Your response should be essentially a shared reaction. Participate with the writer by sharing your own thoughts and feelings as you read the writing. Look at the following student writing and our responses to them.

Piece 1

My horse was painted red. The eyes and the bridle and saddle were painted on with black paint. I could ride that horse for hours. When I was mad or excited—I'd hop on that horse and ride it so hard that it would leave the floor and bang back down with a wonderfully loud wood-on-wood, spring-breaking ka-plam! One thing that really pleased me then was that the horse was always in the same mood I was. If I wanted to ride her hard—she seemed to want to fly and crash on the floor—if I was tired and rocked very slightly back and forth—she sometimes went to sleep before I could rest my head on her neck and "rest my eyes." She died one day in a fire at my aunt's house—but then I was "too old" for my horse and too young to be told about the fire.

—Rita[1]

Response 1

Your horse story brought back memories of an old, yellow horse that used to stay on our screen porch. He, too, was always ready for a rough ride. I particularly like the way you captured the sound of the horse hitting the floor: "wonderfully loud wood-on-wood, spring-breaking ka-plam!" Good job of using personification to make the horse come alive. The irony of your last line "too old" and "too young" is also well done. Maybe you could do something with that in another paper.

Piece 2

An Asylum of Sorts

I remember tight trampolines that would decay
          after
bounce   bounce
as the young ones showed
their courageous skills.

I remember the cops and robbers
ambushing the streets. The ditches as fortresses,
an asylum
of sorts. The guns fired back
and forth.
                          Sneakily
the robbers made for the break.

I remember cool Halloweens. Halloweens never lasted long enough,
except for the crying children
that scurried away from the garage. The MONSTERS inside had
ordered their exits,
as the candy sacks were shaking.

But most of all, I remember the swinging branch. The boys,
and even the girl, would afford a time of day for such a wondrous
pleasure.
The branch gripped
firmly to the tree
as we gripped firmly to the branch
with perspiration from fear on our brows and
smiles from our stupidity. We never took its life away, but
that
blizzard sure did.

—*Brett*[2]

Response 2
Nice work here playing around with line breaks and special effects with fonts
to add extra dimension to the words . . . you're showing us what's possible. Your
lines about the ditches as fortresses brought back to mind the forts we'd make
out of snow piles in the winter up north, a fairly similar concept. I got pretty good
at the rock-inside-the-snowball trick. Same with the meditation on the branch
and its fate; reminds me of the tree my cousins and I would swing on.

Finally, here's how this kind of approach can work in a more academic kind of writing. These are just the first and last pages of an essay, but notice how Erica DiMarzio responds to Sarah[3] as both a teacher and a reader (see Figure 8-1). She offers encouragement and critique in a balance that works for her.

Mr. Llewellyn

WELCOME TO MATH CLASS

"Hello. I'm Mr. Llewellyn," says the man in front of the classroom, clad in an argyle sweater vest and khakis. "I'll hand out your notes for the first chapter. Come up row by row." He takes a seat in a tall, metal stool and stares at us, his fingers drumming impatiently. I sigh, annoyed with the thought of taking notes on the first day of eighth

I love this. Great imagery

grade. My shiny new sandals tap impatiently along with my new Ticonderoga number two pencil which drums out a tattoo on my fake wood desktop. Mr. Llewellyn shuffles over to the smartboard, and takes a fat red pen, as thick as a cigar, in his hand. "Alright, can anyone tell me the answer to the first question on the board?" he asks gruffly. Silent and apprehensive students wish for summer sun. Math books seem to radiate heat in the dense warm air of the last remnants of summer's 80 degree temperatures. I should go

Comma splice - Should be a semicolon

swimming today. I shouldn't be here, it's too cool outside. Ice cream sounds sooo good! I wonder if the Dairy Bar is still open... Suddenly a loud voice interrupts my mint

☺

chocolate chip double scoop. "Hello! Anyone? Wake up!" He taps angry red marks on the board. "If you don't know the answer to this, you *definitely* do not belong in this class." He smirks, and then shakes his head. He turns around, his bald head glistening in

good

the glow of the projector, and scribbles the answer. This is the beginning to what seems like a *very long* year.

— Good direct characterization in intro!

Figure 8–1. Erica's Response to Sarah

The most effective responses are personal and specific. We're not suggesting that you should use every student paper to tell a story of your own, but you do need to find a way to let the writer know her story, her writing, has touched you personally. Recounting a personal memory, giving examples of times when you reacted to a similar situation differently, or simply saying, "I can really tell you feel strongly about this," are all ways of letting the writer feel the impact of a personal reader. When you respond, remember your humanity.

Looking for the Good

The most significant role of any teacher or reader is that of skilled responder, one who offers concrete, helpful suggestions about specific aspects of the writing. To respond means simply to react—orally or in writing—first as *reader* rather than as teacher. If we're looking for the real reason kids don't learn to write, it's right here. Most teachers are not practiced as responders to students' writings. They know how to be editors, proofreaders, critics, raving lunatics, and error counters. But responders? No.

Most student writers, sadly, never hear any specific, human, teacher-as-responder comments about what they write. First, teachers must discover the power of responding. Forget grading and evaluating for the moment. That kind of responding is less than helpful with beginning writers. Real responding differs from evaluation because it is personal and shared. It is here-and-now feedback. Rather than a to-do list of what the writer should fix next time, authentic response is immediate, personalized, individualized comments about what the writer is saying *now*.

The goal of the responder is to help writers discover what it is they want to say, and then to challenge them to say it as powerfully as possible. Offer questions to the writer to guide him toward improvements. "What about a stronger verb than *walk*? Did your brother *swagger*, *stroll*, or *strut*? Or something else? The right word will help you capture and convey his mood." Or, "I get a bit lost here. Why are your mother and her sister yelling?" These responses offer guidance and pose questions for the writer to consider while maintaining some dignity and quite a bit of authority. You don't know the answer to your question; you're asking legit questions as a reader. You're a reader asking questions of the writer and leaving the next-step decisions up to the student writer. Granted, you're responding as a skilled reader who is asking helpful questions to lead the writer toward more control of the writing. That is what teacher-responders do. The best teacher-responders are effective, careful, thoughtful readers who offer suggestions without leaving the student writer feeling criticized, corrected, and coerced.

Modeling appropriate responding behaviors and comments is also important. This is the time when your impact on students' writing is formative, personally, to students as writers and to the emerging pieces of writing. Showing your student writers good examples from their own papers encourages them. Sit down with those papers and look for the good stuff: a word, a phrase, a fresh idea. Then mark it; circle it; say, "I like this because . . ." Excerpt the parts from the students' writings that you like and share them with the class via your blog, a PowerPoint, or by putting them on the document camera during class. These excerpts should be anonymous; that is, don't identify the student writers at this point. Show the excerpts to your students, and say, "Look at what great stuff I found in your writings."

Yes, you will have to look through a world of chaff to find the kernels. Yes, there may be far more bad writing than good. But you start by rejoicing over the good rather than haranguing over the bad. Never lie to your students. Tell them, "I had to mine the slagheap looking for the gems." Sometimes we laugh with our students about the lengths to which we will go to find something good in their writing, but this positive psychology in the writing class changes dramatically the students' willingness to work on their writing to improve it.

If you have not tried "mining the slagheap," wait no longer. Look at this piece of writing by an eighth grader. It's not new, but it's a great example.

If I Were Older

I would like to be older than I am now. Because when I get sixteen I could drive a car. . . . . When I get twenty-one I could drive a transfer truck. I want to become a trucker because I have been on trips with my daddy and I had fun talking to all those trucker's. Once I talked to a lady trucker. Her handle was "The Lady Buttermilk." She had came from VA. headed toward Big 'A' town (Atlanta) with a load of frozen food. We was her frontdoor until she got behind schedule and she put the pedal to the metal. Then she passed us and she became our frontdoor. One other time I was with daddy on a trip and we was in the rockin' chair. The old "Yellow Jacket" was at our frontdoor and the old "Halk Eye" was at our backdoor. We was just riding along because when ever a smokey was coming, my good-buddies would call for me over the old radio. Then we would slow down to double nickles (55 m.p.h.). We stayed in the ol' rockin chair until we got up to ol 'Sparkle City (Spartenburg South Carolina). Boy we had fun that day.

—Dylan[1]

Maybe all of those run-ons and fragments and usage errors catch your eye first. Maybe you're tempted to label this a hopeless case. Remember, though, that you took the pledge. You said you would look for potential. Plunge in. First, look for *anything* you like about this writing. There's a lot to like. We like the trucker talk and the fact that the student is the expert and the teacher is the novice. Dylan seems comfortable with writing. You could suggest that the writer give you a dialogue between "The Lady Buttermilk" and old "Yellow Jacket." Point out the expressions you like. Skip the bad stuff. Listen to what the writer—as a person—is trying to tell you. Stay with him. Point out the good things in his writing and be patient.

As we discuss in Chapter 5, *good* in writing is not a static quality. *Good* is a growing thing. *Good* for the halting writer is different from *good* for the fluent writer. *Good* for the unpracticed writer is different from *good* for the effective writer. Goodness in writing is not an absolute standard and does not have a moral equivalent.

Teachers' Responses

There's no way to escape it; your response to your students' writing remains very important to them. In a traditional class, your response is important because you control the grade. Whatever your response ("review semicolon usage"), students who want a good grade do what you tell them and the rest mentally zone out. We don't think that the teacher should be the only audience for all student writings; having only a single audience focus is inhibiting to a writer's development. When the teacher becomes the only audience for student writers, many will learn to give the teacher what he wants, but then they can't write for the next teacher, the next year. Additionally, some Genghis Khan types who teach writing can damage students' motivations and development. We don't think, however, that teachers who are merely insensitive responders do irreparable damage. One writing class with a skilled teacher-responder restores confidence and awakens latent language talent even in the oppressed. Teachers' responses are absolutely critical to student writers, and such responses do not necessarily stifle and enslave students. Our observations of successful writing teachers confirm this point. They move students to make insightful observations and to offer helpful criticism of writing by example, by talking students through the processes of writing firsthand.

Students need to hear your opinions, and they expect you to deliver content knowledge to them. They need your sophisticated and caring responses. Grow better student writers by sharing your knowledge and responses with them.

■ What Kind of Response Is Helpful? ?4

The writing teacher has to be willing to play a number of different responder roles, changing these roles as the writer develops. Tailor responses to suit your goals as a writing teacher, the student's progress as a writer, and the context in which the writing occurs. As you come to each piece of writing, ask yourself a series of focusing questions, such as the following.

How far has this student progressed as a writer? Is she still working on developing written fluency, or is she ready to apply more control and precision in her writing?

When promoting *fluency*, your responses will be focused on places in the piece where the writing is going well: "I like this part about your uncle!" When moving the student toward more *control*, you might begin to focus on stylistic techniques and bring along the student's familiarity with literary terms while still offering encouragement: "This detailed description and characterization of your uncle makes him come alive on the page. Way to go!" You might even push toward more *precision* if the student is ready for it: "Love the details about your uncle! Let's hear him talk rather than just having you report to the reader what he said. What were some of his favorite expressions that you might include? How will you punctuate his speech to capture his hesitancy?" All three responses are about the uncle in the piece, but they guide and encourage the student in different ways, causing the student to focus on various aspects of her writing.

For what reason is the student writing this particular piece?

If the writing is a journal entry to promote development of written fluency, respond as a fellow reader and writer, as a person, as an encourager. If, on the other hand, this is a final draft to which you have previously responded—perhaps several times—as the student progressed through several drafts, you are ready to respond in ways that lead the student to increasing levels of control and precision. "You've really focused your main points. Nice work! Which persuasive techniques that we discussed in class might really nail your points and convince your readers? Review your notes and try one or two here."

How often has the student worked with this style or genre of writing?

If your students are trying to write literary criticism for the first time, your responses target the elements expected of the genre while still encouraging the students to keep going. The student may be quite adept at narrative at this point in the year, but now she is moving into new territory and working on a different type of fluency. The student is aiming for fluency not just in how the writing flows from the mind onto the computer screen, but for fluency and facility with a specific form of writing that follows certain conventions. Your task as responder gets a bit more complex because you will focus on fluency *and* on control. Respond in ways that address the demands of the genre while also encouraging continued writing and improvement. "I like your analysis of the social class differential between Huck Finn and Jim. Explore ways in which that difference breaks down. When is Jim more knowledgeable than Huck? What does Huck learn from Jim? Why doesn't the class distinction hold up in every instance?"

As the focus of the writing and the abilities of your student writers develop, so do your roles as responder. Let's look a bit more closely at responding to develop with your students the *fluency, control, precision* model that we discuss in Chapter 2.

Responding to Encourage Written Fluency

At the fluency stage, the writer needs attention, encouragement, and support. Responding at this level means seeing potential, drawing out, spotting future topics, learning more about the student, and rescuing nuggets from the slagheap. Three skilled gurus of writing instruction give us clues about what works in most writing. For Ken Macrorie, strong verbs, vivid detail, inventions of all kinds, ironies, oppositions, and a strong, personal voice are signs of development (1984). For Peter Elbow, "cooking"—letting the topic simmer, grow, and develop in your mind while you're not consciously working on the writing—is a natural way for writers to revise mentally, gain insights, and develop new ideas for the piece (1999). For Donald Murray, an abundance of information, sense of order, clarity, and an air of authority are the most important initial indications that a writer has potential (1985). These pieces of advice have been with us for quite some time, but note how very useful and apt they still are.

Responding to beginning students' writings demands more than merely putting gold stars on the papers. Almost immediately, the teacher must respond as an informed reader, pointing to *what works* in the students' writing. To promote fluency, accentuate the positive.

Responding to Encourage Control in Writing

Take a look at Chapter 5 for our list of good stuff in writing. Let those features that we mention cook in your brain awhile. Now, make your own list. How does your thinking about good writing differ from and align with ours? Take your thinking about good writing a step further. Peruse state, national, and/or core writing standards for ideas about the features of good writing.

These sources indicate characteristics of writing that exhibits elements of control and precision. Help your students move toward control in their writing by creating your own examples of good writing techniques. Publish excerpts and demonstrate to students what you're talking about. Look for what works at the word, sentence, paragraph, and whole discourse levels. Keep the classroom awash in examples of good writing.

Try giving your students the task of making their own list of some features of good writing. Ask them to work in small groups with a stack of student writings that represent a complete range of struggling to skilled pieces. Have students sort through the writings, putting the papers in piles to help them identify and categorize the criteria for good writing. The discussion, arguments, and questions that ensue help students find their own voices as responders to each others' writings. Have each group compose a classroom chart that represents their criteria. Display these charts in the classroom as reminders of response topics.

Later in the year when the peer groups are more skilled, ask students to compare their categories for good writing with the ones in Chapter 5. Or, give students simplified versions of the standards used in your state for writing. Ask students to compare their criteria to the published ones. Although students' labels for the criteria may vary from the professional models, it has been our experience that students identify the same broad categories—interest and technical expertise—as well as many of the same subpoints. Such similarities give students confidence that they know lots about what makes writing work, about how writing with control looks, flows, and sounds.

As the student writer gains confidence and a sense of personal voice and worries less about getting words down in writing—that is, as the students gain more fluency with writing—your role changes to focus on helping the student gain control and precision. Your role gradually evolves to that of editor. Our best editors have not been insensitive authoritarians who want us to write in only one way; far from it. Rather, as an editor, offer support to the writer and help writers express as powerfully and effectively as possible what they have to say. Your responses are nonthreatening and helpful if they are phrased as questions or as take-it-or-leave-it advice. A responder uses a very different tone from that of authoritarian or grade giver. The writer is in control of the writing; the responder sees alternatives or offers a second opinion, being careful not to take the piece away from the writer.

An editor is much more than a proofreader. An editor has a vision of what works for the piece, honors what the writer is doing stylistically, anticipates what an audience will need to know, and helps the writer construct the most effective piece of writing. Even in the best writer and editor relationships, writer and editor will sometimes reach an impasse.

For several summers, Dawn taught memoir writing during summer school for at-risk ninth-grade students. One of the students, Marci, was working on a basically strong piece about having her first car wreck and the resulting reactions of her family. (Yes, Marci was over sixteen and still in ninth grade because "social promotions" from one grade to the next were not in vogue.) Thankfully, no one was injured, so the family found it easy to sling biting comments about carelessness her way. The family apparently expressed themselves in highly colorful language that was not fit for public consumption. They had an intuitive sense of metaphor, simile, and adjective placement within sentences, though they didn't use or even know those terms. Marci depicted her family members as beginning many of their comments with "You are a(n) [insert adjective] [insert noun] . . ." or "This is unbe[insert adjective]lievable . . ." (expletives deleted).

The piece of writing had lots going for it, including a good eye for detail, but the inappropriate language was a significant distraction. It added no emphasis or poignancy or insights to the circumstances surrounding the wreck. Dawn pointed out that the R-rated language served little purpose and might offend some readers; then she offered some additional responses to the writing, ending with, "And I advise cleaning up that language." Marci continued to work on the piece and shared it with her writers' group when her turn to do so arose. Raucous laughter ensued. Dawn took Marci aside and said, "Really, Marci, the language needs to be more appropriate." Marci responded, "But that's how they talked." Well. "That may be, Marci, but the language needs to go." Four days later, Dawn read a new draft of the piece, and the language was still there. "Marci, what's going on with this language?" Marci placed her hands on her hips and replied, "My writing group likes it. They think it's funny and gutsy, and they are *not* offended by it. Plus, it's how my family talked."

The language stayed and Dawn didn't lose her job.

So much for the teacher-as-editor. The important point to make here is that the teacher-as-editor is not the same as the teacher-as-God. The give-and-take—the healthy dialogue between teacher and student writers about specifics in the kids' writing—is a worthwhile activity regardless of where it takes the piece of writing—especially when you won't lose your job by letting the student be in charge of the writing.

Responding to Encourage Precision in Writing

With confident writers and advanced writing classes, your role as responder may be more to function as a critic, arguing fine points of diction, asking for a more consistent point of view, and challenging the writer to rework the piece. Even as critic, the teacher-responder realizes that the writer and the writing are closely related. The criticism must clearly aim to improve the piece, not to punish the writer. It will be much easier to function as careful critic if you yourself are a writer. Teaching writing from the inside out builds expertise and credibility; but more importantly, such inside experience gives you a knowing empathy for the difficult task of the writer.

Using Responding to Grow Writers and Responders

You may be thinking, "Well, sure, I could teach writing if they would put overachievers in my class." We hear you. We know that you aren't teaching private writing lessons to one student at a time. You've got the usual 150-plus students in five or six or more motley classes; or, you're trying to keep sixty-five squirming students enraptured during two-hour (or longer), block-scheduled classes. Fortunately, this book is, in part, about teaching writing well in difficult to impossible situations.

One of the keys to providing enough response to student writers is, of course, to involve the students themselves as responders. Student response is often more forceful than your own and certainly may carry more weight. Okay, you tried that and nothing happened. You brought in some student papers and said, "What is good about this writing?" and the kids looked at their shoe tops. Responding takes practice. It may be new to students—or at least the notion that you really do want to hear their genuine, authentic responses, not just the usual school palaver, may be a new concept that you will need to reinforce until your students believe you. Don't be surprised if it takes a little time to get them going. Model the kind of response for which you're looking. Lead them. Cajole them, but don't give up on them. Responding to writing in a variety of ways promotes multiple perspectives and the sense of embarking on a shared journey as writers, a healthy climate in which a writing community thrives.

Developing Effective Writing Response Groups

When you designate class time for responding, students know that you value the positive ways in which responding improves writing. As students respond to writing, they learn what to seek in good writing; as they hear others respond to their writing, they learn how to listen to helpful commentary and how to return to their writing with a fresh perspective. We give students lots of practice at working as responders, but first we teach them very directly how to be effective responders. Here are some of the key points that guide our practice.

1. *Establish the ground rules for responding by modeling appropriate responses to a student's writing.* Your appropriate modeling is the key to effective response groups. Whether orally or in writing, how you handle the words of your students will signal to your students how they are to talk and respond to each others' writings.

2. *Establish a "No Hunting" rule for your responses and enforce that rule with students' responses to each others' work.* We prohibit and cut short cheap shots aimed at writers by their peers. Most writers struggle at some point, if not frequently, to express their ideas. Avoiding judgmental and unkind remarks toward writers must be a value in an effective response situation. Similarly, gratuitous, bland, insincere, and inaccurate comments about students' writings also are not helpful for improving the piece of writing.

3. *Begin appropriate responding by trying to understand what the writer is trying to say.* Summarizing the piece or restating the message or story lets the writer listen to what the audience has made of the piece. Talk about the piece as a whole. "I like the order of events," or "I like the way you wrap up this piece."

4. *Find things to like in the piece.* Point very specifically to sentences, phrases, and paragraphs in the piece that work: "I like this opening," or "I like this verb right here." Point to where you think the piece is going well: "I like the voice in this passage," or "Nice transition here."

5. *Suggest how the writer may elaborate on what is already written.* This suggestion is probably the most helpful editing posture. Rather than suggesting that the writer make changes or correct errors, find places in the piece that have potential for more development. Through a series of questions to the writer, draw out elaboration possibilities. "Is there any more to this story?" "What happens next?" "I'd like to hear more about this." "I'd like to see and hear more of this character."

6. *Provide opportunities for the writer to hear the reader's questions and voiced musings.* Hearing a reader's first impressions is very helpful for the writer. Model and listen to what your students say, looking for comments that begin with "I wonder . . ."; "What if . . ."; "If this were my piece, I might . . ."; "I notice . . ."

7. *Question the writer about what he or she plans to do next with the piece.* "What will you work on next?" "Where do you see this piece going from here?" "Is this piece related to any other thing that you've written?" These are all questions that open possibilities for dialogue.

8. *Give the writer the chance to ask the responder questions.* The writer will no doubt want to clarify response comments, ask advice, and seek counsel about what to do when returning to the piece. Questions help writers clarify what the responder means.

9. *Focus on the* piece, *not the writer.* It's easy to be sidetracked by the emotional content of the piece. Don't be tempted to become the writer's analyst, confidante, priest, or rabbi. Continue to focus on *how* the experience is rendered in writing rather than on the experience itself.

We encourage you to make these principles your own and to construct them in ways that work for you and your students, as did our colleague Larah Buffington[4], who devised a mnemonic device for her seventh-grade students to internalize the principles of using writing groups in her classes. She solicited ideas from students about what they wanted to call this business of responding to each others' writing—"writing groups" was a bit dull for this class—and she asked students to develop a metaphor to go with their ideas. After some initial small-group work, they decided to call their groups Fireworks Writers. Larah and her students reasoned that everyone at a fireworks show says "ooh" and "ah" with each colorful burst. They thought their writing would be filled with fireworks moments as they worked in groups to respond to the writing and make it better. Next, they put their ideas for working in writing groups into a catchy acrostic using "ooh" and "ah," calling them the *OOH AH!* Guidelines:

Open-minded reading and listening.

Objective feedback only, no baggage and no hunting.

Hesitate before speaking about others' works.

Appreciate the good stuff in a specific way.

Helping, constructive feedback is our aim.

To add to the fun, they chanted *Ooh ah! Ooh ah!* several times with great enthusiasm. The teacher next door came over to ask Larah to keep the ruckus down. Larah assured the teacher that they would be quieter, and then she and her students decided they'd need to induct that teacher into Fireworks Writers a bit more gradually.

Maybe you're not ready for fireworks yet. That's just fine. Do what works for you, with this caveat: Students sniff out hesitancy and insecurity. If you haven't run writing response groups before, tell students that you're taking a risk to try this activity and that you'll see, together with them, how well it works. Explain that this responding thing is driven by them but that it needs to fit classroom decorum. After each of the first few times you conduct writing groups, debrief with your students how it went and what needs to change to improve the functioning of the group as *responders*.

Students as Responders

Students become more reliable, knowledgeable responders to the writings of fellow students if you take the time to teach them how to do so. In addition to the ideas mentioned elsewhere in this book on how to have students interact with each other and respond to each others' writings, here are some ideas for how to model responding for students and for teaching students to give constructive responses to their peers.

■ Helping Circle

Begin demonstrating the art of responding to students by using your own writing. When students are first asked to talk about each others' work, it's basically one incompetent writer talking to another incompetent writer. "Well, wha'd ya think?" "Oh, I liked it." This type of response is far from helpful for improving writing.

So hand out a piece of your own writing and ask them to give you some help. Tell them to point to good stuff first and then ask you some tough questions about your piece. What does it need more of? What to leave out, what to leave in? Take notes on what they say. Be accepting of their comments, not threatened. Listen; don't talk back to them in defense of your own written words. Then, bring in successive drafts of the same piece, showing them how you have incorporated their suggestions; invite further response and questions. It doesn't take much of this kind of modeling to have a dramatic effect on the quality of students' responses in peer editing.

The next step in the *Helping Circle*, a term coined by Macrorie, is to move from public critique of your writing to that of students' writings. We usually begin with a student whom we've asked in advance to be the first public participant, someone who is a rather confident—but not arrogant or defensive or necessarily perfect—writer. Because leading a group of students through public responding to other students' writings is a bit frightening the first time or two, it's important to begin with some rules or structures and then be prepared to enforce them. Our basic rules are simple: Be positive; be helpful; assume nothing—if you're unsure, ask the writer; be as specific as you can.

Sharing a piece of writing with a large group is definitely growth producing, but it may also be very frightening. Lessen the tension by making public miniresponses a routine part of your class structure. When you spot good writing, jot a note encouraging the student to share it with the group. Some students are understandably reluctant in this setting, but if you get them to try it once, the thrill of seeing thirty-two heads bobbing up and down in response to their writing will get them hooked. The key to this type of responding is the teacher's skillful enforcement of rules and sensitive attempts to help the novice through the experience.

Responding to Published Writing

Any writer will tell you that what he or she has published could still be improved. Writers' skill levels and their perspectives on topics continue to develop even after they reach the pinnacle of the writing world and become *published writers*. The work of published writers is also fair game on which your students may cut their responders' teeth.

Just as you did with your own writing to introduce the Helping Circle method of responding, introduce excerpts from published pieces into your writing class. When we bring in excerpts of published pieces, we don't always tell our students up front who wrote the piece. We just indicate that this is yet another piece of writing we will examine together. Students talk about what works in the writing, what confuses them, what they like in the piece, what they would omit or change—just as they do for their writing or for ours.

We use a range of writing styles for the excerpts and a range of authors, from those traditionally placed in the literary canon (William Faulkner and James Joyce, for example) to those who author young adult fiction (Laurie Halse Anderson and Walter Dean Myers) and nonfiction (Paul Janeczko and Deborah Heiligman). After students have responded to the writing and discovered who the published author is—which may lead them to want to read the entire book!—they have not only worked with a piece of rather fine writing but also discovered that, as responders, they learn lots about the sound and feel of good writing.

Publishing Excerpts from Students' Writings

The best way to teach the group to be skilled responders and to point out good writing is to publish weekly or twice-weekly excerpts from their own writing. Read quickly through the writings for the week, looking for particular pieces that work. Select a few, keeping the excerpts anonymous. Then, read some of the excerpts aloud to the class and ask for comments and "I like . . ." statements. The group members feel free to open up because they do not know the identity of the writer. We focus our comments on what makes the piece of writing work and what, if anything, the piece needs. Students look forward to the excerpts and take genuine pride when they "get published."

Partners

We frequently use response partners in our writing classes because they are much more efficient than are larger groups. Debates about fundamentals such as whether the teacher should choose the partner pairings or let the students choose their own partners occur among teachers. We've done it both ways and have success with both methods. We usually mix the two methods within the same class, sometimes assigning partners and sometimes letting students choose their partners. The key is that they're being productive. To promote productivity, Dawn has students prepare for their partner time. Each writer composes three to five specific questions about his piece of writing, questions that cannot be answered by a simple "yes," "no," or "maybe" response. After the writer reads his piece aloud to the partner, the partner offers responses to the piece, and then the writer asks his specific questions. The questions extend the discussion and help the writer to generate ideas for dealing with troublesome spots in the writing.

To build some self-reliance within the partnerships, we delay answering most of the tough questions students ask about their writing by saying, "Check with your partner on that," or "What did your partner say?" Students soon realize that the teacher is not the first line of response in our classes, thereby empowering the authority of the student writers in matters concerning their own writing. We give "partner of the week" awards and generally celebrate good collaborations. Of course, some kids prefer to work alone, and that has to be okay, too; but we generally continue to encourage them to seek out a partner.

Standing Groups

Small, supportive groups that function well together can be a comfortable place for a writer to get helpful responses. The key is to build groups who have confidence in one another and then keep them together for the tenure of the class—or at least for an entire grading period or completion of a major paper—letting them meet on a weekly basis. The group gives the individual writer a home base and a comfortable audience on whom to try something before it goes "public." In our experience, the respect and caring attitudes that form among these standing group members as a result of their prolonged work together is really quite remarkable.

Occasionally, groups will cease to function well. At that point, consider reassigning group members, especially at the beginning of a new grading term, unit, or major paper. Or, sit with that dysfunctional group and provide some modeling, again, about how to work together as effective responders. Despite the occasional pitfall here and there, we like working with standing groups because of the varying responses (that is, more than just the teacher's opinion) that emerge about the writing and because they help students to develop greater courage to take on new audiences/responders.

Editorial Boards ? 6

If you're a well-organized type who doesn't mind an involved set of procedures for responding, the editorial board approach may be helpful. Appoint groups of five or so students who are responsible for selecting good writing and suggesting editorial changes. The board's problem is to publish an excerpts edition by a certain deadline. All student writers are required to submit a finished piece to the editorial board. The board reads the submission, selecting pieces that have potential and notifying authors of their editorial decisions. Authors whose pieces are not selected are sent "rejection" notices. By simulating the actual process writers go through to become published, the teacher takes some of the mystique out of it, and students learn firsthand the joys and pains of getting published. Rotate the editorial responsibilities among your writers so that each of them experiences the processes, responsibilities, and pressures of editing someone else's writing.

Holistic Ratings

Another technique is to divide the class into groups and appoint a group leader. The groups read the papers from another group, responding and rating with a holistic rating guide. (See Chapter 11 for more information on holistic ratings.) This approach is especially well suited to Advanced Placement classes because the essays that students write when they take the Advanced Placement test are graded holistically. Specifically, each member of the group reads each paper, underlining examples of good writing and writing helpful and positive comments in the margin. The reader also makes general comments on the effectiveness of the piece, suggesting changes to the writer or simply asking the writer questions.

The entire group rates the paper on a five-point scale. The rating is assigned to the paper, and the group writes a brief defense of the rating. Such cooperative response develops the students' abilities to recognize effective writing, and it shifts much of the burden of careful response from the teacher to the students. As students continue to practice pinpointing the good stuff in others' writings, they begin to transfer those successful techniques into their own papers. Our goal is to make students more independent of our help. By relying on us less and on themselves more, students hone their confidence as writers and their own sense of what constitutes successful writing.

Writers' Groups by Other Names

Students are a quirky but usually malleable bunch. Perhaps they have participated in "writers' workshops" or "writing groups" since they were in fourth grade. Just hearing those familiar phrases again may make students groan.

Just as Larah invented Fireworks Writers, our colleague Renee Basinger[5] decided that her writing groups needed a new name for public sharing of writing, something to grab her fairly tough, streetwise students' attention. She coined the term "Burn Out." Sounds illegal, we know. Renee's idea was that her students' writings were so intense, so hot with truth and honesty and keeping it real, that the airing of them was a form of combustion. Students looked forward to hearing what writing had "caught fire" with their peers.

If you teach potential pyromaniacs, we don't recommend using the same term that Renee used. The point is that she found a term that inspired her students. We encourage you to do the same.

Beyond the Writers' Workshop

What we are about to say is heresy for some teachers: Writers' workshops are not a panacea for all of your students' writing woes. And more heresy: To improve as writers, students need more than writers' workshops. When the notion of writing workshops first appeared, teachers were seeking ways for students to have more authentic audiences for their pieces of writing. They were seeking audiences beyond the teacher-as-evaluator. Writers benefit from responses from living human beings in close proximity to them shortly after they complete a draft of a piece. That truism has not changed over the years. Students are available as a captive audience, so students' responding to other students' writing was and is a good idea. Like so much else in teaching, however, many methods lead to learning.

Writing workshops are not the only way to work with post-draft pieces of writing. We began this chapter by saying that students will, inevitably, want to hear your responses to their writing. They want to hear your ideas for what they need to do to improve. Having peers chime in on this process is valuable; they do not, however, take your place. Peers are about as knowledgeable as any beginning responder, and peers whom you have coached in the ways of responding are better than other novice responders. Nonetheless, students benefit from knowing what multiple audiences think about their pieces of writing.

Look for other ways to bring legitimate audiences to your students' writing. Are your students in tenth grade? What do the seniors in class with the English teacher down the hall have to say about your students' writing? Set up writing response groups with students in a nearby college or university who are studying to be English teachers. Use technology to set up response groups with others who are practiced writers, even if they live in the next state or another country.

Wikis and blogs are well suited as venues for online responding to writing. Online—or asynchronous—responding works very much like face-to-face—or synchronous—responding. Writers and responders are not required to be in the same room at the same time (synchronously) to offer useful suggestions and feedback to a piece of writing. For online responding, just as with face-to-face responding, the same guidelines apply. The same types of modeling and the same nature of responses are helpful. The groups benefit from knowing that you are checking on their commitment and keeping a sharp eye and virtual ear on this responding work. Doing so online or in person helps writing to grow and improve.

Writing workshops have been in use long enough to become routinized unless we safeguard against such complacency. We regularly hear students in writing workshops operating on autopilot: "Try adding detail," "I like the opening," "I'm a little confused by the conclusion." These comments are probably valid for any first or second draft of anything written by anyone. To what extent, however, are comments like these helping the individual student writer in this particular writing context for this specific written piece? Reponses are most helpful when they are tailored to a particular writer and a specific piece of writing.

Venture beyond the typical arrangement to others like the ones we suggest earlier in this chapter. Vary the routine. Change up the response venue and technique. Responses are valuable tools for writers only if writers are awake and attuned enough to hear and use what the audience has to say.

Varying Responses to Writing

We think it's important to vary response modes, audiences, and strategies to keep the whole responding business as fresh as possible. Students sometimes get lazy as responders, or they get into ruts with formula responses. Jog their complacency every once in a while by looking at the quality of their responses. Spend some time evaluating students' responses as a whole class, talk again about what kind of responses are helpful, and challenge them to read closely and ask good questions of the writer. When these factors are in place in your classroom, the skills associated with quality writing and effective responding show marked improvement.

Making Time to Save Time

You may be thinking something along the lines of "This is all well and good, but I don't have time for such responding." We hear you. There's no way around it: Responding takes time. Like other abilities, however, your capacity to respond well and quickly improves with practice.

What we know as longtime teachers of writing is that taking the time up front to respond to our students' writing—and doing so consistently—builds better writers and saves us time in the long run. Smooth, skilled writing is easier, quicker, and more pleasant to read—and to grade, if necessary—than is unpracticed and slipshod writing. Are the next William Faulkner and Laurie Halse Anderson sitting in our class, benefiting from our responses? We hope so, but we may not be able to identify those students in the early stages of their writing development. What we *do* know is that all writing improves with careful, targeted, skilled responding. Go for it.

NOTES

1. Rita and Dylan are fictitious names of student writers who preferred not to be identified.
2. Brett was a student in Darren's Principles of Writing Instruction course at Kennesaw State University in Kennesaw, Georgia.
3. Sarah was Erica DiMarzio's student at Delaware Valley High School in Milford, Pennsylvania.
4. Larah Buffington, a Kennesaw State University English Education undergraduate student with Dan Kirby, developed this idea while student teaching at Lovinggood Middle School in Powder Springs, Georgia.
5. Renee Basinger, a Kennesaw State University English Education Master's and doctoral student with both Darren and Dawn, developed this idea while teaching at South Cobb High School in Austell, Georgia.

Works Cited

Elbow, Peter. 1999. *Writing Without Teachers*. New York: Oxford University Press.

Macrorie, Ken. 1984. *Writing to Be Read*. Portsmouth, NH: Boynton/Cook.

Murray, Donald. 1985. *A Writer Teaches Writing*. Boston: Houghton Mifflin.

9

Revising Writing

The writer of any work . . . must decide two crucial points: what to put in and what to leave out. —**Annie Dillard, "To Fashion a Text"**

Revision can be tricky to teach and to learn. In some ways, moving into revision seems to put brakes on the fun students have with writing. Revising means getting down to some serious work with the writing.

When we work with students and their writing, we find that they adjust to writing in their journals, gaining fluency, so that their entries grow from only a sentence or two to a page and more of writing each day. Their writing in the journal and in class, with practice, becomes spontaneous, alive, creative, self-revealing, often entertaining, and sometimes very good—*but* it also is often sloppy, plagued with spelling errors, punctuated indifferently if creatively, written as one rambling paragraph—and it needs cutting. Verb endings have evaporated, sentences run into each other, verb tenses and pronouns are erratic, conclusions don't conclude, introductions don't introduce, descriptions don't describe—in short, the writings are first drafts and need to be *revised*.

Okay, you say to yourself, it's time to get *serious* about this writing stuff. The fun and games are over; it's time to bear down and get to work. These kids can obviously write; they're just being lackadaisical or lazy.

So you return that last batch of papers, give your students a little speech about cleaning up their act and maybe even getting ready for college English. You tell them to go back to their computers and correct their errors. You even generously offer to help them make corrections, not wanting to be too much of an ogre.

The students groan but get to work readily enough and rewrite the papers in a suspiciously short time. They ask only two questions while they work—one about whether you want their first drafts turned in with the revisions, the other about whether they get "credit" (a grade) just for *doing* the revisions. When you face the batch of "revisions" after school that day, the results confirm your worst suspicions. Most of the papers are very neatly retyped, carefully preserving every error in the original draft. A few kids have made a half-hearted attempt at correcting misspellings and punctuation. By and large, however, their papers get worse about as often as they get better. Only two kids seem to have done any effective revision of their papers, and they always do the best writing in the class anyhow.

You wonder where to go instructionally from here and think maybe your students are just too irresponsible to do any really good writing, and maybe you'll take that want-ads job as a clerk at the bookstore and forget the whole English teaching business. Or that's how it looks right now, late in the day, fatigued, frustrated, and feeling dead-ended.

We know the feeling. That's why we work to keep in mind that revision in writing is more than eliminating surface errors in spelling, punctuation, and usage; it's harder than it sounds and looks. Before you sigh and reach for the grammar book and those *serious* writing exercises, remember that revision does not have to be drudgery. Revision is just that— *re*-vision, "seeing" it again. When we revise our writing and do a good job of it, we see it anew and from a different perspective. We become our own reader, and we become critical and questioning, at least as much as we are able. We also read with appreciation and enjoyment. Even we English teachers weren't born with that innate ability; however, we *learned* to ask such questions and read with such a stance. When students don't revise in detail a paper that has been given back to them with the terse command to redo it and make it better, it's not because they are lazy. They simply haven't been taught *how* to revise yet.

Learning to revise writing is part of the larger developmental process of learning to write. Because learning to revise is a growth process, it needs to be approached systematically and with some knowledge of how it's likely to take place. Our job is to help students become competent *revisers*, and therefore better writers, rather than to turn them into error correctors. In this chapter, we suggest some good places to start the process of revision with students once you have them writing, and we point out some ideas about revision that will help you teach this potentially frustrating part of writing more systematically and with more success.

Thoughts on Revision

If we communicate nothing else about revision, let us make this statement upfront and clearly: Revision must be *coached*.

Working with students to coach their writing into being better is tremendously time-consuming. Doing so will sap your energy. Discussing with students their pieces of writing and what the pieces need to be better is hard work. We sometimes think we'll go live in a cave instead of work so hard again. And then we read our students' reworked, coached, revised papers—and it's all worth it again. Our energy is renewed.

Several central ideas guide our thinking about revision and how we teach it. We invite you to think about how you work with students to teach them how to revise writing, and to see if these ideas resonate with you.

Revision as a Series of Related Activities

Revision is really a series of closely related activities. A term describing writing, and especially revision, that you will often hear is *recursive*. Writing is recursive because the writer keeps circling back on the writing, tinkering, changing things, rethinking, rearranging mentally and on paper, and anticipating what is coming up. This act of recursiveness complicates writing wonderfully, making the actual act of writing practically impossible to describe with complete accuracy. To set aside the theorists and researchers for a moment and say it another way, when we write we also read and fix. We read in chunks the stuff we've just written, checking spelling, adding a word, moving a sentence, putting in details, and crossing out words, all in an effort to get the writing to sound right. We run ahead of ourselves down the page, already thinking of what we will say next. We write, pause, reread, reflect, and write some more. Fluent writers complete these recursive activities very quickly as they write; it's part of what we do to make meaning and to keep the flow of ideas and of meaning going. Without this recursive capacity, writing would be virtually impossible, as would talking, thinking, and even reading.

If writers engage in so many activities quickly and all at the same time, how do we teach an intervention process like revision? Knowing students are going to be all over the place at once in a piece of writing does not mean that we cannot point out to them revision strategies that will help them make their writing better. The teacher's job is to simplify the complexity of activities associated with revising and to chop it up into pieces so students can handle the process of revising in manageable chunks. Because writers are doing a lot of things at once does not mean that writers can't be taught. Fly-fishing is a rather compli-cated activity too, but Dawn's cousin Becky can teach you how to do it. Many complicated activities require simultaneous and numerous activities that can be taught, especially when we break them down into steps, moves, and actions that we learn discretely and then piece together for an effective end process or product. Like fly-fishing, revision is complex, but workable. When we teach writing as *craftsmanship*, and not as a body of knowledge to master, the job becomes manageable and we teachers can coach our students to do it.

It helps us to think of revising writing as occurring in four steps, knowing they overlap and can happen at the same time. The four steps are *in-process revision, re-vision, editing,* and *proofreading*. At some point in our work with writers and in our teaching, we focus attention on each revision step separately, coaching young writers in the tricks of the trade, demonstrating to them how revision works for us as writers.

Four Steps of Revision

Step 1: In-Process Revision. *In-process revision* takes place as the writing is going on, and it is part of what makes writing such a complicated business. Writers ask themselves questions as they go along, questions such as, "Is this what I really want to say?" or "Is this part clear?" or "How can I say this part better?" and then they make adjustments to try to get closer to their intended purposes. They add words and phrases and sometimes sentences; they delete and cross out; they change and reorder and alter. They listen to the *voice* of the writing and make adjustments so it will sound right. They become their own *readers* even as they write, often stopping to reread part of the paper from the beginning. They look back to see what has already been done, and they look ahead, anticipating what will be said next.

With various computer programs and research processes, we can observe in-process revision; when we watch students write by hand, scratching out sentences and drawing arrows to move paragraphs around, we see evidence of in-process revision. What we can't see, however, is the thinking behind these changes in the text. What did the student see, think, read, connect, or reject that caused her to make the revision? That's the part that we have a hard time understanding *as it happens*, even if students can talk to us later about what they recall of their reasoning or fleeting impressions. In-process revision is probably impossible to measure, and it is certainly as individual as the writer; but we do know that it grows with practice. As writers reach maturity, they interrupt the writing more and more and spend substantial time as readers and in-process revisers. They write, but they revise as much as they write.

For us, revising takes more time than does writing. We are able to generate a flow of words and capture our thoughts, but then we need time to make our writing more precise, accurate, vivid, or coherent. Skilled writers tinker with the finer points of expression as they write, getting that first or second draft closer to what they want to say than they were able to do as novice writers who struggled just to get thoughts and ideas onto paper or the computer screen.

Reading out loud is one way to enhance in-process revision in the classroom, but reading aloud has so many benefits for growing writers that it's difficult to isolate its effects on revision. Once students have spent some time reworking their pieces of writing, we model how our processes of revision work. We project our pieces on the document camera or projected computer screen and "read with a pencil in hand," marking our pieces of writing as we read from them. We try to make our thoughts visible to student writers, interrupting ourselves as we read our writing to tell our students what we're doing to the writing as we read it, showing them what we are changing and talking about *why* we think the changes need to be made. We talk about our struggles, writer to writer, and our efforts to "make it sound right." By hearing us talk and think through our pieces of writing, students see that all pieces of writing benefit from revision.

Step 2: Re-Vision. *Re-vision.* We write the word like this to remind our students and us that a good bit of revision is seeing the writing again in a different way. There is value in trying on several different perspectives, of literally writing whole drafts from scratch. Most teachers, anxious that the writing job be done by Friday, have never encouraged enough of this type of work in their classrooms. Deadlines are necessary. All writers have them. But we also need to teach our students the option—and even the necessity—of trying the writing in a different way.

Students tend to balk at the idea of rewriting a whole draft from scratch, so we often begin reinforcing this notion of re-seeing the writing by working on writing leads. Students can have better papers instantly if they will just do something about how they start them. Authors grab a reader or lose that reader in the first paragraph or half-page. It's a simple matter to write three or four leads for a piece of writing that is off to a rough start. No, we're not talking about topic sentences. We're talking about working on the device and on crafting the writing that is the opening of the paper. Is the piece of writing improved if it begins with a scenario? A rhetorical question? A startling statement? How might the writer best draw the reader into the piece?

Once students get some practice in crafting opening sequences that reel in readers, try the same kind of process with other paragraphs or sections of the paper. Now that they have readers, how do they keep them? Students will sometimes drift into autopilot, churning out material to reach a page or word requirement or just to be *done.* Talking about both what a paragraph *does* along with what it *says* helps students re-see their writing and its impact on a reader. Does it explore a related idea? Illustrate or extend a point? Entertain a different view? Transition to another section? How does each paragraph relate to the ones before and after it? We often examine these questions in detail with our students and find the resulting list enlightening. We call this activity *text mapping*. That is, we map the route through the piece as formed by the purpose that each paragraph accomplishes within the larger piece of writing.

Our job as teachers of re-vision often is simply to be alert to possibilities that student writers might have missed. That's what coaches do. They have fresh ideas and ask a lot of questions. Have you thought about doing it this way? Are you satisfied with this order? How will you end the piece? Where does your writing gain momentum? What are you really trying to say? Does this piece of writing do what you want it to do? Those questions are seeds of revisions waiting to emerge through the chaff of unnecessary words, cluttered sentences, and unfocused images.

Step 3: Editing. Editing, to us, involves at least two people, writer and editor, working on the piece of writing. The relationship is a special one, supportive, helpful, nonthreatening, probing, and sometimes challenging. We work as editors with our students, but we prefer to teach them how to be editors for each other in Writers' Groups.

This task takes time early in the class, but it saves time later. Plus, the rewards go far beyond teaching writing. We often model response groups after the techniques we learned when working with fellows from the National Writing Project. Each group has a leader, responsible mainly for seeing that each member reads and participates. When we lead a group, the first question we often ask before each member reads is "What help do you need from this group for this piece of writing?" We want the writer to put into words specifically how the group might help her before she reads. Doing so keeps the group from shotgunning—from commenting on anything and everything just for the sake of commenting—and it keeps the group from making vague comments like "That was nice." To enhance this part of the responding and editing process, Dawn has the writer prepare in advance three to five specific questions about the piece of writing the group is to consider. These questions ask for specific advice and cannot be answered with a simple "yes" or "no." Instead of asking, "Do I have an effective introduction?" a better question is "How can I make the opening scene more action filled?"

After the reading, we make sure each person around the table responds to the writer's request for help. We at least want those in the group to speak to the writer's stated problems or questions with the piece, but these are usually the catalyst for discussing the writing, not the sole points of the discussion. At first, addressing the writing in this manner is not always easy; but the members of the group keep at it, and it doesn't take the response group members long to become pretty good editors—not merely error hunters—for each other. Because everyone in the group takes part as responder, and as writer and reader, all have ownership in the group.

At the same time, as the teacher, we rotate from group to group, concentrating mainly on modeling responses after members read. We use a fishbowl approach to teach response groups how to be true editors and responders. In this approach, we pull a group of experienced student writers into the center of the room, their five desks facing each other in a tight circle. The other students circle close behind them. Then, we simply lead the group in reading and responding, pausing now and then to point out to the audience at their backs why and how they are doing certain things. It looks weird at first, and the first time in the center of the fishbowl most assuredly feels odd, but we have found that it works.

Step 4: Proofreading. Proofreading sometimes takes place with editing. It's the job of cleaning up the paper and eliminating surface errors. It's the least important activity of revision until the final stages of the paper. Traditionally, some writing teachers have taught only this kind of revision, leaving their students with the impression that learning to be a good writer is learning to avoid or correct errors. It's a narrow and narrow-minded approach to teaching writing, and alone it produces properly correct and uniformly dull prose because it teaches students to edit out the risks in their writing in favor of correctness.

Writers work on several of these "steps" at different times in their writing processes and sometimes on several at once. The steps are not rigid, but we find that delaying a focus on proofreading helps our students truly *revise*, not just *correct* writing.

Developmental Processes of Writing and Revising

Revision should be taught in terms of what we know about the processes of writing and in terms of what we know about the growth of young writers. We don't get frustrated and angry when the novice violinist saws out squawks and screeches. We encourage the novice to practice, and we endure the assault on our ears with patience, knowing this racket will grow into sweet music with time, regular effort, and proper direction.

A lot of our problem is solved when we quit thinking of revision as correcting mistakes and start to *teach* student writers how to revise. When we do that, we discard the old prejudice that students are lazy and have to be forced to make their writing better, and we become able to see just what they do when they write and revise—if we are willing to take the time to watch them. We also start to see how they develop as writers and how revision fits into that development.

Kids are not lazy. They want to write good papers, and they work hard at it. We have done a lot of formal and informal research on students' writing. We've watched a lot of students writing and revising papers. We're amazed at how hard they work. We have watched students plan, draft, revise, and rewrite a paper in one class period, after instructions. One senior made fifty-three effective changes from the original to a revised draft as she worked, and we've found that many of our students can work at that level. Using the computer to help us track the number and nature of the changes is not especially difficult, and doing so helps us understand her writerly concerns and see what, specifically, she thought needed to be changed.

We have seen students make powerful changes by revising and editing their writing when their peers or we have clearly demonstrated to the student writers what they are to do and when they work in an atmosphere that is nonthreatening. During one semester of work with a well-trained editing group, we have seen students grow from halting, damaged writers barely able to fill part of a page with unreadable prose into good writers with style and sometimes brilliance. As with any successful activity, students can learn to approach revising with excitement and joy.

Forget the notion that student writers can't revise. Take some time to watch them. Then, structure your class to help them do a better job. Show them how to revise, and plan ways for them to help each other. Make sure that what you ask them to do is appropriate for them as writers and for the writing job at hand.

Start with the Familiar

Revision cannot be successful until students are practiced in a particular mode of writing. Students cannot be confident enough to tinker with a piece of writing until they have practiced enough and know they will not destroy what they have worked so hard to write. If you're getting resistance from normally willing students when you try to get them to work on revision, then you may need to go back to writing activities such as those in Chapter 4 for more practice before pushing revision too hard.

Remember, when your students begin a new mode or form of writing, they need time to practice this new experience before they might reasonably be expected to revise it with any success. Students who happily write and revise personal narratives into flawless form may not nimbly write and effectively revise a movie review the first few times they try—although both are legitimate kinds of writing for your class. Let them get comfortable with the new kind of writing first. Let them get the feel of it and find out what they have to say before you expect them to do a good job revising it. That is, let them *get it down* before you ask them to *get it right.*

Choices, Importance, and Frameworks

The piece of writing to be revised needs to be important to the student. The usual situation in the classroom is that students want to finish papers as quickly as possible and turn them in so they'll not have to fool with them anymore. This attitude is especially apparent when your students feel that their writing is not good enough. School has encouraged this get-it-done-fast approach to writing with days neatly divided into roughly sixty- or ninety-minute-long class periods and teachers insisting, "Turn it in at the end of the period." Because we're not willing to take extended time with a piece of writing, we get hastily done and shoddily produced two-draft papers (one class period for the explanation, prewriting, and first draft; then one more class period for the rewrite; and too often, older kids get to do *both* drafts in one period!). We teach our students to write fast; and, with such an approach, we teach mediocrity. There is no reason why we can't spend more time teaching revision on fewer pieces of writing that lead into an elaborated piece of writing. Often, less really is more.

If the piece of writing is meaningful to them, most students are willing to revise extensively and will seek your help in making it better. Your interest in what they're writing and your encouragement of the good things you find in their writing are the most important factors in keeping students going through the work of several drafts, but there are a few other simple ways that you might encourage revision.

Choosing from several pieces to edit is one way of getting something the student is willing to work on longer. After all, *selecting* is an important form of editing. If we expect our students to take a paper through more than one draft, we always try to make sure they may choose from at least three pieces they have written.

Better yet, we encourage you to work from within a framework of writing, such as memoir. Within the memoir framework[1] students write several short pieces such as a name piece, a map piece, a neighborhood piece, a parent piece, a piece about an artifact from childhood, and several others. Then, students choose several pieces to weave together for inclusion in their final memoirs. This type of revising is effective for student writers for several reasons. First, it allows the writer to select pieces for revision with a theme or focus in mind: What is it that the writer wants the reader to understand about him or her as a result of having read the memoir piece? Second, it allows the writer to work from within a sound knowledge of a genre of writing because we have read thirty or more excerpts from published memoirs as we wrote our own pieces. Third, it allows the student writer to work on meaningful transitions and other devices to weave the separate pieces together into one final product in an effective manner. Finally, the writer is completely in charge of choosing what goes into the memoir, so that the writer cares about the writing and is the authority on the writing. These factors encourage student writers to work on revision following processes used by real writers. This approach to selecting and crafting writing also allows the student to choose for revision only those pieces that are personally significant and important to the writer. Then, of course, we move into deciding how to publish the students' memoirs.

Revising a piece of writing for publication gives the work a new importance, and the student is more interested in getting it right. Publishing makes the writing real to your students, no longer only an exercise to submit to the teacher. In-class publishing is essential to any meaningful work on revision because it gives students a valid reason to revise their writing. Suddenly, the stakes are higher when work goes public in some form.

Working together in groups to revise papers is another way to give students an audience for their writing and, therefore, a reason to revise. Reading aloud the papers on which they are working is an important tool in revision work, but you'll have to structure opportunities for it in your classroom carefully. Students need to hear their writing, and the immediate response of a group of classmates may be very valuable in editing a paper. We don't hesitate to use the grade to get students to revise their writing. Part of many students' willingness to work hard on papers instead of turning in the first draft and forgetting it is that we assure students they will earn better grades if they work to improve their pieces. Sheer logic indicates that our statement is accurate, and notice that we say *improve* the writing rather than merely correct the errors. We ask students to do more than purely proofread their writing. We have found that our students do a better job and work harder when we point out the good things in their writing and ask them to expand on those, rather than telling them, "This is what you did wrong." There are times when we might even withhold the grade—any grade—for poorly written papers from capable students until they try again. Sometimes, we resort to whatever works. Our best successes with revision in the classroom, however, have always come when we've emphasized what the student writers are doing right.

Using a Focused Conference

A short, focused conference can be very effective in teaching revision. Conferences don't have to last twenty or thirty minutes per student to be effective. A short conference of three to five minutes, conducted by a teacher skilled and practiced at asking pointed questions to help focus the conference and the student's ongoing writing, can let you confer with most of your student writers each time that you conduct conferences. Just like in the response group, we ask the student writer, "How can I help you?" The writing belongs to the writer, not to us. We do not take papers out of their hands and show them how to fix them. We do not talk first, unless it is to ask students to tell us about their pieces of writing and the help they might need as writers and as revisers.

If students draw a blank and don't know what help they need, then we ask them to read the piece to us quietly. We tell them what we hear and ask them again, "What help do you need?" Usually that gets us going. Sometimes we send the student writers back to their response groups, and in some classes we will not confer with students if they haven't tried their pieces out on their groups.

During revision, we continue to stress the fact that students own their writing. We don't want our student writers to be overly dependent on us. Students' questions such as, "Is this good?" or "Will you read this and tell me what you think?" or "Can you fix this for me?" get merely a look from us. Students soon learn that they are to go *first* to their groups for responses, that they need to work on elaborating and crafting and otherwise revising their papers based on the in-class activities we have explored together as writers, and that *then* they might come to us for a more extended conference on what the paper needs. We are not in the business of reading most first drafts, other than for a general impression, and we are not in the business of being the only responder in the classroom. We *are* in the business of offering meaningful writing opportunities to students, of teaching them how to write and revise effectively and how to respond to each others' writings, and of using short, focused conferences with our student writers *at the point of need.*

We frequently use conferences in our teaching of writing and revising, and we see some real growth in students' writings as a result of that technique. We enjoy conferences because they let us work as writers, one-on-one with our students. What we like best about this technique, however, is that it is directed by the students according to what each one needs for a particular piece of writing at a particular time and within a particular context.

You Are the Model

You're the first model for your students. We advise you to write and *to revise with them.* Let your student writers see you struggle with writing. Talk to them about what you're doing as you revise. Go through the whole process with them, talking about your problems and the way you try to solve them with each step. Show them the different drafts of your work and the way your writing changes from one draft to the next. Document cameras and computers are very helpful for doing so.

Individual Differences in Revision Processes

Remember that there are individual differences in the ways students revise. Revising is one of the many processes of writing; therefore, it is as unique as each writer who undertakes it. When you teach revision, allow enough flexibility for these differences among the student writers who are in your classroom.

Look at this original and revised paper by Lynn.

Original Draft

The jumps are coming and the horse breaks into a dead run. Low again the rider prepares for the jump. Up and over, the horse's legs stretch outward and down for the ground making a huge arch.

Revised Draft

The jumps are nearing and my horse breaks into a dead run. Staying low on its back I prepare for the jump. Up and over. My horse's legs extend. Stretching and reaching for the ground on the other side. Making a huge arch in the air.

—*Lynn*[2]

No two students will revise in the same way. For this paper, Lynn only wrote two drafts, but she does a great deal of in-process revising. She does little editing (she changed the point of view on her teacher's suggestion), but she's a near-perfect proofreader. Being able to do a good job in two drafts is rare in the high-school classroom, but you'll have a few students who work well in a short time.

Let's take a look at some more substantial revisions. In the extended example below, Marie[3] revises a paper about a literary work after receiving feedback from her teacher, Ryan Dippre. We'll start with how she opens the essay.

Original Draft

Beauty is to be admired; it is the nature of human beings to do so. However, there is a line that should not be crossed by society. Society makes many allowances for those who are beautiful. The line that should not be crossed is between ignoring harmless deviations from what is socially acceptable and ignoring the actions of a morally corrupt individual. Oscar Wilde's *The Picture of Dorian Gray* poses the question, how important is beauty, and it also demonstrates the willingness of society to cross the line. Superficial beauty allows for those who possess it to act immorally more often than those without it, but how much societal forgiveness of an individual is too much?

Marie is off to a decent start, with some tentative insight about Wilde's intentions in the novel. She seems to have a handhold for speaking about the text: the possibly dangerous allowances we make for the beautiful. But at this point, she is still in the process of sorting out her thinking, evidenced by the choppy sentences, jumbled order, and generalities. The writing here doesn't flow. Such is to be expected in early drafts; it's okay.

In responding to her writing, Marie's teacher Ryan suggests that Marie is dealing with two questions at once ("How important is beauty?" and "How much societal forgiveness of an individual is too much?"). He also asks her to elaborate on her claim that admiration of beauty is a quality of human nature, and prompts her to be more specific. Here's Marie's revised draft of the opening.

Revised Draft

It is in the nature of human beings to admire beauty. In fact, society makes many allowances for those who are beautiful. Frequently, people use beauty as a measure of quality, even when they probably should not. This beauty can perhaps become dangerous when it is given too much credibility by society, or when beauty replaces all other meaning in life. Beauty can allow those who possess it to act immorally more often than those without it. Oscar Wilde's *The Picture of Dorian Gray* questions the importance of beauty in life, and examines the impact it has on the lives of those who possess it.

In this novel, the main character, Dorian Gray, answers that question for himself. He realizes that in his world his beauty takes priority. That is what people see when they look at him, and frequently that first impression never changes into a true impression of him. He realizes this, and decides to take advantage by continuing to use his beauty as a cover-up for his evil practices.

There's rarely a quick fix in revising. Marie has changed most of her original introduction, breaking it into two paragraphs and elaborating on her ideas. Especially noticeable is the improved *pacing*. Marie is working with complex concepts that take some time to unfold. This revision shows improvement in helping move a reader through a series of propositions, likely due to Ryan's suggestion that she deal with one question at a time. The result isn't perfect. Marie seems to be using the typical "funnel" model for an introduction, which follows a general-to-specific formula. Although a conventional approach for academic essays, it doesn't make for particularly compelling reading. If we were working with Marie, we might discuss some alternative strategies such as beginning with a specific scene or example from the book, using narrative as a means to engage a reader, or asking questions that challenge us to think.

Let's move on to look at how Marie revised one of the interior paragraphs of her paper.

Original Draft

Society's true view of Dorian Gray was what he wished them to believe. Despite his becoming more and more morally depraved as time went on "he was not really reckless, ... in his relations to society" (Wilde 145). He kept his standing in society by inviting guests to lavish dinner parties. "To [his guests] he seemed to be of the company of those whom Dante describes as having sought to 'make themselves perfect by the worship of beauty'" (Wilde 146). He kept up appearances quite well in society, so, despite the rumors of his immoral side, they never abandoned him and his youthful perfection.

In this paragraph Marie explains Dorian's talent for maintaining appearances despite rumors of depravity. Here's her revised paragraph after feedback from Ryan, who asked her to expand on how society influences Dorian's actions. We've italicized the changes.

Revised Draft

Society's true view of Dorian Gray was what he wished them to believe. Despite his becoming more and more morally depraved as time went on "he was not really reckless, . . . in his relations to society" (Wilde 145). He kept his standing in society by inviting guests to lavish dinner parties. "To [his guests] he seemed to be of the company of those whom Dante describes as having sought to 'make themselves perfect by the worship of beauty'" (Wilde 146). He kept up appearances quite well in society, so, despite the rumors of his immoral side, they never abandoned him and his youthful perfection. *Society's continued support of Dorian as the years went by proved to him that he was right in his thinking. Evil really was just as acceptable as good when one does it right, and Dorian definitely had that figured out. His peers did not believe that someone as beautiful as he could possibly hide a dark side, and they showed that by continuing to invite him into their homes and going into his home. They never went so far as to publicly shun him. They chose to not believe any evil could come from his beauty. Essentially they chose beauty over morals, just as Dorian himself did.*

In this instance, Marie chose to build on her writing by extending the paragraph. We think the elaboration is effective. Through exploring the complicity of Dorian's acquaintances, Marie connects the threads of her argument instead of just assuming the reader gets it.

Students often struggle to determine how much explanation readers need, usually erring on the side of "not enough." If your reader is always the teacher (i.e., the "expert"), this tendency sort of makes sense: Why go into the details of explaining something that your reader (that is, the teacher, the expert) probably already knows? By gently helping students imagine the needs of a broader audience, we help them see the responsibilities they take on in making a point.

Marie's work on the conclusion to her essay is also revealing.

Original Draft

The acceptance of society is something most in the setting of this novel desire. Sometimes who society accepts can go a bit far. This book raises the question of how much acceptance is too much. The society in Wilde's novel turns a blind eye to suspected evil acts so as to feel right accepting the superficially beautiful Dorian Gray. This act answers the question of how much with the answer that there isn't much that would be too much evil in this society.

Like her original introduction, this paragraph has some classic draft hallmarks: passive phrasing, awkward syntax, and more general statements. In his feedback, Ryan identified the sentence structure as problematic. Here's Marie's revision. Again, we've italicized the changes.

Revised Draft

The acceptance of society is something most in the setting of this novel desire. *Sometimes society accepts those who are too evil to be worthy when instead those individuals should be rejected on principle.* This book raises the question of how much acceptance is too much, *specifically with Dorian Gray. It raises the question of how much weight should be placed on something as seemingly superficial as beauty.* The society in Wilde's novel turns a blind eye to suspected evil acts so as to feel right accepting the superficially beautiful Dorian Gray. This act *vaguely* answers the question of how much *importance is given to beauty by showing that it is important, but the beauty needed to cover-up actions and what actions are allowed to be ignored is not stated. Assumptions are the only way to truly answer the question: first to assume about the beauty of a person and then about the society.*

Here, Marie uses overall paragraph structure while again offering some further elaboration. We think the changes improve clarity though additional challenges remain. Marie seems to be still working out what she thinks and how best to say it. It's not easy.

To illustrate further the point that we are all different as writers and as revisers, look at how we write. Darren keeps several notebooks around for jotting down ideas and observations. He uses a site such as Diigo.com to bookmark socially any items of interest. He typically has several pieces of writing "fermenting" at once, and he uses a journal or the computer to begin writing. He gives himself plenty of latitude to chase down stray thoughts once he begins serious drafting on the computer, and he usually only prints a hard copy when the piece is ready to be reviewed by a critical reader. Dawn waits to write a first draft until she is sitting at home with her laptop, and she engages in lots of retrospective reading and in-process revising. Even so, she writes a first draft straight through, shaping her writing more at the point of utterance rather than mentally in advance. She's not a detailed advance planner, nor is she a one-draft writer. Dawn prints her draft, rereads with pen in hand, and then returns to the computer for more drafts, seeking feedback from a partner after her second or third complete draft.

Our personal examples illustrate that despite our individual differences as writers, we all go through the agonies of prewriting and revising. We think these processes in some form are universal for writers.

The point is that all kinds of writer-revisers will populate any class you teach, and all of them need your suggestions and encouragement to get better at writing.

Choosing Not to Revise

Students should have the choice not to revise. Remember that students can't really do a good job of revising unless the piece is important to them. If they are not ready for revising, or not really involved in the writing, then pushing them to edit in depth and proofread in detail will be a frustrating experience for them and an exasperating one for you. As you work on revision, be sensitive to when students have had enough. We have worked with students with whom we could have exchanged six or seven or more drafts had we the energy to do so, but both our students and we are often tired of a piece after three or four substantive drafts. Some may return to the same writing later, but they reach a saturation point at which they are done for the moment.

Remember, also, that sometimes the piece of writing itself is not worth the trouble. Sometimes, filing the writing in the writer's notebook is enough.

Keeping Revision Going

Most students we teach come to us knowing nothing of revision beyond hunting for errors in a first draft, and they're not very good at that. What we have to do first is get them to work on a paper for a longer period of time than a class period. Sometimes more than fifteen minutes.

Students want to finish the thing and turn it in. We want them to write something real for them and for us and turn it into a quality piece of work. How do we keep them working, writing, revising, and editing?

First, the writing must be important *to the students* because *their writing belongs to them.* You will save yourself and your students a lot of grief—and your students will write better—if you accept that idea.

Working in response groups in an inviting and encouraging atmosphere shows students possibilities and lets them know that their writing is appreciated and is taken seriously. For most students, their peers' approval makes the difference between writing that is merely a class exercise, something to get done and turn in, and writing that is an expression of who they are.

We push our student writers. Nancie Atwell "nudges" her students. We shove ours. "Tell me more. Tell me more." They hear that more than anything else from us. We tell them frankly, "You are used to finishing it and turning it in. I want you to try to stretch it. There's something here you haven't said yet," and we tell them, "Write more. Tell it all. Take the reader with you."

Our students write lots of short, exploratory pieces, looking for important writings that will grab them. Then, we have them work on what Kirby and Kirby (2007) have termed *elaboration* and *crafting*. These are two types of revision for which Kirby and Kirby have devised specific activities suited to the type of writing that students are doing.[1] Take a look at the personal narrative, the kind of writing done in the "Anatomy" (see page 31). The following are brief samples of these types of revisions as devised for the memoir framework.

Elaboration: First-Revision Options for Personal Narrative

Read your piece aloud to a partner. Listen for places where you can add more stuff. Mark these places as you read. Try at least two elaborations. More is better.

1. *Character*. Flesh out a person in your story. Describe the character in more detail. Select one or two things about the character and develop them like a cartoonist would. How do his hands look? How does her mouth work when she smiles or talks? What about hair, eyes, clothes? Favorite sayings? Where do you see the character when you close your eyes?
2. *Dialogue*. Let them talk. Don't tell us what they say. Let's hear it from them. Don't worry about how you punctuate it now. Just use real voices.
3. *Scene Setting*. Develop scenes in your piece in more detail. Look for parts where you mention a place but don't give us a picture of it.
4. *Looping*. Find the best parts in your piece, and take off on another freewriting from there. See what else you know about this memory. Run the movie in your head again.
5. *Write More*. Finish it. Tell it all. Pick up the story right where you left off and ride it to the end.

Remember, the key is to *write more*. After students have worked with another draft that includes their elaborations and with their response partners, they're ready for further revisions called *crafting*.

Crafting: Second-Revision Options for Personal Narrative

This is the tough part. You have to work alone, and you won't always know what you're doing. You can try these revisions out on somebody later, but right now you have to hack it out alone.

Begin first with chunks, pieces of text that are several sentences long. Choose at least one of these to work with.

Beginnings (Try at Least Two)

1. The hook: "I should have known Mrs. Swartz hated kids."
2. Scene setting: "It was a dark and stormy night."

3. Telling detail: "There on the pavement was a small child's tennis shoe."
4. Character throwing: "Teddy Howland was the skinniest, ugliest kid in Eureka."
5. Walking: "Giving credit where credit is due, if it hadn't been for my mother, I never would have gotten him in the first place, mainly because my father didn't like dogs" (Goldman 2001).
6. Dialogue: "I'm not even sure I like you."
7. Intentional fragments: "Identical rows of desks. Gray shirts everywhere you look. No bright patterns, no variety, no uniqueness. This is no kind of school for me."
8. Hypotheticals: "Imagine a girl who's just deleted her Facebook account and tossed her smartphone off a bridge. Social suicide, or a new beginning?"
9. Questions: "What's more important, preserving a friendship or telling the truth?"

Endings (Try at Least Two)
1. Circle: End where you began.
2. Aha!: Sadder but wiser, or "Gee, look what I learned."
3. A feeling: Stuck in Mobile with the Memphis blues again.
4. Drawstring: "And that's how it happened."
5. Surprise: The strange twist at the end.
6. What now: Where do we go from here? What's the next step?
7. Curiosity: The next thing I want or need to know.

Moving Chunks (No Limit; Cut and Paste)
1. Movement: Pacing readers, making them play your game.
2. Paragraphs: Have some. Keep them short unless they have pictures.
3. Scenes: Shuffling the story.
4. Subheadings: What would they be? Help the reader follow your thinking.

Deleting Chunks (No Limit; Follow Rules)
1. Nice but doesn't fit. Save it.
2. Not nice and doesn't fit either. Cut it.
3. Eradicate chaff words: -ly words, being words.
4. Compact and compress. Cut the "telling."
5. Conclusion: If it only repeats information, cut it.

Now that the hard part is done, turn to some relaxing sentence-level revisions. Make at least ten specific changes.

Sentence Level
1. Concrete detail: Add sensory stuff.
2. Specificity: Name stuff.
3. Adverbs: Minimize using those adverb props.
4. Strong verbs: Search and destroy every *is* and *was*. Replace with specific action verbs.
5. Direct expression: Cure a serious case of *would*. Search and destroy.

Notice that whether you teach revision strategies like these in two formal steps coupled with response groups and conferences, or whether you work with revision informally in conferences and editing groups, your students are still writing and you haven't gotten to proofreading yet. Do it last, as we suggest, and you will find it is less of a problem than it once was. Try it. It may surprise you.

Technology and Revision

When revision is technically easy, students are more likely to do it. Rather than just retyping the piece and fixing the commas, students can move chunks of text with ease with the computer. They can save one opening paragraph (perhaps in another document) and write two more to see which one works best. They see how the piece sounds when it starts in the middle or even with the last paragraph of the piece, all with cut-and-paste options that they can undo if the writing isn't enhanced. Word processing, of course, allows students to re-see their papers each time they drop text in or out of the draft, helping them understand real revision, not just minor correcting. With writing platforms such as wikis and Google Docs, they can easily track changes from draft to draft, using a split screen to see the same portion of their text written in two different ways to help them judge which one is more effective.

Our digitally comfortable students—which are almost all of them at this point in time—learn computing at an early age. We commonly see two-year-olds sitting with an iPad or other tablet, learning letters, numbers, a second language, and just playing games that, if nothing else, increase their fine motor skills. The long-term impact of such immersive, interactive technology is unclear, and although we are by no means uncritical cheerleaders, we do see opportunities for writers, revisers, and editors. It's clear that today's students know lots about useful computing that can enhance their writing and academic lives—not just their knowledge of games—with the right encouragement and guidance.

Document Sharing

The sheer convenience of a document-sharing system makes working in online writing groups, editing, and responding to writing accessible and relatively easy. With just a bit of instruction, most teachers and students who are not familiar with document sharing will pick up the essentials of using the system. Student groups collaborating on a project may use a system like Google Docs, part of the Google suite of applications, without worrying about working on separate versions of the same piece of writing (all versions are automatically saved and are retrievable), or which draft was most recently updated (all are automatically dated), or who had what where and in what condition. It's all there for anyone with whom the documents are "shared" to access. All it takes is a willingness to learn and experiment. The convenience of document sharing blurs the lines among creating, drafting, writing, revising, editing, and publishing in ways that may be constructive for our student writers to consider.

Cloud computing is a trendy term, and we know firsthand the potential for convenient collaboration and publishing this kind of technology presents. In this context, a *cloud* is a server that you don't own or maintain but to which you have access. Your documents, videos, and pictures may all be stored and viewed on the cloud. Some services, like Google

Docs, are free; other companies charge a fee. The specific platform doesn't matter, but the concept does. It's one that is here to stay—until something even better takes its place.

Writers need readers—a community for praise, suggestions, feedback, and responses. Audiences who access written work online may do so at anytime (24-7) from anywhere (school, home, the parking lot) and on any device (computer, laptop, smartphone) that has Internet connectivity. Document-sharing technology invites collaboration and meaningful interaction about written pieces while they are being developed and after they are published.

If you haven't yet tried out the cloud, we encourage you to do so and then to explore ways to use it effectively in your teaching. You may be surprised to learn that your students already work in such environments frequently and that they are able to answer some of your questions about how to navigate the system. As you give Google Docs or something similar a whirl, notice how it affects the ways in which you plan, write, organize, revise, respond, collaborate, and create with other people. Notice how you feel when you receive a plethora of responses to your posted (published, even if still in-process) work. Discussing such topics with your students will help them understand how medium and mode impact written and visual published products. Learning how to make that outcome a positive one is essential.

Jumping In

We use technology extensively as writers and revisers. Coauthoring a book, as you might imagine, can be challenging. We met regularly in person, but those meetings were for talking through and hammering out problems and new ideas, not for hours of silent side-by-side writing. We wrote individual chapters, editing and revising and adding completely new material to the third edition of this book, incorporating new theories, technologies, student work, and new or updated ideas and practices. Once one of us had a draft of a chapter or of a section of a chapter in good enough shape to share with the other, we uploaded the draft to a shared cloud-based workspace. We revised each other's work within that space, giving us the ability to see drafts as they emerged, trace and compare versions of the piece, tinker with it until we thought it was basically done. Our own processes, then, are recursive within and among chapters as we write.

We like using wikis and blogs in our teaching of writing for some of the same reasons. Students more readily own the work, and we are able to be an observer and/or active responder within the site as the work and nature of the collaborative technology and its uses evolve. We certainly understand that moving to such paperless environments can be intimidating for teachers. At the same time, learning how to use a wiki, blog, or cloud-based program is becoming simpler all the time. You can create a blog or wiki in thirty seconds; sites such as Wordpress and Wikispaces have simple to follow tutorials to get you started. Seriously, it's as easy as going to the site and clicking on a button that says "Get Started." Rather than detailing the procedures here, we invite you to read up on the topic either online or in some very thorough books. Will Richardson's *Blogs, Wikis, Podcasts and Other Powerful Web Tools for Classrooms* (2010) and Dana Wilber's *iWrite: Using Blogs, Wikis, and Digital Stories in the English Classroom* (2010) both provide specific and pain-free instructions for getting familiar with these tech possibilities.

We like the ways in which cloud or Web-based virtual environments allow our students' writing groups and us to provide asynchronous, always available feedback to writing. These technology-based contributions expand our workshop space far beyond the hour on

Tuesday that we give it in person in class. By having the work available to those within a peer group, and as appropriate, to all in our classes and to other writing groups within the state or internationally, we have the ability to allow students to interact with a range of readers, responders, writers, and revisers. These virtual audiences, who may be readers and responders for our students' writings, help us create a bit of leverage and stress the value of revision. Working in a group much larger than the one in our physical classes increases the sense of accountability students feel for editing, revising, and proofreading their writing. Students often find that they enjoy writing for virtual response groups even more than for face-to-face ones. Either way, our student writers increase their levels of responsibility for their writing and revising.

One of our colleagues who teaches middle school brings revising and technology into a perfect blend by having her students use a SMART Board to revise. Students are able to highlight chunks of text, move them around, or slide them out of view as their peers look on. Several students may write individual revisions of a sentence or two and project their revisions next to the original. Doing so provides a powerful visual as students discuss the relative merit and impact of each revised bit of text. One student's revision sparks another's thinking, so that student has her turn at the SMART Board and demonstrates how her ideas for revision alter the text. This teacher is very adept with the interactive technology of the SMART Board and teaches her students how to use it effectively, too. This is one of the better ways we've seen to make revision visible and somewhat tactile for our students who benefit from such learning modalities. Plus it's just plain fun, a benefit for any type of revising work.

What Works for Revision

We encourage you to bring your authentic writing and revising processes into your classes. Let your students see you at work, thinking and revising, crossing out and moving chunks of text around, and revising by writing entirely new parts of your pieces.

What works best for us is modeling, discussing, and working on all phases of writing together with our students as writers, revisers, and teachers. We use computers and other technologies because we like them and think they are valuable tools for revision. We read real writing on which we're working to our students, and we seek their feedback and ideas for revision, as appropriate. Mainly, we try to be the writers at work that we are in real life, and we encourage you to do the same.

NOTES

1. For more information on the memoir framework and how to teach it, see *New Directions in Teaching Writing: Memoir* (2007) by Dawn Latta Kirby and Dan Kirby.
2. Lynn Aaron was a student at Gainesville High School, Gainesville, GA.
3. Marie (a pseudonym) was Ryan Dippre's student at Delaware Valley High School, Milford, PA.

Works Cited

Dillard, Anne. 1998. "To Fashion a Text." In *Inventing the Truth, the Art and Craft of Memoir*, edited by William Zinsser. Boston: Houghton Mifflin.

Goldman, William. 2001. *The Temple of Gold*. New York: Ballantine.

Kirby, Dawn Latta, and Dan Kirby. 2007. *New Directions in Teaching: Memoir*. Portsmouth, NH: Heinemann.

Richardson, Will. 2010. *Blogs, Wikis, Podcasts and Other Powerful Web Tools for Classrooms*. Thousand Oaks: Corwin.

Wilber, Dana. 2010. *iWrite: Using Blogs, Wikis, and Digital Stories in the English Classroom*.: Portsmouth, NH: Heinemann.

10

Publishing Writing

In the age of hypermaterialism . . . and thousand-dollar "It" bags,
perhaps making stuff is the ultimate form of rebellion.
—**Jean Railla, *The Punk of Craft***

When writing is going really well in your classroom, students will naturally want to share what they have written and get a "live audience" response from their peers. Peer response groups, writers' groups, and conferences provide some of that response. There's absolutely nothing like "being published," however.

We're not talking about agents and book contracts for your students. The idea is to make your students' written pieces available to real audiences within and beyond the school, to recognize the hard work and sparks of inventiveness and acts of analysis that your students successfully bring to fruition. Once students have wrestled a piece of writing into an acceptable degree of control and precision, publishing and celebrating are the icing on the cake. In fact, we sometimes serve cake during our celebrations when we unveil published works from our students. Depending on your students' responses to sugar, that may not work for you, but you're getting the idea that publishing students' work is important and a special time in the writing classroom.

In a culture accustomed to purchasing and buying, the notion of *making something*— such as a classroom-produced book of your students' writings or a wiki on which they publish their pieces (we discuss how to do both later in this chapter)—may seem a bit surreal to your students. One of our colleagues literally makes guitars by hand. They are practically pieces of art and produce full and rich sounds. Some of our students cannot fathom why he takes hours and hours to make that which can easily be purchased at a nearby store. The notion of something handmade may seem quaint or unnecessary or unrewarding to students. Many adolescents are focused on fitting in with their peers by wearing the "right" brands of clothing, listening to the popular musical groups, carrying the flashiest and newest gadget—or the "It" bag, as cultural observer Railla points out. If I *make* something, then, by definition, it isn't the "right" brand with the proper bling.

We like to disabuse our students of these notions as much as possible, at least as they relate to writing, by talking about writing as a craft and as an art, as a work that they call into being. Human beings, not factories and robots, produce writing. Sharing in the rewards of both *making* and *celebrating* that which is created is essential to the writing community.

All work and no play make all of us cranky and dull. Celebrate what your students accomplish often; celebrate by publishing some of their work—even if it is not yet Hollywood or *New York Times* ready. Many options for publishing students' texts exist, some of which may not have occurred to you yet. Our aim in this chapter is to explore some of the many ways in which you are able to publish students' writings.

Why Publish Students' Writings?

Publishing and celebrating writing are essential phases of writing. Writing becomes real when it has an audience. Except in those isolated cases when we become our own audience in the diary or private journal, our purpose in writing anything from a note taped to the refrigerator to a Petrarchan sonnet is *contact* with other human beings. Responses guide the growth of our writing. We learn ways to make our writing better by seeing its *effect* on others.

Publishing is far from an add-on element in writing instruction. It may actually be the most important step, especially for young or novice writers, because it's how we see our writing actually go to work on other people. Is it making them laugh or consider options as the student author intended? Is it entertaining or scary or informative or unsettling—that is, does it achieve the student author's purposes and goals? Writers will know the answers to those questions best when they see real audiences responding to their finished pieces of writing. We publish students' writings for lots of reasons, including the following:

1. Publishing gives the writer an audience, and the writing task becomes authentic—a real effort at communication—not just writing to please the teacher.
2. Publishing is a primary reason for the writing to be important enough to engage in the hard work of editing and proofreading.
3. Publishing involves the ego, which may be the strongest incentive for the student writer to keep writing.

Publishing writing and garnering the accompanying positive reactions, kudos, praise, and recognition create the moment of truth. It's serious stuff—important business—to get that live audience reaction. Skipping it (as traditional assignments often do) conveys the message that what we're doing with this writing in school doesn't much matter to real people. That is not a message we want to convey.

Ways to Publish in the Classroom

Provide *regular* opportunities for students to publish and celebrate their writing in class, and include all students. Several publishing and celebrating methods are relatively easy. We recommend using a variety of them, selecting, as appropriate, what works for the piece of writing, the amount of effort students have put into their writing, your particular students, and the learning objectives you are trying to achieve.

One caution: Just as you read a book before you teach it to your students, read all students' writings before they are published in any way. The idea is to celebrate writing and reward students, not to anger administrators, parents, and fellow teachers and students.

Reading Aloud

Sharing writing by reading aloud should be a frequent part of any writing class. It's the best way for students to get immediate reactions to their writing. It's a good tool for checking responses to revisions and edits. But writings simply need to be shared and enjoyed. Reading aloud grows writers.

Provide opportunities for students to work daily—or at least weekly—with a reading partner with whom they feel comfortable and on whom they try out their works in progress. Also provide regular in-class opportunities for your students to form small groups for reading and responding. These groups may consist of four to six students (or two or three pairs of reading partners). Also find times when the entire class is the audience.

The Faithful Photocopy

We have found that what our students look forward to most eagerly and read most carefully are the photocopied sheets we pass out weekly at the beginning of a class, usually each Monday. Selecting and duplicating student writing should be done often. The selections from journals or in-class writings do not need to be long, but try to include as many students as possible. Select good writing, even if it's only a sentence or two with a vivid image, an unusual twist, or the surprise of humor. Select writing with creative possibilities—not necessarily mechanically perfect—writing. Talk about the selections with your class and tell students what you liked about the writing, why you picked these specific pieces, and why they're good.

Make sure, especially when duplicating selections from students' journals, that you have a clear understanding with your students about what types of writing will be published in class. Always get their permission before sharing their writing with the class. We recommend publishing journal selections anonymously; their authors will often take credit when others respond positively in class.

Using Student Editorial Boards

After you've selected and published excerpts from students' writings for several weeks, turn that job over to the students themselves. Set up small groups as editorial boards (see Chapter 8) to pick writings and prepare copies each week. Rotate the responsibility from group to group so that all students experience regularly the job of editing during your course. Work closely with your editorial boards, but let them pick *what they like* to publish. Engage students in discussions about the appropriateness of content to be published, and then go with their choices as much as you feel secure in doing while still remaining gainfully employed. Their selections will come from in-class writings and not from journals. Pieces of writing that are word-processed rather than handwritten are easier to read, making editing much easier, and they take on that professional look that connotes a "published" piece.

■ Room Displays

You have probably already designated one or more places in your room to display students' writings, and you have probably found that displays of finished products attract attention and stimulate talk and thinking about writing. As we pointed out in Chapter 3, room displays have other possibilities. A Works-in-Progress section of the bulletin board—or wall or reserved corner table—is an easy way to encourage growing writers. Displaying works that aren't finished yet helps to dispel notions that writing is quickly done in two drafts for the teacher and that what's important in writing is always the final product. Some teachers we know regularly post works-in-progress because doing so meets certain school, district, or national standards. We applaud posting students' works for the reasons we indicated— and if doing so makes standards-watchers happy, so be it.

With the cooperation of the principal, there's also the possibility of displaying students' writings in the school's hallways. We like to create hall displays with short writings like Name Pieces (see Chapter 4) and concise poetry such as cinquains. Short writings are easy for students to put up on butcher paper. Hang the writings high to keep them out of the reach of the curious. Displays are a fluid medium; both students' interests and the displays themselves benefit from frequent change. Your writing might also appear on display with that of your students. Remember that these displays are celebrations and recognition of writing. Keep it fun and never *insist* that students display their writings. We've never had a student who resisted for long the opportunity to join in once the praise, recognition, and positive comments begin flowing.

■ Projection Publishing

Darren regularly displays outstanding student work (particularly well-written or creative sections, sentences, and phrases) with the class by using the LCD projectors and document cameras that are fairly common in contemporary classrooms. If you work without access to this type of technology, using a simple overhead projector and transparencies also gets the job done. Whatever the technology, publishing writing in a format for all to see works well for talking about good writing and for helping writers gain confidence while exploring effective writing techniques. Engage in this activity often so that students understand that good writing is not just the stuff expert authors mysteriously create. Good writing is what your students are doing right now. Try starting the week with great lines from recent student work.

Caution: Please notice that we're not suggesting that you slap a kid's paper on the LCD projector and begin criticizing its faults in front of the entire class. Use the whole-class viewing of writing as a way to celebrate, publish, and share the good stuff your students are writing.

Making Books the Simple Way

If you want to see your students' eyes light up with pride, have them prepare their best writings and bind them in their own books. All you need are some inexpensive bookbinding materials—wallpaper samples, glue, construction paper, cloth tape, scrapbooking extras, and so on—and patience. Folding a piece of wallpaper over the written pages makes a simple soft cover for students' writings. Trim the wallpaper to be slightly larger than the sheets of writing. Then it's a simple matter to staple the spine two or three times and cover the end with cloth tape. Though simple to do, the process may get a bit messy—scraps of wallpaper on the floor—but a bit of a mess is worth it. Create your own book first to show students the steps. Alternately, make the book project an extended affair and allow students to experiment with their own materials, media, look, and message. The exact organization for what students might include is up to you, but they might take their cue from what we'd expect from a professional volume. Typical elements might include a dedication page, a table of contents, notes that accompany particular pieces, photography and other visual and design elements, and a page about the author.

The resulting bound books are attractive. Illustrations and font style or calligraphy for student-made books are limited only by students' imaginations. We're always impressed with the creativity and artistic savvy of our students, many of whom invest hours in this work and turn out impressive collections. As evidence for what students have accomplished in your class, these bound books are quite compelling. Darren has had a lot of success with these projects, and students are often so proud of what they've created that they'll make an extra book for him to keep. Before long, you'll have quite the library of models to spark your students' imaginations.

Publishing Outside the Classroom

Publishing outside the classroom might be the most significant writing experience you and your students share, but it's something to approach carefully. Even if students are using a simple protected wiki or some other online writing space that's been made private or semiprivate, new responsibilities and concerns present themselves as their work goes "out there." It's not always easy moving from the relatively safe class environment, where publishing is part of a common and shared experience, to the cold world of public writing potentially judged by strangers. It's a scary transition but an important one—and your support and encouragement (and example) help your students to mature as writers.

The Literary Magazine

If your school already has a flourishing literary magazine, then count yourself lucky and enjoy its benefits. Encourage students to participate in it as fully as their inclinations and other activities permit. Help them select, edit, and polish their best pieces to submit to the literary magazine. Rejoice loudly with them when their stuff appears in it. Mourn with them when they don't make the cut. Use the literary magazine for its full effect with those students in your classes who are ready for a larger audience.

Because you're a teacher who encourages and supports writing, chances are that you'll be approached sooner or later to sponsor the school literary magazine. Or the bug to start a miniversion of the literary magazine just for your own classes may bite you. Because that day will likely arrive, we offer a brief primer in doing the school (or class) literary magazine.

Our experiences in producing literary magazines for the entire school give us a certain bias, perhaps; but our Basic 12 premises for creating a literary magazine have kept us sane and clearly focused in our conversations with parents and administrators.

The Basic 12

1. Everyone is creative and potentially has a place in the literary magazine. It's not just for the precious, gifted few.
2. The literary magazine begins in the classroom with the journal and the pieces that students write there.
3. We invite and encourage students to participate and publish. We do not pressure them.
4. An effective literary magazine is not a miniature copy of *The Kenyon Review* or *Poetry*.
5. Most students are shy about their writing and about having it appear in print. Encourage them.
6. The literary magazine belongs to the students.
7. The literary magazine can be expensive, but it doesn't have to be.
8. If you produce a literary magazine primarily to make money, you'll lose money.
9. Administrators sometimes don't like literary magazines.
10. The literary magazine is vulnerable to censorship.
11. The literary magazine is a *lot* of work.
12. The literary magazine offers a lot of reward to teachers and students.

■ How to Produce a Literary Magazine

There are four practical methods for producing a literary magazine. Each requires a great deal of time and work, each requires the willing help of students, and each requires the cooperation and support of the principal.

Method 1: Desktop Publishing

This is the simplest route to getting literary. Basic publishing software may already be a part of your school's resources, and we find many of them to be quite user-friendly and effective. If the software isn't already installed on school computers and you're the experimental type, an open-source (i.e., free) alternative such as Scribus may be for you. Even without a special desktop-publishing program, pieces produced and published with just a standard word-processing program usually look quite professional, complete with color, various font styles and sizes, columns, graphics, and other features associated with published works.

Even if the pieces are produced with computers, you'll need many copies of the final products.

Method 2: The Photocopied Literary Magazine

The cheapest kind of literary magazine is simply photocopied, stapled together, and passed around the school. It's spontaneous, easily produced by students, and given away. If you want to be fancy, get the class artist to do a silk-screen design on heavy stock paper for a cover. It will be an attractive product and cheap.

Method 3: Offset Printing

The offset press is relatively inexpensive, and the result looks professional. The cost depends on where the printing is done and whether you include fancy extras like photographs, color, and artwork. It's often possible to get a local printer to give you a considerable price break. Many schools have their own graphics department with an offset press. Your school or one in your area may be able to print the literary magazine quite reasonably.

With offset printing, of course, your copy has to be "camera ready." Proofreading and careful word processing are essential. Again, the computer is invaluable in readying your product for offset printing.

Method 4: The Full-Blown Technicolor Special Whamdoodle

Color photographs and slick, clay-based paper and typeset printing—when you add these special touches, the literary magazine usually becomes very expensive. It may cost literally thousands of dollars to produce.

That's out of financial reach for most of us, but we have a fantasy that someday there will be a public high school somewhere in America with creative arts and literacy booster clubs and budgets equal to those of a successful athletic program. Hey, it could happen, right?

Method 5: Digital Literary Magazines

With the advent of numerous software programs that allow students to produce highly sophisticated documents from their computers, teachers in some schools are trying the e-zine, or online magazine—in this case, the literary zine. Zines are not printed; they are posted to a school's website, distributed to a listserv, or otherwise made electronically available. Zines may include all the features of printed literary magazines, including photographs. One advantage of zines is that using color, various fonts, and visual images is free and relatively easy to do; this functionality is built into the desktop publishing software that you purchase (see Method 1).

When teachers and student groups opt for zines, they usually do so as a service to their community and stakeholders, not for the purpose of making money. It's possible to charge for zines, but the response rate and technicalities of doing so are often not worth the work; charging may also dramatically decrease your audience. If you and your students want to try this method, be sure you have updated email addresses for those who will receive the zine and/or the notice and link that the zine is available online.

When to Begin a Literary Magazine

Begin a literary magazine when a group of kids says, "Hey, why don't we put all this good stuff in a magazine of some kind?" In short, you begin it when the students want it and are willing to work together to produce it.

It's not an easy job, and students need to know that fact when they begin. Help them, advise them, encourage them—*but don't do the work for them*. It's their magazine and will be effective only as long as the students know it's theirs and take responsibility for it. It ends when students are bored with it, are tired of working on it, or want you to do the work of producing it.

When *Not* to Do a Literary Magazine

Never make the literary magazine a crusade. Suggest it as a possibility to students when you see that they're ready for an audience larger than those in their class, but don't insist on it if they seem uninterested. They may not be ready to move their writing beyond the audience of their peers yet. Or it simply may not be as important to them as it is to you.

If your principal—perhaps still worried about the most recent censorship case in the neighboring district—is opposed to the idea of a school literary magazine, then look for and suggest alternatives, such as those in the following section. It's not going to help the cause of writing in the school if you lose your job.

Sometimes there's simply no way to find the money to produce a literary magazine. Literary magazines rarely pay for themselves, and you shouldn't go into debt, assuming you'll sell enough copies to pay for it. You'll need some kind of financial support. Advertising, patrons, a deal with the school library or English department or school board or even the football coach—there are possibilities for paying the costs, and we've seen all of them (and some other bizarre schemes) work in one school or another. But if there simply is no money, look for other possibilities for publishing students' writings.

Alternatives to a Literary Magazine

Many schools have literary editions of a school newspaper that feature student writing. Another, and perhaps better, alternative is a regular literary column in the school newspaper. Suggest this possibility to the editor or sponsor. Your classes may even volunteer to edit the column and, cooperating with the newspaper staff, provide a regular place for student writing to appear.

A similar alternative is a literary section of the school yearbook. And, of course, the school website or class blog is a fine alternative to printed publications.

Publishing Outside the School

Your local newspaper may sponsor writing contests for students, or it may even regularly feature student writing in its pages. If it doesn't offer opportunities like these for young writers, don't hesitate to approach the editor with ideas for regularly printing students' pieces of writing. It's good PR, for one thing. If you live in a larger community, chances are that your local paper has an educational editor (or consultant) whose job is to work with the schools. You'll usually find this person receptive to these types of suggestions.

If your community has a local access or local television station, approach the manager with the idea for a program of students' reading their writings on the air. You may get a positive response. Locally owned radio stations may also be receptive to such a weekly or monthly show.

If you have a shopping mall or a local library in town, they often are willing to display students' writings. Work with the art teacher in your school to create visually appealing displays that do more than merely pin pieces of writing to the wall. Sometimes, the local grocery store or all-purpose store (think Wal-Mart here) may even be willing to display students' writings, to sponsor writing contests with a donation in exchange for having their name mentioned as the sponsor, or otherwise support students' efforts to publish their writing.

In most towns and cities, there's at least one literary group or group of professional or semiprofessional writers. They probably sponsor contests for young writers. Find out about them. These writers' groups are usually happy to offer assistance to student writers and teachers of writing.

Check with the professional organization in your state for writing contests and opportunities for publishing that they may sponsor—many such organizations do. The National Council of Teachers of English (NCTE) also sponsors annual writing contests for students. Additionally, ask the language arts coordinator in your school district to send you any flyers on writing contests that come through the central office. There are many of these each year, but *examine the ones unfamiliar to you carefully and critically*. Be especially wary of any contest requiring some sort of fee for entering. Have a regular place in your classroom where you post notices of writing contests.

Coping with a Publisher's Rejection

Even those of us who've been writing for years may grind our teeth in frustration and disappointment when a newspaper, professional journal, creative outlet, or other publisher rejects our writing. You know how those rejection letters go, right? They're on lovely letterhead stationery and say something highly useful like the following:

> Dear Sir or Madam:
>
> We regret that we cannot use the enclosed. Although we should like to send an individual answer to everyone, particularly those who request special criticism, our staff and time are insufficient for detailed correspondence.
>
> All contributions must be accompanied by a *stamped and self-addressed envelope*. Otherwise we cannot return them or make any other form of reply, and they will be destroyed. Stamps alone are not sufficient. Contributors living abroad should enclose a return envelope and international postage.
>
> —*The Editors*

Consider carefully before you expose your students to the writer's ultimate rejection: a "thanks, but no thanks" letter. For those very few, very sophisticated young writers whom you feel are ready to venture into the impersonal publishing world that adult writers experience, your role is to give them as much support, help, and encouragement as possible.

One point that needs to be reemphasized here is that *you* share the experience of submitting writing for publication *with* your students. Whenever possible, send something somewhere yourself when your students do. Most of the time, writing is rejected—in fact, almost all the time. Sharing the disappointments—and sometimes the triumphs—makes the experience easier and more meaningful.

The so-called *little magazines* offer student writers the best opportunity to appear in print. Editors of the littles are usually individualistic and idiosyncratic, but most of them do take the time to respond personally to writers who submit work to them. Many of these editors are writers themselves and encourage beginners.

The *International Directory of Little Magazines and Small Presses*, published annually, is the go-to resource for noncommercial and *avant-garde* writers. Listing hundreds of addresses and descriptions of magazines and small presses, it's a supermarket of places to send manuscripts.

One warning about little magazines, however: Supervise your students carefully and be frank with them about the kinds of magazines that often print experimental—and sometimes antisocial—writing.

Finally, there are the commercial magazines. A few, such as *Seventeen*, offer some opportunities to young writers. All are highly competitive, impersonal in responding, and very difficult—sometimes impossible—to break into.

Writer's Market is the best source for addresses and descriptions of commercial markets. It's published annually by Writer's Digest Books, who also publish *Writer's Digest* magazine. Get your school librarian to order a copy. It's expensive.

The same cautions apply to having students submit their work for publication in online magazines (zines) or digital spaces sponsored by those outside of your school. Not all Web publications are what they seem, so careful screening and parental permissions are essential.

Publishing in Digital Environments

When we were in elementary school, the act of writing had a fairly universal look to it: A person sat at a desk and, with crayon, pencil, pen, or some other utensil, scratched words across a sheet of paper. Typewriters allowed us to peck away at the keys of a machine instead of scribbling, but the product was basically the same: words inscribed across paper. During the 1980s, computer-based word processing became readily accessible. Sitting at a computer caused writers to shift attention from paper to a screen, from scribbling to typing/word processing. Overstating the impact of using computers for writing is practically impossible. Computing created, quite literally, a paradigm shift that is continuing and evolving still. Writing, revising, editing, and creating multiple forms of written and visual expression will never be the same acts that they were prior to computing.

Most of us cannot begin to take full advantage of all that a computer is able to do. We learn how to jump through a few hoops and create a few bells and whistles, but we often don't go too far beyond putting words on the screen, which are then printed onto paper. Our children capably produce far more sophisticated products on computers than we know how to create, a trend that is likely to continue.

Though words that ultimately appear on paper may be the default expectation for students now and in the near future, the rise of inexpensive digital technology that is ubiquitous, social, and seen as the global norm, as futurist Clay Shirky notes, is changing expectations and possibilities. Technology that is easily accessible may also be changing how we view what it means to be *literate*.

New technology develops daily. We won't even try to name and discuss all of the new software, devices, and techniques that aid student writers and enhance written products. Any such list would be out of date before you read it. Nonetheless, here are some of our ideas for using technology to great effect for publishing students' writings.

As you read our ideas, be sure to jot down your own additional thoughts. Discuss your ideas with your students and colleagues. Odds are that you and your students will use computers for writing and for publishing writing in ways that we haven't yet conceived.

Tips Related to Publishing Students' Pieces

Regardless of how you end up using digital sites, if students' writings are to appear on them, use only each student author's first name or perhaps just the student's initials—not full names—to identify each writer's work on the blog. Students may be vulnerable to unscrupulous Internet users, from salespeople to predators. The less strangers know about the individual student, the safer the student probably is.

In addition, before posting *any* student work on your blog, wiki, or other Internet site, whether public or private, send students home with permission slips and get them back, signed by parents or legal guardians. Doing so is a must.

Some school districts include a blanket technology form in student handbooks or in the materials that parents receive at the beginning of each school year. By signing, parents or guardians allow their child's likeness and work to be posted on public websites used and maintained by the school district or by teachers. Most parents will sign the forms. After all, they are accustomed to technology, too, and like seeing their child's work; but some parents refuse to grant permission for a variety of reasons. Whatever the parent indicates on the form is law—sometimes literally.

Noticing the E

Have you noticed that the letter *e* may precede almost any word? E-business. E-publishing. E-mail. In this context, *e* simply means "electronic." Business and publishing conducted online, electronically, digitally. Mail delivered electronically rather than by a live mail carrier. E-everything is fast and usually cheaper than using hard copies. E-everything may also be suspect, spam (like junk email), or shoddy. The availability of e-everything doesn't always mean it's better, but sometimes it is. Screen carefully e-anythings that you use with your students.

Class Blogs and Websites

Publishing students' writings on a class blog or website that students maintain offers them the opportunity to negotiate responsibilities that come with having an online presence. Parents and students expect teachers to maintain blogs for their classes. Some blogs are quite elaborate and creative, but most teachers use their blogs as online bulletin boards, posting assignments, deadlines, and other reminders for students and parents. How the blogs are generally used is analogous to using laptops as souped-up typewriters. Both get the job done, but both fall short of maximizing the medium.

With a little forethought and leveraging of effort, the whole concept of maintaining class blogs might reasonably be shifted to students rather than shouldered by teachers. Blogs are ideal platforms for posting updates, summaries, project reports, public displays of writing, and other demonstrations of learning. Blogs may rather easily become the platform on which students demonstrate their learning in compelling and relevant ways.

Online Platforms, Communities, and Similar Publishing Venues

While working on this book, we debated how to address digital platforms and the potential forms of digital composition. Bundling the topic into a single chapter seemed unwieldy and inappropriate, especially given the infiltration of digital interactivity into our personal and professional lives. Every aspect of teaching writing now has virtual, online, or other e-implications. Why wall off in a separate chapter that which is not walled off in our everyday lives? So, we didn't. Nonetheless, our general ideas for teaching with technology warrant full exploration of the good, the bad, the ugly, and the pretty elements of using technology for teaching adolescents.

We also considered our options about referencing specific platforms, products, technologies, and websites given how rapidly technology evolves and how easily something new becomes "so yesterday." Anyone remember Webquests and MySpace, for example? We haven't completely resolved this dilemma. We mention certain kinds of digital technologies that seem to offer some longevity and relevance to what we do. Although none of the digital options are the Hot New Thing anymore (who could predict *that* most of the time?), we think they currently hold the most potential for what we do as writing teachers. Specific how-to texts and online tutorials abound for these topics. We don't write that stuff and don't plan to try to do so here. Instead, we'll stick to an overview and trust you to know what the newest, hottest e-everything is and to figure out whether bringing it into your teaching will enhance students' learning.

◼ Blogs, Wikis, and Other Socially Networked Spaces

Blogs and wikis have been around for a while and continue to evolve. About three years ago, Dawn presented a workshop to high school and college teachers in which she gave time for them to Tweet. Over two-thirds of the audience had no clue what she was talking about, and some thought it illegal in their state. Most of us are now more familiar with "microblogging" sites such as Twitter and Tumblr. Whether you're using full-strength or micros, these tools seem especially suited for helping students explore various texts and forms of publishing.

Blogs offer students the opportunity to take the concept of the journal and transform it, at least potentially, from the private to the semipublic through immediate connectivity with readers, other writers, and visual media. Wiki technology also unshackles collaborative efforts from time and space restrictions, easily allows for multimedia integration, and opens our students' work to wider audiences and conversations. With wikis and blogs, students may engage in collaborative writing, maintain ongoing research logs, access stable project areas of district servers, and create public demonstrations of their work that are easily accessible. Students' work may be published—made public— in a trice.

Like conventional publishing, being "socially networked" comes with expectations about quality, credibility, and responsiveness. These real audience expectations are the stuff with which real writers must contend. For our student writers, it's where fluency, control, and precision (see Chapter 2) eventually lead: to crafting and publishing at least some of our writing for a real audience.

Even when students are restricted to quarantined online venues for their writing—some schools' "intranet" spaces, for example—the audience for the writing is both authentic and expectant. They want to see what we have to say. Words matter, representing us for good or ill when they go out into the world. That's the cautionary part of using these publishing venues. The ease with which we email, update, post, Tweet, and text doesn't take into account the effect of our words on our public image and on an audience's perceptions of us.

As coaches of our students' writing and as those who work with students to publish writing for celebratory purposes, we face a challenge when working with our students in these spaces: helping students realize the potential of online writing while also analyzing with them the meanings, impact, and consequences of publishing—of any texts (writings, photographs, videos) going onto any live, digital venue. We use these digital spaces with our student writers, but we also educate them about the power of the written word and of the visual text, especially in instantaneous e-environments. For a couple of interesting examples, take a look at Figment.com and Cowbird.com. Figment is a story-sharing site for young people. Cowbird is similar but features a visual/audio component. Both sites leverage social networking as a platform to write, publish, share, and learn. Give these sites (and others like them) a trial run yourself before considering ways they might fit in your classroom. Even just suggesting that students might take their work public in these ways reinforces the idea that audiences help student writers improve.

◼ Digital Media-Making

The ability and savvy to manipulate images, video, sound, and graphic elements were once reserved only for the experts and professionals, but no longer. The stupendous variety of online applications, sites, and programs—most available for free, and all offering ways for people to *create*—makes this a golden age for innovative writing teachers. (Lists of such digital resources abound, but see the online Additional Resources for a few starting points. You'll find the link to these online resources at www.heinemann.com/products/E04195.aspx, on the Companion Resources tab.) Whether the available software is used for simple moviemaking, graphic renditions of stories or character, dialogue creation, screen casting, or any similar options, students who access these programs have opportunities to practice and apply literacy and communication techniques in a digital form for multiple purposes and audiences. As they do so, they enhance the appearance and import of their published products.

The wide range of media-making options is much more a partner than a substitute for writing and for publishing students' work. Asking students to consider how an image evokes an emotion, how a melody conveys tone, how a video montage puts forth an argument, or how narration and image combine to aid understanding helps students to recognize the integrated nature of writing and technology. The skills and insights needed for one also apply to the other. Working in digital media benefits students when they return to writing—to words—alone. Concepts like editing, revising, audience awareness, precision and control, and crafting are germane across media forms. Understanding mood, tone, style, and metaphor in constructing or analyzing visual texts aids students' capabilities to do the same with written texts—their own and those of others. This is knowledge that enhances the published product, whatever it may be. Explore digital media and its instructional uses with your students to spark their interests and creative inclinations.

Reaping the Rewards of Publishing Students' Writings

Many options for publishing your and your students' writings exist and many more are being developed as you read this chapter. Whether you're involved in publishing student writing in your classroom, in the school literary magazine, in your community, in the national press, or on a website, hold in mind the instructional point and psychological benefits of publishing students' pieces. It's *the students*, and not the pieces of writing *by* the students, that are important in this process. It's the response of an authentic audience to the student's published work that inspires her to try again and to improve her writing. This type of energy in the classroom is invaluable. When you write and publish *with* your students, you model habits of mind, benefits of writing for real audiences, and the blazing power of the written word—whether in print or digital form. These lessons will serve your students well.

Work Cited

Railla, Jean. 2006. "The Punk of Craft." Modern Craft column in *Craft Magazine*. Vol. 2, p. 10. Available at www.make-digital.com/craft/vol02/?pg=12#pg12. Viewed May 1, 2011.

11

Grading, Evaluating, and Testing Writing

Assessment should begin conversations about performance, not end them. —**Grant Wiggins, *Assessing Student Performance***

Grading students and evaluating their progress are sometimes the most demanding jobs in teaching. The traditional version of grading is enough to make us pull out our hair and to drive our students to the wailing wall of stress. Grading doesn't have to be that way, however. It can be much more humane and effective.

Part of the problem with grading is that it's usually so . . . final. Few teachers give formative—that is, in-process—*grades*. We give formative *responses* and *feedback* and *suggestions*, but not *grades*, which may be how grading should work. The only problem with this approach is that once it's time to grade students' writing, there's nothing left after that point. The grade is the grade and not much can be done to change it. Okay, we may allow our students a rewrite for a better grade, but after a while those papers build up and wall us into a hoarder's nest, demanding our attention. We're soon back to tufts of hair flying around the room and wailing. How do we avoid this dilemma?

We've discussed throughout Chapters 1–10 the ways in which we avoid this finality of a one-size-fits-all grading process. You've read about our ideas for what to do while writing is being shaped and is emerging, moving from idea to draft to revised product, from fluency to control to precision. We have shown you some of the ways we pour our effort and time into the journey toward a finished piece with our students. We coach our students and confer with them repeatedly. We use peer response groups and allow choice in topics for students' writing within a reasonable framework. We put lots of time into working with our students as they write, and that time generally pays off. Our students' writings are far better with such care and attention, with our efforts to help our students move into precision and control prior to submitting the final pieces of writing for a grade.

If we have a relapse, lose our minds, and drift into our old ways of galloping through mere writing *assignments* and moving to the grade as though it were the point of our instructional efforts, we inevitably find the whole writing and grading ordeal to be tiresome

219

and highly frustrating. In such situations, we've rushed through what we know to be best practice in the interest of *finishing*—finishing the unit or the era or the genre or whatever else it is we need to get done. *Getting done*, however, is not the aim of effective writing instruction. *Writing well* is the aim of effective writing instruction, and anytime we forget or abandon that premise, our teaching and our learning objectives are in conflict.

Handling the paper load of the writing classroom is no mean task, but we have managed to do it—better at some times than at other times—throughout our entire careers, without drifting into senility and brain damage. When done the old-fashioned way, grading and the paper crunch take up too much of every teacher's time and energy; the grading process itself becomes a futile and defeating experience. In contrast, when grading is relegated to the final step in a process of coaching, drafting, responding, conferring, and coaching again, grading becomes less arduous. Time spent up front in the initial instruction surrounding the work of producing written pieces pays off in the reduced time we spend on actually grading written products. By the time we need to grade final pieces, we already have numerous in-process grades, and we have worked with the students' pieces of writing numerous times and seen how they have taken shape and developed. Similarly, students know the time and effort they've put into their writing and the feedback they've received along the way. By then, the grade is almost anticlimactic.

The teachers to whom we talk are frustrated by grading because they often see little improvement in students' writings even after hours of hard work. Our question is, "When did you put in the most effort?" If your response is "When the papers came in and I lugged them home to grade them," we ask you to reevaluate your practice. Coach more, respond more, confer more as the pieces are evolving. Another question we pose for you to consider is "How do your students feel when they see the grade you've put on their written pieces?" If your response is "They react negatively, find it difficult to accept the grade, and find it demoralizing to think that grade represents their work with writing," we urge you to reexamine your instructional and coaching processes. Something about what is happening during evaluation is helping students view the whole writing-to-grading process as a plot to make them feel inferior and inadequate. This is the point at which you might sense big trouble. How is your hard work—your writing instruction, and yes, your evaluation and grading of students' written pieces—helping your student writers? If you hesitate to answer or think of an old adage like "That which does not kill us makes us stronger," we think there's room for reconsideration.

Transitioning from Coaching *to* Grading *Writing*

Grading does not have to be a one-size-fits-all straightjacket that derails our teaching and the values we work to establish in our classrooms. We carefully consider our assessment and evaluation plan in every class we teach, making adjustments for the students, content, and context in which we are teaching. Are we teaching at the beginning of the term when students are still learning about us and how we teach writing? Are we teaching highly fluent students who are ready to move into control and precision? What specific theme or focus or genre of writing is our instructional focus? What's happening in pop culture and current events that provide interesting connections to authentic topics for our students?

These are just some of the contextual questions we contemplate as we work out a specific assessment and evaluation plan.

We are acutely aware that the people sitting in our classes are just that—people, not automatons lacking feelings and preferences. Throughout the time we are coaching writing with our students, we remind them that their work leads to a finished piece of writing that is eventually subject to review—to assessment and evaluation—and yes, to grading. When our coaching and responding moves students toward better writing, we are guiding their growth as writers while helping them bear in mind that their writing will ultimately be subject to assessment and evaluation. As we work on writing together, students have a rather clear idea of what's coming when it's time for grading. If our students think that one day we're Dr. Jekyll—having a fine time exploring writing together—but the next day we've morphed into Mr. Hyde—the harsh grade-giver—we've likely rushed instruction and truncated the important talk about how and why writing benefits from review.

When you first begin teaching writing in the ways we discuss in this book, you may experience some Jekyll and Hyde bumpiness as you transition from teacher-as-reader to teacher-as-grader. Students who hear you say, "That's good. I like it," might feel betrayed when they see a C grade if your coaching of their writing hasn't been consistently honest, developmental, and instructive—if you haven't also said something like, "This paragraph will engage your readers more if you use action verbs." Responding and evaluating are not mutually exclusive teaching activities, but it may take some practice to work out the conflicts these two roles present.

General Principles for Grading Writing

The following general principles guide our grading in the writing class.

1. *Grading should be deemphasized*. Students are often very grade conscious, and they may bludgeon their teachers with the "Is this going to be graded?" question. If your answer to them is "yes," that's the universal signal that the assignment is important, and they grudgingly set out to give you what you want. If your answer is "no," they may decide that the assignment is not worth doing. At its worst, this grade-grubbing becomes a kind of "We won't work unless we're paid [with a good grade]" statement.

   Careful planning and deliberate strategies to deemphasize grading go a long way toward changing the grade-grubbing syndrome. We begin all writing classes with the "Not everything you do in here will be graded" speech. We talk about the importance of practice and the establishment of a rigorous conditioning regimen. We tell our students that practice pays off eventually in better grades because some major writings will be graded, and the practice or shorter writings lead up to and prepare them for the graded assignments. Some of you have given the same speech. Such a speech works, however, only if you actually deemphasize grades in your class by finding a set of strategies to put such talk into practice.

2. *Drafts should not be graded*. The standard composition format—students write papers, teacher takes papers home and grades them, students see grades and trash the papers—teaches students very little about how writers work and how good writing grows from draft to draft. One of the surest ways

to involve students in viable composition processes is to resist grades until students complete a final draft. Comment and respond extensively to drafts without grading them. Don't use the grade as a threat or an ultimate weapon. Don't talk about grades much. Focus on the piece of writing itself. After a student has worked on several drafts of several pieces, ask her to pick one for careful revision and then evaluation.

3. *Develop grading criteria with students.* In Chapter 5, we talk at length about developing criteria for *good* writing. These criteria, when developed cooperatively with students, become a grading scale that students understand and accept. Furthermore, by using such cooperative criteria, students have the opportunity to see more clearly how to improve and grow as writers. It's more than showing them what you want. It's developing their own critical sense and evaluative judgment.

4. *Involve students as graders and evaluators.* There's perhaps no more dramatic way to help students understand the pitfalls of grading than to ask them to participate by grading one another's papers. We're not suggesting, of course, that a teacher abdicate the role of grader. We are suggesting that students can and should *participate* in the evaluation process, not only to develop empathy for the grader but also to become better readers of one another's papers. We don't necessarily count student-given grades in our grade books, but we use that peer grade as a springboard for discussion and revision. If a peer partner grades a paper as a C, then the writer and the partner discuss what the paper needs to improve, thus indicating to the writer what revisions are still needed.

5. *Grade processes as well as products.* We value both process and product. That letter grade on the paper carries meanings all out of proportion to its importance. We advise developing grading strategies that reward students for careful preparation, extensive revision, and practice. We often ask students to compile portfolios for each finished product, portfolios into which the students put their jot lists, drafts, research notes, peer responses, revisions, experimentations with the writing, and anything else that indicates their processes as writers. These in-process products indicate the students' work as writers and show their efforts with writing prior to achieving a finished product. We grade these portfolios separately from the final products so that process receives an individual, and usually equally weighty, grade as does the finished paper. The portfolio is evidence of effort as a writer. We know that a rich process might still result in a poor product (Have you ever worked long and hard on a paper and received a grade of C– on it?), and that a skimpy process may sometimes result in an A paper (Did you ever write a paper the night before it was due and get a good grade on it?). When we grade the portfolio separately, we are demonstrating to students that we value both products and processes.

6. *Focus your grading.* Begin with a few criteria. Grade only the specific structures of writing on which you've been working. If you have spent all week on concrete detail or strong verbs or beginnings or transitions, let your grading of that week's writings reflect your teaching emphases. Don't try to grade everything all at once. Start small. Slowly add criteria to your grading scale, carefully demonstrating to students exactly what you're looking for.

7. *Give ideas, inventiveness, and content an important weight in your grading scale.* Most of us have tried the two-grades approach at least once. You know, A over C; A for content, C for mechanics. We've never found that method very helpful. Students either average the two or see the A as a gift and the C as an insult. Instead, use a scoring guide that values both content and inventiveness.

We offer multiple opportunities for our student writers to experiment with ideas, explore options, and take chances. Remember, they are apprentices learning an art. They stretch further, try new tools, or follow an unlikely vision when they trust that we are their supporters. We want our evaluations to reflect their increased confidence, their willingness to tackle difficult subjects, and their ability to analyze the strengths and weaknesses in their own writing. This approach may appear to deemphasize correctness, but we want writers to concentrate on shaping their subjects first; fluency precedes control and precision. We know from experience that the development of fluency through extensive writing practice brings with it growing control of language.

The more students write and receive careful feedback, the better they become and the fewer problems they have with correctness. That is, they gain fluency first and then begin moving into control of their writing. With precision and control come an increased focus on correctness during the final stages of students' composing processes when they are finalizing the final version of the paper. Note the repetition of *final*. It's one of the last aspects of writing to which students attend.

Even as students gain control of most of their usage and surface errors, any college composition teacher will tell you that some errors stubbornly persist even in the writings of college students. At least a few subject-verb agreement and pronoun reference problems, for example, seem to plague most students' papers. Considering how complex some of the rules of usage are, it really is understandable that those students who don't devote themselves to the study of proper, conventional English usage have habitual misuses. Many are also so much a part of oral language use that students seem to have difficulty deleting them in written language.

As a few examples of persistent usage errors, we invite you to consider the use of *this* as a catchall for any and all ideas previously mentioned; singular pronouns that cause awkward constructions of *he or she* rather than the commonly used *they*; and the absolute fear of using *me* or *I* incorrectly, resulting in the ubiquitous reflexive pronoun in all instances: "Darren and myself wrote this book." Ugh.

We sometimes approach these stubborn errors directly through minilessons that address not generic errors but the precise, contextualized errors students have made in their writing. Dawn has even resorted to insisting that all in the classroom join her in a choral chanting of one or two usage rules at the beginning of editing sessions. She laughs while students indulge her exasperation, and the precise errors that drive her to this madness are the fodder for future blog entries.

Nonetheless, we absolutely do *not* emphasize such surface considerations at the expense of real and powerful expressions of ideas and feelings. Content and correctness are both important, but it makes a big difference to your success as a teacher of developing writers where you begin and where you put your emphasis.

There is a place for rigorous grading in the writing class. It is at the end of students' writing processes—after practice, trials, and revisions.

An Important Distinction

We talk to many colleagues and parents who think that *assessment* and *evaluation* are just two words for the same thing—grading. Not exactly. Think of the distinction this way: If you hire a personal trainer to help you increase your activity level, the trainer will first *assess* your current health, level of customary activity, and other factors. He doesn't refuse to work with you based on the assessment; instead, he adjusts the activity level and exercises to suit you, the individual client. After a few weeks of training, he may *evaluate* your progress. Are you able to run five more minutes than when you began? Are you able to perform a more advanced level of push-up? Based on the evaluation, the trainer adjusts your program, either continuing as is or increasing your activity level or changing to different types of exercises—and then he continues to work with you and assess how you're doing. If the trainer had a rubric of 1 to 5, with 1 meaning "no progress at all" and 5 meaning "ready to leap tall buildings in a single bound," he might assign you a *grade* of 4.

Assessment considers progress. *Evaluation* compares specific progress against some sort of standard or established criteria. *Grading* is a type of evaluation. Schools encourage teachers to grade frequently and sometimes harshly. We encourage teachers to assess and confer, evaluate and adjust instruction, and grade only at the end of thorough writing processes.

Start with a Personal Evaluation

A good place for any teacher of writing to begin thinking about grading is to engage in some self-evaluation. How do you grade your students' papers? What are your primary emphases? Have you worked out a grading scale? Does it overemphasize surface features? Do you respond to ideas as you grade the papers? What do you hope your grading methods will develop in your students?

Maybe you're not ready for an introspective look at your grading procedures, but success in the teaching of writing demands that you have a grading system compatible with maximum student growth. Take a look at that stack of papers you've just finished grading and answer the following questions as honestly as you can. Write your answers down so that you can argue with yourself later.

1. Are the papers graded in the *deduct* manner? (You take off points for errors, and sometimes the kids end up owing you points.)
2. Do some papers in that stack make you feel uncomfortable because either good papers have bad grades or bad papers have good grades?
3. What was your *primary* emphasis when you graded those papers? What were you looking for? Do the grades reflect that emphasis? Do your comments reflect that emphasis?
4. Is the grade *final*, or does the student have the option of improving the paper and thus the grade?
5. How have you responded to *what* the writers are saying? Do your comments question, confirm, and show interest in the content? What percentage of your markings identifies errors? How many positive comments, on average, have you written on each paper? Do only the *good* writers merit positive written comments from you?

6. What do you hope your grading will accomplish with these writers?
7. What type of follow-up teaching have you planned for after you return the papers to the student writers?

Perhaps the most seriously damaging habit we get into as graders is mindlessness. The sheer volume of papers and their frequent drabness have a kind of hypnotic effect that may rob the evaluator not only of objectivity but also of sensitive and insightful reading. If student papers are important enough to be graded, they deserve the best reading we can possibly give them.

Now that we have shared parts of our basic philosophy about assessment, evaluation, and grading, we move into the nuts and bolts. The remainder of this chapter is dedicated to practical alternatives for making grading and evaluating less loathsome activities.

Grading Options

The most satisfactory answer to the grading headache may be to present a number of grading alternatives and encourage you to take your pick. Our guess is that you'll end up using all of them at one time or another, perhaps arriving at some personal, eclectic system.

The Nongrading Approach

Some writing theorists (none of whom work in the public schools) recommend strongly against any kind of grading in the composition class. Several teachers we know have tried the nongrading approach, focusing exclusively on constructive responses to students' papers, carefully keeping each of the students' papers in a folder or portfolio to serve as a record of progress. Several times during the grading term, the student and teacher sit down to confer and discuss the student's progress in concrete and specific terms, referring to the collected writings. The advantages of such an approach are rather obvious. The teachers spend most of their time focusing on writing behavior rather than agonizing over grades. The students are weaned away from writing for the grade and are encouraged to practice and experiment with their writing. Progress is emphasized; evaluation is positive and helpful.

Unfortunately, the realities of most schools demand that even the teacher who deemphasizes grading in the composition class give some kind of grade for the permanent record when the course is over. This means, of course, that the teacher must grade *something*. We suggest that, at least with younger, less skilled, and less confident writers, you grade anything but their writings.

The disadvantages of the nongrading alternative are principally the hassles teachers face using such a system. Students exhibit withdrawal symptoms, parents think your course lacks rigor, and your principal thinks you're lazy. In the end you still face the difficult task of translating progress into a letter grade for the report card.

As a middle ground, we suggest that you have a number of assignments that are not graded. Call them *practice activities* or better yet *explorations* or *jottings*. Steal liberally from the ideas earlier in this book. Train your writing students to expect frequent practice activities and explorations. Culminate this practice by responding to, sharing, or publishing the writings rather than grading them.

A Performance System

The performance system is quick and simple for the teacher and clear and concrete for the student. If the student does the assignment, she gets the grade (or points); no value judgments are made about the quality of the work. You establish an acceptable level of performance in your class and students meet it. You may specify that you want five pages in the journal each week or two short writings each week with a revised piece every two weeks. Whatever your performance criteria, the student either does the work and receives credit or fails to do the work and receives no credit.

The advantages of such a system are its efficiency—it's easy to record who did what—and the psychological effect of transferring the responsibility of grading to the student. "You want to do well in my class? Do the work." Teachers spend their time responding and commenting on students' papers rather than counting errors or debating between a C+ and a B−.

The disadvantages are few but not unimportant. A performance system does not give the teacher the flexibility to recognize exceptional works, bad or good. Such a system could lead to a lessening of incentive to do good work unless the teacher uses other enticements to motivate writing. Motivation comes through *publishing* the writing, perhaps in class books that contain the best work from a particular assignment or by celebrating an outstanding piece through oral reading. Publishing excerpts on the bulletin board or the class website gives credit for excellence. A performance system might lead to the complacency of just getting the job done unless we find ways to celebrate excellence and quality.

Holistic Grading Strategies

Charles Cooper and Lee Odell, with characteristic clarity, give a classic definition of holistic evaluation:

> [Holistic evaluation is] a guided procedure for sorting or ranking written pieces. The rater takes a piece of writing and either (1) matches it with another piece in a graded series of pieces or (2) scores it for the prominence of certain features important to that kind of writing or (3) assigns it a letter grade or number. The placing, scoring, or grading occurs quickly, impressionistically, after the rater has practiced the procedure with other raters. The rater does not make corrections or revisions in the paper. Holistic evaluation is usually guided by a holistic scoring guide which describes each feature and identifies high, middle, and low quality levels for each feature. (1977)

Holistic grading has been around for a long time. It is used in specific situations that don't focus on direct feedback to the student, such as on a district-level writing test. The positive point of holistic grading in the classroom is that it focuses on the piece of writing as a whole and on those features most important to the success of the piece. It also helps the teacher to evaluate more quickly, more consistently, and more pointedly. The rating is quick because the rater does not take time to circle errors or make marginal notations. We have known entire faculties who have undertaken training to grade writing consistently across departments using specified criteria.

The rating is consistent because raters are rigorously trained to apply quickly the same carefully developed criteria to all pieces of writing. This consistency is evident not only from piece to piece rated by the same rater but also between different raters rating the same piece. This means, of course, that students might reasonably expect their English teachers to be more consistent in their grading, thus reducing the grading idiosyncrasies that so often frustrate student writers.

Holistic Sorting

Using this technique requires that you read students' papers with your criteria for an effective product clearly in mind. Read a paper and place it in one of three or four piles based on the extent to which the paper meets the criteria you are using. Don't take the time yet to mark anything on the paper. When you've read all of the papers, go back to the piles and argue with yourself a bit, perhaps moving papers from pile to pile as you tweak your mental evaluations of each paper. When you're satisfied that the papers in each pile are generally of the same quality, assign grades by piles (the A pile, the C pile). Finally, reread each paper, writing some pithy notes to the student about the paper.

Impression Marking

Perhaps the simplest and fastest approach to the holistic grading of student papers is to read them quickly without circling errors or suggesting editorial changes. The experienced teacher/rater/reader scans the paper and grades it based on some general feelings about the paper's effectiveness. Common impression markings are not the usual letter grades. More often, impression marking uses a scale of 1 to 3, with a mark of 1 indicating poor effort, achievement, completion, and/or writing; 2 indicating average or pretty good work; and 3 indicating that you want to shout, "Wahoo!" because the student has put forth lots of effort and definitely gets the right idea. Another commonly used impression marking system is the "check" system of putting a check, check plus, or check minus on the paper.

The impression marking system is efficient and surprisingly reliable because readers have a clear set of criteria in mind as they read the papers. This set of criteria must, of course, be in the writers' minds as well as those of the readers. Impressionistic criteria are shared and illustrated for writers as part of the full-range instruction about writing processes.

We use impression makings to indicate whether our students are keeping up with their written responses to readings, are writing thoughtful journal entries, or are bringing all of their materials to peer conferences. Some teachers might call these minor or *daily* grades as opposed to the weightier *test* or end-of-unit grades.

Evaluation by Peers ?.4

We involve students in the evaluation process and train them in using several holistic systems. When students are responsible for assigning a grade or some sort of mark (check plus, 2 out of 3) to a peer's work-in-progress, they tend to take their reading of their peers' work seriously. As students are moving toward their final drafts of a product and assessing peers' drafts, our student writers also come to understand how their own writing is stacking up, what they are doing well, and what they might revise further. We emphasize the point that peers' evaluations are indicators of what is working well in the paper and of what the paper still needs. Because our students have worked on the pieces of writing extensively and are all moving toward submitting the paper for evaluation, they seem comfortable with the fact that their peers are trying to help them achieve the best writing possible.

Grading by peers is controversial and has even been the subject of court lawsuits. Many teachers feel that they abdicate their responsibility as evaluators when they ask students to grade one another's papers. Other teachers feel that students are not capable of careful judgment of the work of their peers. On the positive side, we involve our students in the evaluation process with quite favorable results. We teach students to evaluate one another's papers not to make our job easier or lessen the paper crunch (although both are side effects of peer grading) but because the process teaches them specifics about several aspects of writing better than we can.

First and foremost, grading by peers teaches students that grades belong to them. They come to realize that those letter grades do not flow out of the diseased mind of a cruel teacher. The grade represents a reader's estimate of the worth of the piece. A grade is simply a calibrated personal response. Second, careful reading of a number of student papers sensitizes them to problems in their own papers. As they offer editing and proofreading advice to peers, they are also learning. Perhaps even more encouraging is the fact that students use peer papers as creative sources for borrowing (which is not the same as plagiarizing; see Chapter 6) ideas, rhetorical and syntactic strategies, and even vocabulary. Taking students through the evaluation process not only makes them better proofreaders; it also teaches them how to make critical judgments of written products.

We've found that students take the responsibility of peer evaluation very seriously and work as careful critics. Likewise, when they write pieces they know will be read and graded by their peers, they seem to take more care and work with real purpose on the assignment.

The key to the successful involvement of students as peer graders is the careful specification of evaluative criteria and careful modeling of the criteria so that all students recognize and understand them. It takes time to develop this kind of sophistication, but we think the results are worth the trouble. The following are some ways to structure peer grading.

■ Elbow's "Center of Gravity"

Peter Elbow suggested what has become a classic method for giving writers group feedback on a piece of writing (1998). Although Elbow did not intend such a system to lead to grading, we've found that students can and do use Elbow's criteria for evaluative judgments. Groups of five work best for this process, but groups of anywhere from three to seven members are able to function effectively. The groups begin the process by *responding* to a student's paper. Elbow calls this *pointing* and suggests that readers point to words and phrases that work well or have a unique effect in the piece. Responders may draw lines under these words and phrases or simply note them on a separate response sheet. Likewise, student readers may point to weak or empty words or phrases. As students begin this process, suggest that they limit their negative pointing to only a few serious problems.

Second, Elbow asks readers to *summarize* the piece, using the following steps:

1. First, tell quickly what you found to be the main points, main feelings, or centers of gravity.
2. Then summarize the piece into a single sentence.

3. Then choose *one word* from the writing that best summarizes it.
4. Then choose a word that isn't in the writing to summarize it.

Once the pointing and summarizing are complete, ask students to evaluate the piece, giving it a 3, 2, or 1. A 3 piece has a readily understandable center of gravity and solid supporting detail. A 2 piece has a center of gravity, but it's not powerfully stated and is lost within the verbiage. A 1 piece starts anywhere and goes nowhere. It's not a centered piece.

The point of this kind of peer grading is to involve students in animated discussions about what works and doesn't work in their writings. The pointing and summarizing format keeps the discussions on track and helps students to become more specific in their responses to one another's papers. The 3, 2, 1 scale gives the paper a relative value in a low-threat and helpful manner. The emphasis of such an approach is clearly on discussing written products rather than assigning grades.

■ Roundtable Grading ?4

Using roundtable holistic grading lets students into the evaluation process. Students read papers, establish criteria, and evaluate nearly final drafts. We find that our students are motivated to make measured, constructively critical remarks and suggestions. Each student becomes a better judge of her own work and has a clearer idea of her own performance. Because of the necessity of working closely with the features for good writing that they established, students form a clearer idea of what they might do to improve their pieces. Considering peers' markings and the teacher's input, students then take steps to revise the paper for the final time.

The criteria that students generate will vary with the type of writing they are doing. For expository or research-based writing, our students have generated categories for evaluation such as the following:

- A coherent plan is evident behind the text.
- The writer resists tangents or straying from the subject.
- Focus is maintained.
- Explanations give the reader what she needs to know to be satisfied.
- Errors do not distract attention from content.
- Natural transitions grow out of content discussed.

We've found that our student writers have a healthy notion of the pitfalls and problems involved with a particular piece of writing. By working together, they generate good ideas about what might turn the problematic into the successful piece. After roundtable evaluation, students see what they need to revise and are more motivated to do so.

Many teachers accomplish some of these same goals through the use of peer conferences. The difference between roundtable grading and peer conferences, however, is the focus on grading, not responding, which has a tendency to increase the stakes a bit. Students tend to take it more seriously than a rather friendly peer conference. The *roundtable grading model* comes from the procedures the Educational Testing Services (ETS) has used to rate students' writing samples.

Be aware that evaluation by peers must be thoroughly structured and patiently implemented. In most districts, peer grades cannot affect the final grade a student receives on a product. The grading is, for our purposes, a way of raising awareness about effective writing. Even then, we have sometimes been forced to admit that in some classes it just doesn't work.

Grading Criteria

If any type of holistic grading is to be effective, we need to establish a list of criteria to guide *readers'* thinking as they read students' papers. These criteria give the reader a focus and suggest specific features in the piece of writing to key on; but the reader still strives, in holistic grading, to read quickly and carefully to arrive at a feel for the piece and a grade. We have had success in using the following general criteria to evaluate effective writing.

Holistic Guide for Evaluating Students' Writings

We strongly recommend that you do not create a scale of these criteria. A scale or ranking system funnels students toward assigning a score—that is, to thinking *atomistically*— rather than considering the holistic, overall impact of a piece. Instead, use the list as a reminder of important characteristics of good writing. When you are providing opportunities for students to respond to peer writings, help them recognize and value excellence and experimentation in any aspect of the writing.

1. *Impact.* The writing has an effect on the reader.
   - The reader's interest is engaged.
   - The writer has something to say and is imaginatively involved.
   - The idea or experience is conveyed with fluency or intensity.
   - The writing is convincing. It may have a sense of immediacy, a completeness, or a rightness of content and form that makes it effective.
2. *Inventiveness.* The reader is *surprised*, finding that the writer has not followed the usual or the trite but has introduced elements that are new and unexpected. Evidence of the writer's inventiveness may include:
   - coined words (onomatopoeic, portmanteau, etc.)
   - tag names (allusive or symbolic)
   - unusual point of view (often to add humor or irony)
   - figurative use of language (to clarify meaning, not to adorn)
   - significant title—one that augments the meaning of the writing
   - original, surprising, and appropriate element in content or in arrangement
   - use of unconventional punctuation, spelling, or format to achieve desired effects
   - insightful (rather than simply decorative) use of non-print elements.
3. *Individuality.* The reader is aware of a distinctive speaking voice. This sense of persona, or individual flavor, seems to come from the writer's control of tone and point of view and/or distinctiveness in the ordering of ideas or in using the resources of the language (figurative language, vocabulary, syntax, etc.). The sense of a distinctive persona is usually strong in good monologues— expressive, expository, or dramatic. In narration or dialogue, the sense of control comes from the appropriate meshing of all parts into the whole.

Standards-Based Grading

With the onslaught of high-stakes testing and the development of core standards for writing, many districts are using standards-based grading. As any teacher will attest, the numerous standards that apply to each content area are written for an audience of informed educators, administrators, and perhaps parents, not for the direct instructional benefit of students. Each standard is divided into detailed features. How does a teacher know that a student has achieved a specific standard and when the student has mastered each subfeature of that standard? How does the teacher track those achievements? By using standards-based grading. Teachers reference each detailed feature for each writing standard and evaluate each student's final product based on the extent to which the student exhibits mastery of that feature. The result is sometimes a fifteen- or twenty-item scale of features that teachers must use to grade each paper.

Tracking the levels of achievement for each student on each feature and overall standard can be nightmarish. In fact, some colleagues have confessed to us that they grade every final product by every student twice: once for the official district file, using the official standards-based criteria; and again using a rubric or other evaluation tool that students actually understand. A system in which teachers find it necessary to maintain two sets of evaluations, one of which district officials never see, is most decidedly broken. Such a system has clearly abandoned the true purpose of assessment and evaluation: to provide information that helps teachers target and improve instruction.

On the other hand, some of our colleagues, usually those in the early stages of their careers as teachers of writing, readily accept standards-based grading. The advantage, in the ideal context, is that the standards themselves provide all that a teacher needs to say to a student about his writing. The teacher doesn't need to create a rubric or figure out comments to offer students. The standards do the talking. However, when teachers are more experienced as authentic readers and responders, when they understand how to guide students to become more skillful and nuanced as writers, they realize that the wording in the standards falls far short of what teachers need to say and of what students need to hear.

We think of the analogy of legalese rather than plain English in contracts. When you are buying a car, agreeing to make monthly payments, and attesting that you comprehend the legalities of what will happen if you don't follow the precise stipulations in the contract, do you sail easily through reading and understanding the pages and pages of legal verbiage? If so, perhaps you need to stop teaching and head to law school.

Use standards-based grading if you must, but foreground your comments and responses to students' drafts and revisions if you want to grow stronger writers.

Portfolios

One means of gathering students' papers into one place and evaluating them is that of portfolios. Portfolios have been used in schools for quite some time now. In fact, it's become difficult to use the word *portfolio* without next using the word *assessment*. There are probably as many types of portfolios as there are teachers who use them. If you want to use one or two versions of portfolios to enhance your assessment plan, the following are some ideas for using portfolios effectively.

▇ Performance Portfolios ?6

Performance portfolios indicate a student's point of mastery in learning and/or with writing processes. The teacher establishes certain criteria that the students are to master, and the students compile products that indicate their level of mastery of those criteria.

For example, in one college where Dawn taught, all English majors were required to produce a senior portfolio. Students in secondary English education included products in their portfolios that indicated that they had mastery of the areas of literature, composition, language, and communication, including the ways in which theory influences practice and the ways in which they will apply their knowledge to their future teaching. They may have included lesson plans, tests, finished papers, response log entries, or other products that show their mastery of these criteria.

The evaluation process for these portfolios was multitiered. Faculty members, two per portfolio, independently rated each portfolio as showing that students had met or failed to meet the specified criteria. Dawn held a follow-up miniconference with each student to discuss the student's areas of strength and weakness in content mastery, knowledge of theory, and ideas for future teaching. The faculty surveyed the overall results to see areas in the program that needed strengthening as they prepared students to become future teachers. These performance portfolios thus helped with program evaluation, students' self-assessment of their own work and knowledge, and with planning future instruction in specific courses. For the students, these particular performance portfolios were rated as pass or fail, and students were given a chance to revise and work to improve an area of knowledge that was weak or failing. By the end of the process, both students and faculty had a better understanding of individual achievement and of the link between instruction, student performance, and program assessment.

In the secondary school classroom, similar uses are possible. The teacher establishes criteria for mastery and the student compiles products showing such mastery. Then the teacher and perhaps other colleagues rate the portfolios for passing or failing achievement of the competencies. Given those ratings and comments by the rater, the teacher then discusses achievement and performance with each student, offering an opportunity for continuing to work on areas of weakness. Students see what areas they have mastered and on which areas they still need to work; teachers have indicators for future instruction; and the data are available for use in departmental reports to parents and administrators about programmatic and curricular efficacy.

Showcase Portfolios

A showcase portfolio gathers together and highlights the student's best work for a period of time such as a unit of study, a type of writing completed, or a grading term. Think of a model who is trying to land a job. He may go to the job interview with his portfolio in hand, one that shows various pictures of him in different manners of dress, with different lengths or colors of hair, and with or without a beard. He's trying to show prospective employers all of the many ways that he can look good and meet their needs.

The showcase portfolio generally features the completed, final products that students feel are their best work. Process is not represented in this type of portfolio, so the reader doesn't see drafts, notes, or response logs—only finished, polished products. The showcase portfolio requires students to cull through their finished products, select the best ones, and then arrange them effectively in the portfolio. Sometimes narratives or explications of how and why the student wrote and chose the particular work accompany the showcase portfolio.

Showcase portfolios are often graded holistically. The best work indicates fluency, precision, and control; it represents a quality written product and polished writing; it fulfills the requirements of the type of writing included in the portfolio—or it doesn't.

A showcase portfolio may follow a student into the next grade. Next year's teacher receives the portfolio at the beginning of the year to assess each student's competencies and weaknesses as a writer by examining what the student thought was her best work at the end of the previous year. Such portfolios can be informative to teachers and help teachers determine peer groupings for workshops, initial minilessons on usage and mechanics with which to begin the year, or the types of writing that students have previously mastered.

▩ Process Portfolios

Process portfolios are in some ways the opposite of showcase portfolios. Process portfolios include the full range of pieces, drafts to finished papers, produced during the processes of writing a specific type of paper or produced during a specific grading term. The purpose of such portfolios is to profile the particular student writer at work. Perhaps during the course of completing an action research paper, the student worked as a writer, thinker, researcher, interviewer, and responder to peers' writings. Indicators of all of those roles should then appear in the process portfolio. The reader would therefore see drafts, Thinker's Logs, research reflections, interview questions and results, and evidence of having worked as an effective responder of others' writings in the portfolio, as well as the finished product. The student keeps "every scrap of paper," as Dawn terms it, composed during the process of producing a particular finished product, organizes the papers, and presents them as a portfolio at the time of product completion.

The Importance of Reflection

The difference between a process portfolio and a mere class notebook or some other comprehensive form of collecting papers is the element of reflection. We use a reflective writing guide to help students think critically about their processes and work as writers. This reflective piece opens the portfolio and is the first piece that we read when evaluating the finished products and accompanying process portfolios. We tailor the prompts in the guide to suit the specific body of work that the students have completed for their process portfolios, but the general nature of the questions remains the same. Here's an example of a reflective writing guide for memoir writing:

Reflective Writing Guide for Memoir Piece
Please respond fully to each prompt in an essay format. This is your opportunity to reflect fully on your work as a writer, thinker, and memoirist. Tell me what you've done, how hard you've worked, and what you think about your accomplishments. You may use an informal tone in your writing. Provide elaborated responses, not simplistic "yes/no/sometimes" ones.
• What were your work habits as you produced your memoir?
• How helpful were your peer response groups in helping you shape your final product?

- How helpful were our in-class activities in helping you brainstorm pieces for your paper and craft your finished product?
- What was the most difficult part of this process?
- Of what aspect of your finished product are you most proud? Why?
- If you had more time for this project, on what would you continue to work? Why?
- What other comments (not grade whining!) would you like to make about this product and process?

We like these reflections for a number of reasons. First, they cause students to think seriously about their work as writers, revisers, and compilers of finished products. They are asked to be honest in their assessments of their own efforts and to pinpoint areas of difficulty and pride in their work, adding both a metacognitive and self-assessment component to their process portfolios. As teachers, we like knowing what students thought was difficult so that we can adjust future instruction; and we like knowing the area of pride that a student identifies in a piece of writing so that we can respond to that aspect of the writing with extra attention and sensitivity.

After students have completed several different types of finished products accompanied by process portfolios and reflective pieces, we ask students to survey their reflections. Are they consistently having the same problems in writing? What are their areas of growth as writers? What new skills have they mentioned in these reflections that they have learned? What new areas of achievement have they noticed in their writing? We have each student chart progress, difficulties, and accomplishments. In this way, learning becomes concrete for students and for us. We both, students and teacher, have a record of what has been accomplished and learned—not just, "I wrote three finished papers this grading period," but "I worked on the openings of my papers, on using more specific details, and on enlivening my writing with action verbs. I'm still working on conclusions and comma splices." Such awareness of the craft and techniques of writing helps to build more confident and effective writers.

Grading with Analytic Scales

Analytic scales are precise and carefully articulated grading scales that direct the reader's attention to specific features of the piece of writing and suggest relative point values for each feature. The grade for the piece is calculated by summing scores on the various subparts. Such a scoring tool is more pointed than impression marking because the rating guide defines and illustrates the grading criteria to writers and raters alike and keeps raters on track during the marking procedure. Such guides, when carefully shared and explained to students, help to demystify the final grade and highlight strengths and weaknesses in their writings. The guides also ensure that certain surface features in the piece (proofreading, spelling, punctuation) do not influence the rating of the piece out of proportion to their importance to the piece's effectiveness.

An analytic scale is one that specifies traits of good writing. All analytic scales are based on the classic Diederich Scale (Diederich 1974) that Diederich and his colleagues at the ETS developed for scoring SAT essay examinations (see Figure 11–1). Because several raters read the essay exams, Diederich needed a scoring tool that would provide a quick and reliable evaluation. Originally, his analytic scale was intended for use by staff or faculty who rated students' writings. Diederich's traits, rated on a 1 to 5 scale, with 1 being a low score, included (a) quality and development of ideas; (b) organization, relevance, movement; (c) style, flavor, individuality; (d) wording and phrasing; (e) grammar, sentence structure; (f) punctuation; (g) spelling; and (h) manuscript form and legibility. Some of our more analytic students enjoy being graded with such a concrete and carefully articulated scale; they like to feel that their grades "add up." We also discuss similar scales with students and explain to them the basis of how many college entrance essays might be evaluated.

DIEDERICH SCALE FOR EVALUATING WRITING

1—Poor   2—Weak   3—Average   4—Good   5—Excellent   Reader_____

Quality and development of ideas	1 2 3 4 5	
Organization, relevance, movement	1 2 3 4 5	
		Subtotal _____ × 5 = ___
Style, flavor, individuality	1 2 3 4 5	
Wording and phrasing	1 2 3 4 5	
		Subtotal _____ × 3 = ___
Grammar, sentence structure	1 2 3 4 5	
Punctuation	1 2 3 4 5	
Spelling	1 2 3 4 5	
Manuscript form, legibility	1 2 3 4 5	
		Subtotal _____ × 1 = ___
		Total Grade: ___%

Figure 11–1. Diederich Scale for Evaluating Writing

The 6-Trait Scale

Now that you know a bit about the original Diederich Scale, you will no doubt recognize it as the root of similar analytic scales, including the 6-Trait Scale. The advantages of the 6-Trait Scale are similar to those of all such analytic scales: Students and parents become familiar with it; it's quick and efficient; and it allows the teacher at least the illusion of consistency in grading, a fact that may be important to teachers, students, parents, and administrators. Many districts with which we work have adapted the 6-Trait Scale to be the 6+1-Trait Scale. Such scales generally evaluate components such as ideas, word choice, conventions, sentence fluency, organization, voice, and presentation, considering the extent to which these features are proficient or deficient in the written product being evaluated. Like the Diederich Scale, 6-Trait Scales use scores of 1, 3, and 5 to indicate deficiency or proficiency in each area.

The disadvantages of this particular scale, to us, outweigh its advantages. First, it has become institutionalized and industrialized. Dawn, who began teaching in the late 1970s, likens the advent of 6-Trait Scales to that of *writing process* in the 1980s. When the concept of writing process hit language arts pedagogy, it was the hot, new terminology. Every class-room displayed a chart featuring *the* steps—in precise order—of *The* Writing Process as though all writers compose every product in exactly the same way, using the same steps in the same order—which is not the case in real, individual composing. Teachers even began referring to writing completed in this manner as *process writing* as though it were a *genre* of its own.

Something similar happened with 6-Trait Scales. The notion has taken on a life of its own. We see charts in classrooms, telling students the precise traits that all of their papers should contain and on which all of their papers will be evaluated. We hear teachers tell their students that they'll be "writing 6-Trait papers in here" as though it were a *genre* of writing rather than an evaluation scale. Our preference is for something else that recognizes the teacher's expertise in teaching and evaluating writing.

Teacher-Created Scoring Guides

All forms of writing certainly share some of the same characteristics. We want all writing to be quality writing. You may not be surprised that we think classroom teachers are best able to assess the quality of students' writings and to affect the seamlessness between instruction and assessment that is most conducive to students' learning. *Only criteria that teachers establish for their own instruction reflect the uniqueness of each writing situation and the demands of each written product.* That previous sentence is an important point. Reread it and discuss what it means.

Poetry and research papers, for example, seem to make different demands on the writer and seem to call for different considerations from the evaluator. Correct use of quotations, documentation of sources, and clarity of argument are all essential to an inquiry paper; and use of figurative language, imagery, and precision of thought are all essential to poetry.

Yes, some of the criteria overlap for both types of writing, but we far prefer to tailor our evaluation guides to the particular demands of the specific written product, as you'll see in the next section on scoring guides. We also prefer that our evaluation guides be coconstructed *with* our students so that evaluation and instruction move toward becoming seamless activities in our classrooms. And finally, we prefer to be able to emphasize particular factors of each writing situation so that any one aspect of writing is not stressed to the detriment of others. For example, if we've already stressed a particular use of quotation marks in the last three assignments, which were research-based, we don't want to continue to stress only that feature of mechanics in upcoming assignments that are more expressive in nature, thus giving students the impression that quotation marks are the only important surface features of which they should gain mastery.

Teacher-created scoring guides are responsive to the needs of students and to the context in which instruction occurs. Teachers know what they have taught, what they have stressed in their teaching, and what their goals and objectives for students' learning are. If evaluation is to inform instruction, it is the teachers in the classroom who, perhaps with some guidance, are best able to create rubrics to measure students' progress with writing.

Why are teacher-created scoring guides effective? Why do they help students *learn*, not simply feel *judged*? Teacher-created scoring guides can be content-specific, focusing the evaluation on those aspects of writing that you've been trying to teach. Such guides should be used after you have demonstrated them, devised practice activities, and given students a chance to revise and improve their pieces of writing by using the criteria in checklist form.

Figures 11–2 and 11–3 are two characteristic scoring guides, originally termed "checkpoints," developed for seventh graders, one for memoir and one for opinion papers (Olson et al. 1981). Notice that in addition to numbers, some specific suggestions are included for improving the paper. If students are rated low on vivid, concrete detail, they are encouraged to add more specific detail. The scale focuses on specific aspects of writing instruction and also allows the teacher considerable latitude by including an Overall Impression section that makes up 30 percent of the rating.

A further advantage of this type of scoring guide is that teachers are able to standardize their grading and instruction at particular grade levels. Seventh-grade teachers could work to develop five or six assignment-specific scoring guides to focus composition instruction during the year. Eighth-grade teachers could build on seventh-grade criteria, and so on, thereby developing a cooperative and compatible schoolwide curriculum and a consistent grading system.

These scales are quick to use (averaging about three minutes per paper), self-teaching, and positive. Using these scoring guides decreases the number of papers that need detailed comments. When we are able to spend less time on grading, we have more time to devote to coaching writing in its early stages, working with students on first drafts and revisions. (See Chapter 9 for a full discussion of the importance of coaching revisions in the early stages of writing.) Use of specific comments under the ratings of 1, 3, and 5 on the scoring guide also reduces the number of repetitive comments that teachers must write on each student's paper.

SCORING GUIDE FOR MEMOIR

Your revised writing was rated as follows:

I. *Honest Writing*

1	2	3	4	5	× 4 = _____
Try again. Write fast. Use the words in your own head.		You're moving. Keep working.		Yes! Fresh honest language. Good!	

II. *Vivid, Concrete Detail*

1	2	3	4	5	× 4 = _____
Try again. Your writing is bare. Add more specific detail.		Some good stuff in your writing. Add specifics. Stay away from generalizations.		Surprising words. Concrete word pictures. Good!	

III. *Strong Verbs*

1	2	3	4	5	× 4 = _____
Try again. Use verbs that paint a picture.		I see you've been working at it.		Good. I like those words!	

IV. *End Punctuation and First-Word Capitalization*

1	2	3	4	5	× 2 = _____
Many sentences do not begin with capitals. Many sentences do not end with appropriate punctuation. See me for help.		Several errors. Proofread carefully.		All sentences begin with capital letters and end with appropriate punctuation.	

V. *Overall Impression*

1	2	3	4	5	× 6 = _____
You really haven't given this assignment a fair shot. Spend more time developing ideas for writing.		Yes. I see potential. Keep working.		I was touched by your writing. You connected with your audience.	

Total = _____

Comments:

Figure 11–2. Scoring Guide for Memoir

From *Inside Out, Fourth Edition*. Heinemann: Portsmouth, NH. Copyright © 1982 by Allyn and Bacon, Inc. from *Composition and Applied Grammar* by Miles C. Olson, Daniel R. Kirby, and Gale Dugas. Reprinted by permission of Pearson Education. Inc.

SCORING GUIDE FOR AN OPINION PAPER

Your revised writing was rated as follows:

I. *Evidence*

1	2	3	4	5	× 4 = _____

Ideas unsupported. Rethink your reasons. Back to brainstorming.

At least one of your pieces of evidence is strong. Support more completely.

Yes! Good. Solid support. Fresh, convincing.

II. *Arrangement*

1	2	3	4	5	× 4 = _____

Be sure you have each bit of evidence in a separate paragraph.

Check your conclusion or beginning. You can find a stronger arrangement.

Each paragraph fits with others. Your arguments build to your conclusions.

III. *Language*

1	2	3	4	5	× 4 = _____

Weasel words. Use more forceful language.

Better. Some words are strong.

Good, strong, concrete words.

IV. *Punctuation and Spelling*

1	2	3	4	5	× 2 = _____

Proofread carefully. Too many errors. See me for help.

Still have a few errors. Check and double-check.

Good job. Careful proof-reading pays off!

V. *Effectiveness of Your Opinion Paper*

1	2	3	4	5	× 6 = _____

I'm not convinced. Develop your paper more completely. Use good evidence.

Yes. You're making progress. Keep working.

I'm convinced. Good support. Solid paper!

Total = _____

Comments:

Figure 11–3. Scoring Guide for Opinion Paper ?8

From *Inside Out, Fourth Edition.* Heinemann: Portsmouth, NH. Copyright © 1982 by Allyn and Bacon, Inc. from *Composition and Applied Grammar* by Miles C. Olson, Daniel R. Kirby, and Gale Dugas. Reprinted by permission of Pearson Education. Inc.

Cooperative Grading ? 9

The cooperative grading process involves the teacher and two students. Student readers are picked at random. Each reader reads and evaluates a paper, assigning it a letter grade. Specific criteria are discussed prior to the grading. Readers might consider surface conventions, arrangement, illustrations and examples, and the care the writer took with the piece. A simplified version of the Diederich Scale might serve as a good guide. After each reader has assigned the paper a letter or numeric grade, the three grades are averaged for a final grade. The teacher's grade counts as a third of the final grade.

In her composition classes with English education students who are preparing to be teachers, Dawn uses a similar three-person grading system in which the teacher, the student writer, and a peer chosen at random grade the paper using the checkpoint devised cooperatively for the specific writing assignment. Each rater makes comments on the paper and completes the checkpoint; then, each rater's score is totaled and the average for the three ratings becomes the score for the finished product. Students report that this process gives them helpful information as writers and as prospective teachers who will be grading their own students' papers one day.

In Dawn's use of cooperative grading, the student's paper receives a careful hearing by the three graders, and the weight of collective judgment is often more forceful as an evaluation tool than the teacher's grade alone would be.

Round-Robins

Students sign up for or are assigned to round-robin groups of three members. Each group member takes the responsibility for reading and responding in writing to the text written by the two other group members. We find that the procedure establishes a minicommunity that provides keen evaluation along with sensitive understanding.

Each responder writes evaluative comments and assigns the paper a grade. The group holds a conference, after each writer has had time to digest the comments, for each individual's paper. When the group reaches a consensus about a grade, the papers are given to the teacher with comments and grade attached. We have found that the grades a group gives reflect honest and caring evaluation. Students receive the implicit message that their ability to evaluate is respected by the teacher. Students take these groups seriously and nurture one another's progress.

A Psychological Boost

One technique that we use is to tell our students that an 87 on a paper represents how much they already have done with the paper. The 13 points they didn't get represents the tinkering and tuning that they could still do on the paper. Thinking about a grade as reflecting what is still to be done with 87 percent complete helps the writer tackle the fine-tuning with enthusiasm. For any of us, it's a boost to think that we've accomplished 87 percent of the task and that we still have a chance to get more of the task accomplished through future revisions of the product, provided we value it enough to work more on it. There's also a boost in letting students choose which papers to revise. Maybe a student will choose to revise a paper that is 76 percent complete but is satisfied with the one that is 87 percent complete—or is just too exhausted with that particular paper to work more on it.

Dawn often allows students in her composition classes to choose up to two papers per semester to revise for a possible better grade, using the comments on the original paper, conferences, and peer responses to help the student writer target areas and techniques for improvement. Darren has conducted writing classes in which every student had the option of revising a paper at least once and sometimes even more frequently. The psychological boost of such an attitude toward grading and evaluation of the writer's work is significant, and students seem to enjoy knowing that the focus is on degree of completion and on continued growth as a writer rather than on a deficit model of grading.

Self-Evaluation

One of the important goals of any writing class is to make the writer feel more responsible for the quality of the piece of writing. One of the more unfortunate side effects of having the teacher as the sole grader is that students either prostitute their own writing abilities to please the teacher or they rationalize the teacher's judgment with an "I wrote a great piece, but he didn't like it" attitude. Real growth toward precision as a writer comes only when students are willing to look openly at their own writing, judging, evaluating, reworking, and tuning the piece in the light of such examination.

Asking students to grade their own writings is difficult to do for most teachers and is a difficult task to accomplish for most students who want to get good grades, perhaps at all costs. There are many ways that students might be involved in making judgments about the effectiveness of a piece they have written. Donald Graves (1979) suggests that student writers look carefully at first drafts, asking themselves two questions:

▨ Question 1: What Is This Piece About?

At the end of a first draft, a writer needs to be able to formulate a clear and pointed answer to this question. If she has an answer, the piece probably has focus.

If she's not sure what the piece is about, the drafting is incomplete. Many times we've seen first drafts with real potential, either because of a strong personal voice or a patch of strong sensory description or a telling character sketch, that have been submerged in circular verbiage. The writer has hit a few hot spots but has not discovered exactly where the piece is going. By asking writers to answer question 1, you save yourself the trouble of telling them this point, and the lack of focus becomes clear as they stutter and stammer about the focus of the piece. We usually smile and the student says, "Looks like I need to write some more to find out where this piece is taking me." Sometimes just the act of talking through this question helps students form the piece in their minds.

▨ Question 2: What Am I Trying to Do?

Graves' second question is rhetorical and stylistic, and asks the writer to examine purpose and audience. For instance, the writer is trying to evoke sympathy in a reader but is actually alienating the reader by using overly dramatic or maudlin examples. Writers who function as critical self-readers should be able to spot the problem as they answer question 2. Again, the discussion of this question helps the writer to clarify purpose and examine specific rhetorical strategies in the piece.

Susan and Steven Tchudi offer a number of suggestions for engaging students directly in the process of assessing their own writings, including:

- Encourage students to serve as each other's editors. One doesn't need to be an expert in composition and rhetoric to make useful suggestions about the clarity and effectiveness of writing. Although students may not know terminology, they are certainly capable of spotting editorial problems and talking about them in their own language: "Hey, I don't know what you're talking about." (Translation for teachers: "Lacks clarity.") "That's crazy." (Translation: "Lacks logical structure.") "I don't believe it." (Translation: "Needs more supporting evidence.") Students are highly perceptive in these ways, and when their editing has real purpose, they can take over the process and make genuinely helpful suggestions to each other.
- Leave proofreading to the students and treat it as something to be done quickly and efficiently, rather than as a climactic step in the process of composition. Only when proofreading is made a mysterious, complex part of the mastery of standard written English does it become intimidating and therefore difficult for students.
- Help the students learn to react to each other's work. Small- and large-group discussion of completed compositions should be a regular part of any English class. At first you may find that students are a bit hard on each other, no doubt imitating previous teachers. It may take some practice before the students can respond to the substance of each other's writing, but it will come with time and guidance.
- Encourage students to develop criteria of excellence, in advance, for the work they are doing by putting themselves in the position of the audience and asking questions the reader would raise.
- Read some of your own writing to the class, and share your own satisfactions and dissatisfactions with it (Tchudi and Tchudi 2000).

◼ Editing Checklist

A more concrete and less sophisticated way to involve writers in self-evaluation is to provide them with an editing checklist to use as they rework first drafts. Although it's possible for students to use the checklist in a cursory and superficial manner, it does give them a tool and an opportunity to improve their writing before the final grade is determined.

A checklist may be useful for less motivated students, offering the potential for a better grade if the student wants to do a careful editing job. "The paper is about a C as it stands now. If you want to clean it up a bit, I could go a B. But if you're really willing to work on this thing, I'll consider an A. Get out your editing checklist and start working through the piece."

Editing checklists can be easily compiled by turning the scoring guide for the specific written product into a series of questions or bulleted items. Students then get an opportunity to interpret the rubric from a more personalized perspective. The rubric will seem familiar and right to them when they see it, and the important features of a particular writing assignment remain as the focal points of the students' writing processes.

Conferences ?9

Throughout this chapter, we've used examples of grading and evaluating that involve the reader and the writer in face-to-face discussion and negotiation. We honestly believe that the only consistently helpful and effective evaluation of students' writings comes as the two of you—student and teacher—sit down with the piece of writing, focusing directly on what's on the page. Extraordinarily successful teachers of writing have one thing in common: They spend very little time in isolation, reading and marking papers, and a great deal of time responding to and discussing students' writings with the writers themselves.

There is some disagreement on the use of conferences, to be sure. Donald Murray advocates for the one-on-one conference. Ken Macrorie advises working in a helping circle, using the writers themselves as a larger and more diverse audience. Macrorie suggests that the one-on-one conference intimidates beginning writers. Nancie Atwell has her own version of how conferences work in her classroom. We prefer to run the writing class more like a writing workshop, getting groups together whenever helpful and holding many thirty-second conferences with working writers as we walk around the room. All of us agree that looking at the writings and discussing strengths and weaknesses are far more effective evaluation strategies than taking stacks of papers home on weekends to grow blind and bitter as we puzzle over grades that many students will ignore or rationalize away.

Many researchers confirm our gut instincts about grading and evaluation: (1) It's nasty work, but schools are unlikely to abandon the practice of giving grades, so we need to find ways—such as those suggested in this chapter—to make grading an informative part of learning; and (2) Remember, positive comments do more for building confidence and for promoting learning than do all the red ink marks teachers will ever put on papers.

High-Stakes Testing ?10

The current autocratic, unbending, depersonalized, and detrimental atmosphere of educational testing is deplorable. (Catch us at a conference, and we'll elaborate.) It postulates that education and learning processes are easily quantified and containerized. It contends that simplistic tests are valuable indicators of outcomes associated with the complexity of teaching and learning. It gives the illusion that the material tested is the ceiling, not the floor, of learning in our schools, that if students do well on *the test*, they have learned what they need to know to be successful students and productive citizens. Worst of all, such tests have become the proverbial tail wagging the instructional dog in that teachers spend inordinate amounts of time teaching students how to take the test and how to pass the test as though the test was all that mattered in learning. Content areas for which the tests have yet to be developed receive less curricular emphasis and cuts in funding.

To this volatile, intense, and politically charged situation, add the fact that writing is not a simplistic activity, easily and quickly learned, effortlessly and efficiently evaluated. Writing is complex, learned developmentally, and best evaluated with specific scoring guides designed by knowledgeable professionals with the precise writing contexts in mind—none of which occurs with the use of 6-Trait Scales or standards-based grading.

So, what's to be done?

Preparing for Standardized Writing Tests in Authentic Ways

We generally avoid giving explicit advice about prepping students for high-stakes writing exams, for good reason. Almost everything involved in traditional test preparation flies in the face of research about best practices, as well as our own philosophical grounds as writing teachers. The best way to prepare students for standardized exams remains a rich and relevant curriculum that values authentic writing for multiple purposes.

Still, the exams are out there, and explicit test prep is increasingly an expectation, if not a mandate, in many schools and districts. If you're going to prepare students explicitly for writing tests, there are good and not-so-good ways to do it. As you consider our ideas, we invite you to think about ways in which you will authentically prepare students for the many testing situations they will face.

Demystify the Context to Gain Control

Students pick up on our subtle cues. When we're negative, uptight, or anxious about standardized exams, expect students to adopt similar attitudes. This doesn't help in preparing them for the contextual realities of these tests.

The best remedy for your own misgivings about high-stakes exams is knowledge. Why not become an expert about these tests: why they exist, what's on them, who reads them, and what is expected from students. Departments of education usually provide plenty of online information about state exams, and although it may be no picnic scanning this documentation, you might be surprised about what you learn. State prep material for the Georgia High School Writing Test, for instance, explicitly states that *formulaic writing is not acceptable* as a student writing strategy on such exams, which is exactly the opposite of what many teachers think "the state wants" (Georgia Department of Education 2011, 17).

Demystifying test expectations for yourself is the first step in demystifying the experience for students. Think for a second about the highly secretive and quarantined nature of this phenomenon. Students are stuck in a room to write about a surprise topic using a sealed-for-sanitation test booklet under a rigid time limit. They can't talk, seek out feedback, consult outside material, or use a computer. What they scribble is confiscated like a lab specimen, never to be seen again. Months later, an isolated score determined by anonymous raters arrives. Students receive no specific feedback on the writing itself, no recommendation for concrete improvement. It's almost as if the system is designed to keep teachers and students off balance and in Orwellian suspense.

Speak candidly with students about exam writing. Examine different expectations that may exist for *voluntary* versus *mandatory* tests. Examples of the former, such as the writing sections of the SAT and Advanced Placement exams, will generally expect more from students than the latter, which include state-mandated exams and end-of-course tests.

Students benefit from knowing—and from knowing that we know—that high-stakes testing is an artificial but still important situation. It can be refreshing for students to hear the unvarnished truth for a change—that they'll never be asked to do such writing in their adult lives and careers (outside, that is, of more educational testing)—but also that understanding the testing context is the key to mastering it. We share our own experiences as test takers and standardized exam readers, and we ask students to share theirs. Engage your students in thinking about what *standardized* means and what these tests are designed to do, practically and politically. In a sense, such tests are much less about singling students out as inadequate and more about districts and states protecting themselves from public criticism. We think it matters for kids to see this bigger picture, to understand what's happening to them and why.

To some extent, a game-oriented approach may help students with standardized exams. The state (or district, or testing organization) has, in essence, created a moderately challenging but common-denominator task that requires certain "moves" to overcome. We're reminded of *Star Trek's* holodeck scenarios, or small-scale sports scrimmages, or the regular "boss" levels featured in many video games. Thinking of the experience as a simulation or gaming challenge to test baseline ability may lessen anxiety and put matters in perspective. The system is beatable through strategy.

In short, ease students into thinking *strategically* about the reasons for such tests as a backdrop for putting into practice the *tactics* that will get them through it successfully.

◼ Understand What Counts: Balancing Safety and Risk

You might think that a standardized writing exam is the last place to encourage students to take risks—better to deliver a sufficient, if uninspiring, effort than to swing for the home-run and whiff. Maybe so. But then again, trying to aim for the dead middle, for some vague definition of average, may itself be a risky proposition. Will a safe, formulaic response get a student a minimal passing score? Or are students expected to deliver something more thoughtful, stylish, or comprehensive to pass muster? Indications may lie in the materials provided by the state or testing organization. Especially important are the model essays offered as examples for certain scores. Do formulaic responses earn passing scores, or are they scored lower? Are creative or unconventional responses that are technically correct rewarded or punished? Are students expected to support their assertions with legitimate reasons and evidence, or is a series of claims good enough? If students literally make up facts, statistics, and other forms of evidence to support the points they make, how is their writing scored?

Knowing the answers to these questions gives students information to use when they're gazing down at that exam writing prompt and planning a response. Fluent, confident writers make game-time decisions based on the specific circumstances; they don't commit to one and only one approach beforehand, regardless of the details. If students have been writing authentically all year, of course, this self-awareness has received strong, regular practice. Your students will be accomplished at justifying their decisions, weighing multiple potential approaches, and knowing why they're opting for one approach over another. The exam is then just another situation calling for informed, personal choices. Moderate risk is a normal part of success, as is knowing when to play it safe; but students ultimately must learn to make these decisions for themselves.

◼ Practice with Perspective

We've said it before and we'll say it again: The best exam preparation is a classroom filled with regular and meaningful writing for a variety of real contexts. Believing this principle is difficult for many conscientious teachers who want to do the right thing for their students. Work at it; believe it. While you're strengthening your believing muscles, consider these practical ways to prepare for exams without devolving into tedious writing drills.

Authentic Preparation Strategy 1: Give Students Real Experiences with Both Writing and Reading Exam Writing

Prepping students with practice-test prompts and timed writing is most effective when they learn to become good *readers* of exam writing as a foundation for their own written efforts. Dissect typical prompts, brainstorm writing ideas, analyze sample essays both strong and weak, apply the scoring guide as a scorer might, and create "memos of advice" to a hypothetical writer. All such activities help to demystify criteria and set students' thinking in a *surplus* rather than a deficit perspective. No need to carve out only sixty-minute blocks for full-on examlike conditions. Try five- or ten-minute microburst writings in response to a sudden question, mixed in with longer planned episodes of writing. As is consistent with the fluency, precision, and control model we are using throughout this book, your goal is building fluency with writing for test situations, giving students a kind of plasticity when it comes to a stop-drop-and-write event. Students become familiar with this context as something to handle without too much sweat, instead of something to fear and loathe.

Authentic Preparation Strategy 2: Embrace a Social and Collaborative Approach

Just because students have to face high-stakes testing in isolation doesn't mean preparation has to be a lonesome enterprise. Any writing begins as an individual act, but movement to small groups and then to the class as a whole helps students recognize idiosyncrasy in their writing that is two standard deviations from the norm (not good), and then to learn from one another. An effective tactic involves keying on evolving student mastery and cultivating a collegial spirit. Because most writing exams are not zero-sum affairs or scored on a curve, there's *no point in hoarding good ideas or tactics*. A collaborative groundswell of sound strategy, writing options, and shared insight boosts success rates for all writers.

Corporations, the military, and other real-world organizations understand these notions and leverage them quite well. They use the *debrief* as a regular part of group information gathering and self-assessment. We debrief most writing projects several times in the course of students' working on them. Doing the same for testing brings authenticity to your strategic discussions. Students have the opportunity to explore the applied skills of problem analysis, proposal vetting, and project evaluation as they discuss test-taking and writing strategies. Treat the work as a serious group effort—thirty minds tackling a universal problem from multiple perspectives—and students will usually respond.

Authentic Preparation Strategy 3: Read Widely, Think Critically About Reading and Writing, and Talk with Students About Both

Reading and writing often constitute the most effective methods for developing students' fluency in reading and writing. Sounds redundant, we know. With literacy, as with many other skills (riding a bike, playing the piano), practice makes perfect—or at least highly proficient. Involve your students actively in literacy practices, and don't stop doing so with or without the test looming over you and your students. Consider ways to build your classes around opportunities to capture your students' imaginations, and offer them contexts for literacy engagement about which they may actually care. When such engagement and active, constructive learning occur, what happens? (Say it with us, now.) Test scores go up. Believe it. This result is no surprise to any teacher who has watched students in action, discussing, researching, reading, and writing about ideas that are personally meaningful.

Thriving as a Teacher of Writing amid High-Stakes Testing

It's deplorable to us that legislators, commissioners of education, and politicians can't think of much else to do with writing in any official way other than grade it, score it, assess it, or make a contest out of it. We offer throughout this book many more wonderful things to do with writing, beginning with sharing it, celebrating it, talking about it, crying over it, and maybe even cussing it when necessary. Mainly, *enjoy* it and *struggle* with it together. Together. That to us is what teaching writing is about. We're not pushovers who care little about quality in writing. We just think there are different—and better—ways to achieve and reinforce quality than through high-stakes tests, the results of which are often published in the local paper for public criticism.

We invite you to start with our ideas and words for teaching writing, but then to derive your personal methods and examples for talking about a range of writing with your students. Use the words that flow though your thinking to help your kids look at their writing as writers and then to see the quality that resides in their writing.

Yes, the quality is there. Our job is to give students the vocabulary for talking about what they do well and the confidence to assert their capabilities.

When we look at our own writing—and we put off judging it critically for as long as we can—we ask ourselves three questions before we ask somebody else, "What do you think?" We look at it hard and ask, first, Does it tell the truth? In other words, is the piece as *honest*, as true to emotion and experience and sense and logic, as it can be? Once past that question, the other two questions are usually asked and answered quickly: Does it say enough? and then, Does it say more than it needs to say?

What we expect from all of our students is that sooner or later they—every one of them—will read something to us and to the class that will knock us off our feet because it's so honest and revealing—and surprising. We wait for that moment when our students write something better than they know they can or expect to achieve. Then we begin to talk about voice and movement and a light touch and all of these other strategies writers need to talk about together. When we work together as real writers and when we write what is real and honest for authentic audiences and in authentic contexts, students learn—and their test scores on any test that any politician or administrator throws at them will show their growth as writers and their efforts to learn.

Works Cited

Cooper, Charles R., and Lee Odell. 1977. *Evaluating Writing: The Role of Teachers' Knowledge About Text, Learning, and Culture*. Urbana, IL: NCTE.

Diederich, Paul. 1974. *Measuring Growth in English*. Urbana, IL: NCTE.

Elbow, Peter. 1998. *Writing Without Teachers*. New York: Oxford University Press.

Georgia Department of Education. 2011. "GHSWT Interpretive Guide Fall 2011." Georgia High School Writing test (GHSWT). Available at: www.gadoe.org/Curriculum-Instruction-and-Assessment/Pages/Georgia-High-School-Writing-Test-(GHSWT)-aspx.

Graves, Donald. 1979. Workshop at Georgia State University.

Olson, Miles, Dan Kirby, Carol Kuykendall, et al. 1981. *The Process of Writing: The Allyn and Bacon Composition and Applied Grammar Program*. Boston: Allyn and Bacon.

Tchudi, Susan, and Stephen N. Tchudi. 2000. *The English Language Arts Handbook*. Portsmouth, NH: Heinemann.

Wiggins, Grant. 1999. *Assessing Student Performance: Exploring the Purpose and Limits of Testing*. New York: John Wiley and Sons.

12

Writing About Literature and Other Texts

We are a species that needs and wants to understand who we are. Sheep lice do not seem to share this longing, which is one reason why they write so little. —**Anne Lamott,** *Bird by Bird*

Literature: That one word captures the heart of many English teachers. Most English teachers recall the first novel that they stayed awake all night to read, the one that transported them to another world or era, the one that introduced them to their favorite fictional character. Literature opens readers' eyes and allows readers to experience—even if vicariously—a cornucopia of viewpoints, cultures, time periods, belief systems, ways of living, and ways of thinking. The characters and settings and cultures may resemble our own lives or be vastly different. Ultimately, we read to understand better ourselves and others.

As Anne Lamott points out, we write for the same reasons. We explore who we are and who others are by engaging in writing and by reading the writing of others. Literature and writing go together like cake and ice cream. Both are delightful, and putting them together in one serving is sublime. Reading fiction and poetry and essays is essential to understanding the world around us, to figuring out who we are, where we come from, where we may go. We enrich our cognitive and emotional lives by exploring ideas in our own writing, by reading the writing of others, and by writing about what others have written.

Reading and writing are parts of the processes of understanding, imagining, exploring, thinking—in short, of being capable, literate beings who live rich lives well beyond what, say, sheep lice need or want. In her usual droll way, Lamott uses humor and hyperbole to trigger our thinking about the importance of writing—and, by implication, of reading what is written—in our cultural and personal development.

In this chapter, we explore multiple texts and what to do with them. We explore varied ways to write about literature, methods for linking writing and the texts your students read. In short, we explore a variety of ideas for purposefully integrating reading and writing a variety of texts in your classroom.

As you read our ideas, we invite you to envision your students. What do they like to read? To what extent and in what contexts are they already working with reading and writing as related processes? What activities will they enjoy, and which explorations will yield richer insights about themselves and others? We encourage you to read with pen or pencil in hand and to add your ideas to ours, respond to what we write, and to fashion your own ideas about engaging your students with writing, with literature, and with other texts. In short, we offer you opportunities to participate in the activities we indicate above; that is, to read our writing, write about what we have written, and to explore your ideas through your own jotted notes.

A Caveat About Literature

In the English language arts classroom, we encounter many types of writing and many types of texts. Some are *literary* without being *literature*. The word *literature* usually connotes, in its most restrictive sense, the great works of fiction exalted by one or more cultures. In a more inclusive working definition, *literature* might include contemporary classics (*Beloved, The Color Purple*), popular fiction (*Water for Elephants, The Help*), and young adult fiction (*The Hunger Games, Speak*). Essays are rarely considered to be, strictly speaking, *literature*. In fact, as *literary* as it may be, most English teachers would indicate that nonfiction falls into some realm other than that of *literature*. Poetry *might* be literature. After all, it's included in those ginormous tomes we call *literature textbooks*. (We discuss poetry further in Chapter 4.)

We invite you to define *literature* in a way that best suits your teaching context and your goals, objectives, and standards for teaching all texts. Throughout this chapter, we refer to writing about a variety of texts, including fiction, nonfiction, poetry, and other texts that students read and encounter in your class. The methods and activities we use to engage students with texts work for all types of texts, regardless of genre.

One Goal: Transactions with Texts

You may be wondering why English teachers need to work with so many types of texts if fiction—literature—is the coin of the English classroom realm. It's for the same reasons we've discussed before: Our students aren't sentenced to stay for life in our classrooms—a relief to all of us, no doubt. They leave and enter the teacher's classroom next door, the next grade level, and the real world. Our goal is to prepare our students to deal with texts they will encounter in our classes *and beyond* them.

Students are surrounded by texts in school, on the computer, in text messages, on TV, in movies, and in the books and magazines they read in physical or electronic form. We have tried out lots of texts in our teaching and lots of ways to work with texts, and we have discovered one primary goal that serves us well in our teaching. Transactions with texts—fiction, nonfiction, poetry, informational, visual, nonverbal, and a broad range of others—are at the core of contemporary schooling and life. We want our students to notice the abundance of texts that they encounter daily. Beyond mere noticing, however, a primary goal for us is that our students *transact* with texts as they read them, write them, and respond to them.

A transaction is more than an *interaction*, during which two or more parties converse, exchange pleasantries, debate, or otherwise talk, listen, and respond to each other. Interaction connotes an exchange, a back-and-forth. *Transaction*, on the other hand, connotes a *change*. Not only does someone read a novel, but the theme and characters from the novel are so compelling that the reader also alters her point of view, thinking, or perception. Not only does someone hear a speech, but he is also moved to take specific action (such as joining and contributing time and money to an environmental project) as a result. Transactions with texts are perhaps the ultimate learning achievement: What we learn changes what we do, how we think, perceptions of ourselves or others, and insights about our own or another culture.

Affording students the opportunity to transact with texts is no simple matter. The text must be compelling to reach students on a conscious level as motivation and as a change agent. We know that not all students like the same books and magazines; some students prefer not to spend their free time reading much of anything. Not all students spend their free time online, blogging, texting, or writing fan fiction, either. Like anything else, the diverse students in our classes will be interested in a range of texts.

The vast array and nature of texts—including those written by students—in the contemporary English classroom may be almost overwhelming when you consider how to use each in your teaching. In this chapter, we offer you a tsunami of activities and ideas for connecting reading and writing, for responding to texts, and for inspiring your students to transact with all manner of texts

Writing and Literature

Writing and literature just naturally complement each other; it's difficult to think of one without also thinking of the other. Many English teachers enter educational settings because they love literature—reading it, discussing it, responding to it, writing about it, and maybe even writing some of it (a short story, novel, or poem) themselves. A majority of English teachers' favorite courses as students were probably literature courses. They daydream about teaching literature, and only literature, for their entire careers. What bliss.

But it's certainly not reality. The longer we teach, the more we look, not for *separate* literature and composition units or classes, but for ways to *combine* literature and composition. After all, both are active meaning-making processes. Good writers write with their readers in mind ("What will my audience need to understand what I'm trying to say here?"), and good readers read with the writer in mind ("Why did the author use *that* image and *that* word? What does she want me to think here?").

Reading and writing are reciprocal processes; that is, one informs the other. Writing helps us make sense of a text we have read. Reading a romantic sonnet may inspire us to write our own poetry. Writing about literature is one way to support our analyses and close readings of literary texts. These are purposes and techniques that English teachers learned as students of literature and of writing. We teachers want to enlighten our students to the value and joy of reading and writing; to grow lifetime readers, writers, and thinkers; and to share and enjoy good literature and good writing experiences with our students. For most of us, that desire is what bought us into the English classroom in the first place.

Considerations for Writing About Literature and Other Texts

One of the most common activities in an English class involves asking students to write about literature and other texts they read. As with everything, there's a preferred and a not-so-wonderful way to entice students to think about texts by writing about them. As you think about how you will link reading and writing in your teaching, consider the following points:

1. *Our job as English teachers is to help our students* experience *literature and other texts through writing, as well as reading.*

Use writing to help your students discover *what* they know about the literature and other texts that they read. Writing is a way of exploring ideas, of organizing perceptions, of expanding intuitions about experience—including *reading* experience. Encourage students to explore, clarify, understand, and relate *in writing* to what they read. Writing is a way of approaching meaning in literature and other texts analogously, backward, or even sideways. Writing about what students have read is designed to yield greater understanding about texts and more enjoyment with texts.

2. *One of the best ways for students to experience literature and other texts through writing is the "creative response" (CR).* (See the CR sequence in the activities explained later in this chapter, beginning on page 257.)

Though we offer more detail later, one example of the CR is spontaneously writing a poem or composing a song in response to a short story or other text. You do so because you want to, because the literature moves you to do so, because the literature sparks your creative thinking and abilities. There's something almost magical about encouraging students to react personally and honestly in writing to a text that moves them. The CR simultaneously helps students grow as writers and as readers by easing students into writing about literature and other texts, first with free, open responses and then with guided responses.

As with freewriting (see Chapter 4), your students may need some time to become accustomed to the types of writing indicated by the CR. It's a type of writing that they may associate only with creative writing, not with insightful literary study. The analogical thinking required by the CR, however, works well as a tool for a close reading of text, for writing well about literature, and for focusing on a *response* to literature and other texts—not just critiques of them. CRs are one of the many tools that help students become more perceptive and willing readers of texts.

3. *Students of literature benefit from writing every day, just like students of composition.*

Most of us no longer teach literature classes separately from composition classes, but the point is that writing about literature requires practice for students' acumen as readers and writers to develop. Perhaps one reason that you like to teach literature is not having all of those piles and stacks of papers to grade. Sounds attractive, we agree. But integrating writing into literary study enhances both processes. Daily responses in writing to what students read are essential for their growth as writers and readers.

The journal (see Chapter 4) is a good way to encourage daily written responses, and we've had success using the first ten minutes of class for a quick journal response to the literature or other text we're talking about that day. It's better than the threat of the dreaded pop quiz to keep students current with assignments. They often look forward to the writing, for one thing, and it has the extra advantage of giving us a daily monitor of their under-standings, or confusions, about the material the class is studying.

Consider substituting a variety of responsive writings about the literature and other texts your students are reading instead of giving tests that focus on recalling facts (What color was Hester Prynne's embroidered letter?), with maybe a discussion item thrown in (Discuss the gender inequities in the novel). One way to re-vision what students do to engage with literature is to extend the writing workshop metaphor into literature study.

One technique is for students initially to respond individually to something specific in a text (Blau 2003)—a plot twist that confuses them, a quote they think might be important, a passage that seemed odd or that caught their attention. Next, move students into groups to discuss with peers their incipient struggles with meaning. Students sometimes think—just as they may think about writing—that two kinds of readers exist: those who "get it" right away, and those who don't and probably never will. Guess to which group many of your students think they belong. Talking through uncertainties about a text helps students toler-ate their initial feelings of confusion and ambiguity.

Using a literature workshop, like a writing studio or writers' group in workshop con-texts, helps students build meaning and realize that understandings of texts may occur gradually, through stages, and in discussions with other thinking people. Through this pro-cess, writing becomes a constant tool to sort out thinking, refine or revise tentative conclu-sions, and order our thinking for others.

Finally, whether the class you teach is called English 9 or American Literature and Composition or something else, we have a responsibility for the growth of our students as writers and as readers who know how to work with and write about multiple texts in a variety of ways.

4. *Model writing about literature and other texts for your students.*

Share with your students several examples of responsive writings about literature and other texts. Seeing a specific example gives students confidence that this stuff is possible to do. Also, remember that *your* example is important to your students. You're the literary expert in the room, you grade what they write, and they want to know what you want by listening to an example of what *you* wrote in response to a piece of literature or other text. As often as possible, write with your students about the literary works you're studying together. Share your writing with them often.

5. *Writing about literature and other texts and sharing writings with one another al-lows students to compare insights, perceptions, attitudes, and even problems about what they read.*

Instead of seeing the teacher's interpretation of a difficult poem or an obscure passage in a piece of literature as the alpha and the omega, we want our students to realize that many interpretations exist and are probably documented in scholarship about the literary work. Because we give our students many choices of what they read for class, we use our writings to share with our students what we particularly like to read. When students hear these shared responses and interpretations, they experience a variety of viewpoints and an introduction to multiple authors' works: short stories by Poe, Hawthorne, and Hemingway, for example, instead of just the one read by the entire class. If someone in the class likes a particular book, story, or poem, others are more likely to read it than if just the teacher recommends it.

Comparing our initial thoughts about and responses to a text is just a starting point. Discussion inevitably includes referring to the text, seeking passages that help to refine our thinking about what the text says and means. Every reader may not agree on literary interpretations, which leads to productive discussions. Work with your students to show them how their assertions need to be—and can be—supported by textual evidence and strong enough for peer scrutiny.

A recent national study (Stotsky 2010) suggests that many teachers do not ask students to perform close analyses of literary texts, with troublesome academic consequences. We are all for considering texts closely—when it's done effectively. Any literary analysis benefits from connections to frameworks of personal meaning and ways of making sense; otherwise, to your students, the analysis is just one more empty exercise.

6. *Variety is essential when writing about any text, including literature.*

Students (and teachers) easily fall into ruts when interpreting a piece of literature. As English teachers, after all, we still have our college notes about the symbolism in *Hamlet*, and teaching that stuff to our students is bound to be good for them, right? We're betting that your college notes represent only one perspective, the one the professor wanted you to have and the one you needed to do well on the test. That was then. This is now, and your students aren't English majors in an advanced college literature course. They need the freedom to *choose*, at least sometimes, what they read and how they will construct their responses to their reading.

Given the limitations of literature anthologies and most school libraries, shoo your students out the schoolhouse door to find engaging quality literature and contemporary, fascinating texts of all types. Equip them with an annotated list of choices to help them out, perhaps, but get them looking at books to determine what they want to read. Think about that point: Students must read the back cover, thumb through the book, and perhaps read a few paragraphs to determine if they like a book. They similarly peruse online books. That's more engagement with literature—with the text—which is a good thing.

Once they've read the book, show students examples of written responses and offer them a range of options for analysis (student-created videos, multimedia projects, and, okay, written papers). Brainstorm with them additional suggestions for writing about the text. When you do, you're much more likely to learn what students really think and really want to say about what they've read.

Motivating Writing Well *About Literature and Other Texts*

If you want students to write avidly and well about literature and other texts, consider incorporating the following ideas into your practice:

- Let students read, at least sometimes, for sheer joy and pleasure. Not every reading assignment needs a writing assignment.
- Use writing before reading or during the time students are reading a literary selection. Although written responses *after* the reading are standard practice, in-progress writing is helpful for sorting out ideas and responses to literature and other texts, for making inferences and predictions, and for building on the ideas of other students.

- Encourage creative expression about the text. Avoid making critical essays the only writing choice your students have.
- Realize that students' responses to a piece of literature or other text won't be as sophisticated as what the professional critic might say about the selection. Student writers are *students*, not professional critics.
- Grade less; *respond* more to their writing about literature and other texts. When you *do* grade what they write, don't grade their writing as if you were trying to decide whether they should go to hell or heaven.
- Offer options. Students have unique preferences in literature, in other texts they read, and in writing. Not everyone in the class has to complete the same assignment. (Reread that last sentence; let it soak in and affect your practice.)
- Let the response or other writing grow out of the conversations you and your students have about the text. Writing grows naturally out of talk, and that includes writing about literature.
- Offer students the option of modifying an assignment based on their understandings of the text, their writing preferences, and their strengths as learners.
- Let students know clearly what you expect from their writing about literature and other texts—formal or informal, response or critique, essay or poem or drawing, for example. Coyness or cat-and-mouse games just frustrate students. If what you *really* want is a formal analysis, say so. And then try *really wanting* other types of responses next time.
- Read and respond to the students' writings as you do to the writing of established authors—somewhat humbly, somewhat tentatively.
- Make writing about literature and other texts a pleasurable experience that students will want to repeat, not avoid.

When your classroom is filled with these sorts of options and attitudes, students are far more likely than not to enjoy reading and writing about literature and other texts.

Tracking Text Selections

When students are avidly reading and writing in your class, you will sometimes need a method for tracking the selections that students read independently, not just the selections that you all read in common. In fact, you may find that students have several simultaneous reading and writing projects underway, so tracking who is doing what and when may quickly become an issue.

Designed by our colleagues Tom Liner and JoAnn Lane, Close Out Questions are a good method for tracking students' progress as they finish books they're reading. Figure 12–1 is a sample of the Close Out Questions that Tom and JoAnn used, but adapt the questions to your own tastes and students. We like using Close Out Questions because it's a quick method for determining how well students have comprehended what they have read.

Name _____

Date _____

Bibliography

1. Situation. What is the book about? _____

2. What is the narrative point of view? Who is the narrator? _____

3. Setting. _____

4. Why is the setting important to the plot? _____

5. Characters. Identify the main ones, including name, age, features, and quirks. _____

    a. _____

    b. _____

    c. _____

    d. _____

6. Plot. What is unique about the plot (i.e., the way the action develops)? _____

7. Ideas. State in one or two sentences the theme of the book. _____

8. Quotable quotes. Give us two. (This is not dialogue.) _____

    _____

    _____

9. Vocabulary. Three words you learned, and a sentence from the book using each.

    a. _____

    b. _____

    c. _____

10. Your turn. What is really unusual, gripping, awe inspiring, weird, funny, heroic, moving, disgusting, or comic about the book (anything but boring!)? Or what about the character(s) or situations in the book do you identify with? (100 words, please)

    _____

    _____

    _____

    _____

    _____

    _____

    _____

    _____

Figure 12–1. Close Out Questions

From *Inside Out, Fourth Edition*. © 2004 by Dan Kirby, Dawn Latta Kirby, and Tom Liner from *Inside Out, Third Edition*. Heinemann: Portsmouth, NH.

Writing Responsively About Literature and Other Texts

These activities draw on students' responses—their insights, feelings, perceptions, and even negative reactions—to what they read. They begin with the student and his response to the text rather than with a traditional interpretation of the literary selection. You probably have already noticed that we don't say much in this chapter about analyzing literature or literary criticism. We left that kind of stuff out on purpose. Although writing critical essays about literature may be expected for Advanced Placement classes—and later for graduate seminars—many more productive (and less painful) ways exist to stimulate and nourish students' written responses to literature and other texts. Literary and other forms of close analysis too often put the cart before the horse; it's just busywork if students can't relate to what they've just read.

The following activities give you some ideas to stimulate thinking about how to have students respond to writing: to literature, nonfiction, poetry, and a host of other texts. Our goal is for students to use responding as an entrée into thinking and expressing their insights about what they read. Too often, English teachers who love literary criticism of one type or another analyze literature into shreds. Little is left of the story or plot or point of view to *enjoy*. We try hard to use a variety of activities to stimulate critical thinking without making writing about literature and other texts deadly dull and woefully serious.

For most of these activities, we have indicated a few specific American literary selections that work well for us. What other works come to mind as you read these ideas? What titles in British lit? Young adult lit? Other genres like graphic novels, poetry, or essays? Jot some notes about your thinking, your ideas for additional texts for which these activities may apply, and then try them out in your teaching.

▣ The Creative Response (CR) Sequence

We use the CR with our students in the same way that we use freewriting (see Chapter 4). We usually begin the class with this kind of writing, and we return to it often, especially when we're working with difficult and unfamiliar material—or whenever the students seem to be having trouble finding something to say about what they're reading.

Class begins with the free response, and from there we lead students into guided responses of various kinds (some of the most successful are listed). The CR works well in the journal, but we recommend collecting the first responses and responding to individual students to give them the immediate feedback they need to get a good start and a solid foundation for writing about texts, including literature.

▣ Phase 1 of the CR: Free Response

Try beginning class with a short selection, such as a song that is related thematically to the other reading the class will be doing. A poem or short story works just as well. Play the chosen song for the class, supply them with copies of the lyrics, and give them these instructions: "You're to write a creative response to this selection. You may write anything about it that you wish—except you may not say 'I like it' or 'I don't like it' or anything like that. It's a *creative* response, which means I'd like you to *create* something of your own. Write a poem, write a short sketch, draw a picture, tell me how it makes you feel, write the daydream you had while listening to it, freewrite while I play it again—respond to it any way you wish, but try to get something on paper this period."

Be patient with students at this point. They may be initially confused by the freedom inherent in the assignment. It's so *not* school. Reading to them examples of CRs to the same selection done by another class will help, as will reading your own CR.

Take the first few sets of free responses and "mine the slag heap," just as you might do with freewritings, looking for the good stuff to praise and ignoring their errors in usage and mechanics. When your students seem comfortable with these free responses, move into guided responses.

When choosing songs to play for students, you don't necessarily need to choose the hottest iTunes hits. Share what *you* like with them. Storytelling songwriters—Dylan, Springsteen, Johnny Cash, Billie Holiday—work well to promote creative responses about literary and thematic connections. The same goes for artists who operate in nonverbal realms, such as Miles Davis (innovative straight-ahead jazz), Brian Eno (being the originator of ambient music is just one of his accomplishments), The Rippingtons (smooth jazz), and Trent Reznor's recent soundtrack work (scores for *The Social Network* and the U.S. release of *The Girl with the Dragon Tattoo*).

■ Phase 2 of the CR: Guided Responses

We use a plethora of guided responses to texts as writing options in our classes. We like to offer several of these activities at a time as choices to students for pieces that they may write in response to the literary selections they've read. As always, add your favorite activities to our ideas.

■ Quotable Quotes

After students finish reading and talking about a piece of literature or other text, write several quotations from the work on the board, choosing ones that are especially evocative. Then, ask students to write a CR to the piece, using one of the quotations in their writing in any way they wish. Often the papers that grow out of this activity are interpretive. It's a good approach to use for literature or other texts with which the students are having some difficulty.

A variation of this activity is to have students pick their own quotations, swap them with one another, and then write CRs to them. Selections from such writers as Hemingway, Tennessee Williams, Faulkner, Longfellow, Blake, Welty, McCullers, Kesey, Morrison, and Cisneros are good for this activity. Any clearly stated theme works well. We've also used this device successfully with films/videos (*Romeo and Juliet, Precious, The Lovely Bones*), nonfiction (Thoreau, Rick Bass, Loren Eisley, Rick Bragg), and poetry (Hansberry, Angelou, Alexie, Li, Plath).

■ Imitation in Kind (Vignettes)

We watch for texts that lend themselves to student imitation. Quite simply, the assignment is to do *the kind of* writing the author did, but *in each student's own way*. It should be a try-it-and-see kind of activity.

One successful imitation-in-kind activity begins with books that are collections of vignettes, such as Hemingway's *In Our Time*, Cisneros' *House on Mango Street*, and O'Brien's *The Things They Carried*. After reading and talking about a number of these vignettes, ask students to try three or four vignettes of their own. Encourage them to draw on their *memories* and write about episodes that involve *action* and *drama*. Encourage students to put the reader into the scene to create compelling material. The results of this activity are usually good enough to follow up with revisions.

Any work with brief, self-contained episodes work well for this activity: Brautigan, Lopez, Flannery O'Connor. Kafka's riddles are good for advanced classes.

Narrators

Lots of literature features a narrator with a strong voice. This type of literature is ideal for generating a focused CR. Many young adult novels feature memorable narrators and work well. Strong narrators and narrative voices (*I* as narrator) raise the question of why authors employ them for certain pieces but not for others.

After students have read several literary pieces with strong narrators, have them respond to this literary technique by trying their own narrative skills and role-taking perspectives when writing a story or other piece using a narrator who is not themselves. If students get stuck while attempting this activity, tell them to look back at one of their favorite books or excerpts featuring a narrator and to try doing it like that. Sometimes, you may need to read the first few paragraphs of a book with the students who are having difficulty and discuss with them the author's use of the narrative voice. Here is Sadiqa's moving and emotional story in which she uses a narrative voice that is not her own. Note how the appearance of the piece, including its surface errors, enhance the narrator's voice:

> my mama said its cause im a BAD GIRL. i don't much care. she can beet me all she want to. long as she dont beet Sweetie. that what i call my Brother. i luv Him and He love me. its my duty to keep Him safe. sometime he pee in His clothes. mama get real mad and say she gone beet Him. i tell her she better not cause He just a lil baby. He dont no better. she dont take no time to potty train Him anyway. when i tell her she slap my mouth and say i be dissrespectfull cause i talk back to her. she hit me hard. i taste the saltyness of the blood coming from my lip. but i just be happy its me and not Sweetie. mama say i aint nobody. i know i aint but Sweetie gon be somebody. He gon be prezadent or somethin won day.
>
> won day i came home from school and saw that mama had left Sweetie home alone. i hate when she do that cause He dont no how to care for Hisself. He only two. well Sweetie had got sick on Hisself and He had spilled some milk on the floor. i tried to hurry up and clean it up fore mama got home but i couldnt. i could tell by the way she slammed the dorr that she was pissed about somethin. another one of her mens probly left her.
>
> so i picked up Sweetie to leave so wed be safe from mama. cause she get in a beatin mood when she pissed. when i was walking out of the room she called to me in that mean voice, Bitch i thought i tol you to clean up when you got home from school! come in hear so i can learn you a lesson! well i knowed what that meant so i put Sweetie on my bed hopin He would fall asleep or somethin so He wouldnt hear the sound.

when i got in the room mama had the strap in her hands. she looked mad as hell. i seen that look and i started shakin cause i was scared shed beet me bad this time and then who would protect Sweetie? well mama took that strap to me and she beet me all over till i couldnt hardly hold my head up. i was hurtin everywhere. i felt the tickle of blood running down my face. i got up to check on Sweetie. i hurt bad but i just be glad its me and not Sweetie. cause He aint did nothin to nobody and mama just hit me cause im a BAD GIRL.

—Sadiqa[1]

Once students know how to manipulate narrative selves and voices with such skill, they begin to understand fully the distinctions between the narrator and the author.

Tall Tale Telling

This is a good activity when your students are reading Mark Twain and other authors who write from a strong oral tradition. Most families have their own legends—many of them exaggerated memories—that relatives like to tell when they're together. The student's assignment is to think of a family story (or make up a convincing lie), and craft it into a piece of writing for a partner or a small group.

The works of Irving, O'Connor, Faulkner, Thomas Wolfe, and Morrison are also useful for this activity. It's worth noting that such stories are often culturally bound and culturally revealing. Branch out to writers who explore diverse cultures and discuss what in their tales seems mythic rather than literal. Look to Amy Tan, Maxine Hong Kingston, and Alice Walker for examples. Gene Yuen Lang's graphic novel *American Born Chinese* also explores similar territory.

Considerations of Texts

We think that writing a traditional critique of a text is just fine—as long as that is not the *only* kind of writing you invite students to do as they think about and transact with texts of any type. Most schooling and standards of various types push—verily shove—teachers toward assessment that is formal, formatted, constrained, and familiar. Traditional critiques fall into those categories and are still valued by a system of schooling that loves common denominators. What do we all know how to do that, in turn, we know how to teach our students to do—and yes, that we know how to evaluate and assess and format as well? Sure, the traditional critique. We know you've had lots of practice with critique.

But what do you do to change it up a bit in your class? To kick the lead out and generate some energy among your students as they transact with a variety of texts? That's what we've been exploring. What we have offered so far in this chapter are ideas for exploring literature and other texts by writing about them in ways that are perhaps nontraditional. Going beyond the known, the familiar, the comfortable, can be challenging. That's why we've offered a multiplicity of ideas for dealing with texts, ideas that we have used with success. We hope to stimulate your creative juices as you plan to work with a variety of texts in multiple ways in your classes.

So far, we've talked quite a bit about literature, but we also include "other texts" quite deliberately in this chapter to nudge you to think about what those *other texts* might be.

Essays, creative nonfiction, informational pieces, editorials, narratives, memoirs, and any number of other pieces of writing come to our minds when we mention "other texts." Beyond literature, what other texts do your students routinely encounter? What other texts beyond fiction do you bring deliberately into your teaching? What is the advantage of having an English Language Arts classroom awash in all varieties and genres and styles and forms of texts?

We'll ease into our considerations by starting with a type of text that is familiar, if not universally beloved: poetry.

Writing and Responding to Poetry and Other Texts

Poetry: That word creates trepidation in many an English student's—and teacher's—heart. Some teachers dread teaching poetry and stuff it all into one two-week unit. Others thrive on all sorts of poetry, from playful to romantic, contemporary to classic, famous to obscure, rhyming to free verse. Regardless of your reaction to *poetry*, you will encounter opportunities in your teaching to work with your students as you teach poetry and as both you and they write some original poetry. Earlier in this chapter (see page 250), we briefly toyed with the question of whether most English teachers consider *poetry*—or any text other than fiction—to be *literature*; we are confident that most do. It may not be most teachers' favorite literary genre, but teach it and read it and—yes—write it, you no doubt will. We have been careful thus far to refer to *literature and other texts* in this chapter to indicate that good writing about text is good writing. The genre—fiction, essay, nonfiction, poetry—of the text affects motivation and enthusiasm, perhaps, but not the basics of why and how to write *about* texts and why and how to *practice writing a variety of texts* in our classes. We turn now to considerations of how to excite your students about poetry as text, form, genre, and creative expression.

Easing into Responding to Poetry

Wordsworth. Blake. Ezra Pound. Tennyson. Dante. Neruda. Plath. Clifton. Vallejo. Sexton. What do these poets have in common? In addition to being canonical poets widely studied in schools, they are notoriously difficult for students—and sometimes teachers—to understand, read with rich insight, relate to contemporary life, and otherwise just *get*. We're betting a few dozen other poets' names also come to mind, names of those poets you didn't get, don't like, and have few clues how to teach.

We're also hoping that at least some poets come to mind whom you truly enjoy and can't wait to share with your students.

Whether you're a lover of poetry or just tolerate it because you must as an English teacher, we next offer some strategies for making poetry come alive for students. No doubt, you will need to teach some of the technical stuff of poetry: rhyme scheme, formats (sonnets, haiku), scansion, meter, literary devices, and the like. That's fine. Knowing that stuff helps students understand and appreciate the intricacies and sophistication and highly compressed visual nature of poetry. But that may not be where you want to *start* working with your students and poetry. If you're like us, we find that many of our students need to tiptoe into poetry rather than plunge head first into its arctic waters. That is, they need some time to become *fluent* (see Chapter 2, pages 26–29) with the genre—as readers, responders, and writers—before they are ready to jump into the control and precision of thought, insight, and use of technique needed to delve deeply into the most sophisticated and complex poetry.

We begin by reading poetry and responding to poetry with our students, just as we do with literature and other texts that may prove challenging. We generally begin with contemporary poetry in somewhat plain (though not simplistic) language that students have a shot at understanding and liking. Many poets come to mind for this initial foray into poetry: Billy Collins, Ted Kooser, Donald Hall, Rita Dove, Kay Ryan—all of whom just happen to be recent U.S. Poet Laureate Consultants in Poetry (the official title since 1985). Once our students have an inkling that not all poetry is impossible to understand, we try out a few activities for letting them discover poetry they personally like, poetry that resonates with them on a personal, emotional, realistic, or other level.

◾ Shopping for Poetry

Once our students are at ease with writing Creative Responses (CRs) (see pages 257–260 in this chapter), we use this activity to add some variety to how students find poems with which to relate.

We make copies of several very short poems and cut the pages so that each poem is on its own small square of paper. After you've done this activity a few times, you'll have a collection of these little poems. Then, spread about twenty of them out on display on desks or bookshelves or some other convenient place before the class comes into the room. As the students enter, invite them to shop in the poetry supermarket. Let them take awhile to mill around and read the poems and talk about them. Finally, advise students to select at least three for CRs.

Poems by Brautigan, Cohen, and Plath work for this activity. Work in your own poems as well as some by students. We also like to include some poets who write specifically for young adults such as Mel Glenn; some contemporary poets such as Billy Collins; and some poets of color, such as Maya Angelou, Nikki Giovanni, and Jimmy Santiago Baca.

Grappling with Literary Terms

What if you're expected to teach students conventional literary terms and assign conventional literary analysis essays? You don't need to shelve personal relevance if you find yourself in this situation. Tone, character, setting, mood, theme, foreshadowing, irony—all of these concepts and more can be translated and explored in personal ways before or during textual discussions. This is one way that we scaffold instruction, starting with the familiar and moving to the more complex or unfamiliar. Without a personal stake in or perspective on such concepts, the writing that students do will likely be empty of voice, care, connection, and importance. By exploring these terms through activities like the ones we offer below, students also are learning more of the depth within a text, which will help them respond with more thoughtfulness, truthfulness, and thoroughness (see Chapter 8 for our discussions of these qualities of effective responses).

Let's say that you're dealing with the themes of identity and stereotype, perhaps as they appear in a text such as *The Catcher in the Rye* or *To Kill a Mockingbird*. Along with the many activities mentioned above, you might consider more elaborate explorations, such as the two activities described below.

▓ Stereotype and Beyond, Part I

This activity, borrowed from Jeffrey Berman (2001), is effective in getting students talking about identity and misconception. It's also a brush with reality to bring a complex term like *stereotype* into focus for students.

First, ask students to recount in writing an episode in which they felt they were stereotyped or otherwise labeled on superficial merits. All kids have felt unfairly judged—about their appearance, speech patterns, clothing, hairstyles, names, interests, or something else—and most are willing to share these experiences.

Now, it's time to flip the script. Their next task is to write about an experience in which *they* stereotyped or unfairly judged *someone else*. Moving from considering oneself as the victim of unfairness to being the perpetrator is not usually easy for kids to do, so they may need a little extra time with this one. Small-group sharing may follow, and students who volunteer to read their episodes for the class should be commended for helping to promote risk taking within a safe classroom climate.

Be careful with this activity. Some students are simply not ready to write or speak about issues of stereotyping, let alone volunteer themselves as perpetrators. Doing so may be too risky or too unsettling. A significant number of your students may claim that they simply don't think of themselves or others in this way, or they may reject the mental exploration altogether. Other students will seek a politically correct response, and yet others may be brutally honest in their writing (though *honesty* may be difficult to differentiate from *prejudice* in some cases). Power dynamics in any classroom can be complex and challenging to negotiate. We recommend allowing students to opt out of such self-disclosure if they're not ready. At all times, both you and your students should be clear about your ethical responsibilities; a safe classroom environment is not one in which potentially hurtful language is allowed.

Certainly this invitation is a challenge. As with all literacy activities and materials, use your judgment to determine if this activity is a good idea for you and your students. New or preservice teachers will want to be especially careful about beginning such work. What's the vibe like in the room? Are students open and friendly with one another, or closed off and wary? Students who have been enthusiastic about participating and sharing in previous activities may be ready for this challenge. Other classes won't be. Although you may be excited about trying out this kind of writing, remember that trust and community cannot be imposed.

▓ Stereotype and Beyond, Part II ("If You Really Knew Me")

This activity also features one method for exploring *stereotype* and similar complex literary terms. For other terms—perhaps *sarcasm* or various sorts of *irony*—the activity would need to be adjusted to work with the literary device you want students to know.

We borrow this idea from the Challenge Day movement (www.challengeday.org) and the MTV show *If You Really Knew Me*. Each episode of the TV program features a "Challenge

Day" at a school, in which students personally confront stereotypes through writing and come to know each other a bit more authentically. Starting their writing with the phrase "If you really knew me, you'd know that . . ." students have the opportunity to address discrepancies between how they're viewed (and judged) by others, and how that view is inaccurate, oversimplified, or just insufficient. Similar in theme to the 1985 classic high school film *The Breakfast Club*, the underlying idea is that once you come to know the unique stories of others, it becomes nearly impossible to reduce them to stereotypes. They emerge as real people rather than objects, as valuable human beings rather than abstractions.

Again, be cautious with this kind of exploration. Don't rush it. Students should not feel pressured to self-disclose if they prefer not to do so. Inviting confessional kinds of writing and sharing may open many emotional doors for students. Oftentimes, once a community of writers has been established, reluctant students will decide to share more of themselves, a true indication that they are feeling safer within the class. As much as we value the organic and affirming potential of this kind of writing, we are not counselors or therapists. There are some subjects best handled by trained counselors, psychologists, and other professionals. Foster relationships with the counseling staff at your school so that you may freely call upon their expertise should the need ever arise.

What You Accomplish with Activities Like These

These kinds of activities ask students to grapple meaningfully with broader concepts and themes that resonate in literature. When they return to the specific text under study, they bring with them the immediacy of these personal explorations. That means that when they're analyzing why Holden Caulfield or Mayella Ewell react the way they do, or how an author deals with issues of identity, they have a fresh personal angle to provide some perspective. For several compelling examples of how students might blend conventional literary analysis with detailed personal connections, take a look at the student essays by clicking on the online Additional Resources link at www.heinemann.com/products/E04195.aspx, on the Companion Resources tab.

Alternatives to the Book Report

Ah, the time-honored and time-worn book report! Kids hate it, and teachers are bored reading it. But your students ought to read books, right? So what we suggest are some alternative activities to make the chore more tolerable for your students and for you. Whenever possible, of course, students should have several activities from which to choose. Many of these suggestions also work well with short stories or plays. Most are good activities to use with films.

These activities may seem simplistic. Look for sophisticated touches in students' products that will convince you students have read and understood a text. The analysis of the text that the student must perform to produce a quality product is more complex than students are likely to realize until they begin trying to complete the products. The subtleties and intricacies of the products clue you in rather quickly if the student hasn't read the book, or hasn't read carefully. Remember, just because an activity is fun doesn't mean that students aren't learning, being challenged, and demonstrating their knowledge.

Advertise the Book

Have students write advertising blurbs (like those on the back of paperback books) and then display them in your classroom. Encourage students to make them as racy as possible (well, within what is acceptable in your teaching context), just like the real thing. This activity is quickly done and generates talk about books and reading. A variation is for students to make advertising posters for the books they've read, with a drawing and a blurb, and display these around the room. If you want to go higher tech, go for videos or PowerPoint slides that can be shown to all students.

Continue the Story

One of the most successful writing activities for novels that we've found is to have students continue the story for a few pages. We encourage them to keep the writer's style and approach intact as much as possible when they do so, and to include some dialogue if they can. The point, of course, is not to get them to write like professional novelists but to generate thinking about the writers' techniques and the whole business of storytelling. Many novels lend themselves to this activity. Favorite authors for this activity are Hemingway, Steinbeck, Robbins, and Potter.

Dawn has had great success using this technique with young adult authors' books that don't end happily ever after, such as Robert Cormier's classic young adult novel, *The Chocolate War*. Students rewrite the ending or extend it for a chapter and then discuss which ending is better—theirs or Cormier's—and why.

For students who are a bit younger, have them write either a future-based extension of the book—say, five or ten or even twenty years into the future of the characters—or an intervening chapter among the novel's existing chapters. This activity works particularly well with young adult novels such as Cushman's *Catherine, Called Birdy*, which is told from the first-person point of view and is written as a journal. Dawn's students have written intervening chapters that take Catherine, the protagonist, on another adventure, or a future-based final chapter that features Catherine as a grandmother. Both types of chapters give students practice in maintaining the novel's unique journal format and protagonist's distinctive voice.

The challenge is to create prose, dialogue, descriptions, and other aspects of text that emulate the original, so that this continuation connects seamlessly with what's come before. Harry Noden (2011) notes the positive potential of imitation for practicing sentence structure forms, voice, and tone. This task requires a solid sense of both content and style.

A Family Tree

Working with a family tree helps students build understanding of the interrelationships within specific novels. You're probably familiar with the elaborate diagrams of family relationships among characters in Faulkner's novels. Cleanth Brooks' *Yoknapatawpha Country*, for example, also contains detailed and accurate examples. On a smaller scale, novels like *The Grapes of Wrath* lend themselves to this way of looking at characters, with a family tree of the Joad family giving students a better grasp of the characters' relationships. We invite students to construct a character's family tree with brief notes on each character. The graphic representation helps students to clarify characters' roles in a long or complex novel. Creating the family tree also requires students to read and reread the text to get the details right. A modified version of this activity to show relationships of military rank in Heller's *Catch-22* also works well.

Authors such as Bobbie Ann Mason in her memoir *Cold Springs* begin with the family tree and a chronicle of where the family has lived throughout several generations. Then, she goes on to recount her own memoir by authoring stories of her extended family and her relationship to them. Students can do the same sort of thing by generating their family trees and then telling stories of their places within the family web.

Further, completing a family tree for the characters helps students to explore important issues of cultural dominance and interrelationships. When students look at the family tree of Sethe in Toni Morrison's *Beloved*, for instance, they begin to explore the ways in which slavery violated family bonds. The family trees for many of the characters in the novels of Louise Erdrich and Barbara Kingsolver similarly generate discussions and raise issues about Native American families.

As a follow-up, ask students to select a particularly interesting feature of the family tree and reflect on its importance in the work. Again, *Beloved* works well as an example for discussion before students try this analysis of the family tree they created.

The Newspaper Interview

We sometimes have students conduct an imaginary interview between a reporter for a specific publication or television program and a character from a novel. For example, have a student imagine herself to be a reporter for *Cosmopolitan Girl* and then interview Janie from Hurston's classic novel *Their Eyes Were Watching God*. To what questions would the readers of that particular magazine be interested in hearing Janie respond? How does Janie as a character fit the profile of the modern woman as defined by that magazine's perspective? How is Janie a role model for today's teenaged females—and how is she not? All of these questions, and more, will come into consideration as students determine how the imagined interview would go.

As additional examples, a reporter from *Sports Illustrated* could interview Ender from Orson Scott Card's young adult science fiction futuristic novel *Ender's Game*; or a reporter for the school newspaper could interview Melinda, the main character in Laurie Halse Anderson's young adult novel *Speak*, after she again decides to speak.

A good approach with this activity is to pair students who have read the same novel, with one student acting as the reporter, and the other as the character. They can make a taped interview, or merely write it. The results can be remarkably insightful, sometimes hilarious. Try this activity with classics and young adult classics such as *The Great Gatsby*, *Go Tell It on the Mountain*, the Twilight series, *The Outsiders*, *Ordinary People*, *Winter Girls*, *The Lovely Bones*, or even for characters in Shakespearean plays. This activity, by the way, also works extremely well with nonfiction biographies, autobiographies, and memoirs.

Shifting Points of View

A simple but effective activity is to have students rewrite a brief version of a narrated novel from another character's point of view. It promotes a lot of talk and thinking about characters and values. For example, feature Catherine Barkley as the narrator of *A Farewell to Arms* instead of Frederic Henry. Other examples include a consideration of how *To Kill a*

Mockingbird is altered if Atticus is the main narrator. In young adult literature, consider how *The Chocolate War* changes if Brother Leon or Archie tells the story, how *Ender's Game* changes if one of the military commanders is the narrator, or how *The Book Thief* works if Hans or Rudy relate the story. Examples abound.

Obituaries

Ask students to write obituaries for characters who are dead at the end of a novel. Real and imagined obituaries serve as models, and students write their own for a scandal-mongering, yellow journalism newspaper. We get started by brainstorming together as many sensational headlines as we can recall. A variation of the assignment is to write an exposé news story for a tabloid; some very funny ones have been done on *The Scarlet Letter*.

Suitable novels are almost endless. Authors frequently kill off characters at the end of their books; check out the novels of Heinlein, Styron, Vonnegut, Kesey, Wambaugh, and Jones. Older students may be intrigued with writing an obituary for Susie, the main character in *The Lovely Bones*. As always check out books before your teach them because all plots are not appropriate for all cultures, schools, and students.

Don't Forget the Little Guy

We like to focus some of our discussion on the *minor characters* in novels. This activity requires students simply to forget main characters for a while and "tell me about the unimportant characters, the ones you usually don't remember or notice or discuss much." It's a good sideways activity for getting students to look at a book from a different perspective.

Many, many books have interesting minor characters worthy of notice. Some favorites appear in classic books such as *Dune, Exodus, Sometimes a Great Notion, Wise Blood*, and *The Heart Is a Lonely Hunter*. We also enjoy the minor characters in the works of Amy Tan, Barbara Kingsolver, Maya Angelou, Mark Twain, Michael Ondaatje, Larry McMurtry, Cormac McCarthy, and Annie Proulx, to name a few.

Book Quotes

In this activity, students collect quotations from their literary selections. Students choose the quotes because the words resonate with them in some way. The quotes just grab them as readers. Students wish they could have written those lines. The object is to make connections to our real lives by reacting and responding to the quotes. We like to use double-entry journal formats for the book quotes, with the quote on the left-hand side of the page and the student's response to the quote on the right-hand side. This activity provides lots of starting points for discussions of character and theme, symbols and metaphors, foreshadowing and irony. The responses also are often the beginnings of more detailed written critiques of the literature. This activity works well for all sorts of literary selections, including fiction, essays, short stories, poetry, drama, and film.

A Defense

Students will often find a book more compelling when they hear that some people would prefer that they did *not* read it. In this activity, students imagine both the reason the book under study might be challenged along with a sustained defense, detailing why a particular work is appropriate for/should be taught to young adults. This option obviously works well with controversial, challenged, and censored titles, but even seemingly innocuous, well-loved, or accepted titles may undergo scrutiny. Consider, for instance, allowing students the freedom to reverse the situation, arguing that a stalwart of the classroom canon should go. We often time this particular activity to align with Banned Books Week. Titles that work well for this activity include *Brave New World, Of Mice and Men, The Hunger Games* (any book in the series), *Twilight* (any book in the series), *Nickel and Dimed, Crank,* or *Lush.* Remember: These books have all been controversial or banned in certain situations, so know your context before you embark on having students read and defend titles like these.

Switching Genres/Disciplines/Contexts

For this writing, students take a "meaty" or significant excerpt from a work written in one genre and "switch" it to at least three other genres. For instance, a short scene from a play might be switched to a short story, a poem, a business memo, a rap, a comedian's monologue, and so on. Alternatives include the following:

- Switch from one discipline to several others (English to biology, history, psychology, math, etc.). What would a biologist or other scientist focus on from the text? What psychological profiles do the characters display? What is the larger history of the time period surrounding the text? Sometimes, our students have simply used wordplay from the discipline to consider a text: The alibi of the main antagonist just doesn't *add up*. Considerations such as these will help students switch out the text. Some of these switches require research (for historical times, for example) and some turn out to be humorous for one reason or another. Students discover just what knowledge and writing ability it takes to repurpose a text so that it focuses on another content area.
- Switch contexts (time periods; cultures; locations; circumstances). How would a scene from *Wuthering Heights* need to be rewritten if it were set in contemporary times? How would a scene from *Fahrenheit 451* need to be altered if it were set in a contemporary repressive dictatorship in Rwanda? What would need to change if the plot of *Speak* were set in a country with strong religious laws and mores? The possibilities for changing significant features of a piece of fiction and then determining how the piece would need to be altered provide an excellent opportunity to engage your students in considering the features of text as they relate to plot, setting, era, and culture.

Along with their transformations, students include a one- to two-page introduction explaining the relevance of the selected excerpt, rationales for their alternate genre/discipline/situational choices, and what they hoped to accomplish with their decisions.

Texting/IMing/Facebooking

Go digital. Invite students to use digital deliveries to demonstrate their understandings of aspects of a novel. They might create a series of emails or IMs that two of the characters would have sent to each other if they'd had the technology to do so. The emails or texts should not be simply a matter of copying dialogue from the piece of literature but newly created by the student to show additional action, emotion, or events not fully presented in the book. Alternately, they might create a pen-and-paper rendition of a Facebook page for a character that suggests the same sort of subtle interactions (print-based profiles allow for many more creative possibilities than does an actual online account). Students follow this creative work with a written summary that explains their decisions and makes the case for their relevance.

Cast the Movie

For this activity, students consider which actors they would cast in a movie made of the book or story they've just read and write a rationale for their choices. Many books have been made into movies, so we begin by discussing with students which castings were apt and which were woeful. Does it matter that in the book, the main character was short with blonde hair and in the movie, the actor is tall and a brunette? Consider classic books and movies, such as *To Kill a Mockingbird*, and which actors would have each role in a contemporary remake of the movie. Who, for example, is the contemporary Atticus/Gregory Peck? The discussions are always lively and sometimes choices are hotly defended. After the discussion, have students list their cast members and write a clear rationale for their selections, including referring to specific details in the book to justify their choices.

Word Cloud

Sites such as Wordle allow users to generate a word graphic, or cloud, from any text, including texts created by students. Challenge students to create word clouds that in content, size, arrangement, design, and font accurately depict the mental state of a character or the thematic tensions of a text. To accompany the visual representation, ask students to write an explanation of why they chose specific words, why they emphasized some words and not others, and how the overall tone and mood of their word cloud relate to that of the original text. When students include specific references to details in the text, they are honing their eye for detail and abilities to critique.

Nonwritten Responses to Literature

Not all responses to literature need to be written. Drawing is also a valid form of nonwritten response. Encourage students with drawing abilities to respond visually to what they read whenever it seems appropriate. Remember, too, that there are some artistic nonwritten responses that don't require much artistic talent. Clip art and free downloadable pictures from the Internet make a tech-savvy kid seem to be a brilliant artist (and maybe she is). Visualizations help keep things interesting in the literature class. They stimulate talk about how we *see* what we're reading. "That character doesn't look like *that*," someone in the class says about an illustration we put up. "I don't know," we might respond, defending the artist, "I kinda see the person like that." And the class is off, talking about their *perceptions* of the work.

Visualizations, like drawings, should always be only *one* choice among several that are available as responses to literature. After a rousing class discussion, ask students to capture the discussion in their journal entries about the text by responding to questions such as the following:

- Which visual representations among those offered by everyone in the class were apt? Why? Refer to specifics in the text to support your assertions.
- How did talking with the entire class and defending your choices influence your perception of the text?
- How did the class discussion give you insights about how your visual representation may benefit from specific changes? What aspects will you choose to revise? Why?

We also offer for each activity in the next section an idea or two about extending students' thinking through writing about their choices. The type of thinking in which students must engage to complete these activities is quite detailed, symbolic, and complex. These activities are fun—and they generate lots of reflection, talking, writing, and learning.

Character Portraits/Illustrations

We've always gotten good results with giving students the choice of responding to a story by drawing an illustration or a character's portrait from the story. This is an activity that allows the artists in your class to shine, even if they aren't gifted readers, and it works well for almost any literary selection. Ask the artist to explain verbally or in writing why he sketched the character as he did, perhaps using descriptions from the book for at least some of his justifications for his choices.

The Character Locker

Students create a locker out of a shoebox by covering it with construction paper or even with aluminum foil. Then, students select one character from a novel they have read and place real items into the locker to represent key events in the novel, items important in the character's life, and items symbolic of the values of the character. If the real item is too large to fit into the shoebox, students may create smaller versions of the real object (substituting a drawing of an axe in place of a real axe for a book like *Hatchet*, for example). Websites such as Glogster and Museum Box open digital avenues for the character locker concept.

Our students love this activity and have created lockers for a wide range of characters in young adult literature, especially; but it works well for just about any literary selection with strong character development. It also works well for biographical and autobiographical selections. For example, one of Dawn's students who read a biography of Marilyn Monroe created a locker that contained an empty prescription pill bottle, pictures of John and Bobby Kennedy, a miniature poster created by the student for one of Marilyn's movies, pictures of her husbands, pictures of the young Marilyn in a swimsuit, the lyrics to Elton John's song "Goodbye, Norma Jean" rolled up as a scroll, a bottle of peroxide, and a tube of bright red lipstick. Watching the result of students' creative interpretations of what is important to a character is fun and enlightening for everyone in class.

Along with the locker and its artifacts, ask students to write an explanation of why they chose each item, what it represents about the character or real person, and how the item symbolizes a specific aspect of the character or person. By reading these pieces, we learn tons of useful information about how our students think about literature and about biographies or autobiographies.

The Illustrated Map and Draw the Neighborhood

These activities are highly successful with our students as they explore literature. Students work in pairs to trace the action of a story by drawing an illustrated map (it does not have to be elegantly done—stick figures will work just fine) and labeling important actions.

Draw the Neighborhood is a variation of the Illustrated Map idea. Here, students draw the neighborhood where most of the action takes place in a novel or story.

These activities sound deceptively simple, but you will notice your students reading and rereading the text to get all of the details on the map just right. Adding color, landscaping, or other features the author mentions is also helpful to encourage close reading of the text. To accompany their maps, ask students to write an explanation of their process for creating the map. They might also write about what they learned about the setting of the text and about the significance of using meaningful details in writing.

Steinbeck's and London's classic stories work well for the Illustrated Map activity. Alfred Brooks' neighborhood from *The Contender*, Bumper Morgan's beat in *The Blue Knight*, and the neighborhood in Cisneros's *The House on Mango Street* work well for our Draw the Neighborhood activity. We further recommend the stories and memoir of Bobbie Ann Mason, Bebe Moore Campbell's memoir *Sweet Summer*, and Annie Dillard's memoir *An American Childhood* for these activities. You'll also find stories in your literature anthology with a strong sense of place in them that will work well for students who want to experiment with these activities.

Book Jacket Design

The idea of this activity is for students to design an original and, hopefully, an attractive and interesting book jacket for a novel. We encourage them to stretch their imaginations and be as sensational and bizarre as any book designer (again, as your school context will permit). Display the finished products around the room to stimulate a hub of book sharing. Along with each book jacket, post the student's written explanation, complete with references to the text, of why she selected the images, colors, graphics, layout, lettering, and other aspects of her design.

Digital Trailers and Opening Credits

For your more tech-interested students, offer the option of creating a digital trailer for the book they've read. Easy-to-use and ubiquitous programs such as Photo Story and Movie-Maker lower the technology bar, which means that students spend less time on mastering the software and more time on meeting the expectations of these activities: generating interest in the book to get others to read it. To do so, students might include text, high-quality images, color, video, and narration (if appropriate) to generate mystery/tension/intrigue in the manner of TV show and film trailers. Student-created book trailers are fairly common, with lots of decent examples available on YouTube and similar sites. Students usually find that writing and planning out a storyboard or other planning document is invaluable as they undertake this activity.

A variation of this project asks students to create the *opening credits* of a film version of the text. Credits obviously list the names of people involved in a production; but more importantly, they set the stage for the story to come. Where trailers typically stoke interest through dramatic scenes drawn from the text itself, credits usually work to begin building a mood or to establish a setting. Examples—again easily available online—will help students get a sense of how this happens. Many TV shows do this work well; *Dexter*, *Mad Men*, and *The Sopranos* come to mind—though some of these shows' opening credits may serve better as an example or a model for *you* rather than for your students.

In the realm of film, the credits for the *Mission Impossible* flicks contrast nicely with more sober fare such as *To Kill a Mockingbird* or animated comedies such as the *Toy Story* films. The opening credits of Spielberg's *The Adventures of Tintin* are noteworthy. Let students watch just the opening credits in class and then discuss with students what points of the plot or character development the scenes behind the opening credits foreshadow. Alternatively, if your students haven't seen the films you select or don't recall details, ask them to make inferences from the opening credits about the plot and characters. They may then watch the film to see if their inferences were accurate.

As students consider these professional models, ask them to write about the connections between the images of the opening credits and the plot, characters, and theme in the original book. For their own creations, these are the precise types of connections they will strive to achieve. They may reflect in writing about the extent to which they were successful in introducing the viewer/reader to important aspects of the text.

Integrating Literature and Writing

When teaching literature *and* writing, we're looking for *connections*—points of contact between the writing and the reading, and with the student and the writing and the literature. When you teach literature (and reading) with writing and writing with literature, you will naturally integrate the language arts, which is what most district curriculum guides and standards require. We've never thought that it makes much sense to teach literature without writing about it, too.

We want to develop lifelong readers, just as we want to develop lifelong writers and thinkers. To this end, go beyond the literature series and writing textbooks. Do something real with your students. With every reading selection, the relevant questions are, "What's in it for the student? How do I put the student in touch with the literature? How might I bring the experience of an adolescent together with the written word?" One way to do so is to give students choices, choices, and yes, more choices about what they do to respond to literature as we have indicated in this chapter.

Another way to develop lifelong readers is to talk with enthusiasm and passion about what *you're* reading with your students so that they see a real person doing real reading and loving it. We bring our reading into the classroom just as we bring in our writing. We read and share with our students what we like, and we encourage them to do the same. As appropriate, we give our students short excerpts from works we've read—from fiction to nonfiction to newspapers to book reviews—and we read aloud to our students because none of us outgrows the pleasure of being read to.

As you think about ways to blend reading and writing in your classroom, think also about the objectives, standards, and goals that you want students to meet. One rich, meaty unit helps students to accomplish many reading and writing goals. The following is an example of such an integrated lesson.

A Literary Conversation: A Literature/ Writing Lesson

This lesson is about blending literary experiences. It is about reading well and writing well and enjoying each more because of the other one. It comes from having fun with a favorite writer. We like Barry Lopez and use him in this example; feel free to choose a favorite author of your own and follow the same basic model for working with the text. This is a favorite activity because it allows students to explore several possibilities with the selection, taking the reader back to the work again and again. It starts in the journal but will not stay there. It has removable parts, and it's simple. What more can you ask?

1. *Setting the scene.* Write about a favorite place. List or cluster details about the setting before you write. Try to visualize the place at a particular time, maybe when something special happened there.

2. *The pictorial display.* More scene setting. Put together a series of PowerPoint slides or a collection of photographs or some streaming video with shots of the setting—in this case, nature shots. For this particular literary selection, Lopez's *River Notes*, they will all, more or less, be shots of rivers. Then, select music to go with the visuals; for this particular literary work, consider using modern electronic jazz with no words.

3. *Reading aloud.* Next, choose short excerpts from Lopez's writings and make a copy of each excerpt. Give one excerpt to each student and have the students read the excerpts in a kind of unscripted conversation, each student reading when the spirit moves her to do so. This part of the activity takes a while. Let it. Listen for the interplay of voices and images.

4. *Short reading.* Now give students a copy of "The Log Jam" section of *River Notes* to read silently; then read it out loud to them. (There are six vignettes in this section; there's one of them that you may want to censor for use in the classroom.) Read and talk, sharing what you each like about the selections. Don't push students too hard. The point is to make contact with the writing, not to explicate it or find the true interpretation. You don't need to feel compelled to point out the symbols or explain the elements of fiction or any of that stuff. Just enjoy Lopez's clever and beautiful prose as readers experiencing it together for the first time.

5. *Summary.* Have each student write a summary of one section, focusing on literal understanding—on comprehension. Look also for students having some problems understanding the piece. Usually, at least a few students

will have a bit of difficulty comprehending all of what Lopez is saying. Lopez is not easy.

6. *Character.* Next, ask students to tell you about a character and briefly to "sketch" that person in their journals. It's always surprising how differently we see people.

7. *Mister Author.* Then, ask students to read the piece again and think about the kind of person who wrote it. After a five-minute freewrite about Lopez, share your collective insights of him. No need to google the author and tell students the real facts; they may do that on their own if interested. The point here is to develop *perceptions based in texts.*

8. *Creative response.* The point is to create something of your own suggested by or modeled after the piece. "The Log Jam" section from *River Notes* is particularly good for a CR.

9. *Wrapping up.* Share the drafts of the responses, looking over the other writings for other good things that have presented themselves. Revise, edit, and publish the writings.

10. *Finally, circle up and read to each other.* Some students will choose to read more by Lopez and to keep talking about him in their journals. Some will opt for other writers.

Consider the writing on as many different levels as possible. Get analytic if you want to, but do analysis last. It takes a good, thought-provoking piece to sustain interest through all of these activities. That's a matter of feel; encourage your students to stick with a piece of literature, not turning it loose too soon. There is always something else in there that the readers haven't seen yet.

For another example of a CR, see Courtney Cook's final assessment of a unit involving *Huckleberry Finn* (Figure 12–2).

We like her approach for a number of reasons. On the surface, the assignment may not seem drastically different from a conventional "literary analysis" essay. Courtney, however, has carefully transformed the task, tone, and direction to create a richer and more engaging experience. She expects students to demonstrate their understanding of *Huckleberry Finn* in multidimensional ways: analytically, creatively, conceptually, personally. She gives students a wide range of creative choice while still insisting that they "*must, must, must* be sure to exhibit a firm grasp of the material we have discussed and covered in regards to *Huck.*" She expects creativity, but not without critical engagement. (In effect, she asks students to read and write both imaginatively *and* analytically.) We also like how her voice resonates through her instructions: She speaks *with* students rather than *at* them, offering guidelines, models, suggestions, and encouragement. It's no surprise that, given this framework for demonstrating how and what they understand, her students produce interesting and engaging work. Emily and Bennett's examples (included in the online Additional Resources—find the link to these online resources at www.heinemann.com/products/E04195.aspx, on the Companion Resources tab) indicate further possibilities.

Huck's Journey, My Journey   Due _____
Final Assessment *The Adventures of Huckleberry Finn*

"Lessons, there are always lessons"
-Bill Peden

      Your final assessment for *The Adventures of Huckleberry Finn* is to craft a visual artifact that communicates your *thorough* understanding of the text. I'd like you to focus on <u>Huck's moral development</u> throughout the novel – consider his journey down the river (literal and figurative) as an adventure in learning life's lessons. Huck learns about human nature, himself, and society. I imagine that you have learned a few lessons in your life – I expect that, whether you realize it or not, many of the most important lessons have occurred somewhere other than the classroom. Consider these, consider the more formal education and exposure you have had, and make connections between the lessons Huck learned and your very own lessons.

The Assignment
- Choose three life lessons that Huck learns. As always, *be specific!*
  - Weak: Huck learns that Jim is a good person even though he is black.
  - Strong: Huck realizes, through his personal interactions with a person who has been marginalized by society, that stereotypes do not always hold true and traditions can be challenged.
- Through a conceptual interpretation and representation (video, painting, collage, performance, diorama, sculpture, illustrations, etc.) clearly exhibit the parallel experiences between Huck's Journey and your very own.
- You have unlimited creative freedom, but *must, must, must* be sure you exhibit a firm grasp of the material we have discussed and covered in regards to *Huck.*

The Process
1. Brainstorm (the most important step in *all* of your writing, right?!):
   a. The many lessons Huck learns. (Tip: It could be helpful to consider larger themes in the novel and how Twain explores these through Huck's character.)
   b. What specifically (events, relationships, etc) led Huck to learning particular lessons.
   c. What price he paid, if any, in order to learn those lessons.
   d. Think of similar lessons you have learned (think big!).
   e. What led you to learning those lessons – be specific!
   f. What similarities are found in your respective journeys?

2. Choose *one* lesson from the three to analyze and represent in your final presentation.
   a. The focus you choose should be the strongest and clearest connection you have; you will need to support it artistically and in a more formal writing assignment.

3. Create your conceptual piece! Conceptual art places emphasis on the ideas behind the art. You can create whatever you wish…whatever it is *must* have a visual component (If you choose to write a song, there must be a visual element that compliments your words and presentation and it *must* be essential to defending your argument).

4. Presentations begin **Monday, April 11ᵗʰ.**

(continues)

Figure 12–2. Final Assessment on *Huckleberry Finn* Unit

The Assessment*:
While this is a creative assignment I expect you to exhibit evidence of an in-depth understanding and engagement with the text. It must be *clear* to me in (1) the product that you present, (2) the presentation of that project, and (3) the artist's statement that you have a thorough understanding of *Huck Finn*. I'm interested in your ability to critically engage with a work of literature and draw connections between your experiences and the text. Keep in mind this is your final assessment for this unit.

*Rubric forthcoming.

Figure 12–2. Final Assessment on *Huckleberry Finn* Unit (continued)

Final Thoughts on Transacting with Literature and Other Texts

The key to integrating reading and writing is to do so in a way that will enhance your students' understanding and thinking about both of these meaningful processes. Doing so is based on relationship: the relationship of the teacher and the students, and that of the literature and the writing to each other and to you.

This chapter is full of our ideas about how writing and literature are reciprocal, meaning-making processes that fit naturally together and that are most suitably taught together. We can't imagine trying to teach writing without reading excerpts and books and plays and poems and essays by published authors. We can't image teaching literature without writing about it in a variety of ways. We've worked literally decades on devising strategies for incorporating the two, and we've shared pieces of those strategies in this chapter.

We encourage you to think about your own goals as literature and writing teachers and to reflect on how the strategies, activities, and ideas presented here might work for you and your students. We also encourage you to devise your own activities suitable for your students' explorations of literature and writing. It's important, we think, to share your enthusiasm for reading and for writing with your students. Let them see you love what you read and write. Let them see you struggle with what you read and write. Let them see you reflect on what you read and write. That's how to grow lifelong readers, writers, thinkers, and learners.

NOTE
1. Sadiqa Edmonds was a student at Albany High School, Albany, GA.

Works Cited

Bean, John C. 2001. *Engaging Ideas: The Professor's Guide to Integrating Writing, Critical Thinking, and Active Learning in the Classroom*. New York: Jossey Bass.

Berman, Jeffrey. 2011. *Risky Writing: Self-Disclosure and Self-Transformation in the Classroom*. Amherst: University of Massachusetts Press.

Blau, Sheridan. 2003. *The Literature Workshop: Teaching Texts and Their Readers*. Portsmouth, NH: Boynton/Cook-Heinemann.

Lamott, Anne. 1995. *Bird by Bird: Some Instructions on Writing and Life.* New York: Knopf Doubleday Publishing Group.

McCann, Thomas M., Larry Johannessen, Elizabeth Kahn, and Joseph M. Flanagan. 2006. *Talking in Class: Using Discussion to Enhance Teaching and Learning.* Urbana, IL: National Council of Teachers of English.

Noden, Harry R. 2011. *Image Grammar: Teaching Grammar as Part of the Writing Process.* 2nd ed. Portsmouth, NH: Heinemann.

Stotsky, Sandra. 2010. "Literary Study in Grades 9, 10, and 11: A National Survey." *Forum 4* (Spring): 1–75.

13

Engaging with Nontraditional Texts

Who sees . . . correctly: the photographer, the mirror, or the painter?
—Pablo Picasso

Weigh the meaning and look not at the words. **—Ben Jonson**

English teachers are fortunate. We work with our students—and within our own minds—on the big themes and ideas of the world through the literature, nonfiction, research, and nontraditional texts that we read, write, and reflect upon. We have the freedom to explore ideas that may be taboo in other subject areas. We have the ability to discuss touchy subjects and have courageous conversations and delve into unusual texts all because we teach English and work in the realm of literacy. Even if we're expected to teach nothing but the classics followed by the standard literary analysis essay, we have the ability to bring dimension, curiosity, immediacy, and relevance to the traditional materials by using supplementary texts and introducing our students to new forms of writing. When we shift the notion of *text* beyond print on paper or screen to include almost anything that carries meaning and is open to interpretation, our classroom walls become permeable. We have unlimited resources to get our students busy with thinking and writing.

Over the last decade or so, a whole galaxy of new literacies has been proposed: digital literacy, information literacy, media literacy, news literacy, visual literacy, multimodal literacy, and many others. We leave it to you to determine whether these are truly *new* ways of making and communicating meaning. It's a great conversation for the teachers' lounge one rainy Monday afternoon. Go for it.

We venture into new literacies in this chapter, looking at the potential for writing and literacy explorations that these concepts, media, and nontraditional texts present. As you explore this topic with us, be prepared to venture beyond the realm of print-based text and paper-based writing. Picasso and Jonson have been there before us, interrogating vision and meaning and text without using a computer, the Internet, or presentational and digital editing software. They focused on *seeing* and on *meaning*, and rightly so. Our experiences with incorporating new literacies into our teaching has taught us that whether students are transacting with a short story or a short film, a poem or an advertisement, an essay or an email, the quality of their thinking and responding is what matters most, not the specific form or medium they use.

What new literacies are you comfortable with using? What unique ways have you brought them into your teaching? How have your students introduced you to new forms of *text* and meaning making that you had not previously considered? How can your understanding of effective writing help them with digital forms of communication? Reflect on these questions as you read, building on our ideas about new literacies in the classroom to create your own ways of bringing these "new frontiers" into your teaching. Be prepared for your students to know more about some of these new literacies than you do. Let them teach you and each other. Let them lead the class into new ways of "weighing meaning" and "seeing correctly."

Exploring Nontraditional Texts

When we bring nontraditional texts into our teaching, we often follow a path similar in spirit to the Creative Response described in Chapter 12. We want students to think critically and creatively about specific texts and then to communicate their understandings in writing and in a social forum. This pathway helps guide our planning. We encourage you to experiment with and adjust these components of teaching with new literacies and nontraditional texts as you see fit.

▆ Immediate Reaction/Response

A curious but common reaction to visual texts exists: In a matter of seconds we notice, comprehend meaning, make a judgment, and then move on to the next stimulus. As an ancient talent, this immediate meaning-making process has served us well across the millennia; we are visual creatures, evolved to read our environment and look constantly for new signs of danger and opportunity. Interestingly, this natural ability to look and assess quickly is the opposite of how we go about understanding print-based texts. When we come across a page of dense text, it's almost impossible to gain much meaning from it with a single glance. Comprehending writing takes time and concentrated effort. Sitting down to read requires us to assemble meaning through a complex and learned process, turning those ink-on-paper symbols into sense in our heads.

For this reason, how we react to writing and how we react to visual texts may be very different, at least on the front end. Although most people anticipate spending some time and effort to understand writing, such is certainly not the case with image-driven media: We see a photo, an image, a few seconds of film; we understand instantly what they represent. What else is there to talk about? Much of our challenge when dealing with image-driven texts, then, is getting students to *remain open to meanings* instead of ending their thinking too soon.

Asking students to write about their immediate reactions to visual texts reveals overt meanings articulated in the text and exposes assumptions we bring to our meaning-making processes. Take a complicated visual text, such as a classic work of art, and share with your students your impressions of the work. You will likely find that the same images don't have universal meaning. When we combine this awareness with the idea that images (and image-integrated texts) serve specific rhetorical purposes, then we're beginning to go beneath the surface in search of intent and meanings.

Critical Investigation, Analysis, and Questioning

Our next general step with visual texts is a process of systematic inquiry and investigation. We want students to apply particular critical questions as a way to dig deeper and speculate about how the text operates and what it's trying to do. Central to this inquiry is the idea that image-centered texts, just like written works, are *purposely created human phenomena*. Someone created these texts, and they did so for a certain reason and to create a certain effect on a certain viewer, reader, or auditor.

A framework of questioning tools helps students as they begin this thinking. Variations of the Five Questions of Media Literacy (at www.medialit.org) help pry open students' thinking and are particularly useful:

1. Who created this message?
2. What creative techniques are used to attract my attention?
3. How might different people understand the message differently than me?
4. What values, lifestyles, and points of view are represented in, or omitted from, this message?
5. Why is this message being sent?

Although students usually begin thinking and writing about these texts individually, much of this work relies on collaboration and "social checking" of emerging interpretations. These starting questions work on all kinds of visual texts, from YouTube spoofs to classic works of art. It may take some practice for students to grasp the idea that a sculpture or painting can act as a "message" complete with intended statements, assumptions about audience, and biases. Stick with it. A few times through and your students may be surprising you with what they notice, infer, and interpret.

If you begin such work in the classroom, you'll inevitably run into complaints from students that asking such questions amounts to "overanalyzing." It might seem that way to someone who's rarely probed the implications of visual texts. We invite you to be patient with that kind of literalism. Although we may believe that audience manipulation is central to many visual texts, no one likes feeling gullible or ignorant. Instead, join the conversation by asking questions and offering your own partial interpretations while pointing out that the resonant, unspoken power of the image has long been recognized by artists and advertisers, politicians and propagandists.

Product Options and Novel Situations

Where does this targeted inquiry and informed speculation lead? Several options exist. Darren has had success with asking students who are working on analyzing particular phenomena—advertising campaigns, Internet fads, parodies of famous artwork, and so on—to prepare public (or semipublic) "guides to interpretation." As guides, they take on the role of experts by helping others make sense of their specific text. Hosted on blogs, wikis, or other online platforms, this assignment allows students to demonstrate a wide range of understandings as they create polished, insightful, and interesting projects. (Some of these projects are detailed in the discussion that follows.)

Another intriguing possibility involves leveraging what students have learned for the solution of an invoked problem. We borrow this particular approach from John Bean's *Engaging Ideas* (2011) and McCann, Johannessen, Kahn, and Flanagan, whose book *Talking in Class* (2006) details how to use scenario-based lessons as the foundation for classroom discussion. Essentially, we create real-world, fictional-yet-plausible situations to which students must bring their newly acquired expertise to bear to make a well-reasoned and justified recommendation (again, see the discussion that follows for examples).

Visual Texts: Some Challenges

Students may struggle to grasp visual texts analytically for a number of reasons. Even though we are surrounded by visual representations in myriad forms in our wired mass-media culture, this fact may actually work *against* the idea that images are worth discussing in depth. The complex meanings of many visual texts are, like Poe's purloined letter, often hiding in plain sight.

The ease of text production may also create some tensions. Anyone with a phone can take a snapshot and distribute it instantly across social networks; anyone with a computer can make a movie and post it online. The formerly specialized and protected realm of experts and artists has had its doors thrown wide open to the great unvetted and uncredentialed masses. Meanwhile, just as they've always done, corporations fill every media outlet nonstop with all manner of image-centered product pitches. How does anyone begin to make sense of all this content, let alone critique or judge it?

The obviously nonverbal nature of images challenges critical viewers to find words for the wordless, using a lexicon and grammar of image composition that is unfamiliar to most people. For some, visual texts may seem simultaneously too obvious ("It's just a picture of a woman with her kids"), too speculative ("There's no way to know what this film is supposed to mean for sure, so why bother?"), and too arcane ("I don't know how to explain this painting").

Take a breath and relax. You don't need to be an expert on media or visual literacy to use a photograph, a flyer, or a fashion advertisement as a text for students to analyze. *And you don't have to have all the answers.* Remember, effective teachers regularly pose questions and create situations in which students progressively demonstrate what they understand and can do. As you grow accustomed to having conversations about what the combinations of messages, images, texts, and graphics convey, you and your students will gain increased confidence in this area.

At the end of this chapter, we include a list of relevant readings on the topic of visual and media literacy. Delve into them when you're ready to learn more. Although students may not need an introductory unit on the principles and elements of visual design to tackle these texts, eventually a basic grasp of some specific terminology (concepts such as unity, contrast, balance, line, movement, gradation, and dominance, for example) might help them understand these texts more completely.

The following ideas for using visual texts with your students move beyond simple personal response to more elaborate involvement through writing. As you read our ideas, consider adaptations that will work for your particular students.

Exploring Photographs as Texts

Writing teachers have been using photographs as writing prompts for ages. Let's venture a bit beyond the obvious "look at this picture and write about what you see" activities.

What Is Real?

Most photographs are not value neutral, meaning that angle, focus, lighting, and (in the case of human subjects) facial expression easily communicate particular attitudes. Try a Web image search for Barack Obama, George W. Bush, Bill Clinton, or Ronald Reagan. You'll see dozens of photos that portray each president positively, and just as many that seem to suggest something suspicious or sinister. The same goes for images of nature, industry, technology, specific cultures, and just about any other subject. Asking students to articulate these tonal differences through writing helps them understand how image control (print the positive or the negative image?) communicates intentional meaning. These discussions also lead naturally to more technical matters of visual composition, such as color, balance, perspective, and considerations of what is—and is not—within the frame. Try using different photographs of the same subject and challenge students to articulate how each conveys a different message. At the heart of talking about photographs are questions about reality. As the filmmaker Errol Morris puts it, "When does a photograph document reality? When is it propaganda? When is it art? Can a single photograph be all three?" (2011, 133) These provocative topics will encourage your students to consider photographs in a number of ways.

Pairing Text and Image

Juxtaposing a photograph with a word or phrase stimulates students to think about how meaning shifts according to context and circumstance. For example, words like *genius*, *terrorist*, *hero*, and *phony* have conventional meanings that students already know. But what happens when we superimpose one of these words on a photograph of a teenage boy? Or the Queen of England? Donald Trump? LeBron James? Ronald McDonald? Or an American flag? Such combinations are a form of *intertextuality*, a process of creating meaning among and within texts. Text plus image forms a more explicit statement than does an image alone.

Challenge your students to figure out the unstated implications of the text and the image in combination. What is literally before them? What does it imply? Why and how does the image/text combination evoke those inferences? Advertising and propaganda largely rely on these kinds of image-word associations. Why? What does the advertiser or the propagandist gain by relying on implications rather than direct statements within their visual texts? Grappling with these slippery meanings helps students recognize metaphor, connotation, and inferences at work. It also helps them evaluate the purpose behind common texts such as ads and political cartoons.

Using Classic Photos and Venturing into Remixes

Some photographs are especially interesting subjects for analysis because of their fame, longevity, historical significance, or pop culture appeal. Photos such as Dorothea Lange's *Migrant Mother*, Charles Ebbets' *Lunch Atop a Skyscraper*, Joe Rosenthal's *Raising the Flag on Iwo Jima*, Arthur Fellig's *The Critic*, Richard Drew's *Falling Man*, and Kevin Carter's image of a vulture approaching a starving Sudanese child (among many other photos) carry both an immediate visceral impact and a more complex story worthy of more intensive exploration. Classic photos often provide insight into a particular cultural or social moment.

They provide an opportunity for students to draw inductive conclusions about the dominant values of the time. Because classic photos are often parodied, each new remix often puts forth a new twist on meaning to consider. Ask your students to convey the meaning of the original and then the meaning of the new, remixed visual text. What does the difference say about the culture and time in which each was produced?

Power and Responsibility

The immediacy and ubiquity of photography—now that nearly every cellphone doubles as a camera—raise interesting ethical considerations. Does someone need to give permission for his or her photograph to be taken? How do we control images of ourselves in public spheres? What are the implications of living in a digital surveillance culture in which *every image*, potentially, may live forever? Should digital camera use be restricted in certain spaces?

The common humiliation of a mismatched outfit, a bad hair day, or a moment of teen-aged inanity was once easily forgotten, erased by the flow of time. Now, a surreptitious pic or video may be uploaded and distributed instantly, generating teen angst and peer pressure gone viral and global. (Look up "Star Wars Kid" on Wikipedia for the quintessential example.) Modern teenagers have to deal with a whole new set of image control worries, making this topic an excellent and a vital focus for writing.

Operating at the crossroads of art, taboo, and propriety, Richard Billingham's work might raise not only some eyebrows but also questions worthy of consideration with your students. Know your teaching context and proceed accordingly with what you select to bring into your classroom. If the materials we suggest won't work for your context, look for materials that will convey similar ideas with less eyebrow action. These questions may be quite provocative: Are photographs of one's drunken, unconscious, and frail father acceptable as art, or do they cross a line of ethical violation? Show one of Billingham's photos to your students and ask them to respond in writing to the following, one by one:

1. Describe the scene in detail.
2. What is the relationship of the photographer to the people and things in the scene? How do we know?
3. What obligations, if any, does a photographer have to his subjects?

Accident, crime scene, and mug shot photographs—all increasingly published online or incorporated into art—generate similar questions. Who owns the image? Who decides when and where the image is made public? What ethical considerations come into play? What insight from their own lives might students bring to this discussion? We like using scenarios for pathways into this type of writing. Ask your students to rank the following situations from most to least acceptable as a way to begin writing and talking:

- A person takes a photograph of you in public without asking your permission.
- A friend of yours tweets pictures of you from a rather wild party. You don't remember the photos being taken.
- During a student body election, a close-up photograph of a student from the yearbook is remixed onto the body of a donkey by an opponent. Posters featuring the image appear around the school.
- An underground school paper publishes pictures of unsuspecting students in a recurring section called Nerd Alert.
- A blurry photograph of a naked person appears online with a student's name attached, but it's impossible to tell the individual's actual identity.

- For her eighteenth birthday, Alison's mom has an embarrassing picture of her as a three-year-old published in the local paper next to the family's happy birthday wishes.

By considering these and similar scenarios, students explore ethics, visual media, and distributions of power and responsibility in their use of one popular medium.

Working with Paintings and Other Visual Artwork as Texts

Just as our classes are replete with students' writings, we routinely display numerous visuals—paintings, artwork, photographs—in our classrooms. The images brighten the room and serve as conversation starters. Once conversation begins, it's generally not too difficult to steer the conversation into productive channels. Try one or more of these activities with your students to stimulate their thinking about texts.

Before and After

With the exception of abstract expressionism and a few other styles of modern art, almost all paintings can be "read" (interpreted) from a narrative perspective. Start by posing a general question to students: *What story is being told in this painting?* This question naturally invites continued inquiry:

1. What was happening before the scene in this painting?
2. What will happen afterward?
3. What is central about this moment in a broader story, the time in which it was produced, or the event that it depicts?
4. If this is one painting in a series, what other scenes might we expect to see by the artist?

Writing about and discussing a painting in this way defuses anxiety about the "right" answer and opens up possibilities for multiple meanings.

How do we decide which stories are more plausible than others? We go back to the text itself, looking closely for details that serve as support for our ideas. ("See, he's *holding* her hand, not *pulling* her along behind him.") Through this process of observation, inference, meaning making, and then testing out hypotheses by observing additional details in the visual text, students grow more comfortable with offering reasons based on evidence. Students see the value in analyzing their assumptions and in revising their ideas that don't pass a public airing.

Pair the Painting

This activity encourages students to grapple with abstract concepts. Ask students to choose an abstract or impressionistic painting that best expresses the theme or tone of a literary work, one that you are currently reading with the class, perhaps. Unless your students are art aficionados, give them a list of suggested paintings to view the first time or two that you use this activity. Once a student has selected a painting, invite him to articulate the rationales for his choice. Again, guide the student to cite evidence from both the text and the painting as he presents his proposition. Not only does this activity help students understand metaphor, inference, and symbolism, but it also guides them to see the helpfulness of an authentic thesis—a central idea that expresses the analogy between the written and the visual works.

Try starting with the well-known pairing of Sondheim's musical *Sunday in the Park with George* and the painting that inspired the musical, Seurat's *A Sunday Afternoon on the Island of La Grande Jatte*. Choose one of your favorite pieces of writing to pair with a painting, modeling for students the connections you see between the two, how you locate the painting (perhaps by a key word search on the Internet), and how you go about writing your comparison of the two. Almost any story, poem, or essay invites cross-media connections and applied thinking. We've had success with Chopin's "The Story of an Hour" (paired with Edvard Munch's *The Scream*, for example) and Eliot's "The Love Song of J. Alfred Prufrock" (paired with Gozzoli's *The Dance of Salome*, for example) to stimulate discussion of each work.

▓ Choose the Book Cover

Try a Google Image search for a novel typically taught in school: *1984*, *The Scarlet Letter*, and *To Kill a Mockingbird* come to mind. You'll come across a variety of book cover designs from various time periods, publishers, and countries. As with the Pair the Painting activity, choose six or seven examples and ask students to select which cover best fits the novel, justifying their decision in detail. As an alternative, invite students to critique two or three covers they did *not* select. These activities move students away from the "right answer syndrome"—because *all* of the options have been used as book covers and are potentially "correct." It's the thinking, evidence, and explanation that students muster that really matter. See the online Additional Resources for this chapter for a sample assignment. You'll find the link to these online resources at www.heinemann.com/products/E04195.aspx, on the Companion Resources tab.

▓ Poetry and Painting

Not surprisingly, artwork has served as poetic inspiration through the ages (see "The Poet Speaks of Art" in the Resources section at the end of this chapter for a solid list of examples). Begin by sharing Uccello's pairing of *St. George and the Dragon* and U. A. Fanthorpe's clever poem "Not My Best Side." Fanthorpe's three stanzas provide the viewpoints of the characters in the painting—dragon, princess, and knight—to humorous effect. (Alternately, ask student to write from each perspective before showing them Fanthorpe's interpretation.) Then move students to creating their own poetic commentary (humorous or not) about another piece of artwork, perhaps a very familiar painting such as da Vinci's *Mona Lisa* or Vermeer's *Girl with a Pearl Earring*. Defusing the seriousness of written critique, artwork, and poetry helps make normally intimidating texts more accessible.

Seeing Video and Film as Texts

YouTube and similar sites have blown the lid off the potential for using videotexts in the classroom. VCRs and DVD players may still be common equipment in schools, but digital files and streaming video are quickly making such hardware obsolete. A creative teacher has quick access to millions of potential texts for any number of teaching purposes. Here are a few ideas to get you started.

▣ Explanations of Tone

Tone and mood are notoriously slippery terms for students. Videotexts—with their combination of musical tracks, sound effects, and film—may render these concepts into immediate, felt experiences. For a few excellent starting points, search for "Doll Face," "Henri," "Mr. W," and "Pencil Face" on YouTube. These short but evocative texts rely heavily on tone to create a certain mood. Challenge students with a short scenario:

> Explain the tone-mood relationship in a video to a friend who doesn't get it. Avoid jargon, rote repetition of definitions, and generalities. Provide a clear and concise explanation with specific detail in real, authentic language.

This activity is not as simple as it sounds. Students must consider how to strike the proper balance between information and explanation for something that seems obvious to them, without making the reader feel inadequate, illiterate, or completely uncool.

▣ Close Analysis of an Advertisement or Thirty-Second Commercial

Easy access to digital video means that the familiar advertisement analysis assignment may be easily adjusted to apply to film-type commercials. Analyzing the techniques within a print-based ad is a staple of many teachers' lessons on propaganda, distinguishing fact from fiction, red herrings, and the like. Ads provide a readily accessible place to start talking about how images, text, and graphics combine in persuasive ways. Kick up the fun and interest level by giving students the opportunity to look at thirty-second commercials, selecting those appropriate for your teaching context. We look to the Super Bowl broadcast for familiar and sometimes celebrated commercials. What makes a specific commercial click with the audience and potential buyer of the product? If you remember the commercial but not the product, how effective is the commercial? How do commercials for the latest tech gadget, for example, differ from those for office supply stores? How does a commercial for an ecologically "green" car differ from one for a gas-guzzling monstrosity? What distinguishes one sporting goods brand from another, making one instantly recognizable and the other an also-ran product? Breaking down the components in an engaging thirty-second commercial takes the tried-and-true ad analysis to a more sophisticated level.

▣ Questions of Quality

Students love the idea of making films, and easy-to-use moviemaking programs now provide viable options for student projects. The key is that students recognize elements that contribute to a *good* digital film. Plenty of student-made films are available on YouTube, but most are not that successful; they are interesting right now, but not so interesting in a few months or to a general audience. Audiences allow a very brief window of opportunity for the film to grab and hold their attention. One point to explore with your students is that good short movies almost always focus on audience experience from the first frame. Spend five minutes searching on YouTube for "student project" and you'll come across plenty of rough, uninteresting, or ineffective examples of student work. Once you've located several, use them to help your students understand quickly what *not* to do. Challenge your students to articulate *why* a film flops ("The opening shot takes too long and pans too much scenery; get to the close-up of the chef in action"). Then, invite them to revise the negative points to become positive criteria ("Set the scene quickly and focus on the chef at the stove, in frenetic action") for shaping their own work.

Global Messaging and Its Implications

As we write this chapter, the short film *KONY 2012*—intended to raise awareness of Ugandan war criminal Joseph Kony and thereby lead to his arrest—has been viewed over eighty-five million times in the three weeks since it was uploaded to YouTube. (Yes, those numbers are correct—and increasing.) We expect this kind of back-channel messaging—basically, advocacy through expository forms of digital media—to become more common. The *KONY 2012* phenomenon has been especially popular among young people, which makes it and similar texts ripe for analysis. We like to play the "believe/doubt" game with these kinds of texts. Ask students to respond in writing sympathetically first, looking for points of agreement, persuasion, and emotional connection. Next, urge them to get skeptical. For every advocacy video gone viral, there's typically a significant backlash as researchers question claims, characterizations, and implications. If you're looking for something a little lighter than *KONY 2012*, the short films created by the Story of Stuff Project (www.storyofstuff.com) make good texts for considering bias, truth claims, and authorial intent.

Extending from this work, we encourage students to view moviemaking as a form of *digital writing*, sharing in common with pen-and-paper writing many of the same techniques, processes, and purposes. Because almost everyone is wired in to almost everything, digital forms of writing often have significant immediacy and impact. Done well, a visual argument can go viral and reach an audience of millions, something a standard English class argument essay has rarely (if ever) done. Even with a modest viewership, just having one's work accessible for others to see ups the ante for many students. We've seen firsthand the transforming effect that tech-rich options for students' products have on the terminally bored and the tragically alienated. We generally encourage students to develop their own focus for such work. Consider, for example, the activist, socially oriented possibilities advocated by educational consultant Dr. Tim Tyson (http://drtimtyson.com). Tyson—a former middle school principal—asked his students to make "meaningful contributions" to the world through their video projects. If we expect schools to create well-rounded adults with a sense of civic and even global engagement, this is the sort of work we might encourage our students to do.

Selling It: Commercialism and the Visual as Text

One benefit of the immediacy inherent in digital and other media is their potential to enhance capitalistic gains. You know, to sell stuff. Most of us don't spend money on offers from total strangers that arrive in our inboxes or snail mail boxes, and for good reason. Nonetheless, visual adventures into commercialism bombard us, usually in unbidden ways. Because escaping them is nearly impossible, we might as well use them for positive, instructional purposes. That is, we repurpose them with activities such as those below.

Junk Mail

Almost every day viable texts for classroom study are hand-delivered to our mailboxes. Junk mail—grocery store flyers, sweepstakes notifications, postcard coupons, businesslike envelopes with mysterious contents—makes a compelling text for close analysis. Once students get used to the idea that each element of a mailing serves a purpose, answering the "why" question helps uncover the rhetorical dimensions of these "everyday texts." Keep your eye on your mailbox and collect the interesting examples you find; ask your students to do the same. Then use classroom discussion of samples as the basis for an extended small-group analysis or photo-essays that deconstruct the tactics at work in particular pieces.

Product Packaging

The stories manufacturers tell about their products don't stop with standard advertising. Open your refrigerator or cupboard and take a look at the container of a typical store-bought food item. Chances are, it's a complex piece of communication. Its shape, design, colors, images, fonts, and narrative information help define what's inside and the kind of person who consumes it. (The weirdness of black-and-white generic food labels emphasizes how much we're used to seeing these sophisticated designs on our containers.) Close analysis of these real-world texts turns the supermarket into a multimedia library. We follow close inquiry about a particular product's packaging with a scenario-centered assignment in which students pitch a solution to a real-world challenge. For example, ask students to design the bottle, packaging, and pitch for a celebrity's or musical artist's new line of fragrance, but give them specific parameters: The product's look must mesh with the celebrity's image, convey certain values associated with the celebrity, and stand out on the shelf without looking tacky. Working creatively within a set of expectations is what professional ad agents, product designers, and image managers do every day.

Product Names

As we like to tell students, professional experts earn lots of money to consider all aspects of a product's advertising, marketing, and branding. Their considerations include niche companies that charge large fees to name new products, using word associations and connotations to build positive impressions. Consider names used for pharmaceuticals (Viagra, Flomax, Levitra, Benadryl), snack foods (Doritos, Funions, Go-Gurt), and SUVs (Escalade, Sorento, Durango, Pathfinder, Highlander), for example. Every major industry spends time and money to create names that appeal to and resonate with targeted consumers. Invite your students to speculate about these decisions, and in the process, to articulate a plausible rationale and intent for the name of a product they know well.

Logos

Much commercial messaging happens without words at all. The importance of branding and logo design in defining and reinforcing a company's values is hard to underestimate. Implicit logo associations can be rich and varied; therefore, they make interesting subjects for analysis. Again, online search engines make finding past and current logo examples a snap. Ask students to speculate in depth about the reasons for specific logo redesigns; Apple, KFC, Burger King, and Walmart, among others, offer good examples. We've also had success asking students to take on the hypothetical role of a design team tasked with re-branding a tired logo, including providing a complete rationale for the new look.

Understanding Everyday Texts

Almost everything may be considered as a *text* if you use a broad definition. What does the car you drive say about you? The clothes or shoes you wear? Whether you travel in first class or coach? Two examples follow of how to make texts/meanings out of what we encounter daily.

Clothing and Accessories

Every day, kids walk into schools wearing and carrying a whole set of texts. What, precisely, our clothes and accessories say about how we see ourselves in the world is a fascinating topic for discussion. Because initially students may be uncomfortable casting the analytical eye on themselves ("I only wear this because it's comfortable" is the typical default comment), ask students to begin by identifying and investigating a broader trend to uncover the reasons for its popularity as a "safe" first step. For example, they might research and speculate about why Abercrombie and Fitch became such a force in teen clothing, why ankle socks replaced tube socks for many athletes, and how people "own" or redefine certain clothing styles in ways that the original manufacturers may not have intended (the urban popularity of Timberland work boots is a good example, as is the hipster embrace of Chuck Taylor basketball shoes).[1] Even young people who reject branding themselves in this way may still communicate a message about themselves, perhaps with clothing choices from thrift or consignment stores. As students become accustomed to thinking and writing about these wearable texts, they'll refine their questioning eye and be more apt to consider the possible implications in their own choices. Eventually, we want students to consider how their personal product choices can be, at heart, a means of telling the world and themselves a story about who they are.

As always, use these activities only if they are appropriate for your teaching context. Not all kids have the resources to make clothing choices and therefore to choose the message they convey through material possessions.

Architecture and Public Space

Like clothing, three-dimensional texts—including sculpture, architecture, monuments, and public spaces such as parks, town centers, campuses, and neighborhoods—carry particular unspoken meanings. Asking students to assess what a building's facade "says" or what message a housing development conveys is, indeed, advanced thinking; but once students get the hang of noticing and speaking about subtle associations, they are very capable of this kind of analysis. One simple way to begin is to snap photos of local buildings in your area—banks, gas stations, restaurants, shops—and ask students to write about what they think is intended by specific elements of design. Is a bank an imposing multistory marble structure or a streamlined drive-through, and what ideas (about customers, access, wealth, the bank's role in the community, etc.) are communicated by each? How does the look of a particular steakhouse—stone exterior, timbered roof, wrought iron fences, old-style lettering—tell a certain story, and is it believable? How do the layout and features of a park encourage certain recreation while discouraging others (for instance, if there are plenty of baseball fields but not a basketball court to be seen, what might this mean?).

There is an intent to all of these creations, an intent that can be defined, critiqued, and evaluated. Each one conveys an identifiable story and meets (or ignores) the needs of a particular community. As you work with your students on activities like these, consider inviting to class a guest speaker who is an architect, museum curator, sculptor, or another planner who considers space in inventive ways. These design warriors may not be accustomed to being noticed, especially by high school students. They will likely be delighted to speak to your class and discuss with your students the meanings inherent in their work.

Analyzing Digital and Web Texts

The amount of information available online and the number of websites you might spend hours browsing are almost beyond comprehension. Here are several fruitful ways for your students to work with reading the texts of websites and the digital culture.

Commercial Sites Aimed at Kids

Commercial websites are often sophisticated and multilayered texts that make for rich, interesting, and relevant subjects for student analysis. Visit sites for typical brand-name youth-oriented products—snacks, candy, games, toys, clothing—and you'll usually find very high-end and interactive experiences designed to keep kids engaged in a product-centered universe. Small groups working on deconstructing a site (or a page on a site) may use wiki platforms to build their analyses and publish their work, taking screenshots to focus a reader/viewer's attention. As you work on helping students flex their sense of critical distance and develop an eye for rhetorical intent with activities like those in this section, they are likely to become more incisive critics of texts targeting them directly.

Campaign Websites

Ask small groups of students to brainstorm about what they'd expect from a typical politician's website, and they may find that they know more than they think they do. Patriotic colors, pithy slogans, flattering images of the candidate, short statements about various issues, a timeline of appearances, a donation feature, and social media options for "connecting" with the campaign are all typical elements of such texts. Ask students to visit several candidates' sites to compare their lists to what they find. Follow this up with a comparison of competing candidates' sites. What is similar or different, and what is the resulting impact? What recommendations about design might they make to a friend contemplating a political run?

Gaming

Video gaming dominates the leisure time of many young people. Yet, with rare exception, the subject of gaming is nowhere to be found in school curricula or classrooms. In *Reality Is Broken*, McGonigal (2011) explores the repercussions of this willful dismissal of gaming and how the sort of problem solving used in gaming applies to real life. Millions of people find compelling and rewarding reasons to devote significant time, energy, thinking, and problem solving to digital entertainment challenges. What do gamers have to tell us about reinvigorating our face-to-face lives?

Many rich opportunities may help you leverage students' gaming interests, channeling them toward demonstrations of learning. Work with your students to delve into the attraction of their favorite games in ways similar to the ones below, thinking also about ideas that you will generate for your students and teaching context:

- Ask experienced gamers to explain the contexts of gaming to newbies or to create practical guides to their favorite games.
- Invite students who play similar online games to debate the merits of two or more titles. (By the way, we see abundant opportunities for teaching students actual debate protocol and ways of reasoning when the topic is as compelling as gaming.)
- Create a project in which your students propose and design a new game based on literary, historical, or social events. Alternatively, ask your students to render skills-based learning (usage and esoteric punctuation rules come to mind) into gaming environments. These activities allow students to transform conventional tasks into a context that is far more interesting and contemporary. You might find yourself enjoying the resulting products as well.
- If you need to teach methods of comparison, do so by asking students to compare the worth of analog and digital games. Thinking about the relative worth (or worthlessness) of board games in a digital age might stimulate some provocative discussion.

We find that our students have myriad ideas for connecting to gaming culture. Just get your students thinking about options, and they will create their own activities.

Recently, while watching a movie with her daughter, Dawn was fascinated to hear her teenager comment repeatedly, "This would be such a cool video game." She didn't stop there, however; she ventured into analysis, critique, and synthesis: "Look at how these scenes could become different levels in the game. Look at all of the special effects you could take from the movie and use in the game. Gamers love to find treasure; look at all of the different types of treasures in that room. These Scotland Yard agents are dressed so conservatively, so stereotypically; gamers would love creating different costumes for them. This is totally a video game waiting to be made." Her imagination was clearly piqued, and she was dissecting—analyzing—the movie in ways that only experienced gamers would.

Creating a successful new game—determining the number of players, the goals, the obstacles, the rules, what counts as winning, what keeps us playing, and so on—is an applied creative and critical act. It offers a good definition of what we'd expect from various kinds of high-level learning. Invite your students to undertake such a project. You and they will enjoy the results. We wager you'll also be surprised at how many standards you are able to meet by working with gaming and similar devices.

▨ Affinity Spaces

Social relationships are certainly one area that digital technology has transformed. In pre-Internet days, finding people who shared your similar interests—especially if those interests were esoteric, alternative to the main culture, or eccentric—could be difficult or even impossible if you didn't live in a big city. Digital interaction, however, has changed all of that. No matter how rare, different, or unique your interests, the Web has a place for you to join a virtual community of like-minded folks. Chances are, many of your students will belong to such networks. Ask your students to consider how they interact in these digital environments with these "friends" they may never have met in person. What tone is appropriate for their conversations? What uses of humor are common? What conventions and nomenclature do group insiders use? How do you ward off pretenders who don't really share your interest and depth of knowledge? Work with your students to delve into the relationships of an affinity group to demystify it for nonmembers. This type of thinking, writing, explaining, and informing is both challenging and potentially rewarding because it will bring to life stereotypes and how to dispel them, and other complexities associated with the group's interactions.

Memes and Online Culture

Digital technology has spawned a wide and diverse online culture with its own lingo, rules of interaction, and phenomena. The rise of Internet "memes"—humorous, ironic, or iconoclastic online phenomena that usually involve remixed images and quirky attempts at wit distributed across online platforms—is a good example of a unique cultural movement. Even if the term *meme* is unfamiliar to you, you've likely encountered examples, from Honey Badger references to pictures of cats with grammatically impaired captions. If you spend significant social time online, you know that memes are a characteristic part of the Internet landscape.

To outsiders, Internet memes may seem mystifying or simply idiotic. And that's the point. "Getting" a meme is an insider thing, a sign of cultural belonging and distinction. Our students are experts in subjects and skills about which we know little. If we slightly shift our notions of authority, we create opportunities for our students to engage in constructive projects that allow students the freedom to show what they know and can do as an insider of online culture. To begin this shift of authority, ask your Internet-savvy students to analyze the popularity of a meme or other online fad distributed through social networking. Some of the currently popular ones are downright dangerous—planking and Batmanning—so give your students the usual "Don't try this at home" speech. Ask them to talk about their knowledge and expertise with nontraditional topics. Urge them to analyze the criteria necessary to achieve the meme or fad, explicate its popularity, and predict its cultural impact and longevity. You may not know what we're talking about. Your students will. Google this stuff so that you don't come across as a total outsider to their discussions. For another example of a student's project analyzing Internet memes and explaining their content and popularity, see the discussion of "How Magnets Work" in the online Additional Resources for Chapter 7. You'll find the link to these online resources at www.heinemann .com/products/E04195.aspx, on the Companion Resources tab.

Satire and Parody

The Web, like much of popular culture, abounds in satire and parody. Practiced in sarcasm, most teens seem to have refined antennae for such humor. Good satire is a sophisticated enterprise, and we've learned that although students may recognize satire when they see it, *analyzing and explaining* how it works—or creating effective satire of their own—is another matter. Laughing at *The Daily Show* and *South Park* doesn't require understanding (or even noticing) the corresponding social and political commentary in an episode. Here's where we offer insight and help. Satire expects quite a bit from a reader or viewer, including the following:

- a solid understanding of the subject of the satire
- an awareness that an intentional dissonance can exist between explicit and implicit messages
- the ability to distinguish literal and implied meanings
- a recognition of humor created by a specific contrast
- the obligation of the audience to help maintain the fiction of literal meaning (i.e., satire is by nature an "inside joke" that is rarely identified as such)

When we challenge our students to examine popular examples of satire and parody, are we killing the humor with dissection? Maybe, but we're willing to risk it. We'll take "The unexamined life isn't worth living" over "Ignorance is bliss" any day. As a powerful form of subversive truth-to-power speech, satire and parody are tactics that students both understand and may employ effectively when they know how to do so.

Multiple options exist for activities that examine satire and parody. For example, ask students to research and track the ironic iterations of a particular cultural artifact to speculate about its resonance and appeal. Grant Wood's *American Gothic*, for example, may be the most parodied and imitated painting in history. What in the painting inspires humor? Why is this painting an easy vehicle for satire and parody? What elements can be manipulated to create satire and parody? Considering what fuels these reactions to the original work helps students better understand satire and parody in action.

Spam, Phishing, Bogus Emails, and Hoaxes

Does a week go by without some new piece of bogus email appearing in your inbox? We're guessing not. Spam and online scamming is an annoying part of modern life, but one that also presents interesting writing opportunities. Bogus email is often identifiable through its deviations from conventional structure, spelling, and grammar. Ask students to look closely at such texts. What mistakes in word choice, idioms, punctuation, and surface conventions do they notice? These considerations drive home the real-world ramifications of failing to use appropriate conventions and format in professional (or pseudoprofessional) communication.

Such work also gets at a form of informational literacy that most of our students don't encounter in any sustained form in the typical curriculum. Garbled emails announcing that we may collect unclaimed millions aren't fooling the typical teenager (or us). At the same time, it's the scam *that doesn't seem like a scam* that's the bigger problem: the website that appears legit, the text that seems innocuous. Engage your students in analyzing and reworking examples of digital cons. Invite them, perhaps cautiously, to imagine and create examples of new forms of trickery to be delivered via email or other digital means. Doing so helps your students hone a healthy sense of skepticism and ask questions about the reliability and validity of what shows up online.

Online hoax phenomena draw upon similar concepts of subterfuge. Whether for purposes of humor, critical commentary, malice, or theft, hoax websites attempt to convey authenticity and legitimacy through textual and design choices. Understanding and articulating how such bogus sites pose as real ones opens students' eyes to the implications of language, image, and graphic choices. Ask students to analyze the persuasive techniques, pseudoscientific language, types of images, and visual layout of sites such as Bonsai Kitten (http://ding.net/bonsaikitten/index.html), the Dihydrogen Monoxide Research Division (www.dhmo.org/), and the Northwest Pacific Tree Octopus (http://zapatopi.net/treeoctopus/). How do the hoax sites mimic the look of legitimate hobby, public policy, and science sites? Why do they so carefully carry out this visual deception? Cull one of those phishing emails from your inbox as a text for students to read closely, looking for clues that it is fake rather than legit. Or use the online examples of common frauds from sites such as Scamwatch to get students to recognize how these texts work. This type of text analysis is critical and engaging; and like it or not, it accomplishes many of the same objectives as do traditional literary analyses of texts.

Possibilities with Texts and Writing

As your students become more adept at thinking about nontraditional texts in analytical ways—moving their initial reactions into provisional responses and then into conversation and extended writing—they're exercising mental muscles that work for any text. It's a simple fact that, for many kids, visual texts are more engaging than are written texts. Why not leverage that interest? Get your students thinking, responding, and writing about media and visual phenomena that have relevance and immediacy in their lives. Then, when it's time to turn to more traditional texts, encourage your students to apply the now-familiar techniques used for nontraditional texts to more traditional texts. Noticing specific phrases and passages in a print-based text and making a case for how they influence overall meaning and purpose is very similar to identifying elements in a visual text and interpreting their impact and intent.

This is not an either/or, zero-sum game. We're working on helping our students become better thinkers, readers, and writers; and all kinds of texts help us get them there. With a slight change in perspective or technique, what works for understanding nontraditional texts also applies to print-based, traditional texts. Working with texts is all about creating and deriving meaning from those texts, written or visual, analog or digital, ubiquitous or rarefied. Just as talk leads into writing, so too do explorations with nontraditional texts build metal flexibility and critical abilities that yield stronger, more competent writers.

The options for opening your students to textual variety are practically endless. We've mentioned a few of our ideas for working with analog, digital, and a host of other types of texts. Explore websites and texts readily found online. Browse books from a variety of fields. Go to a museum and drink in the artwork. Take a road trip. Above all, keep your eyes open. What texts do you notice around you? How do your abilities to understand a variety of texts improve your expression of ideas, in writing and in other media? Get curious, ask your own questions, and then bring a variety of traditional and nontraditional texts into your classroom for your students to consider and interpret, to write and respond to them. It is this type of textual acumen that will yield literate, fluent, competent writers, regardless of medium.

Resources

Your head may be spinning if visual texts and digital environments are new to you, or your brain may be clicking with new instructional ideas if you've thought about visual literacy for a while. Some of you are, indeed, digital culture insiders. Whatever the case, we invite you to explore the resources below and consider the instructional possibilities they afford you and the insights they offer to your students.

▨ Visual Texts: Further Resources and Readings

Art

- The Beinart International Surreal Art Collective (http://beinart.org/)
  An enormous collection of bizarre and disturbing artwork. Lots of potential for creative uses with students. Be warned: This site contains content that could easily be considered offensive to many.
- The Poet Speaks of Art (http://homepage.mac.com/mseffie/assignments/paintings&poems/titlepage.html)
  Good collection of paintings and the poems that they have specifically inspired.
- The Google Art Project (www.googleartproject.com/)
  High-resolution reproductions of famous artwork.

Photography

- The Library of Congress American Memory Site (http://memory.loc.gov/ammem/index.html)
  Offers links to extensive collections—many of them image-centered—focusing on specific studies of advertising, architecture, culture, government, and history. Includes teacher resources.
- The National Endowment for the Humanities Picturing America Gallery (http://picturingamerica.neh.gov/index.php?sec=home)
  Educational repository of classic American painting and photography.
- The LIFE photo archive (http://images.google.com/hosted/life)
  Search the entire *Life* photo archive, which can also be done by adding "source:life" to any Google Image search.
- The National Archives Experience—Digital Vaults (www.digitalvaults.org/)
  Digital selections from the National Archives in an engaging visual interface; includes educational resources.
- *Believing Is Seeing: Observations on the Mysteries of Photography*, Errol Morris (2011)
  Fascinating anecdotal examination about how viewing photographs can shape "reality." Each essay analyzes a specific set of photographs (which are included) for how they've shaped the meaning of events.
- *On Photography*, Susan Sontag (1977)
  Sontag's classic collection of essays about the nature of photography. Often complex and occasionally delving into esoteric subjects, these essays raise essential questions about photography, art, reality, and truth.

▨ Video and Film

- *Reading in the Dark: Using Film as a Tool in the English Classroom*, John Golden (2001)

  Golden offers specific strategies to get students thinking critically about film.
- *Reading in the Reel World: Teaching Documentaries and Other Nonfiction Texts*, John Golden (2006)

  Golden turns his attention to nonfiction film, providing concrete approaches for teaching a range of titles appropriate for multiple grade levels.

▨ Other Resources

- *Buying In: The Secret Dialogue Between What We Buy and Who We Are*, Rob Walker (2008)

  Walker investigates how our choice of products, labels, and brands play a role in building a personal narrative about who we are.
- News Literacy Project (www.thenewsliteracyproject.org/)

  Partnership between schools and journalists to help students develop critical media skills.
- *Understanding Comics*, Scott McCloud (1994)

  McCloud uses the comic book form to explain comics, dwelling upon how image, text, borders, color, shading, perspective, and many other elements interact to create specific meaning. Totally engaging.
- Know Your Meme (http://knowyourmeme.com/)

  Online catalog of every notable Internet meme, including commentary, analysis, and exhaustive examples. Given the nature of Internet phenomena, the site contains content that could easily be considered offensive to many. Proceed at your own risk.
- *New Literacies: Everyday Practices and Classroom Learning*, Colin Lankshear and Michele Knobel (2006)

  The authors make the case that conventional schooling is based on outdated assumptions about what is important in learning; a shift toward decentered, distributed, and collaborative models would result in more student engagement and accomplishment.
- *Reality Is Broken*, Jane McGonigal (2011)

  McGonigal argues that we'd better begin taking video games seriously in terms of what lessons we might learn about engagement, goal setting, collaboration, and risk taking in the "real" world.
- *What Video Games Have to Teach Us About Learning and Literacy*, James Gee (2007)

  Gee is perhaps the foremost scholar on the potential benefits of video games. His work looks closely at the incentives, learning processes, and complexity of gaming, looking for crossovers to the classroom.
- *Web Literacy for Educators*, Alan November (2008)

  Offers concrete recommendations, examples, and exercises for using the Internet more efficiently and critically, especially when it comes to research.

Nontraditional texts abound and are increasing in number even as you read this book. Get out there and explore them, bringing your new learning about new literacies and nontraditional texts into the classroom for your students' edification and enjoyment.

NOTE

1. See Rob Walker's *Buying In* for an in-depth discussion of how consumers sometimes "rebrand" products in this way.

Works Cited

Bean, John. 2011. *Engaging Ideas: The Professor's Guide to Integrating Writing, Critical Thinking, and Active Learning in the Classroom*. 2d ed. San Francisco: Jossey Bass.

McCann, Thomas M., Larry R. Johannessen, Elizabeth Kahn, and Joseph M. Flaganan. 2006. *Talking in Class: Using Discussion to Enhance Teaching and Learning*. Urbana, IL: National Council of Teachers of English.

McGonigal, Jane. 2011. *Reality Is Broken: Why Games Make Us Better and How They Can Change the World*. New York: Penguin.

Morris, Errol. 2011. *Believing Is Seeing: Observations on the Mysteries of Photography*. New York: Penguin Press.

Walker, Rob. 2008. *Buying In: The Secret Dialogue Between What We Buy and Who We Are*. New York: Random House.

14

Mediating Literate Lives: An Argument for Authentic Education

The principle goal of education is to create [people] who are capable of doing new things, not simply of repeating what other generations have done—[people] who are creative, inventive and discoverers. **—Jean Piaget, developmental psychologist**

Ever tried. Ever failed. No matter. Try again. Fail again. Fail better.
—Samuel Beckett

When we're lost in the weeds of teaching, just trying to make it through another week or another stack of papers, the big picture gets a bit hazy. Why do our students need to be creative and inventive, and am I helping them get there? Am I trying hard enough to nurture and nourish my students as writers and as literate people? We're teaching writing, but for what purpose beyond "the test"? What's the larger point? *Is* there a larger point?

Questions and doubts that occasionally plague caring teachers are understandable. Most teachers are too busy with day-to-day matters to spend much time philosophizing, but not too busy to worry a little. We put lots of effort into getting students into, through, and out of the next lesson, unit, exam, class. It helps, at times, to pause and consider, "Why am I working so hard on this teaching stuff? Why am I teaching English?" At such times, words of wisdom, such as those from Piaget and Beckett, sustain us and help us work through doubts that creep up on us.

By now, you probably have a good idea of what we stand for as writing teachers. To encapsulate some of the threads in this book in terms of *adults functioning in the world*, however, here's what we're after:

- creative individuals with a voice
- fluent, context-aware experts with language
- engaged and thinking adults.

If you're ultimately helping students become these kinds of people, we think you're doing your job as a writing teacher (above and beyond what the Standards of the Week have to say on the matter). This chapter takes a look at some of these larger life reasons for writing.

Transitioning to College Writing

Teachers hear it constantly. Some say it repeatedly. It's a mantra in our heads. "We're getting our students ready for _____." Fill in the blank: life, careers; first grade, middle school, high school, college. Part of the joy and challenge of teaching is its expectant nature, the focus on a *now* that leads to a *then*.

As we consider getting our students ready for next steps, such as college, we invite you to take a look at Figure 14–1.

This simple diagram is probably what many people expect for students moving through school. In this dream, students become steadily more sophisticated writers through elementary, middle, and high school. Their experiences build cumulatively to prepare them for college, with the background, experience, practice, and ability to succeed in postsecondary writing situations. The movement to the next level is seamless. Teachers at each level understand and respect the work of others along the path. What could be clearer?

Now, take a moment to compare the idealism of Figure 14–1 with Figure 14–2.

Figure 14–2 reflects the common belief that schools are somehow underpreparing students for college expectations. Kids start off fine, but then somewhere around middle school the wheels come off. Writing improvement slows. Students end up graduating from high school woefully underprepared for the rigors of college writing. Figure 14–2 hints at the historically troubled relationship between colleges—with entrance policies that, in effect, dictated what was important to know—and schools, which were left scrambling to respond to these mandates. In fact, the National Council of Teachers of English was basically formed by teachers a hundred years ago to fight back against this one-sided relationship.

Let's take a closer look at the implications of Figure 14–2. Is it accurate? Many kids do enter elementary school as eager learners. They like writing stories, drawing pictures, and demonstrating what they can do and what they know. And yes, by the time they reach high school, a lot of this curiosity and enthusiasm for learning seems to have disappeared. Some

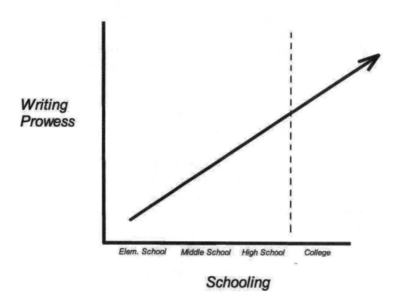

Figure 14–1. The Expectation

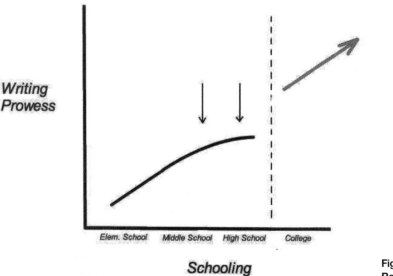

Writing Prowess

Elem. School   Middle School   High School   College

Schooling

Figure 14–2. The Reality?

attribute this evolution to the natural doldrums and upheavals of adolescence. Others note that the nature of school shifts as students get older. The open, individualized, and somewhat pastoral community of the elementary classroom morphs into the industrial, taxonomic system of the high school. It's not a conspiracy theory to suggest that this shift may be intentional. The higher grades are structured to curb youthful exuberance, sort students by narrow measures of potential, channel interests into acceptable academic subjects, and further emphasize obedience and rule following. Fun storytime is for little kids; in high school, it's time to get serious. Some students thrive in this new environment; many more, however, become alienated to writing, to schoolwork, to learning in general. As the old saying goes, "Students enter school as question marks and leave as periods."

So maybe some of the stagnation of writing improvement in Figure 14–2 comes from approaches to writing that alienate rather than foster deeper personal engagement, critical thinking, and meaningful application of what students know and learn.

There's another huge factor at work here as well: the ironic downward pressure of high-stakes testing on college preparation. *Rigorous standards*, *student achievement*, *accountability*, and *excellence for all* are some of the buzz phrases of testing proponents; but the actual effects are more like *mediocrity*, *minimum competency*, and *lowest common denominator*. Not exactly college-prep descriptors.

Draconian testing policies narrow curriculum, hamstring good teaching, and corrupt learning. That's pretty much undisputed. In trying to ensure that schools and teachers are doing their jobs, these policies contribute to undereducated, underprepared, and uninterested students and graduates. Teaching writing in middle and high schools—and doing it well—often means struggling with Orwellian institutional and political mandates that claim to advance student achievement but that actually act as barriers to student success.

Let's be clear. Figure 14–2 is a generalization for the sake of making a point. But we suspect it's a pretty accurate picture of how the testing craze actually acts as a drag on post-school writing preparation for students.

We have, then, some powerful forces at work on the school side of the equation that are sandbagging teachers' attempts to help students get ready for life after graduation. But that doesn't mean that the college side of the issue gets a free pass. Take a look at Figure 14–3.

Regular reports of high school graduates unprepared for the rigors of college writing are full of not-so-veiled criticism of high school teaching while remaining noticeably quiet on the exact nature of college writing itself. The assumption is that college writing is monolithic, its qualities fully agreed upon and universal. But is this really the case?

As Patrick Sullivan and Howard Tinsberg's collection *What Is "College-Level" Writing?* (2006) demonstrates, the reality is far more complex. What counts for good postsecondary writing varies greatly depending on course, instructor, assignment, situation, content area, and institution. Writing conventions shift from field to field, and what is recognized and rewarded in one discipline may be proscribed or punished in another. Ellen Knodt (2006) notes that even if a secondary English teacher's intent is solely to prepare students for first-year composition—the college writing class just about every college student takes—it's still problematic to assume a stable set of skills given the various and sometimes competing philosophies that motivate writing programs. As Sullivan (2006) highlights, even agreeing on *basic qualities* of good writing can be tricky: An essay judged superior because it is clear and uses correct grammar might be failed by the next reader for lack of ideas and substance.

That's why we represent the expectations of college writing in Figure 14–3 as a "probability field" of possibilities and uncertainties that depend on the writing situation. Yes, we know that responding with "it depends" to the question of what college-level writing looks like sounds like a cop-out, but it's pretty accurate. And this is not to exclude college faculty from criticism either, as historically they've been quick to criticize their secondary-level colleagues and slow to seek partnerships that address this topic. The notable exception is the National Writing Project, which through its network of local sites across the country,

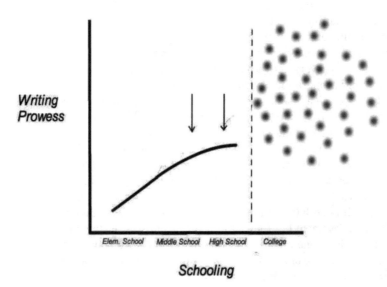

Figure 14–3. The More Accurate Reality?

has brought together teachers at all levels and across fields as writers, partners, and co-researchers.

So what's our takeaway point with this series of rather inelegant diagrams?

It's this: Helping students develop strategic thinking habits and flexibility as writers is more effective than obsessing over specific forms and genres. Mastering the five-paragraph essay won't get you far in college . . . but neither will relying on any other all-purpose template—for a lab report, a business memo, a literary analysis essay, or whatever. The short-cut preprogrammed approach to writing is a fool's game. A practiced ability to evaluate a writing situation and respond confidently, critically, or creatively from an array of options is much more useful. This ability to assess a situation is more a soft skill than a formula, a honed trait, not a fact to be memorized. Sullivan (2006) lists five general traits for successful college writing that reinforce this notion:

1. a willingness to evaluate ideas and issues carefully
2. some skill at analysis and higher-level thinking
3. the ability to shape and organize material effectively
4. the ability to integrate some of the material from the reading skillfully
5. the ability to follow the standard rules of grammar, punctuation, and spelling

The modifiers in this list—"carefully," "effectively," "skillfully"—all suggest the ability to figure out writing contexts and deliver on certain expectations. They most certainly do not suggest that rote, automatic, or fixed responses are suitable.

IDEAS FOR TEACHERS OF WRITING: Throughout this book, we've offered lots of examples for helping students develop these abilities. Chapter 7 features activities and writing ideas that stress careful analysis and inquiry. Chapters 8 and 9 address revision, feedback, and editing through techniques that work. Chapter 11 addresses the place of correctness in written conventions in an overall assessment of writing quality. Chapters 12 and 13 include a ton of ideas for writing about all manner of texts. One critical component must be in place for any of these ideas to take hold for you and your students: For most people to engage in high-quality, effective writing, they have to see writing as a realistic and personally meaningful act. How do you accomplish this goal? We've addressed multiple ways for doing so throughout this book. Look ahead to Chapter 15 to see the thoughts of Sonny Harding, Lisha Wood, Kyle Jones, and others who address how they work to accomplish this goal in their teaching.

College "Readiness"

Consider our predicament as teachers. On one side of an abyss are schools, fellow teachers, and students who are burdened with tests and mandates that prescribe limited forms of writing as appropriate; on the other, varied expectations for postsecondary writing that presume lots of experience with creative adaptability and critical responsiveness. We run students through a *convergent* secondary system that narrows writing to a few school-specific forms and artificial situations. Then we send them to college with all its *divergent* writing possibilities and contexts, and what a surprise, they can't handle it. We expect poise and confidence and strategic awareness and craft, all from students who've learned that writing is pointless scullery work if not an outright punishment. As the old-timers like to say, you can't get there from here.

Well, maybe you can. There are writing bridges between college and high school, if you know what path to follow. Consider how the Council of Writing Program Administrators has defined "college readiness." (These are the people who run writing programs in colleges and universities, so we can safely assume that their ideas have some merit.) Their Framework for Success in Postsecondary Writing (2011) first lists the habits of mind that will serve students well in college. These include the following:

- **curiosity**: the desire to know more about the world
- **openness**: the willingness to consider new ways of being and thinking in the world
- **engagement**: a sense of investment and involvement in learning
- **creativity**: the ability to use novel approaches for generating, investigating, and representing ideas
- **persistence**: the ability to sustain interest in and attention to short- and long-term projects
- **responsibility**: the ability to take ownership of one's actions and understand the consequences of those actions for oneself and others
- **flexibility**: the ability to adapt to situations, expectations, or demands
- **metacognition**: the ability to reflect on one's own thinking as well as on the individual and cultural processes used to structure knowledge

Imagine that. Curiosity, openness, creativity, persistence, flexibility, and more are essential to writing well. The traits in the Framework are exactly those we might use to define well-rounded adults who think for themselves. Knowing that you can foster these traits in your students through your teaching methods gives creative, progressive teachers (like you) some real hope that their work with students is relevant in middle and high school, to higher education, and in functioning as literate adults.

The Framework goes on to get even more specific about the kinds of reading, writing, and critical thinking experiences that support these traits:

1. *rhetorical knowledge*: the ability to analyze and act on understandings of audiences, purposes, and contexts in creating and comprehending texts
2. *critical thinking*: the ability to analyze a situation or text and make thoughtful decisions based on that analysis, through writing, reading, and research
3. *writing processes*: multiple strategies to approach and undertake writing and research
4. *knowledge of conventions*: the formal and informal guidelines that define what is considered to be correct and appropriate, or incorrect and inappropriate, in a piece of writing
5. *ability to compose in multiple environments*: from using traditional pen and paper to electronic technologies

These explanations of ideal college writing preparation are exciting for teachers to learn. Even with the pressure to turn the classroom into a test-prep boot camp—to dumb down, oversimplify, and drill, baby, drill in the pursuit of standards and accountability—if you can manage to set your sights beyond the immediate manias and inanities, the horizon holds promise for students whose instruction has helped them become confident and clever, flexible and fluent in their writing.

IDEAS FOR TEACHERS OF WRITING: In Chapter 1, we discuss foundational attitudes and beliefs that foster students' abilities to develop these traits. In Chapters 2, 3, and 7, we offer specific methods for engaging your students in seeking questions that pique curiosity. Chapters 8 and 9 advocate for activities that build persistence, responsibility, and flexibility as students craft writing and engage in a community of writers through peer work, shared writing, and revision as a means of reseeing and reconceptualizing. And the concept of metacognition—that crucial quality of knowing and evaluating oneself as a learner, writer, and thinker—underlies our entire approach in this book. Having students explore language, writing, and texts in ways we suggest in Chapters 12 and 13, an enlightened view of writing as consisting of interrelated processes as we discuss in Chapters 2 and 3, and the ability to write for multiple purposes and audiences that we discuss in Chapters 4, 5, 7, 12, and 13 build and refine the components numbered above.

Transitioning to Work and Career

You may be thinking, "Well sure, everyone knows writing is a must in college. Duh." Reasons for writing and writing well exist beyond school, however, as we've indicated numerous times throughout this book. Really, it's not a huge jump from success in college writing to success in professional writing, whatever one's interest or career. Careful, context-aware writing is rather a standard expectation no matter your profession; and although it's unrealistic to prep students for the specific of any given job, that doesn't mean we have to ignore the subject altogether. In fact, what professionals in all fields do with written language rests firmly on the assumptions in this book.

English teachers can and do help prepare students for this and other transitions. Blau (2003) argues that English teachers, because of our emphasis on interpretation and the process of making sense of texts, are uniquely positioned to be guides for people moving into professional spheres that expect these same abilities (78). Heading toward a career in law enforcement? You'll need the ability interpret crime scenes, write detailed narrative reports, and use language in a way that defuses rather than escalates difficult situations. Those in the legal field need the ability to draw upon evidence and implication to create compelling narratives and arguments, a job that usually requires a refined sense of voice and tone. Students who want a successful career in business should expect to develop a mastery of detail, rhetoric, anecdote, and audience awareness to motivate employees and reach customers. Even the technical, statistics-driven writing of scientists and medical researchers gains context and impact when combined with compelling narrative and relevant examples.

IDEAS FOR TEACHERS OF WRITING: Fluency, flexibility, and the personal confidence with writing in multiple contexts that comes from moving into control and precision in writing (see Chapter 2) are crucial advantages in practically any career. We invite you to focus on seeing your students' writing as developmental, as processes that take time, work, and nurturing. When you encourage students to write what's in their heads (Chapter 2), to write authentically (Chapter 6), and to write in multiple genres and for varied purposes (Chapters 7, 12, and 13), you are preparing them for fruitful work and career pathways.

Writing and the Big Picture

It's almost a cliché to point out that a strong and functioning democratic society—or perhaps any advanced society regardless of political leanings—relies on a well-educated populace willing to take part in civic life and political affairs. For us, one of the broader reasons for developing fluency, voice, control, and confidence with writers is the presumption that having a public voice still matters. This notion doesn't mean that we're prepping students for political careers, just that they will be prepared as adults to participate in whatever public contexts might call for careful thinking, consensus building, and writing that connects, be it a neighborhood organization, a town hall meeting, a PTA, a volunteer group—or a rally, boycott, or protest.

This expectation extends to going public via online media as well. One of the excellent facets of digital writing is the capacity for anyone to share their writing, thinking, and creativity in an easy and massively public way. Digital channels allow a public airing for many more voices and ideas than ever before, and ideally, those of a superior merit, beauty, resonance, power, and artistry will rise to the top. Think it, say it, and express it well, we might say, and your audience can literally be global.

Of course, it's not that simple. No voice exists in a vacuum. As educators such as Will Richardson and professional bloggers such as Andrew Sullivan have noted, success in online communication and writing most often depends on a willingness to read, grapple with, respond to, debate, and build upon the ideas of others. What things mean, what has value, what is true—these are socially constructed conversations that require a willingness to engage and a collaborative spirit. So consider this: If students have had similar experiences throughout their education in classrooms that emphasize the careful refinement of ideas in a social setting, they are in essence getting real-world preparation for the responsibilities and expectations of "virtual" writing. (Re-read that last sentence; let it sink in.)

It's worth noting again that the "anybody may participate" nature of the Internet is not without its drawbacks. In his book *You Are Not a Gadget*, Jaron Lanier (2010) makes an intriguing argument for a new ethos when interacting online. Lanier points out that for all its obvious benefits, the Internet as participatory medium has generally resulted in people taking *less* responsibility for what they write, not more. The potential anonymity afforded in digital spaces such as discussion boards and comment threads often produces a chaos of invective and name-calling, flaming and "trolling," instead of any step forward in reasoned and respectful discussion. Lanier suggests new foundations for how we communicate digitally, including the expectation that online writers accurately identify themselves to assume personal responsibility for their words.

You start building this type of awareness with your students as you and they discuss their writing, work to make it more effective, and then celebrate their authorship—their ownership of the writing—by publishing their writing in some form. Although there is a worthy tradition of anonymity in public writing, particularly when the ideas expressed are revolutionary or politically dangerous to individuals living under repressive governments, we see Lanier's rationale in tightening online expectations for what counts and deserves credibility in our daily lives. With virtual spaces playing an increasing role in our lives, conversations about identity and accountability are essential.

IDEAS FOR TEACHERS OF WRITING: In Chapter 13, we explore forms of new media. New media produce—and perhaps require—new types of *texts*. We offer ideas for using both new media and the resulting texts for writing instruction. We also think that discussions of new media are critical elements for elaborating the concept of literacy with your students. Some of the most fun we have with students is introducing them to very broad ideas of *text* and opening up the idea of what makes a text a text, the metaphor of *reading* nontraditional texts, and implications for their future work with media, literacy, and texts.

Constructing the Narrative: The Importance of Story

An essential reason for learning to write well involves taking charge of and establishing a context for the stories that surround us, the stories from which we construct our lives and in which our lives are steeped. As we move through school, *story* becomes equated with *fiction*, which sadly becomes tagged as *soft, fun, creative,* and other nonserious descriptors. School writing is about *fact, exposition, persuasion,* and *argument*. Look at any district, state, or common core of standards for high school learners, and the nonfiction, expository genres that students are to master leap off the page. *Story* is for fairy tales.

Except that it isn't.

We represent individual reality as story. Life is story. We remember life's meanings and events and lessons learned by the stories we equate with them. Individual identity is synonymous with the story of our lives. Are we the authors of our lives, making changes to plot and character and setting, or are we at the mercy of other forces making these decisions? Depends on each person's circumstance and sense of self. Can we fundamentally redefine ourselves and so rewrite our ongoing stories? (*The Great Gatsby* is one writer's notable take on this question.) We address the value of narrative in Chapters 3 and 4, and how to move students into writing and exploring a range of nonfiction genres in Chapter 7. Seeing the full range of options for writers is important, as is knowing that the importance of story goes well beyond a writing mode. The psychologist Rollo May has noted that "depression, despair, feelings of 'I can't,' and related helplessness can be [. . .] seen as the inability to see or to construct a future" (2007, 243) or to feel a sense of agency about our own story. And if you take away our memories—our remembered stories of the past—we become little more than ciphers as well.

An understanding of the power of story is crucial in politics and government: Those who "control the narrative" by spinning the facts (as storytellers similarly spin tales) define the perception and the reality. Political campaigns often seem little more than elaborate storytelling contests with competing tales about heroes and villains. More ominously, government or military cover-ups are fictions designed to hide truths and so manipulate public opinion, as manufactured or misleading stories such as the following demonstrate: Former pro football star turned Army Ranger Pat Tillman was killed not by enemy forces as first related in the news but by so-called friendly fire in Afghanistan; veteran Jessica Lynch was captured by Iraqi forces and portrayed as a fighting-to-the-last-bullet heroine, but she was actually knocked unconscious when her Humvee crashed; and the prisoner abuse scandal at Abu Ghraib, a U.S. military detention center in Iraq, was covered up for months before being detected. Political rebellion and revolution can be seen as the rise of one "story" over another, as those who have been marginalized, oppressed, or ignored in the dominant narrative suddenly make their stories heard. Without an awareness of the power of story to define what is real and what isn't, what counts and what doesn't, we are much more susceptible to the dangers of demagogues and the disingenuous.

Likewise, history is story—or, perhaps, the selection of certain stories over others. We all learned the conventional "story" of the United States in grade school, complete with dashing characters, pivotal conflicts, themes of liberty and equality, and an uplifting tone. But shift the perspective—to that of an American Indian or a slave—and likely the story becomes very different. The religions of the world are essentially stories about what matters. Myth is a structure for meaning that, on occasion, clashes with science, which has its own stories about how the world works.

Our entertainment choices are determined by the stories that compel us, from whatever TV shows we watch regularly, to the music we favor, to what our leisure activities "say" about us to others. Sports fans know that story is essential, forming the context for rivalries, dramas, triumphs, and failures. (If you find watching a particular sport boring, it's most likely because you don't know about or are not invested in the stories that give it meaning.) Companies seek to create a story conveyed by their name or logo, and advertisers tell stories that seek to connect with themes or identities that resonate with consumers. A current commercial features the narrative line of a dog wanting to protect his treasured bone from theft, so he puts it under the iconic, protective umbrella of a particular insurance company. Another ad features an elementary-aged girl sitting in the driver's seat of a car, listening to cautions and safety admonitions from her father; then the camera cuts to the girl as a teen, pulling out of the driveway in a car the dad has chosen for its built-in safety features. Note that these ads do not stress the *facts* of insurance policies or the numbers of lives saved with a car's safety features. Rather, they tell a compelling story that we remember and relate to our own pets, children, and parents whom we love. In these ways, which stories matter (and how) fuels a host of sociocultural movements, beliefs, and convictions.

One of the most compelling kinds of story, however, is the one we tell ourselves about ourselves. In *Buying In* (2008), Rob Walker identifies the fundamental tension of modern life: We all want to feel like individuals, but we also all want to feel a part of something bigger than ourselves. To resolve this tension, each of us devises a constantly updated narrative, a never-ending story we tell ourselves about who we are and what we value through the things we buy, wear, own, or create.

Walker's incisive thesis fits well with the centrality of story in our lives. How does what I do, own, eat, drink, drive, and know reflect on the perceptions others have of me? More importantly, how do they reflect on my self-image and what I think of myself? What stories do we tell ourselves about our actions, thoughts, and place in the world? These are the constructs of agency and self-efficacy. Any psychologist will tell you that we need a healthy self-concept to be emotionally grounded and comfortable inside our own skins. How do we get there? Part of the journey is contained in the stories we construct for ourselves.

Understanding how stories work—how they may be used to shape meaning, identity, and perspectives—is extremely important business in the making of a life, even if such topics don't show up as prompts on state writing tests. Our approach to writing often starts with personal story because it puts the focus on students: their lives, their views, their world. But it doesn't end there. When we explore our own stories, we inevitably begin to explore those of others as well. Story, then, evolves from a tactic for personal relevance to a much broader strategy for understanding, questioning, evaluating, and arguing.

IDEAS FOR TEACHERS OF WRITING: In Chapters 2 and 4, we offer numerous ideas for using journals and promoting written fluency with your students. These ideas are often grounded in the stories that your students choose to tell about themselves and others who are important to them. In Chapter 4, we invite you to explore all manner of pathways for writing with your students, many of which feature story of one sort or another. Whole books have been written about narrative, story, and the importance of each. Explore some of those as well to seek additional ways for incorporating the fundamental, essential idea of *story* into your students' literacy experiences.

Creative Expression: Dare We Say It?

We dare.

All people have a creative instinct, of which language is an essential part. You may not think that you work with students who are going to become published writers; you may not see the next Pulitzer Prize winner in the hoodie-wearing kid texting surreptitiously in the back row. But every one of your students will become people who, at various important points in their lives, will find themselves in situations that demand creativity with words.

It could be a line to a potential lover. Or a note of condolence. An alibi or explanation. A heartfelt thank-you letter. A eulogy for a parent. A polite note of refusal. A best man's toast. A wrenching good-bye. Or it could be something less defined, a simple human need to put into words the inexpressible: the joy and fragility of life, the pain and the suffering that is bound to come to us all. In these moments, facility with thesis statements will not help, nor will the five-paragraph essay form. No writing formula prepares a person to negotiate in language the emotional vicissitudes of life. What will help, though, is a personal conviction that written expression is possible—is, in fact, crucial—for every one of us.

The greeting card business—which is little more than images on cardboard paired with a few generic lines of humor, condolence, or affection—has grown into a multibillion-dollar industry partly because people don't have the personal confidence, experience, and faith that they can say it any better than some anonymous stranger can. Well, we disagree. Those are the moments we're really preparing students for, the moments that really count after all the exams and the memos and the essays are gathering dust. We want people who speak from the heart with their own unique versions of grace and poetry, wit and honesty. It's not all that much to ask.

IDEAS FOR TEACHERS OF WRITING: In Chapters 2, 3, 4, and 6, we offer many ideas for preparing students to write authentically and meaningfully to personal and public audiences. When you engage in these types of writing with your students, you prepare them to know how to tap their creative abilities.

Homo Creatus

As several English educators have pointed out, we are compelled as humans to make, to create. We are as much *Homo creatus* ("man the creator") as we are *Homo sapiens* ("man the wise"). In a parody of this notion, consider the typical message students get about the point of an education: to gain the skills to get a job to *make money*, which of course isn't really "making" anything at all, but trading the time and effort of our finite lives for credits to use in a consumerist society.

Of course, there's nothing wrong with preparing students for meaningful careers that lead to financial security. We highly recommend such a goal. But if this path means shutting down one's creative potential, if it implies that students need to prune their sense of self until it meets a purely economic definition, then education becomes an unfortunate process of narrowing one's humanity rather than unfolding one's wider potential.

We ignore the urge to create legitimately at our peril, both individually and socially. Our point here is more than just philosophical. We can tap into that innate creative need in practical ways with our students. Consider the collaboration between the National Writing Project and *MAKE Magazine*, in which "teachers and students collaborate on making stuff, document their tinkering, and disseminate their knowledge to a community of other makers" (Reed 2011). Could this type of learning be a viable alternative to the dominant test-preparation culture found in many schools? Would engaging students in a do-it-yourself culture provide better contexts to improve reading, writing, and critical thinking skills? And even better, would such a focus more legitimately prepare students for richer lives as a result of those applied reading, writing, and critical thinking skills?

Likewise, teacher Matt Lintner (2012) points out that if you are a student, you may graduate from high school—with straight As, no less—without ever having done the following:

1. searched for answers to unknown questions
2. budgeted your own time
3. discovered what most interests you
4. initiated a project requiring sustained commitment
5. taken risks or experienced failure
6. led a team in the pursuit of a worthy goal
7. practiced consensus building or the messiness of compromise
8. asserted yourself, even if it meant challenging authority
9. built something of value
10. created art that speaks to the soul
11. explored the natural world
12. interacted with people outside your age group
13. volunteered substantively in your community
14. apprenticed in fields of your choosing
15. started a business
16. traveled and gathered perspectives outside your comfort zone
17. acquired practical skills like saving and investing, handling tools, programming, growing food
18. learned to say "no"

This is a fascinating list that causes us to question what we're all about as teachers.

IDEAS FOR TEACHERS OF WRITING: Systemic changes to incorporate some of these purposes into schooling might be a long time in coming. But in the kinds of classrooms we create, many of these worthy and life-reverberating experiences can happen, if we decide to make it so. Teaching writing from the perspectives and approaches discussed in this book are certainly a step in the right direction.

Living Literate Lives: The Challenges Ahead

The young people we educate today will face some serious challenges in their future. It's hard to predict what kind of world we'll be living in fifty years from now, but it's fairly safe to say that those of us still around will be dealing with some rather significant questions along with some crucial problems.

Take, again, the role of technology in our lives. It's entirely likely that new gadgetry and online connectivity will continue its colonization of our lives to a degree hard to fathom right now. Young people will just as likely be the first adopters of whatever new shiny thing appears. The effects—neurologically, socially, psychologically—of this shockingly fast shift to digital immediacy in our lives are far from clear. Lost in this e-embrace are deeper, troubling questions. What does it mean to be literate with these new possibilities for communication? What habits of mind worth nurturing might be threatened? How is our own self-image shifted or defined by tech use? These are age-old questions, but never more important given how quickly digital culture is evolving.

Another related question about technology reaches into global territory: What moral obligations do we incur when we welcome technology into our lives? After all, modern technology and the power that fuels it come from somewhere, mostly from finite fossil fuels. It may seem passé to point this out, environmentalism being so '90s (or is it '60s?), but the simple fact of limited resources on the planet necessarily raises the question of responsibility. In a world of seven billion people and with an inevitable energy crunch on the horizon, how do we morally position our gadget-filled lives?

And about those seven billion or so other people. One thing that technology has done is remove many of the more conventional barriers to communication. That's obvious enough. What's not so obvious is what this more immediate global reach and possible connection with others mean for conventional ideas of identity and stereotype. Religion and culture are still impassable barriers for many, and yet it's never been easier to communicate. If, as Rollo May has suggested, violence and authentic communication are mutually exclusive (1972), perhaps technology as a channel for writing and speaking and understanding does have some transformative potential to create fundamental connections—across religions, regions, and cultures—where few have flourished before.

IDEAS FOR TEACHERS OF WRITING: In Chapter 13, we discuss a range of digital re-sources and the influence of digital venues for writing and communicating with others. By using such strategies, your students will be better prepared to deal with the advances in technology and literacy that are sure to come.

Inside Out: How It All Begins

To the average kid in the average classroom, these tensions may seem totally irrelevant and impossibly distant, but they link to the central ideas of this book. The issues facing us moving forward are essentially issues of power, identity, fairness, and responsibility. If, as the old saying goes, "All politics are local," we are not very far away from the idea that all politics are also *personal*. Our own stories and voices are, somewhat paradoxically, the same vehicles by which we interact and come to know others as multifaceted, complex, and worthy of dignity, respect, and acknowledgement. Starting with who we are as individu-als in the writing classroom is the first step toward grappling constructively with who we *all* are, as an individual, a community, a culture, and a species in the world. We encourage you to see the "big picture" as you mentor your students' developing abilities. It is teachers, often, who model for their students how to lead literate lives, how to write, respond, read, and interact with clarity and purpose.

Works Cited

Blau, Sheridan. 2003. *The Literature Workshop*. Portsmouth, NH: Heinemann.

Council of Writing Program Administrators. January 2011. *Framework for Success in Postsecondary Writing*. Available online at www.wpacouncil.org/files/framework-for-success-postsecondary-writing .pdf. Viewed May 11, 2012.

Knodt, Ellen Andrews. 2006. "What Is College Writing For?" *What Is "College-Level" Writing?* Patrick Sullivan and Howard Tinsbert, eds. 146-157. Urbana, IL: NCTE.

Lanier, Jaron. 2010. *You Are Not a Gadget*. New York. Knopf.

Lintner, Matt. 2012. "Race to Nowhere." January 11. Available at: http://susanohanian.org/outrage_fetch.php?id=1161.

May, Rollo. 2007. *Love and Will*. New York: Norton.

May, Rollo. 1972. *Power and Innocence: A Search for the Sources of Violence*. New York: Norton.

Reed, Samuel. 2011. "DIY Movement: Teachers and Students as Makers." January 18. *The Notebook: An Independent Public Voice for Parents, Educators, Students, and Friends of Philadelphia Public Schools*. Available at: www.thenotebook.org/blog/113233/diy-movement-teachers-and-students-makers.

Sullivan, Patrick. 2006. "An Essential Question: What Is 'College-Level' Writing?" *What Is "College-Level" Writing?* Patrick Sullivan and Howard Tinsberg, eds. 1-30. Urbana, IL: NCTE.

Sullivan, Patrick, and Howard Tinsberg, eds. 2006. *What Is "College-Level" Writing?* Urbana, IL: NCTE.

Walker, Rob. 2008. *Buying In: The Secret Dialogue Between What We Buy and Who We Are*. New York: Random House.

15

Conversations
with Teachers

Every object tells a story if you know how to read it. —**Henry Ford**

Stories are the stuff from which meaning derives, as we discuss in Chapters 13 and 14. Ford's focus on *objects* in the quote that opens this chapter suits his lifelong work and focus on building cars; his inventiveness permanently changed the automotive industry. We agree with Ford: Objects do carry stories worth knowing. We hasten to add that the same is true for people. People have stories worth hearing and knowing. You just have to ask for them. Which is what we did with a group of our colleagues as we gathered teachers' authentic practices and voices to inform this book.

You've heard from us about writing and how to teach it. In this last chapter, we share with you the insight of teachers who are working every day with young writers. Their voices offer notions for us to question, consider, and perhaps implement. They paint a varied and compelling picture of teaching.[1]

While we were writing this book, we extended invitations to area teachers to participate in a focus group about the challenges and successes of teaching writing today. We all met one evening at Dawn's house, and the focus group idea skyrocketed, turning into several hours of free-flowing, enlightening, and energizing conversation. Although we, Dawn and Darren, had prompts and questions ready in case the conversation strayed or found a lull, our first instincts proved accurate: When you gather English teachers together and add snacks and a few beverages (yes, wine, too), the discussion fuels itself.

We audio-recorded the session and from that transcript and our notes, we mined the data and derived categories (see following headings) to capture significant threads of the discussion. We then invited our focus group participants—along with a few other teachers we've worked with—to riff in writing on any of these topics that resonated with them. Most people responded to several categories; one responded to them all. (Yes, she's the classic Type A overachiever, and we adore her.) We encouraged our teacher-informants to follow their reflections in whatever direction appealed to them.

These teachers run the gamut of experience. Several are newbies in the profession (one to four years in the classroom), and others are veterans with twenty-five years or more of teaching under their belts. Most now teach high school, though some have been middle school teachers. Two have somewhat special career circumstances: Marsha works predominantly with English language learners, and Rob is a former high school English teacher turned English Education professor. Although this group of teachers may not represent the full range of teachers' perspectives and experiences, we think what they have to say is candid, fresh, and useful.

As you read, consider these teachers' perspectives and experiences. What is similar to your teaching and professional experiences? What will be helpful in your classroom with your students? Jot some notes about your thinking. Most of all, let their thinking inform yours as it has ours.

What Works for You with Writing Instruction?

All the following teachers describe moments of epiphany that motivate how they approach writing. They wrote about a range of strategies and techniques, from sharing their own writing and interests with students to using students' commentaries and perspectives as tools of inquiry.

▊ Marsha Kindrachuk

Being a new teacher—I'm in my second full year of teaching, my first year with a full contract—I am constantly looking for ways to improve my teaching, myself, and the ways in which I connect with my students. I buy into the "Write with your students" theory rather than the hypocritical "Do as I say, not as I do" traditional way of teaching. I tell my students that I left a lucrative career and chose to become a teacher because I love learning, especially reading and writing, teaching, and students. I tell them I could be making a lot more money elsewhere, so I promise them that I will not be boring (at least that's the intent) because I could do that elsewhere with far fewer headaches and less hard work. When I assign writing, I pick up my pen and write with them. When I have them share their writing, I share mine, as well. This helps them realize pretty quickly that we are all part of a writing community. I set up the classroom with basic rules and expectations. The class comes up with the guidelines with some gentle (but unnoticeable) prompting by me. When students buy into the rules, they're much more likely to follow them. We begin by writing the very first day, and we never stop writing.

I have tried numerous things from *Inside Out* with varying results depending on the age, level, and student population. Many ideas I've tweaked to work for my class or me. I have done the Name Piece many times now, and each time it's a little bit different. Every time, though, I always have at least one student come up and express appreciation for researching his or her name. I always have students take home their research to share with family members, and they interview relatives and return to school with that information to share with classmates. I've tweaked the Coat of Arms into a Mandala piece, which I just did with my Multicultural Literature class of seniors, and that was a great success. I'm taking that one step further to write about food in students' individual cultures, and we'll create a class cookbook that includes not only the recipe but a student narrative of why this particular dish is so important to the student/student's family. An added bonus: We get to sample everyone's recipe that day in class!

I've done cemetery writing last year with sixth graders and got all sorts of interesting pieces. I've gone on the walking composition, I've tried various pieces of memoir writing, and I've always brought in the whole writing workshop focus into our classroom community of writers.

Basically, anything works in my classroom writingwise as long as I'm willing to experiment, participate right there with the kids, and not be afraid of failure. If it's not working, I merely tweak it until it does!

■ Courtney Cook

I remember it fondly: the nervousness in my stomach, clammy hands, shaky fingers, and a smile that spoke more to terror than genuine excitement. It was my first day of being expected to know things . . . and have people depend on that knowledge.

The students, anxious to see one another after a summer away from halogen lightbulbs and homework assignments, laughed and excitedly greeted each other's stories of summer fun. I felt like a fraud and was unsure of my ability to step wholeheartedly into these shoes as possessor of knowledge and manager of the classroom. Something about the transition from student to teacher felt too big for my britches, and I felt that I still had so much to learn. I wasn't an authoritarian; how could I be a teacher? I didn't own a single crocheted sweater vest with apples and pink things on it. I'd never succeed!

It wasn't just the wardrobe that made me feel like I wasn't "teacher material." It was everything that I felt the apples and bumblebee broaches represented: coloring, smiling all the time, limerick poetry. I didn't want to just read limerick poetry; I wanted to read poetry of protest and explore the human condition. I wanted to share with my students the secrets of the screwed-up lives of writers and read a lot of books. Not books about girl detectives and locker room crushes, but books about hard life stuff. I wanted to dig into the nit and the grit of being human in hard times and find inspiration in other's stories of survival and searches for goodness. The idea that a teacher had to look a certain way somehow suggested to me that a teacher had to behave a certain way, and Lordy, Lordy, I knew it was a long shot for me to step into those bedazzled flip-flops adorned with oversized daisies.

I learned quickly that I could survive without being the authority that I wasn't and that I didn't have to stock up on gold star stickers, that my teacher identity could very closely mirror my nonteacher identity. This comfort with my cowboy-boot-wearing self in the classroom had little to do with that historically situated "teacher image" and had everything to do with me finding my own voice and style on the page and embracing it.

In the early days before I nestled into the identity of writer, I found that I was unnecessarily hard on my students' writing. I would focus on the smallest grammatical errors, red-penning each and every comma splice and misplaced modifier. While I never decided that grammatically correct writing is unimportant, I did recognize the source of that hyperattentiveness to minor errors and the effect it had on my students' confidence in their own work.

My darling tenth graders would receive papers from me with scrunched-up faces, not wanting to look at the explosion of red. After a few weeks in the classroom, it became very clear that I was doing to them what had been done to me—making them feel that there was an agreed-upon, absolute, "right" way to write. I was helping them decide that they were not writers because they did it "wrong," in the same way I had decided I would not be a good teacher because I was not fitting into the "right" identity.

So I backtracked. I started to talk about questions rather than answers and reminded them that writing was a hard and a long process that takes time and practice and intention. We began writing journals and focusing on specific writing skills (writing small, finding our own voices, etc.) and sharing those personal pieces to build confidence. We formed a writing community where we were all safe to take risks and make mistakes and not know how to write "right."

Through this process, I found within myself a confidence in my autonomy and ability as an educator that stemmed directly from my ability as a writer and my student's sense of accomplishment. As I encouraged my students to find confidence in their own writing, I found comfort in mine. It was the comfort with my new writer self that liberated me from the need to use my red pen as a sword in unconscious attempts to protect my own insecurities.

Looking back, I recognize the importance of embracing our whole selves as educators. This means standing strong in your crocheted vest or with your steaming cup of coffee and reminding yourself that you don't, in fact, have to know *everything* to be a good teacher. That being a good teacher means always learning and always learning means always *not* knowing something.

The biggest step toward finding my own teacher identity was finding comfort with my craft and honoring my "not knowing." My commitment to being comfortable with what I don't know has informed my teaching in a powerful way as it reminds me of exactly what I was trying to teach my kids: that writing, much like living, is about being honest, trying new things, making mistakes, and *always, always* learning.

Lisha Wood

It goes without saying that I love to read and write, or I wouldn't be a high school English teacher. My earliest memories of writing include "The Samuels' Episodes," a story of a dysfunctional family, ripped straight from my wild imagination and my grandmother's favorite soap operas. I even bound the first, never-finished copy in army green construction paper for a published effect. Why I chose such mature subject matter (I wouldn't even let my parents read it) or a last name I had to learn how to pluralize, I'll never know. I just wanted to write something.

That story, along with the multitude of unfinished journal entries, vignettes about relationships, and ridiculous attempts at saccharine poetry, all led me to the writing I love: nonfiction, often editorial in nature. I found this love on the high school and college newspapers and again in my master's program, but never allowed it into my teaching. That's not to say I didn't write and share journals with my students because, duh, we all know to "write with our students." As teachers of writing, we've all heard that writing *with* our students is one of the most important and influential techniques we can use as writing teachers to build community and improve writing. However, it's easier as a teacher to spend time grading and planning and copying and grading instead of sitting down to respond to one of our own assignments.

Last year I began teaching AP Language with a colleague, who is also the journalism teacher. One night, while checking her blog, I LOLed to a picture she'd posted of a cat wearing what looked like a lime football helmet. Zealously, I began writing a response to that picture of the cantankerous-looking kitty. Naturally, she responded with her own Rogerian argument, and a teacher nerd-fest began. We decided to use these as models for an assignment for our AP Language students. The students loved it, and we received creative nonfiction pieces beyond our wildest dreams. We've continued to do this with restaurant reviews and other editorialized topics. Each time, I share my own review/editorial and then have students write theirs, thus creating a community of writers; that's right—students who want to write and even *share* their writings with the class. They know I'm willing to put myself out there, share my thoughts of why I chose a certain word or tone, and share a little about me. This has made them braver as writers. In a class where we do not get to do a lot of creative writing, students feel stifled. I realized I can offer them a little treat (in between the horrible AP Language practice essays) that sparks their creativity *and* meets course requirements: creative nonfiction. We discuss all aspects of AP Language—rhetorical devices, tone, diction—while they develop style and voice through these pieces.

I am a cross-country coach, and I run every day with my runners. My participation in the sport enables me to understand any issues my runners may have and how to help them improve. The same is true of writing. I wasn't a bad teacher when I didn't write with my students, just like I wasn't a bad coach when I didn't run with my students, but I wasn't at my best either. Just as runners respect a coach who plays, language arts students trust a teacher who writes.

Ashley Glover

My first year teaching was a bust. All the way around. I was so focused on feeding my students information—*how* to write, *what* to write, *when* to write. I just couldn't understand why they weren't able to translate my brilliant instructions into their formal writing. I thought, "This is so easy. I'm showing them how to do it, and I'm giving them all these easy steps for how to write an essay. How come they aren't *getting it*?"

Then, one day, I started to understand. We were having a class discussion that had gone drastically off topic (as usual), and I was watching them all light up as they bounced ideas off of one another. One kid—the token "loner," who refused to do anything in my class besides sleep and/or text under his desk—was actually engaged in the discussion. Wait, it was more than that. He wasn't just engaged; rather, he was *leading* the discussion. Regardless of how off topic we were, I decided to try to harness both their enthusiasm and the opportunity to try a different approach. I asked Loner Kid to begin to jot down what he thought the most important points of the discussion were. He did so. The next day, I found a way to weave what they had been talking about into a set of themes from the novel we were reading. I took Loner Kid's notes and put them on the overhead. I asked the rest of the class to form these points into questions. Hands started shooting up around the room, and it was one of those moments when I was just *dying* for one of my administrators to walk in and do a formal observation. They were interested because *they* had generated the questions. We spent the entire class period debating these questions, and they were so passionate about their individual viewpoints that none of them even flinched when the bell rang (again, why oh why couldn't this have been my formal observation?). The following day, I typed up all of their questions and asked them to choose one to write about for a persuasive essay. There was some grumbling when they realized that I was using their own gusto and questions as writing prompts (many called me a traitor as they picked up the page of questions and sulked back to their desks), but something incredible happened with their writing that day. They actually cared about the topic, because they owned it.

From that point forward, I decided to structure my class in the following way:

- Always start by letting students talk *first*; they do not want to listen to me talk.
- The class must be 98 percent student-driven. I say 98 percent because there are times when even the most intellectually stimulating and productive conversations can take a wrong turn.
- Take notes about their discussion—especially when it gets heated or passionate (by the way, I've learned that the more controversial the topic, the better).
- Morph the class discussion into a series of "dense questions." Eventually the goal is to get the students to do this themselves; however, there have been several occasions when it works better if I act as the class secretary and develop the questions while they talk.
- Use the dense questions as a platform for their writing.
- Sit back and feel brilliant while you watch them *care* about crazy things like voice, sentence structure, thesis statements, and sentence fragments.

CONSIDERING WHAT WORKS IN THE WRITING CLASS: As you think about what these teachers wrote, consider the following questions:

- What works for you as a teacher of writing?
- What works for your colleagues as teachers of writing? Have you ever asked them? If not, how might you get productive discussions going?
- What do these teachers *do* that makes teaching writing work for them?
- What have these teachers decided *not* to do that makes teaching writing work for them?
- Would you want to be a student in (or observe as a colleague) these teachers' classes? Why or why not?
- What strikes you as fresh and honest about what these teachers say about teaching writing?

How Do You Build Classroom Community?

The diversity of approaches below seems united by several threads. Each teacher speaks about the need to establish personal connections with students as an essential facet of making a classroom work. All also speak about that often-elusive goal of getting students to be responsible.

Marsha Kindrachuk

I have rules for the writing community and a big "No Hunting" sign prominently displayed in the classroom. I also remind the kids "What happens in Vegas, stays in Vegas," so they're more willing to take risks in sharing their personal writing. I make sure to live up to this pledge by deliberately piquing their interests about what students in other classes wrote, but when they ask, I remind them about the "Vegas pledge." Once they realize I'm serious, they buy into it, and most students are very willing to put themselves out there with their writing. Since my kids are constantly writing, they are always engaged. When they come into class, I always have a prompt on the LCD projector so they immediately get their journals and begin writing. I always ask for volunteers to share their writing. When I don't have volunteers, I read mine. Sometimes they ask for me to read mine regardless; other times, they ask for a specific student to read his or her piece. I offer a trip to the treasure chest (my box of trinkets or small candies) for those who volunteer, and many times this is incentive enough to get a kid to open up. We build community through peer review and by not gossiping to other classes about what goes on inside our class. Respect is modeled and expected, and in the three years since I've been teaching (preservice and fully certified), I've never had a problem with building community.

▧ Lisha Wood

I found out my first year of teaching that when I walked into a class and announced that "This is *our* classroom, and I want us to create rules *we're* comfortable with," I really was saying, "Take over! I have no idea what I'm doing." I've learned over the years that allowing students to have autonomy in a classroom, and creating a comfortable classroom environment, means first having a clear understanding of what I'm comfortable with as a teacher. I guide, rather than dictate. I suggest, rather than demand. And ultimately, I get the students to create the rules I would have given them to follow in the first place.

First, I have them complete a handout or note card where they put down rules that make a classroom environment positive for them. Then I type their rules onto one sheet and have the class synthesize the rules into general topics (i.e., these are all about how we treat others, these are about how we treat ourselves, etc.). We always end up going to the same place: *Respect*. From there, we can create a few classroom rules that we can all live with that revolve around respecting each other, the environment, and most importantly, themselves. This helps them hold each other accountable as much as I do. It also keeps me consistent and fair. They have ownership because I've seemingly given up the dictatorship, and instead we're in this community together. The difference between now and my first few years, other than daily tears, is that I know what I'm comfortable with and where I want to go. It's backward design for behavior management. Control is just an illusion anyway, but they don't know that, so I let them think they have control, but there's a clear, intangible feeling when they walk in my room that they know I will expect them to follow rules. It's a presence. A kind, yet firm expectation and guidance.

I have always been fortunate enough to teach multiple levels of English. Currently, I teach AP Language to juniors and a remedial freshman course. Can we say Sybil? I start my day with a small group of students who are below grade level in reading, writing, and all things involving maturity. I spend ninety minutes, every day, all year in what I call "freshman boot camp." The first six weeks are just community building (and bad-behavior breaking) with a little bit of reading and writing thrown in for good measure. I turn from a human to an unknown creature sporting one hundred pairs of eyes noticing every off-task movement to regain control and the one hundred "arms" of a centipede tapping every desk to command attention. The course is as much about teaching these students reading and writing strategies as it is about how to behave appropriately and respect yourself enough to have a chance in this world. My left eyebrow muscle is the strongest on my body, arching daily to signify "I don't think so" for some infraction or violation. My throat is hoarse after my third block each day, and emotionally, I'm drained.

Then, my thirty-two third-block AP Language college-bound students arrive, circling my desk, eager to share their writing, ask questions about vocab and makeup assignments, and just generally get on my good side. I often have to ask them for a minute, just one minute to myself, where I can morph back into a human, a person, someone whose dry sense of humor, high expectations, and relaxed persona can resurface. I change from someone who demands that students ask to get up from their seats to a person who rarely cares if someone needs to go to the restroom. Whenever an AP Language student ventures into my second-block class to turn in an essay early or ask a question about homework, they often leave with a deer-in-the-headlights look and tentatively ask me later, "What class is that?" I love that I have the talent to be more than one person throughout the day. It's a gift we have as teachers to play the roles and don the hats we're expected to wear. I wouldn't trade teaching both ends of the spectrum because they tap into two very different parts of my personality, and I value the opportunity I have to teach very different life skills throughout the day. However, those who don't teach should walk a mile in all of our different pairs of shoes before they patronize us with how "hard" they think our jobs are. Yes, our jobs are difficult, but they have no idea.

Susanne Greenwood

Having taught for twenty-five years, I still consider my first and foremost preparation in the English/language arts classroom to be the establishment of a community that permeates our classroom space with a *joie de vivre*. The ambiance I establish early on in terms of our classroom community is vital. Over time, I have learned that while I want to know my students as the varied individuals they are, they too want to know about me. These mutual revelations contribute to an air of familiarity and comfort in our classroom space, and through the days and weeks of our classes, support and nurture the kind of learning, discussion, interaction, camaraderie, and collaboration I seek among and with my students.

Getting to know my students as readers, thinkers, and writers comes first for me. I want them to hear and see in me the love I have for language and its power to shape, influence, change, connect, move, and inspire individuals, organizations, communities, and worlds. An online survey on our first day of class works well as an "ease-into-school" assignment to gather this kind of information from my students, and they particularly like being able to type out answers in text boxes and "chat" about their likes and dislikes about summer reading as well as rate their love—or apprehension, or dislike—of reading. I ask them what they hope to achieve in our English class and what they think it takes for them to be the students they envision themselves as. And while their responses are informal, I am happy to gather their candid and enthusiastic responses and record a sense of their ideas and written expression, as well as their dreams and goals for the future.

Within days of beginning class, I assign a multigenre writing assignment entitled "An Introduction to Me." Students are given a number of writing prompts and have free choice as to the three multigenre pieces they employ to write further glimpses of themselves. For example, four anecdotes might inform a meaningful photograph; a timeline of important life events might be accompanied by stories exploring these episodes. More than anything, I want them to reflect upon the details and nuances of all their experiences and to articulate them as fully as possible.

As part of my teaching practice, I write every assignment my students do, and share all my writing and revised pieces with them via our classroom SMART Board. This practice contributes quite effectively to the community I seek in my classes. Quickly, my students understand that I am not just a teacher but also an amateur photographer, animal lover, avid cook and baker, voracious reader, and fairly good knitter. We share our likes about music, movies, television, and favorite "reads"—and suddenly we have things to talk and write about! All of us in our class are required to share something wildly unique about ourselves, and jaws drop when I share that I can stand on my head, unaided by a wall. Soon, I am telling them with a poker face that there will be "absolutely no laughing" as I attempt to lift my backside up into the air!

▧ Colette Armstrong

As a new teacher seven years ago, I entered the doors of a high school steeped in fifty years of tradition and unenthusiastic to change. Being an outsider to this community, I was challenged to find my place and make my way within the context of this environment. I began to create my identity by getting involved in coaching and sponsoring student council. By getting involved with some of the crucial events in the community, I built my credibility and became part of the social fabric while getting to know students outside the confines of my English classroom. Planning and executing events like the Pep Rally, Homecoming Dance, Senior vs. Faculty Basketball Game, Talent Show, Relay for Life, and the Mr. High School Mangeant [a fund-raising event] helped me create an identity as a teacher who cares about students not just in the classroom but out of it, and this affected students' perceptions of what I was all about.

Being an involved teacher really impacted my classroom identity. I was able to set high academic expectations because students knew I cared and that I was going to be working just as hard as they were. My work ethic changed the way students looked at me and all of a sudden students were saying things like, "Ms. Armstrong, you have more spirit than anyone at NGHS" and "You are NGHS." Students could see how much love I had for them, the school, and this profession, and subsequently I had very few issues with classroom management and student slacking. They had respect for me and tried not to disappoint me. My teacher identity had been created.

Seven years later I have been able to impact this tradition-driven school by inspiring a change in students' perceptions of community service, spirit, and love for the school, along with high academic performance. Last year my school raised $76,000 for Relay for Life, which brought our five-year total to $208,000. I helped build this spirit of giving over the past five years slowly, and now it is part of the school culture. Seven years ago, we were not allowed to have even one spirit dress-up day. This year during spirit week, virtually every student in the school participated in at least one dress-up day. Each student is now seeing that school can be fun if they get involved because I helped build this school spirit. Academic rigor has also been my priority, and last year I had only one student out of 150 students who did not pass the state-implemented standardized test, despite the fact that I do not teach to the test. The rigor created in my mostly college prep classes allowed students who do not normally pass these tests to rise above and exceed expectations regardless of predictions that they wouldn't.

All of my experiences—both successes and failures—have taught me that teachers need to build their identity by nurturing authentic relationships with students and the school community. I do not think I would have been as successful as a teacher if I did not have my students' trust. Because of the relationships I have built, the example I have set, and the teacher identity I have created, I feel like my students are able to experience a fun, safe, academically driven high school.

◼ Ashley Glover

Okay, so once I figured out how to not hate writing instruction, I then needed a way to make the feedback process relevant for my students. As much as I'd like to think that Loner Kid spent hours poring over all of the heartfelt, genuine comments that I would painstakingly scribble all throughout the margins of his paper, the reality is simply this: he didn't care. He looked at the grade at the top, probably cursed me for whatever punishment his parents might inflict on him if it wasn't an A, and then likely crumbled it into a ball and tossed it in the trash. So why the heck was I spending hours giving him feedback? Why was I killing myself and sacrificing my free time (oh so much free time, as an English teacher) writing it all down for him? Was he learning anything? Did I lose all the ground I seemed to have won with him in class discussion when I wrote "AWK" next to his transition in the third paragraph?

There had to be a better way. And there was. The idea came to me as I assigned their second set of persuasive essays. If I'm being completely honest here, the idea didn't really originate out of my longing for them to "get it." The idea originated out my abhorrence for taking home a crate of essays that weighed more than half my own body weight. I just didn't want to do it again—especially when it seemed so ineffective. So I decided to try a new method of "staggering due dates" with their next set of papers. The idea was that I would put them in groups of five to seven students; they would all have an individual conference with me, and their final drafts of their essays were due on the day of the conference.

During the conference, we would always start off with what they did *well*. This can be a bit of a challenge with some students ("Oh yes, Susie. I just *love* the way you followed instructions and double-spaced your entire paper"). Next, we would focus on five to ten main issues in their paper; some were grammatical, while others related to content. The student would write these items down on the *conference sheet*, and he or she would have the opportunity to ask questions, seek clarification, finally figure out what "AWK" means, and so on. The point is that—once again—it was about *dialogue*. Kids love to discuss things. They actually *do* want to feel like active participants in their own learning; we just have to find a way to allow them to be a part of the conversation. Once we filled out this list—never more than ten items, because you and I both know we will lose them if we go much further than ten items—then I graded the paper. Yes, in front of them. I didn't sugarcoat anything, and I didn't feel self-conscious about it. I was very nervous about this process before I started doing it, but I found that the students actually never put up an argument when I began to grade the paper. I don't think this is due to any magical powers on my part; I think that they simply felt like they were heard in the process, and they understood why points were coming off for certain items.

Finally, I put the grade in the grade book so that the student could see exactly how it would affect his or her grade. If the student felt good (or apathetic) about it, then the grade could stand "as is." However, if students wanted to make corrections, they could submit a revised copy of the paper . . . according to the conference sheet.

I found that this process accomplished several goals. It helped my students to feel like they had a second chance—that it wasn't just "the red pen of death." They could actually show me that they had learned from their mistakes (what a concept!) and make a concerted effort to correct their errors, and that they could earn a better grade. And they really improved. But best of all, *I didn't have to take home crates of papers anymore! I had a life again!* If students decided to resubmit their papers, I simply scanned through their revised copies and their conference sheets to see if they had addressed the issues. Parents were actually writing me complimentary emails about my "unique" conferencing strategy. Students were thanking me for second chances. Glorious!

I have tweaked this process over the years, and I've developed the following documents:

- A Writing Contract: This document outlines the conference process for both my students and parents; I have both of them sign it to be sure that we're all on the same page before I begin conferencing.
- A Conference Sheet: This is the document that I referenced earlier. It is included in the information packet that I send home and post to my blog, so students and parents get to see what this whole process looks and feels like before we start.
- A Grammar Correction Sheet: This aid helps students understand why they make grammar errors, provides rules for how to correct them, and then qualifies that they go through the task of addressing the error and the rule in their revision.
- Schedule of Groups and Due Dates: This document might seem daunting, and it can be annoying to create for each class period. However, I still protest that it beats the heck out of taking home crates of papers to grade all the time.

CONSIDERING TEACHER IDENTITY AND CLASSROOM COMMUNITY: As you think about what these teachers wrote, consider the following questions:

- How would you describe the classroom community you want to create in your classes?
- Jot four words that describe you as a teacher. Next, jot four words that describe you as a person. What do the differences and similarities in the two lists indicate to you about your teacher identity?
- All teachers have "reps" (reputations) among students. What is your rep? To what extent does it encourage you that you are building a compelling teacher identity?
- How, specifically, do these teachers build community in their classes?
- What tips from these teachers might you use in your own teaching?
- Why do you think so many teachers chose to respond to this issue when given the option to do so?
- What do these teachers have in common among their views of how classroom community aids their teaching?
- What strikes you as fresh and honest about what these teachers say about teaching writing?

How Do Standards and Testing Relate to How You Teach?

Our respondents all note some of the paradoxes of standards and testing. As do most effective teachers, they must deal with the incongruities of mandates and exams that seem at odds with good teaching. Here's how they cope.

Patsy Hamby

The English department chair at our school asked me to teach American literature five years ago because students at this eleventh-grade level are faced with seven high-stakes assessments—perhaps more depending on their schedules. Not only does this American Literature class have an end-of-course test (EOCT), which is generated by a testing service, but high school juniors are also administered state writing and language arts assessments in addition to state exams in their other three core class areas and an EOCT in a social studies course. Not one of these exams is created by their classroom teachers, who are also denied access to specific exam content and are even forbidden to discuss the exam after students have taken it. In total contradiction to this practice of top-secret, tightly guarded assessment, professional development training sessions for teachers focus on backward design whereby effective teaching instruction is based on assessment and generated only after we have envisioned the final assessment. Instead, in these mandated testing situations, we are told that the tests are based on the standards, and if our instruction is based on the standards, our students will meet or exceed requirements.

As lead teacher for our American literature/composition team, I helped create the curriculum map for our content area, a course overview that contains twenty days of test-related content, either for review or for actual administration of the tests. While each teacher has the flexibility to determine how he or she will review for the exam, test days are totally inflexible for teachers and for students who are taking the tests, and totally chaotic for students who are not.

Among the approaches to teaching to the test for the language arts exam, teachers often reserve one of our four computer labs for five consecutive days and administer the test-prep software purchased by our district, a drill-and-kill type of program with questions supposedly similar to those on the exam.

Recently, a parent of one of my students insisted that I modify my curriculum plans and insert a monthly assessment of my students' ability to pass the standardized assessment, to be administered eight months from now, an adjustment that would increase the test-prep days on my curriculum calendar from twenty to twenty-eight. She does not worry about her child becoming a lifelong learner or about extending her child's thinking beyond the one assessment that may prevent the child from graduating on time. So I question, is this parent attempting to determine my curriculum? Do testing companies drive our education curriculum decisions? Or on a larger scale, is our nation at risk of limiting our focus to the one-size-fits-all, pass-for-performance philosophy of education? Are my students to be considered statistical data instead of the wonderful individual human beings they are who make my classroom a living, thriving community of learners?

Two students I taught last year failed their high-stakes assessment. Both are labeled as members of two subgroups that traditionally fail: Both are African American males, and both are economically disadvantaged. These two students chose to sit near each other in my class for a paired activity, and during a transition, I was standing near them and overheard their conversation. They were talking about Jason Heyward, a rookie on the Atlanta Braves baseball team. They knew this athlete's history, his statistical averages, and his prospects for the future. I watch Braves baseball sometimes at home in the evening while I'm grading papers, and I know a little about the team's standings, but their discussion was far beyond my intellectual grasp of the sport; I was amazed as I overheard their shared knowledge and wouldn't dare attempt to enter their discussion because they would have to dummy it down to allow me access. Now if only there were a few test items about Jason Heyward on that standardized assessment so they could really demonstrate their mastery!

Lisha Wood

The most authentic teaching I've done in years has been the AP Language course. The reason is that the entire course is taught from a backward design perspective. I know exactly what the test looks like from the first day and what is expected of the students, and I can plan every unit with the end goal in mind. Extensive training was offered before I was even able to teach the course, so I've worked collaboratively with experts who've taught the course for years and seen tests and many student essay samples. Interestingly enough, when we're new teachers, we're often thrown into teaching remedial students, alone, with no prep, no collaboration, and no real backward design. I've used many of the strategies from AP training and the concept of backward design that I've learned/developed through my own teaching of the AP course with my remedial students in the past few years, and I found that my teaching was more effective. As "they" continue to change standards every few years or so, continuing with the backward design template means always knowing what standards are being taught and what the end goal is, which can only lead to student achievement.

Rob Montgomery

How do you incorporate a document you don't trust? For me, that was the hardest part of learning to teach with standards. By the time my [high] school started placing an emphasis on standards (incorporating them in our lesson plans, posting the daily standard in a conspicuous location in the classroom, structuring faculty meetings around their implementation), I had been teaching for several years, had gained experience working with a National Writing Project site, and had come to develop what I thought was a pretty solid understanding of what my students needed in order to become competent, confident, and sophisticated writers. Unfortunately, this understanding didn't bear much resemblance to the standards I was now asked to make a centerpiece of my teaching.

I believe that students should write, and write a lot. They should write about things they are passionate about, curious about, frustrated by. Some of this writing would be formal, but much of it would be informal. It might be written in different genres, and seldom could it be summed up in just five paragraphs. It would be messy but vibrant, disordered but engaged, and from the chaos we'd wrangle their work through multiple drafts into a piece about which they could be proud.

But here's how the state of California wanted me to approach writing in the ninth and tenth grades:

> 1.1 Establish a controlling impression or coherent thesis that conveys a clear and distinctive perspective on the subject and maintain a consistent tone and focus throughout the piece of writing.
>
> *(California Department of Education, 2006, p. 224)*

This clinical legalese continues for two more pages, flinging jargon left and right, and none of it really represented anything that looked or sounded like what I wanted my students to be able to do with writing. If implemented as written, it certainly wasn't going to inspire my students *to want to* write.

My solution—as squirmy as it makes me feel to write this—was to know the standards well enough to ignore them. Standard 1.1 is emphasizing thesis, tone, and focus—all things I can get on board with. But when I taught these things, it wasn't as though I was structuring specific lessons around them. My ninth-grade students had to write personal narratives, and so, instead of thesis, we'd talk about the story's "So what?" moment—the thing that made it a story worth telling. We'd figure out which events and details were crucial to the story's success (focus) and we'd talk about choosing words that reflected how the author felt about the story he was telling (tone). All of this would be done as part of the revision process—a living, breathing, cantankerous beast that looked nothing like the writing process autopsy in the standards document—and it grew organically out of (A) what I wanted to accomplish as a teacher, and (B) what my students needed in the moment to make their writing a success.

Now that I'm working with preservice teachers [at Kennesaw State University], I know I have to be more systematic, but my approach is much the same as it was when I taught high school: Know the core ideas in each standard so you can ignore the rest. Trust your judgment as a teacher, zero in on the items you'd want to teach anyway—evidence, detail, organization—and don't get lost in the convoluted wording that only obscures what the act of writing is really like.

CONSIDERING STANDARDS, TESTING, AND TEACHING: As you think about what these teachers wrote, consider the following questions:

- How well do you know your state's standards and/or the Common Core State Standards? How well do you think you need to know them to be a successful teacher?
- How do these teachers manage contradictions between how they *want* to teach and what the standards and "the test" seem to indicate they *should* teach?
- To what extent do these teachers share your level of concern about the relationships among standards, testing, and teaching?
- What have these teachers decided *not* to do that makes teaching in an atmosphere of standards and testing work for them and their students?
- Select one teacher. What questions would you ask him or her during a conversation about standards, testing, and teaching?
- What strikes you as fresh and honest about what these teachers say about teaching writing?

How Do You Account for Writing Across the Curriculum and in Other Content Areas?

As these teachers acknowledge, *writing across the curriculum* is a term they know well but had to learn to integrate into their teaching. They all did so in a manner suited to their knowledge base and interests.

Kyle Jones

It took me a long time to understand what *writing across the curriculum* meant. To me, the concept always seemed vague, and I never felt as though it was explained in a way I readily understood. In my fourth year of teaching, the meaning of *writing across the curriculum* finally clicked inside of me; still, in my first three years, I really struggled through various roadblocks and obstacles on my way to finding my own understanding.

My first roadblock was my ignorance of the state and county standards I was responsible for teaching students. During my undergrad years, I was expected to explore the Georgia Performance Standards, but I didn't develop a working memory of them. Once I began working in a high school in a large urban school district with their own take on the state standards, I again "explored" the content but lacked a full understanding of what I was to teach students. My failure to know my own [state's] standards immediately put me at a disadvantage for trying to teach *anything* across the curriculum. (Turns out you have to know your own curriculum to teach across it!) Still, I never considered myself a bad teacher. I am passionate about writing and literature, but I may have been a little misguided in those very early years.

My second obstacle was simply inexperience. I'm not sure there is a cure for this particular issue as we all begin literacy instruction as rookies. Thankfully, I was teaching at a school that expected collaboration among teachers, and I worked with a team of teachers of various experience levels who helped me balance my ambition with my inexperience. I would like to think the support I received early in my career is what set me up for later success. I know we are not always so lucky to start our teaching careers in such an environment.

I don't think my experience is very different from most rookie writing teachers. I used my inexperience to my advantage by forcing myself to be creative and to think outside of the proverbial box to be an effective writing teacher. I developed various journaling activities and workshops for my students to supplement the typical essay writing in high school that quickly kills many teenagers' interests in writing at all. I was always looking for alternatives.

During my fourth year of teaching, everything started to finally come together. I had the chance to begin a radical new class that hadn't really been done in a large public classroom before. While developing this class with another colleague, I was put in a position for the first time of having to really look closely at my standards. I spent weeks looking at my state and county standards and wrestling with how to develop each skill within my students. I finally had an "aha" moment just a month before the school year was to start again.

I developed a rubric that encompassed all fifty-three primary standards that my students were responsible for knowing by the end of the school year. I then developed a series of projects that would require my students to pull from the larger rubric and create their own rubric based on the standards they were attempting to learn and the skills they were attempting to increase. Having students take ownership of the standards was how I finally got them to write across the curriculum. My students were led to make connections with drama, poetry, fiction, nonfiction, and even history with their writing by holding themselves accountable to the standards themselves. The entire time my students developed these projects, I worked to become a true subject matter expert by developing my own understanding of the standards and constantly shepherding my students in their research writing and journaling.

I began to think of myself as a writing Sherpa. I was no longer instructing toward my students about good writing practice, but rather I was now guiding them through their own self-discoveries. The new class I had developed naturally required students to write within not only my curriculum but across a social studies curriculum as well. With constant collaboration with my social studies colleague, we had students making connections between various texts with their historical and geographical brethren. I had never been more energized as a teacher than when one of my students developed a mobile device application that allowed users to access the story of *The Odyssey*, critical analysis that the student had created, and historical and modern information about the locales in the epic poem.

I don't want to give anyone the false impression that this process worked for all my students. Many of my students still struggled with writing across the curriculum and making the various connections with our social studies counterpart. There will always be a few students who remain unmotivated or simply unmoved by the empowerment of their own learning. Still, as I enter into my fifth year of teaching, I am convinced that having students take ownership of the standards, guiding them through their mistakes, developing various connections with them, and having them write almost every day is the key.

Colette Armstrong

Finding ways to integrate other content areas into my language arts class has always been a goal because I contend it creates a bridge of relevancy between subjects. It is also a skill students will need when they enter college and all of a sudden have to write a paper in their "Math 101" class about how to solve an equation. If I don't do my job preparing students to do this type of academic writing, what will happen to them in the university system? Because of this pedagogical outlook on cross-curricular writing, I try to collaborate with teachers in other content areas to have students write using another subject's content knowledge.

As an English language arts teacher, I frequently assign literary analysis papers asking students to look closely at the literature we are reading. Part of this analysis is looking into the history of the time period and the author since most literature is affected by the time it was written and the popular styles of that time. The curriculum of our United States History and our American Literature classes are also closely aligned chronologically, which allows students to use the content they learn in U.S. History to add to their literary analysis. This partnership between history and literature is also achieved through a paper the classes collaborate on each semester, which students submit to both their U.S. History and American Literature teachers for a grade on content and writing, respectively. This collaborative team approach allows students to see how the content areas work together to create a bigger picture.

Incorporating science in writing has also been a goal. My district has aided in the development of this goal with a high-stakes standardized test given to all sophomores and graded on scientific knowledge and writing proficiency. However, regardless of this assessment, the merging of science and the humanities has been important to connecting the core subjects for student comprehension. We administer a practice science essay once a year to assess students' abilities to write about scientific concepts, and our science teachers have implemented more writing in their curriculum. For the schoolwide practice essay, language arts teachers graded the essay for organization and conventions, and the science teachers graded for ideas and content, which creates a valuable team approach.

This cross-curricular writing collaboration provided an excellent way to show students how important writing is while creating a dialogue between teachers about how to best help our students succeed. It was eye-opening to see how students needed assignments like this to create connections between content areas, and it was the teachers who needed to help these high schoolers see how all of the subjects they take overlap. Pure collaboration is the best way to create authenticity in writing, and these cross-curricular efforts have helped to improve our students' writing and reasoning skills.

CONSIDERING WRITING ACROSS THE CURRICULUM: As you think about what these teachers wrote, consider the following questions:

- What is your definition of *writing across the curriculum*?
- How effective were the solutions these teachers found for engaging students in writing across the curriculum (WAC)?
- What ideas do you hope to implement to encourage writing across the curriculum in your class and school?
- In some WAC projects involving an English teacher and a teacher from another content area, the English teacher grades writing for surface errors, mechanics, and conventional usage, and the other content area teacher grades the writing for content. What are the advantages of this system? What are its pitfalls? What else (beyond grammar, mechanics, and organization) could the English teacher seek out and coach when she reads the paper? What would happen if the teachers switched their grading responsibilities (i.e., if the science teacher graded surface errors, mechanics, and conventional usage, and the English teacher graded the content of the paper)? What assumptions about WAC do your responses indicate?
- What strikes you as fresh and honest about what these teachers say about teaching writing?

How Do You Teach Writing to Struggling or Apathetic Students?

Every teacher encounters students who struggle with writing and students who don't seem to care much about writing. How teachers respond to these students sets a powerful tone in the writing classroom and among a community of writers. Sonny's insight here is witty and candid, touching the heart of what we do. (P.S. Dawn did not bribe Sonny to write nice things.)

Sonny Harding

If we're going to make any progress with students who don't care about writing, I think it's important that we first stop blaming the students. Granted, at some point we have to put our foot down and demand personal accountability, regardless of the child's background; I'm a firm believer in that, too. However, we can't do anything with these kids' writing until we know where the kids are coming from first.

I teach in a suburban town clinging tenaciously to its redneck past. My high school, where I've taught mostly freshmen for my brief career, is a short drive between two multiplexes and a wealth of fast-food options. Having grown up in the county all my life, I've watched it prosper economically and spread like kudzu (at least the kudzu that it isn't being razed for another megachurch). You'd think that the new subdivisions, strip malls, and their inherent tax dollars would bring about a new day of literate parents who fill their homes with books, raise children to value their education, and demand much from the teachers they employ.

Yet all of this growth hasn't changed the educational culture much, and it's stifling my school system's credibility and rigor. The county abandoned summer reading for everyone but the honors students. When kids fail my Ninth Grade Literature & Composition course, they're usually put in front of computer software to "recover" the credit without having to write a single word. It's a sick, sad world. Don't blame kids for not knowing the fun and power of words if they're educated in a system treating literacy with such levity.

These kids who resist writing are responding to the culture in which they're raised. I recently had to explain to a student not *where* the closest Barnes & Noble is, but *what* a Barnes & Noble is. Some kids insist they won't need any literacy skills when they take over their fathers' auto garages or stump-grinding businesses (I'm paraphrasing actual conversations I've had with actual students). *We* recognize the folly in their arguments, but they don't.

It's one thing to be a lazy, reluctant writer because of the allure of video games or the Internet; we're all guilty of that. I'm about to take a break from writing this to play some Scrabble on my iPhone. Teachers can fix that with structured discipline and fair grading. But it's quite another problem to be a lazy, reluctant writer because of a systemic epidemic of ignorance and low expectations in your community. That's just not the kid's fault, so stop blaming him when he blows off another essay or continues to use that lowercase *i* no matter how many times you underline it three times with your red pen.

So what do we do, Teachers? I can't imagine my classroom climate is all too different from yours. We've got struggling, reluctant writers. They either want to improve but can't, or they don't see the value in improving at all. Having taught these students for only five years now, here's what I can suggest: *Give them a purpose, but give them the tools.*

Dawn Kirby recommends letting students write about their own lives, and she's right. One hundred percent. Not every prompt works for every kid, but stories come much easier when they're from their own memories. But personal narrative isn't the panacea to all their writing woes. Too often, teachers hide behind the effectiveness of memoir in the classroom without properly addressing the real writing issues at hand. Your job isn't over until you're blown away, not by how much of their soul they're revealing, but by their masterful command of the English language. A short narrative of a childhood memory can suck just as much as an analysis of the Christian influences evident in *Beowulf*. Don't believe me? Assign some personal writing with no further instruction and watch the unimaginative, stilted dreck roll in.

Students need tools to create a *good* piece of personal writing. Everybody can spit out their recollection of a trip to the beach; it's your job to instruct them to write a better one. Address their areas of weakness; don't let them slide. Need to see vivid details? Go over how to write some. Show them *tons* of examples. Want active verbs or appositives or paragraphs? Teach them! Focus on one thing at a time, be clear about what you're expecting, and don't let it go until they've nailed it. Maybe it's punctuating dialogue one week, using subordinate clauses to combine sentences the next.

Struggling students need a few boundaries, some rules or a template to follow. Remember, these kids hate writing; you'll be lucky if they care about their grade enough to even attempt to satisfy you, so meet them halfway. Providing *lots* of examples can help. I like showing them a narrative, and then asking, "Now what would *your* story sound like?"

The downside, of course, is that your students might sacrifice their own originality in an attempt to mimic the original. That's okay. Not ideal, but it's okay. We can learn a lot through imitation; artists take their own blank canvases to the Louvre all the time to copy the masters. Grant your struggling students the same frameworks or guides. Your more advanced students will recognize the available margins within which to innovate or insert their own voice. Reluctant students, though, win half the battle if they even turn in the work.

But once you see their work, once they've trusted your methods enough to actually do the work, that's when your job really starts. You've got 180 days to move them as far along as you can. Their writing will be poor; do not delude yourself into thinking that they're all lazy little Hemingways. But they're people, good people who deserve good lives but haven't realized the power their words can have. So teach them.

CONSIDERING TEACHING WRITING TO STRUGGLING OR APATHETIC STUDENTS: As you think about what this teacher wrote, consider the following questions:

- Sonny's response is characterized by his last sentence, "So teach them." How does Sonny reach struggling or apathetic student writers? What clues in his writing lead to your response?
- As a student, with what topics or content areas have you struggled? Which teacher stands out in your memory as helping you improve or as increasing your difficulties?
- Sonny names several sociocultural factors that affect his students and their attitudes toward writing. To what extent is it acceptable for students to decide they don't *need* to learn specific academic content?
- What strikes you as fresh and honest about what this teacher says about teaching writing?

How Do You Handle Grades and Motivation?

We like Colette's questions about the purpose of grades and her comments that we each must figure out for ourselves the value of grades. Her comments connect well to the discussions of grading options in Chapter 11. In a larger sense, she's tapping into the age-old puzzle of how to get students to care, to feel self-motivated, and to find meaning in learning.

Colette Armstrong

The combinations of peanut butter and jelly, summer and the beach, jeans and a T-shirt, and grades and motivation seem to go hand in hand, but from experience I know that grades do not always depend on or impact a student's motivation. When I first started teaching, I followed my teacher's old school rules that students should be punished if their work was late and every missed punctuation mark should result in points off. I was grading students based on what I thought was their motivation, but I was missing the fact that some of these students were really trying, and I was just killing their papers with red ink. It was during this first year that I realized motivation did not always match the grade as I watched some kids try with no hope of meeting my assignment's timeline.

The definition of a grade is different for every teacher, and I think every teacher has to decide what their grades are going to represent. Are your grades a reflection of a behavior? Of knowledge? Of motivation? Of an intrinsic need to learn? Of what you told your class? I decided, after my first year, that grades should show what a student knows at a particular time. I also decided that if students were able to show mastery of a skill, I would reward them with grades that reflected that mastery. With this new philosophy, however, comes the inevitable downside of having all students just retake a test to do better. I combat this by not allowing students to retest everything. In order for a student to retest, the subject matter needs to be a skill the student needs. For example, a grammar test has material a student needs to be able to apply to writing and reading, but a test over the content of *A Midsummer Night's Dream* does not, so it could not be retaken. This approach to grades has helped me motivate students not to give up on the grammar, reading, writing, and language skills they will need, thus allowing them to master the information at their own pace.

A student's motivation is impacted by a lot of different things, and for some students grades do the motivating. I have found, though, that students are more motivated by their interest in the subject as well as the amount of relevance they see in the acquisition of that knowledge in their lives. If high school kids don't think they will need the information, they are probably not going to be motivated to learn it. And I can't blame them. I was the same way, and I still am. We are trying to standardize their education to provide a base knowledge that will allow all students to have the chance to explore all of their future career options, but . . . students need to see the value in the class, and, when they do, they are more motivated to learn. It is really common sense if you think about it.

The tie between motivation and grades is contingent on the type of grades you are taking and the relevance you can create for your class. This is the key to getting my students to buy in. Buy-in is the motivator that pushes my students and encourages them to raise their grades.

CONSIDERING GRADES AND MOTIVATION: As you think about what this teacher wrote, consider the following questions:

- How much experience do you have with grading and assessing students' writings? How will your level of experience affect your approach to grading?
- What similarities between Sonny's response (see How Do You Teach Writing to Struggling or Apathetic Students?) and this response do you notice? What might be the genesis of these similarities?
- What does Colette *do* that makes the necessity of grading students' written pieces work for her students and her?
- Colette gives an example of the type of work she would let students redo and the type she would not. What responses and reactions do you have to her distinction?
- Novice teachers often dread grading student work. Other than the obvious issue of coping with the paper load, what makes grading difficult?
- How do your colleagues handle issues of motivation and grading? How do their strategies inform what you might do as a teacher of writing?
- How will you address the connections between grading and motivating students as you teach writing?
- What strikes you as fresh and honest about this teacher's response?

What Opportunities and Obstacles Does Journaling Present?

Kyle relates his personal journey with the purposes and outcomes of using journals with students. Like his students, he grew into the idea and then made it his own.

Kyle Jones

I've never met anyone who didn't want to have his or her voice heard. I have certainly met a few people who feel their voice is insignificant so therefore why try to have anyone hear it, but it all boils down to our innate desire to have an outlet where our words have authority and meaning—a feeling of our voice carrying gravitas. Journaling, I've found, is how I give my students that weightiness to their words.

In my second year of teaching, I decided I would make journaling a weekly occurrence in my classroom. As most teachers discover, your first year you work hard to stay afloat and manage the gritty details of being a good educator. (You learn quickly that despite all the practice you've had in a college classroom or your limited field experience, you still have a lot to learn about classroom management, timing, and student mentoring.) I had gotten through my first year and realized that I never felt like my students wrote enough on a daily or weekly basis. To me the answer was simple—journaling. During my undergraduate studies, I had grown fond of the practice. It appeared to me that it was a simple but dynamic way of having students write. I wanted to bring the practice into my own classroom, but I knew there would certainly be obstacles along the way.

My new adventure into journaling began at Target. There was a massive sale on one hundred–page spiral-bound notebooks in packs of ten, so I bought as many as I could physically carry to my car. I knew that if I wanted my students to really journal, I would have to make sure I had the proper equipment ready for them. My purchase paid off quickly as many students ended up getting their journals through me rather than through the hassle of going to the store; thus, I ensured they would all have a journal for my classroom.

During my first year of teaching, I really had no idea what I wanted my students to write about; I just knew I wanted them to write! A wonderful colleague of mine let me borrow a book full of interesting writing starters. I liked them simply because they were each unique and in some cases just "out there." (We're talking about prompts that might read: "You just found out your boyfriend/girlfriend of three months is really a vampire and is plotting to turn the school into their lunch." Go!) Many of my students took to writing these odd prompts immediately, but I had almost as many who really struggled to allow their creativity to flow from their brains to the tip of their pencils. I started to realize a few weeks into my journaling experiment that my whacky prompts weren't for everyone.

By year two, I had students write in their journals two to three times a week and my only requirement was that the entry had to fill the entire page. I would collect the journals every ten entries. The time I spent reading through students' journals and finding out who they really were became very important to me. I worked hard to develop trust in my students to encourage authentic writing and journaling. If a student turned in their journal but didn't want me to read the passage for personal reasons, he or she could fold the paper in half and all I would do is glance to make sure it made the length requirement while still respecting his or her privacy. I found this meant a good deal to my students. A few reluctant writers would write pages and pages using their personal voice, in some cases for the first time.

Finally, after nearly three years of trial and error, I feel as though I've nailed down my journaling routine. My journaling prompts now vary more. I inject freewrites from time to time to encourage creativity and genre variety, but just as often I'll devise a prompt that actually pertains to something we're reading or discovering in class. I'm not talking about a prompt like, "Why is Romeo and Juliet's relationship doomed from the beginning?" but rather, "Explain a time you've been blinded by emotion or desire. What was the result of your actions? What did you learn?" I still throw in some of the crazy fictional prompts too, but I attempt to make my students write about their dreams, fears, hopes, uncertainties, mistakes, triumphs, past, present, future, judgments, misunderstandings, and roles in this world. Honestly, I want them to write about concepts and ideas they just don't normally think about like, "What legacy do you want to leave behind once you've graduated from this high school? What legacy do you want to leave your children?" I have made it a priority to push students to be honest.

I knew my press to make journaling a weekly experience in my classroom was truly worth it when I collected them once, and one student began with his intention to take his own life, describing his hardships and intertwining them with my prompt's questions. As his entries continued, his tone and personal voice changed and by the tenth entry he had decided he no longer wanted to take his life. He had finally found his outlet. In the lower right-hand corner of his last entry, he wrote in small, scribbled letters, "thank you."

CONSIDERING JOURNAL WRITING: As you think about what this teacher wrote, consider the following questions:

- Kyle has found primarily rewards in his use of journal writing with his students. What concerns do you have about reading this type of writing from students?
- How many of your colleagues use journal writing with their students? What reasons do they give for doing (or not doing) so? How do their experiences influence your thinking about using journal writing with your students?
- In Chapter 4, we offer many ideas for using journals in the writing classroom. Which types of journals appeal most to you? Why?
- As a student, to what extent have you participated in journal writing? How does your experience (or lack of experience) inform how you will (or won't) use journals with your students?
- What strikes you as fresh and honest about this teacher's response?

As you read these teachers' responses, perhaps you thought of additional topics to explore, activities you want to use with your students, or personal experiences that inform your teaching. We invite you to explore your lines of thought and make notes about them for later reference. Perhaps you'll even start writing a journal about your teaching ideas.

Final Thoughts

All of the contributors in this chapter are working through the puzzles and challenges of teaching writing. What is working for them is not a model of standardization but an individual approach to writing instruction that begins with the rich individuality of the students in their classrooms.

By engaging in this type of deep reflection—whether in a focus group, around coffee on a Saturday morning, or in a personal journal on teaching—these teachers tackle what amounts to an authentic form of professional development. Real professional development consists of "what you need, when you need it." It doesn't hit you like a ton of bricks as the latest top-down bright idea. Authentic professional development evolves from something that's been plaguing you personally as a teacher, from a frustration or inconsistency or inadequacy you've identified in your teaching, from a real need to adjust how you engage your students to help them learn, right now. Authentic professional development also occurs when teachers gather to discuss what works, to share ideas, and perhaps to read and discuss professional articles and books as a group.

Ending with teachers' voices is also where we began because we, Dawn and Darren, are teachers who engage in our own interior monologues about our teaching. Just like the teachers featured in this chapter—and just like you—we participate in dialogues with colleagues about our practice and our goals as teachers. We think about the big picture through written responses and ideas scribbled in the margins of professional books and articles—all with the goal of improving our teaching. Our students bring outside cultural influences, their personal interests and circumstances, and the numerous challenges of living as twenty-first-century adolescents into our classes. Their authentic selves and their written pieces, full of their own voices and interests, permeate our classes and our teaching. Like all teachers, we encourage—and sometimes shove—our students to grow in their repertoire of abilities as thinkers, readers, and writers. Successes, near misses, and failures accompany us as they do all teachers, but we aim to "fail better," as Beckett terms it. Our goal is to encourage our students to do the same as writers, thinkers, and learners.

We invite you to join us on this reflective professional journey. Your discoveries will inform those of your colleagues and vice versa. Together, you will interact to change the culture of schooling. We can't wait to run into you at a workshop or conference and hear about how you are transforming your students' learning and your practice from the *inside out*.

Teacher Contributors

Colette Armstrong and Kyle Jones teach at North Gwinnett High School in Gwinnett County, Georgia.

Courtney Cook teaches at Wellesley High School in Wellesley, Massachusetts.

Ashley Glover teaches at Fellowship Christian School in Roswell, Georgia.

Patsy Hamby teaches at Hiram High School in Hiram, Georgia.

Susanne Greenwood teaches at Marist School in Atlanta, Georgia.

Sonny Harding teaches at East Paulding High School in Paulding County, Georgia.

Marsha Kindrachuk teaches at Osbourne High School in Austell, Georgia.

Rob Montgomery was a high school teacher in California; he now teaches pre-service English teachers at Kennesaw State University in Kennesaw, Georgia.

Lisha Wood teaches at Sprayberry High School in Marietta, Georgia.

NOTE

1. Excerpts from the teachers' written responses are used with permission. The pieces have been minimally edited for conciseness and to correct obvious typographic errors. None of their essential meanings have been altered. Teachers were not paid to participate and were not prompted to refer to Dawn, Darren, and/or *Inside Out* in their responses.

Work Cited

California Department of Education. 2006. *Reading/Language Arts Framework for California Public Schools: Kindergarten Through Grade Twelve*. Sacramento: CDE Press.

Index

spelling and, 5–6

spider pieces, 148

spontaneous, 74

starter activities, 49–54, 78–86

story importance in, 307–309

storyboards, 127–128

student responders and, 178–181

successful college writing, 303

"sum of the parts" and, 5

switching genres or disciplines, 268

talking directly to the audience when, 117

talking pieces, 148

tall tale telling, 260

teacher responses and, 54

technical skill and, 99

technology and, 8–9, 59–61, 109

technology tools, 200–202, 268–269

test-approved formats, 3

thinker's log, 147

topic exploration, 126–128

tracking text selections, 255–256

transactions with texts, 250

visual art, 282, 282–285

visualization and, 56–59, 64–66

voice and, 70, 99, 99–100, 112–115, 119–121, 150–151

white papers, 140–141

word cloud, 269

word play and, 107–108

writer's notebook, 47–48

Writing across the curriculum, 329

Writing Life (The), 147

www.nwp.org, 1

Z

"Zero" draft, 32